Engineering Trouble

Engineering Trouble

Biotechnology and Its Discontents

EDITED BY

Rachel A. Schurman

AND

Dennis Doyle Takahashi Kelso

UNIVERSITY OF CALIFORNIA PRESS
Berkeley   Los Angeles   London

University of California Press
Berkeley and Los Angeles, California

University of California Press, Ltd.
London, England

© 2003 by the Regents of the University of California

Library of Congress Cataloging-in-Publication Data
Engineering trouble : biotechnology and its discontents / edited
by Rachel A. Schurman and Dennis Doyle Takahashi Kelso.
p.   cm.
Includes bibliographical references and index.
ISBN 0-520-23761-7 (cloth)
ISBN 0-520-24007-3 (paper)
1. Genetic engineering—Social aspects.
2. Agricultural biotechnology—Social aspects.
3. Food—Biotechnology—Social aspects.
I. Schurman, Rachel. II. Kelso, Dennis D.
TP248.6.R4645 2003
306.4'6—dc21   2002152991

Manufactured in the United States of America
13   12   11   10   09   08   07   06   05   04
10 9 8 7 6 5 4 3 2 1

The paper used in this publication is both acid-free and totally chlorine-free (TCF).
It meets the minimum requirements of ANSI/NISO Z39.48- 1992 (R 1997) ⊛

For Michael
and Migahm

CONTENTS

ILLUSTRATIONS

FIGURES

TABLES

ACKNOWLEDGMENTS

This book emerged out of a reading group on biotechnology started in 1997 by several of the contributors. At the time, a number of us were based in the Energy and Resources Group (ERG) at the University of California, Berkeley, a place where faculty and students are encouraged to pursue new ideas, eclectic thinking, and socially and environmentally significant research questions. We thank our friends and colleagues both in ERG and in the larger Berkeley community for stimulating the research that ultimately led to this book. We also thank the director of the Institute for International Studies at Berkeley, Michael J. Watts, and Professor Steven Weber for channeling key institutional and financial support to this project, ensuring that we would have the facilities (both physical and financial) to continue working collectively on this book, even after most of the original members had moved on to new cities and occupations. Funds for the project were kindly provided by the John D. and Catherine T. MacArthur Foundation through a grant to the Institute for International Studies at UC Berkeley titled "Globalization and the Rethinking of International Security: Problems of Multilateral Governance and Identity Politics."

The coeditors also thank their current departments, the Department of Sociology at the University of Illinois and the Environmental Studies Department at the University of California, Santa Cruz, for offering supportive environments in which to work. Rachel Schurman gratefully acknowledges the Department of Sociology and the Center for Advanced Study at the University of Illinois, and the Yale Program in Agrarian Studies, for providing her with critical release time to work on this book. In addition, the Program in Agrarian Studies at Yale provided a wonderful place to read, think, and write in a warm and congenial atmosphere.

Several other people also made important contributions to this project.

Emin Adas at the University of Illinois provided essential research and computer assistance during the manuscript preparation, particularly in the last stages as the manuscript was going to the University of California Press. Anne Kapuscinski at the University of Minnesota was there all along (in spirit if not in body) with words of encouragement, insightful comments on several of the chapters, and useful explanations on the science side of things. In putting together this volume, we had the opportunity to work with a superb editorial team at the University of California Press. Blake Edgar showed great interest and enthusiasm for the project from our first contact and has remained a committed and congenial editor with whom to work. Nicole Stephenson, who assisted Blake during the initial stages of this project, was also helpful in many ways. Erika Büky skillfully guided the revision of the text; and she made significant contributions to both the substance and clarity of the book. Carlotta Shearson, our heroic copyeditor, improved the chapters on many levels. The book reflects her ability to expose and correct weaknesses in content as well as expression, and we are grateful for her hard work, engagement, and patience. Finally, we wish to thank the reviewers who provided valuable comments on an early version of the manuscript. Philip Bereano, William Lacy, and Philip McMichael brought to the task a rich blend of experience and scholarship; we very much appreciate their contributions to our thinking. Of course, any remaining errors or other shortcomings in this volume are our own. Robert Devlin at the West Vancouver Laboratory of Fisheries and Oceans Canada, with characteristic generosity, allowed us to use his photograph of transgenic and nontransgenic coho salmon in the design of the cover. To all, we offer our sincere thanks.

Finally, we wish to acknowledge the more personal debts that made this book possible. We are grateful for Michael Goldman's close reading of a number of chapters, his able assistance with the title, and his positive outlook on life and wonderful sense of humor. William Munro played a key role as an editor, a sounding board, and a good friend. Migahm Takahashi-Kelso not only endured her spouse's long absences for field travel but also served as an enthusiastic proponent, thoughtful discussant, and critical reader. And, of course, heartfelt thanks go to our loving and supportive families, who are always there when we need them for emotional and gastronomic sustenance.

Introduction

Biotechnology in the New Millennium

Technological Change, Institutional Change, and Political Struggle

Rachel A. Schurman

In September 2000, the business section of the *New York Times* ran a front-page story about a new problem in the nation's food supply. A new genetically engineered (GE) corn containing the protein Cry9C had been found in several nationally sold brands of corn tacos (Pollack 2000).[1] Although the corn, known as StarLink, had been approved for use in animal feed and in industry, it had not been approved for human consumption. Yet when a group of social activists hired an Iowa-based company to test the tacos, there it was.

What seemed at first to be just another bump in the history of biotechnology turned out to have enormous repercussions. In addition to ending up in the U.S. food supply, where it wreaked havoc, the genetically engineered corn found its way into the food systems of many other countries in which it had also not been approved. Tensions over trade in GE agricultural products flared, and key U.S. agricultural importers, such as Japan and South Korea, began rejecting shipments of U.S. corn on the grounds that they were contaminated with StarLink. When U.S. agricultural importers began to seek non-GE sources of corn from such countries as Brazil and China, U.S. farmers and the U.S. Department of Agriculture (USDA) panicked about the major market losses that would inevitably result.

In the U.S. heartland, where most of the corn had been grown, the contamination problem exploded in another way. The company that produced the seed, Aventis CropScience, tried to blame farmers for not following proper planting procedures and not taking adequate care to keep StarLink corn separate from their conventionally grown crops. Angered and offended, farmers charged that the company had not properly informed them about how to raise and segregate the corn. Both groups were deeply concerned about the liability for losses associated with StarLink. The incident created a rift between these formerly friendly business partners and revealed differences in their interests in and positions on the technology, differences that had not been previously apparent.

Some five months after the unapproved corn was first detected, the USDA agreed to spend up to $20 million to buy back the remaining StarLink corn seed from seed companies. The Bush administration's rationale for the buyback was that the debacle was in part the fault of the U.S. Environmental Protection Agency (EPA), which had agreed to a two-tiered system of regulation on the assumption that GE corn could be grown for animals and kept out of the human food supply (Kaufman 2001a). Despite the administration's efforts to resolve the crisis, reverberations from the StarLink incident were felt long after the problem was identified. In the end, food manufacturers recalled nearly three hundred products, U.S. corn trade with many foreign countries was seriously disrupted, and the industry paid more than $10 million to farmers in Iowa alone (Lin, Price, and Allen 2001, 40, 46-47; Perkins 2001, 8). In March 2002, a federal judge settled a class action lawsuit, brought by consumers who complained of allergic reactions to StarLink corn, with an award of $9 million (Robinson 2002). But perhaps most significantly, the StarLink incident moved agricultural biotechnology squarely into public view.

In many ways, the StarLink corn incident is emblematic of the political, economic, and institutional crises that have befallen agricultural biotechnology at the beginning of the twenty-first century. As we move into the new millennium, agricultural biotechnology—that is, the use of recombinant DNA techniques in food, feed, and raw materials—faces a highly uncertain future.[2] Although there is little doubt that biotechnology as an industrial production complex, a set of material techniques and practices, a cultural icon, and a bundle of social relations is here to stay,[3] the directions in which the technology is likely to go, the extent to which it will become part of our daily lives, the uses to which it will be put, and the political and institutional environment in which it will evolve are more uncertain now than at any time since the early 1980s. Indeed, we appear to be standing at a crucial juncture in the history of the technology, a juncture at which the future is surprisingly open to the actions of a broad range of (human and nonhuman) actors.

Although the StarLink incident can be seen as the high-water mark in the contemporary crisis of agricultural biotechnology, the causes of the crisis are complex and involve deep tensions that have been brewing for decades. These tensions reflect a clash of worldviews about whether such a potentially revolutionary technology should be introduced into the socionatural world at all; who should have the power to decide; what kinds of precautions should be taken to limit the harm that is done to people and the environment; and what kinds of institutional structures should be established to control and regulate these technologies. As a geared-up and heavily invested (in all senses of the word) life sciences industry has moved forward with its technoscientific interventions in virtually every form of life, many have started to challenge the assumption that any one segment of society should have such a prerogative. These challenges have made genetic engineering into one of the most contested technologies of our time.

While social resistance is one source of uncertainty for the biotechnology industry, farmers, food retailers, and policymakers represent another. Will farmers continue to find a market for their products if they use these increasingly controversial technologies on their farms and in their dairies and fish pens? If farmers opt not to use the technology, will they be adversely affected by genetic "contamination" from pollen drift or other sources of genetic change or by the presence of trace amounts of genetically engineered organisms (GEOs) in the food supply chain? Will retailers lose customers by allying themselves with the biotechnology industry instead of with some of their most vocal and concerned consumers? Even government regulators are unsure how to deal with the political sensitivity of these new technologies. Should regulatory agencies continue to facilitate their commercialization, or should they respond to that portion of the public that advocates that we proceed with greater caution? Different groups are clearly worried about different issues, but all contribute to a growing uncertainty about biotechnology at the beginning of the millennium.

One of this book's primary goals is to illuminate the dynamics of this key historical moment, including the concrete political-economic changes taking place in and around the biotechnology sector, the institutional foundations on which those changes have been built, and the political struggles they are generating. Ten to fifteen years ago, a spate of studies predicted a number of important social, economic, political, and environmental changes that would occur as the science and industry of biotechnology developed. These changes included the emergence of a new and closer relationship between industry and universities (Busch et al. 1991; Kenney 1986; Kloppenburg 1988); the erosion of biodiversity (Fowler and Mooney 1990); growing social and economic inequalities associated with the patenting and use of these new technologies (Busch et al. 1991; Doyle 1985; Juma 1989); and their potentially adverse environmental consequences for ecosystems (Goldburg et al. 1990; Krimsky and Wrubel 1996; Rissler and Mellon 1996). Although the industry was still young at the time of these studies,[4] they pointed to the way in which biotechnology was leading to greater economic concentration in the agro-food sector (Busch et al. 1991; Buttel, Kenney, and Kloppenburg 1985; Hobbelink 1991; Kenney 1986); to the privatization and commodification of plant genetic resources and other life forms (Kloppenburg and Kenney 1984; Kloppenburg 1988); and to the further extension of capitalist production relations into the farm sector (Goodman, Sorj, and Wilkinson

1987). The best of these studies took a historical approach to these issues but also identified what was new about the new biotechnologies.

Although this body of literature proved prescient in identifying some of the critical changes biotechnology would introduce into society, the bio-physical world, and the global agro-food system, three important new developments call for a fresh look and additional analysis. First, the technology has moved from the lab to the field—or more accurately, from the lab to the field, the barn, the forest plantation, the sea, and the human body.[5] Between 1996 and 2001, the number of acres planted with GE crops—almost exclusively corn, soy, canola, and cotton—rose from an estimated 1.7 million to an estimated 130 million worldwide (James 2001, 1). Genetic-engineering techniques are also being applied to a growing number of life forms, including insects, farm animals, marine organisms, trees, and humans. Perhaps more important, technology development has been revolutionized—and greatly accelerated—by the advent of genomics and the synergies that have emerged between molecular biology, recombinant DNA techniques, and the bioinformatics sector (see Pueppke 2001; Boyd, this volume; Scholz, this volume).

The second major development has been the extraordinary politicization of the technology. Just when the science and industry of biotechnology began to take off, the technology became a lightning rod for local, national, and transnational conflicts over trade, agriculture, and the environment. These conflicts and the political struggles they have engendered are transforming public perceptions (perhaps most importantly, among investors and consumers) of biotechnology's significance, promise, and future and have shaken the industry to its core.

The evolution of biotechnology, and the public's reaction to it, have strained existing social, economic, legal, and political institutions and revealed critical inadequacies in their ability to cope with the wide array of challenges posed by the technology. These processes are creating powerful demands for institutional change by specific parties and sets of interests. Thus the third major development has been institutional: as such weaknesses and problems are revealed, new institutional arrangements within and among societies—ranging from new food-testing systems to new international regulatory regimes governing trade in GEOs—are being created. These arrangements are changing norms and relations within the sector and are likely to have ramifications that extend far beyond it.

These developments raise many interesting questions, a number of which we seek to explore in this book. How has the biotechnology revolution actually affected the way we produce our food and raw materials? Has it altered the structure and organization of the agro-food sector and the power relations within it? What new social relationships have been forged as a result of the technology? There are also important questions about the institutional changes provoked by genetic engineering. What concrete institutional reforms have been associated with the technology? What are the dynamics of institutional change, and what political struggles are those dynamics engendering? What regulatory structures are becoming dominant within the emerging institutional matrix, and what groups and interests will they favor and empower? How will these new institutions shape the way we relate to the technology in the future?

We also need to understand better the politicization of the technology. What does this politicization mean, what are its consequences, and what is behind it? How broad-based is social resistance to biotechnology? Is this resistance confined to a handful of activist groups and organizations, or are we facing a rapidly expanding popular movement against the technology? How is the politicization of biotechnology influencing the trajectory of technological change? Although the number of academic and popular books being published on biotechnology has burgeoned, none has seriously explored these questions. It is this gap that the present collection seeks to fill.[6]

TECHNOLOGICAL CHANGE

When the first wave of political-economic analyses of agricultural biotechnology appeared in the 1980s, the commercial application of modern biotechnology was still in its infancy. The technology clearly held the potential to transform the agriculture, food, human and animal health, and pharmaceutical sectors, but little technology had actually moved from university and industry laboratories into the commercial sphere. During the 1990s, however, that situation changed dramatically, as a large number of agricultural biotechnology applications were approved for use in the United States as well as abroad.[7]

The two most extensively deployed biotechnologies have been those that render plants resistant to pests and those that confer herbicide tolerance to crops (Shoemaker 2001). Indeed, between 1996 and 1999, herbicide-tolerant soybeans were adopted more rapidly than any agricultural technology in the world, with pest-resistant corn not far behind (Buttel, this volume). Reflecting U.S. farmers' embrace of the technology, in the year 2001, an estimated 68 percent of the U.S. soybean crop, 25 percent of the U.S. corn crop, and 69 percent of the cotton crop were planted with genetically engineered varieties (Agricultural Statistics Board 2001). Also successfully commercialized in the 1990s were chymosin, a genetically engineered enzyme used in cheese production (approved in 1990), and bovine somatotropin (approved in 1993), a genetically engineered growth hormone that causes cows to produce more milk. Because GEOs are widely used by the food-manufacturing industry, they have become virtually ubiquitous in processed food (Barboza 2001a).

Although the adoption of GE crops has been extraordinarily rapid in the U.S., they have not spread around the world as fast or as widely as some of their proponents suggest.[8] Indeed, although farmers in about a dozen countries legally planted GE corn, soy, canola, and cotton (the four most important transgenic crops) in 2001, the use of genetically engineered seeds remains heavily concentrated in only three countries: the United States, Canada, and Argentina. Together these countries account for more than 95 percent of the transgenic acreage planted worldwide. (When China is added, this figure rises to 99 percent; see James 2001.)[9]

Although it is mainly plant biotechnologies that have become a commercial reality in the last decade, molecular biologists and the biotechnology industry have applied their energies and resources to a broad spectrum of living organisms.[10] Currently, scientists are genetically engineering animals for better disease resistance, faster growth, more attractive market traits (e.g., leaner meat or more meat), and higher-protein milk.[11] Some animals—referred to as "pharm animals"—are being genetically engineered so that they can be used to produce body parts for humans and various human therapeutics (e.g., drugs or proteins) in their milk and tissues (Royal Society 2001; Yoon 2000b). Industry researchers are genetically modifying salmon to make them grow faster, and trees to improve market qualities (see the chapters by Dennis Kelso and Scott Prudham in this volume). Even insects have not escaped the molecular biologist's gaze: silk moth caterpillars are being genetically engineered to produce stronger silk, male bollworm moths to render sterile the bollworm moth population in the southern United States, and mosquitoes to deliver vaccines to humans and livestock (Kilman 2001). Although none of these applications has been approved by the relevant government authorities and made it to the marketplace, much of this applied research is quite advanced, and some firms are now seeking regulatory approval for their organisms (e.g., transgenic salmon).[12]

The Growth and Consolidation of the Biotechnology Industry

With the commercial deployment of the technology have come important changes in the size, significance, and structure of the industry. Economically insignificant twenty years ago, the biotechnology industry has become a leading sector in the economy. In the United States alone, the industry generated $20 billion in revenues in 1999, of which agriculture accounted for $2.3 billion (Ernst & Young 2000).[13] And these data include only U.S. companies that are *primarily* engaged in biotechnology activities. The inclusion of industries that provide inputs to the biotechnology sector or utilize the new techniques to produce their products would undoubtedly raise this figure much higher.

Martin Kenney (1998) describes the industrial complex that has grown up around biotechnology as a "new economic space." This space has come to be populated by a handful of life sciences firms, most of which were formerly part of the chemical industry. Although early analysts (see especially Doyle 1985; Hobbelink 1991) clearly perceived the trend toward concentration, William Boyd (this volume) documents the breadth of the structural changes that have occurred as the industry, the technology, and the legal system have coevolved. In recent years, the life sciences firms have integrated vertically and horizontally and now encompass much of the commodity supply chain, from chemical inputs to seed companies to farming (in the form of production contracts). A study by Nicholas Kalaitzandonakes and Bruce Bjornson underscores the degree of concentration that has occurred: during the first half of the 1990s, there were some eight hundred mergers, acquisitions, and other strategic alliances in the agricultural input industry. There were only about a fifth as many a decade earlier (the study is cited in Shoemaker 2001).

Underlying this dramatic shift in industry organization has been the emergence of stronger intellectual-property protection for life forms. In the 1980s and 1990s, patent protection was broadened to include whole plants as well as their constituent parts (genes, gene fragments, proteins, and seeds). Patent rights were also extended, under certain circumstances, to DNA sequences. As the courts extended property rights deeper and deeper into the biological sphere, they created a powerful incentive for industry expansion (Boyd, this volume).

There have also been changes in the nature of competition in the industry (Boyd, this volume; Goldsmith 2001). These changes appear to have been driven by several factors—changes in property law, the fact that a handful of firms control the major segment of the industry, and the emergence of the fields of genomics, bioinformatics, and, most recently, proteomics. According to William Boyd's analysis, the gigantic firms that dominate the life sciences industry now compete by amassing huge property portfolios in the form of patented transgenic organisms, their constituent parts, and the technologies used to create them (see Ratner 1998; Service 2001). Although the industry's use of blocking patents is not new, the application of this competitive strategy to life forms is. The cost of researching and developing new traits and organisms, soliciting patents and regulatory approval, paying licensing fees, and marketing new products has risen so high that few firms can afford to enter the industry.

The Waves of the Future

If the large-scale investments that the private and public sectors are making in these areas are any indication, genomics, bioinformatics, and proteomics are clearly the wave of the future.[14] *Genomics* is the automated sequencing and analysis of genes; *bioinformatics* refers to the inference of genes' functions from information about known DNA sequences in other organisms;

and *proteomics* refers to the science of protein functions and their relationship to genes. All three rely heavily on the new information technologies. The emergence of these new sciences, and their incorporation into plant and animal genetic-engineering research, have raised even higher the barriers to entry that characterize the agricultural biotechnology industry.

William Boyd and Astrid Scholz (both in this volume) argue that genomics has become the driving force of innovation in the biotechnology industry, altering research agendas and augmenting competition over intellectual property rights. These new sciences promise tremendous acceleration of product research and development (R&D)—an all-important attribute in a field in which speed is the essence of competition. Indeed, the language of speed, racing, and getting there first are pervasive in corporate discussions and in descriptions of the industry.[15] Genomics and bioinformatics have enabled firms to analyze many more organisms and traits at a much lower cost, greatly augmenting the number of patents for which firms can apply. The cost of "going genomic," however, is high, which is why most life sciences firms have entered into partnerships, joint ventures, and other strategic relationships with specialized genomics and bioinformatics firms (Boyd, this volume).

The development of these new information sciences has had other consequences as well. The pharmaceutical industry's embrace of these new technologies in its drug discovery process over the last decade has had important implications for the industry's uses of genetic resources from the global South.[16] As Astrid Scholz shows in this volume, the technological changes that have swept the industry have pushed the pharmaceutical sector toward combinatorial chemistry and "rational" drug design, reducing the economic significance of natural products. As a result, the balance of power in genetic-resource negotiations has shifted even further toward pharmaceutical firms, which can now credibly claim that they are less in need of the South's genetic resources. In the future, this reduced dependence is likely to limit the economic benefits Southern countries can derive from their biological diversity.

THE NEW BIOTECHNOLOGY POLITICS

The spread of biotechnology; the consolidation of the biotechnology, seed, chemical, and pharmaceutical companies into a powerful life sciences industry; and the rush to patent genetic organisms and other constituent building blocks of life have all contributed to the recent politicization of the technology, an occurrence that none of the literature predicted. Indeed, the past five years have seen an immense escalation in political activity focused on the use of genetic engineering in agriculture. This activity is starting to shape the development of the technology and may affect it even more in the future. Any attempt to theorize the process of technological change must take this important influence into account.

An interesting question to ponder is why none of the scholars and analysts of biotechnology anticipated either the depth and power of the social response to the technology's development and deployment, or the political, economic, regulatory, and institutional crises this response would precipitate as the century came to a close. In similar fashion, the literature has also glossed over the real scientific challenges—what Andrew Pickering (1995) would call the "resistances of nature"—that have accompanied efforts to genetically engineer specific plants, animals, and marine organisms. Addressing the resistances of nature, although we do not do so here, is a critical next step for agro-food studies, as David Goodman persuasively argues in this volume.

Sources of Resistance

Although the most serious political challenges to the biotechnology industry have come in the past several years, social tensions about the new biotechnologies are neither new nor isolated from other social issues and conflicts (McAfee, this volume). Ever since it became common knowledge that scientists *could* transfer genes across species in ways that were unlikely to occur in nature, individuals and groups have publicly questioned whether they (or we) *should* be doing so. Indeed, a close look at the North American antibiotechnology movement suggests that it has been around nearly as long as the technology.

Social resistance to the use of genetic engineering in agriculture has come from many quarters and is rooted in a broad array of moral, cultural, material, health, and environmental concerns. In Western Europe, where antibiotechnology activism has been most intense, sustained, and effective, activists' critiques have centered on the health and environmental implications of GEOs and the metabolic threats they represent to the living land and the living body (Goodman 1999; Schurman and Munro, this volume). Derrick Purdue's analysis shows how European groups mounted a powerful challenge to biotechnology in the mid-1990s, a challenge based on the mobilization of "counterexpertise" that combined "a situated knowledge of seed science and law with impressive political skills" (Purdue 2000, 11). Coterminous with other food and health scares such as mad cow disease and a growing anti-imperialist (and anti-American) sentiment, public opposition to biotechnology in many European Union (EU) countries has united consumers, farmers, environmentalists, and others in a fierce rejection of the technology and its purveyors. Social activists, particularly the environmental activists, have been instrumental in mobilizing this public opposition to biotechnology—most importantly, among consumers—by tapping into deeply held cultural and aesthetic values with respect to food and its production, and their connection to the preservation of (a simultaneously real and imagined) rural society (Levidow 2000; Schweiger 2001; Thomas 2001).

Ethical concerns about whether human beings ought to be playing God like this, to paraphrase an oft-quoted comment of Prince Charles's, have also figured prominently in the rejection of the technology (Goodman 1999; Frewer 1997; Reisner 2001). In David Goodman's view, the activism against the new agricultural biotechnologies reflects a new kind of biopolitics that rejects the modern ontological division between nature and society and recognizes a "shared community" between human and nonhuman nature (see Goodman 1999 and this volume).[17] Somewhat less sanguine about the anti-GE movement, Richard Lewontin (2001) sees it as embodying a powerful romanticism, in which activists' rejection of biotechnology is associated with a more general revulsion toward the exigencies of late capitalism. Although both views are partially right, they fail to reveal the full range and depth of sensibilities about genetic engineering.

Although no region has manifested a reaction quite as powerful or broad-based as that witnessed in Europe, the politics of agricultural biotechnology have been heating up in other parts of the world as well. In the United States and other advanced capitalist countries (e.g., Japan, Australia, and New Zealand), a broad set of activist groups and organizations has come together to protest agricultural biotechnology on many of the same grounds articulated in Europe (see Schurman and Munro, this volume). Compared with the uproar in Europe, however, social resistance to biotechnology in most other Northern countries is still significantly more activist-based than consumer-based (Buttel 2000), though the threat that the movement could have wider popular appeal presumably goes a long way toward explaining the industry's fierce resistance to GE food labeling (see Guthman, this volume; Alliance for Better Foods 2001).

In the global South, where political struggles over agricultural biotechnology have also grown in frequency and intensity, social resistance has revolved around a somewhat different set of issues. One is "biopiracy," or the appropriation of traditional knowledge and biological resources produced by generations of farmers, particularly indigenous communities. The notion that multinational corporations based in the North want to go to Southern countries to search for genetic material to take home, patent, and then resell to Southern farmers has reignited old resentments about North-South economic inequalities and the history of external exploitation (GRAIN 2000; Shiva 1997; McAfee, this volume). Concerns about biopiracy have been linked to a broader rejection of certain Northern countries' efforts to establish intellectual property rights (IPRs) over life forms (Oh n.d.; Shiva 1997), although the politics of IPRs are intrinsically complicated and reflect a wide diversity of perspectives on political-economic strategies for achieving community, local, and national economic and political empowerment.[18] To many, the notion that life could be patented is absurd and accepting that notion represents a perilous path for indigenous communities and Southern countries to take, given existing world power inequalities (see, e.g., Dove 1996; Kloppenburg 1988; Shiva 1997). Others see the fight against the extension of IPRs as a losing battle. Because the advanced industrialized countries have patent rights to *their* agricultural commodities, they argue, Southern countries and communities should seek to establish such rights as well and should forge agreements that will allow them to maximize the benefits they receive from their genetic resources.

Two other issues—namely, threats to the environment and harmful effects on poor farmers—have galvanized social resistance to biotechnology in both North and South. Worries about the changes that GEOs could introduce into local ecosystems have figured prominently in national and international debates about the safety of GEOs, since many Southern countries are home to the wild relatives of GE species. Critics of the technology have drawn an analogy between the probable social and economic consequences of biotechnology and those of the Green Revolution, which the critics blame for increasing farmers' dependency on Northern corporations for inputs, for reducing the viability of poor farmers, and for harming indigenous communities (Altieri and Rosset 1999; Bryan 1997; Mittal and Rosset 2001; Shiva 1997; Wright 1990). However, the politics of biotechnology, the environment, and the fate of small farmers are far from clear or uncomplicated, since some Southern scientists, academics, and poor farmers see biotechnology in a positive light—as offering a way to lower the costs and minimize the environmental effects of a chemical-intensive agriculture while increasing the yields of local staple crops. Indeed, some Southern scientists have expressed considerable frustration at foreign and domestic nongovernmental organizations (NGOs) for hamstringing their efforts to develop agricultural biotechnologies that they believe could benefit their countries' poorest farmers (Napoleon Juanillo, personal communication).[19]

Forms of Resistance and Arenas of Struggle

Political struggles over the new agricultural biotechnologies and their close cousins, genetic resources, are taking numerous forms and are being fought out on many levels and in multiple arenas. Although colorful protests and the destruction of GE test plots are the actions that have made the most headlines. contemporary biotechnology activism also encompasses lobbying efforts, litigation, regulatory struggles, public education and consciousness-raising, and discursive struggles, as well as politically motivated consumer avoidance of GEOs, or what Melanie Dupuis (2000) describes as a "Not in My Body" reaction to genetically engineered foods (Schurman and Munro, this volume; see also Reisner 2001).

In the advanced industrialized countries, some of the most serious political challenges have been mounted in the regulatory and policy spheres (see Guthman, this volume; Schurman and Munro, this volume). Many Northern activist organizations have focused on food labeling, although as Julie Guthman shows, the politics of labeling are ambiguous, and labeling could easily lead to results that are both politically counterproductive and undesirable to many in the sustainable food movement. In the South, too, political struggles have involved legal and regulatory battles (in Brazil, India, and Chile, for example), though for Southern nations these have been rivaled in importance by activities in multilateral negotiating bodies and forums, such as the UN Convention on Biodiversity (McAfee, this volume) and the UN Cartagena Protocol on Biosafety (Schurman and Munro, this volume). Indeed, the various UN bodies and conventions have been critical arenas of struggle for Southern countries because they represent nodes of control for the transnational movement of germplasm and genetically engineered organisms.

As a number of scholars have argued, the battles over biotechnology and biodiversity are as much about discourse—the power to name and define—as they are about material outcomes (Buttel 2000; Krimsky 1998; Levidow 2001). Business firms, states, NGOs, and local communities are struggling not only over material access to and control over plant genetic resources but also over the meaning of terms such as *resources, nature,* and *the environment* more broadly and over whose value systems, worldviews, and knowledge will prevail when it comes to defining and valuing them (see McAfee, Scholz, and Kelso, all in this volume). Similarly, when activists and the biotechnology industry are at loggerheads over whether GE foods are safe for the human body and other biological systems—and over what kinds of scientific criteria should be relied upon to decide—these conflicts are simultaneously material and discursive. Indeed, in Sheldon Krimsky's view, discursive struggles are ultimately more important than the "surficial" struggles, for "those who eventually gain control over the bio-mythmaking will affect the pathways of innovation for future generations" (1998, 144). Although control over mythmaking is probably best regarded as something that is dynamic and shifting rather than as something that can be conclusively gained or captured, Krimsky's more general point about the significance of discursive struggles is well taken.

Finally, although much of the social resistance to biotechnology is national, there is also an important transnational element to the movement (Schurman and Munro, this volume). The nature and import of that transnationality needs to be more seriously investigated than it has been to date, however. (Indeed, most aspects of the biotechnology politics discussed here have not been adequately theorized.) Toward this goal, social organizing around biotechnology could be fruitfully compared with other transnational social movements, and their modes of organizing and their effectiveness could be analyzed (Keck and Sikkink 1998; Smith and Guarnizo 1998).

Impacts of the New Biotechnology Politics

What effect has the explosion of GEO politics had on the biotechnology industry and on the development and deployment of the technology? Although the effects of biotechnology activism require much more analysis, the studies in this volume suggest that the groundswell of social resistance, both organized and unorganized, is profoundly affecting the industry and the trajectory of technological change. As several of the chapters in this volume show, social resistance has substantially reduced the market for GE products, particularly in Europe; has negatively altered the political climate surrounding the technology by raising concerns about its potential consequences; and has significantly dampened Wall Street's enthusiasm for biotechnology and slowed the industry's momentum. The rising social conflicts have also brought tremendous media and public attention to the issue. In the language of actor-network theory, these new political conflicts have opened up the formerly "black boxed" practices of conventional agriculture—which have now come to include modern methods of genetic engineering—and subjected them to intense scrutiny (Goodman 1999).[20] In the process, private corporations' rights to introduce new technological innovations unimpeded have been challenged.

In our chapter on antibiotechnology activism, Munro and I argue that organized resistance to biotechnology has affected the fortunes of the biotechnology industry and the political environment surrounding the technology in three important ways: first, by pushing supportive states (including the United States) to take more seriously the task of regulation; second, by helping to create new, supranational regulatory regimes for GEOs; and third, by imposing significant economic costs on the industry. In general, our work points to an emerging shift toward the *re*-regulation of the technology and industry, representing an important countertendency to the deregulatory trend of the past two decades.

Dennis Kelso's chapter on genetically engineered salmon demonstrates that the rising social resistance to biotechnology operates in more subtle ways as well. His empirical analysis shows how public perceptions of other GE foods are influencing salmon farmers' thoughts about whether they will adopt transgenic salmon grow-out stock, if and when that GE salmon is approved by government regulators. More generally, Kelso suggests that the commercial adoption of transgenic organisms is not preordained by the mere availability of this new technology and the competitive edge it may offer to some, but will instead depend upon social agency and struggle, including the raging discursive battles over the costs, risks, and benefits the technology promises to convey to different sectors of society and to the environment. Kelso's analysis also shows the real diversity of interests within the salmon sector, reminding us that no industry is totally unified in its interests or behavior and that this diversity may strongly influence the process of technological change, as different groups decide whether or not to adopt the technology or sell products that are made with it.

Thus far, this discussion has focused on how social agency and activism are affecting the deployment of the new agricultural biotechnologies and the economic health of the agricultural biotechnology industry. But the new biotechnology politics will have effects far beyond these realms. As Frederick Buttel points out, the economic globalization regime is now rife with political tensions over GEOs (Buttel, this volume; see also Kelch, Simone, and Madell 1998; and Josling 1999). In his view, the politicization of agricultural biotechnology may turn out to be the Achilles' heel of the North's "globalization project," that is, the organized attempt by a set of globally oriented state policymakers, financial and transnational corporate elites, and managers of global institutions (for example, the International Monetary Fund, World Bank, and World Trade Organization) to stabilize twenty-first-century capitalism (McMichael 1996). Another way in which biotechnology politics has been significant is through its impact on institutional change.

INSTITUTIONAL RESTRUCTURING

As a number of scholars of technology have noted, new technologies are not formed from whole cloth but rather emerge out of particular historical circumstances and existing institutional arrangements (Marx 1967b; Noble 1977; Kloppenburg 1988; Prudham, this volume). *Institutional arrangements* refers to the institutions, organizations, international agreements, and bodies of national and international law and policy that structure the agro-food system, as well as to the informal norms, practices, customs, and power relations that pattern the everyday behavior of relevant actors (Jepperson 1991; Powell and DiMaggio 1991; Veblen 1964). Biotechnology's development has clearly been influenced by a long list of institutions, including prevailing property-rights regimes; the relationship between the public and private sectors (especially between universities and industry) (Wright 1994; Prudham, this volume); scientific conventions, norms, and practices; institutionalized market relations between groups in the agro-food supply chain (Bender and Westgren 2001); the agencies and institutions that collectively create and constitute the regulatory environment (Endres 2000); and trade relations and patterns. It is within this institutional context that biotechnology firms have devised and pursued their R&D strategies, that scientists have developed and tested new technologies and applications, that farmers have decided how and what to plant, and that consumers have made choices about what they are willing to eat.

Yet, as several of the chapters in this volume show, the new biotechnologies not only have evolved out of a particular set of institutional arrangements but also act as springboards for new ones. Indeed, biotechnology—in the broadest sense of the word—serves as a catalyst for the formation of new institutional arrangements in society. Although its catalytic role cannot be seen in isolation from other political, economic, and ideological forces at work in late-twentieth-century capitalism—for example, the material and ideological changes associated with the ascendance of neoliberalism—biotechnology is playing a unique and provocative part in the process of institutional change.

The StarLink corn incident powerfully illustrates this observation. After it became clear that neither the relevant U.S. government agencies (the USDA, the EPA, and the Food and Drug Administration) nor the agro-food industry was capable of keeping the unapproved corn out of the human food supply, new norms for genetic testing, new protocols for growing and handling GE crops, new regulatory standards, new labeling requirements, and new systems of distribution were developed. In general, the stresses generated by biotechnology created demands for the institutional reforms that are now being pursued.

New Governance Structures

Examples of the institutional changes provoked by the scientific, social, economic, and environmental aspects of the biotechnology revolution are many and range from relatively insignificant changes to profound changes in the social norms, relations, and governance structures characterizing the agro-food system. Perhaps the most obvious arena in which biotechnology has generated a demand for institutional change is that of intellectual property rights. As the life sciences firms have sought to capitalize on their enormous investments in genetic engineering, genomics, and drug discovery and development, they have demanded greater protection of private property rights. The need to establish proprietary rights over living organisms is seen as paramount, since such rights remain the primary means by which firms can profit from their investments in research, development, and acquisition.[21]

This push for institutional change in the intellectual-property sphere is not a new phenomenon; nor is it associated exclusively with modern biotechnology or with the biotechnology industry.[22] As Jack Kloppenburg (1988) showed in *First the Seed*, private plant-breeders in the United States and Europe have long sought to establish proprietary rights to plant genetic resources and have been quite successful. Yet some features of the present period—and of the biotechnology industry's involvement with this effort—

are particularly notable. For example, efforts to extend IPRs to life forms are now being carried out at the *international* level as well as the national level. In response to the concerns of the biotechnology industry (as well as other key industries), the United States, supported by other advanced industrialized countries, is pressuring other countries to adopt systems of private property rights that are commensurate with its own. These systems will extend protection for the new seed, plant, animal, and process technologies into developing countries, most of which have patent, copyright, trademark, and trade-secret protections that are far less comprehensive than those in the United States. The primary (but by no means the only) vehicle for this effort is the World Trade Organization (WTO). During the Uruguay Round of the GATT negotiations (the precursor to the WTO), the advanced industrialized countries pushed for the Agreement on Trade-Related Aspects of Intellectual Property Rights (TRIPS), which will impose minimum IPR standards on all countries by 2006. To remain in compliance with the WTO, countries will have to change their national laws to meet these standards (Oh n.d.).

A second noteworthy change is that whereas in the past it was primarily independent seed companies that were pushing for proprietary rights in germplasm, it is now a vertically integrated and economically powerful life sciences industry that is pushing for proprietary rights with regard to a much broader array of life forms. The marriage of the agricultural biotechnology, chemical, pharmaceutical, and seed industries has created a coalition whose interests in IPRs are similar and who collectively wield tremendous political power. The progress made in recent decades in extending private property rights to life forms testifies to the power of the life sciences sector to shape the institutional environment in its favor.

The public's reaction to biotechnology is significantly changing two other institutions: the food-supply and food-distribution systems. The rejection of GEOs by European consumers, along with the fallout from the StarLink debacle, is stimulating the development of a new "identity preservation" system that will eventually make it possible, at least in theory, to segregate genetically engineered crops from non-engineered crops. Although it is not clear that such segregation is feasible in practice—particularly in open-pollinated crops, such as corn and canola—new storage facilities, farm management practices, transport and processing systems, and even easier-to-clean machinery are being developed. These changes will extend and complicate the commodity supply chain as existing industry actors alter their crop-growing and crop-handling methods, as new businesses offer new services to grain growers and suppliers (e.g., genetic testing, certification, and separate storage systems and facilities), and as specialized markets are established.

Another sort of institutional change is reflected in the plethora of initiatives taken at the local, regional, national, and international levels to deal with the economic, environmental, and human-health concerns raised by this new technology. Interestingly, much of this change is about (re)regulation and undoubtedly reflects as much a reaction to two decades' worth of neoliberal policy reforms and national *de*-regulation as it does the challenges posed by the new biotechnologies. In the United States, some localities have passed ordinances that ban or require labeling for GE food distributed in public programs, and states have considered (and in some cases passed) bills that would place temporary moratoriums on the planting of GE crops and make it illegal to raise GE fish in lakes and ponds connected to other waterways. Although most of these efforts represent small and highly circumscribed challenges to the biotechnology industry, they do represent institutional change. Much more sweeping, however, are the changes that have taken place in national and transnational regulation of GEOs. For example, the growing demand for GEO-free products in many countries has created significant pressure for national labeling systems that institutionalize this aspect of postproduction "choice" (see Guthman, this volume). At the international level, the growth of trade in GEOs has led to the Cartagena Protocol on Biosafety, an international agreement to regulate the international movement of GEOs, and the establishment of an intergovernmental task force on genetically engineered foods within the Codex Alimentarius Commission, the UN organization that sets international food and safety standards. Within the Codex there is considerable pressure (particularly from Europe and Japan) to establish a system that will allow GE products to be traced from field to market ("Japan's Stand" 2001). The establishment of such a system would represent a major shift in the way foods are identified, labeled, and internationally traded.

The Process of Institutional Change

Although little theorizing has been done about these processes of institutional change, many of the reforms spurred by biotechnology have clearly evolved out of existing institutions that have been modified to fit new circumstances or extended into new spheres, or both. For example, as Scott Prudham shows in his chapter in this volume, the genetic-engineering research now being done on trees in the U.S. Pacific Northwest reflects a long history of public-sector involvement in and support for research aimed at increasing commodity production. Yet the institution of the silviculture research cooperative itself is changing, both in response to IPR developments and to changes in the broader political economy of public science, which have made public funds more difficult to come by while offering new opportunities for the commercialization of publicly supported research through the Bayh-Dole Act of 1980. Although the future of such cooperatives is difficult to discern, the old model of cooperation in tree improvement and the free sharing of plant genetic material among co-op members is likely to be supplanted by new models of academic-industrial relations that "emphasize more-formal management of research as intellectual property . . . [and] more-exclusive relationships, public and private" (Prudham, this volume).

Historical continuities are also evident in the area of intellectual property rights, which, as already noted, have been a long-term concern of private seed companies in the United States and Europe. In this case, the efforts of the biotechnology industry and the governments of advanced industrialized countries to create more comprehensive—and increasingly global—IPR systems can be seen as an attempt to extend the authority of an institution into new geographical and biological spheres. In the process, however, such institutions tend to change significantly as they are adapted to new circumstances and are reshaped by local social and environmental forces. We need to study both aspects—efforts to extend particular institutions, and the process of transformation by local actors—if we want to understand processes of institutional change.

Although biotechnology's coming of age has stimulated the transformation of existing institutions, wholly new institutions, patterns, and relations are also being established. As Scholz describes in her chapter, the demand for genetic resources by the large pharmaceutical companies has generated new institutional arrangements in the form of bioprospecting fees paid to various state and nongovernmental institutions (see also Gamez 1993; Kloppenburg and Rodríguez 1992). These fees follow certain norms established by pioneering agreements such as that between Merck and Company and the Costa Rican biodiversity institute named INBio. The Cartagena Protocol discussed in several chapters of this book also had no historical precursor and was a direct outcome of the new environmental challenges raised by biotechnology and concerns about its deployment on a world scale.

Tremendous political struggle characterizes the process of institutional change because particular groups seek to promote, protect, and institutionalize their interests. These political struggles are being fought in a variety of settings, from the informal, grassroots, and local, to the formal, national, and international. But it is not only their ubiquity and diversity that should command our attention; so too should the fact that the process of struggle itself can lead to new and unanticipated agreements and alliances between stakeholders and, in some cases, to unexpected institutional outcomes. Yet, while struggles over institutional reform invariably reflect existing power dynamics and relations, they do not necessarily (or perfectly) reproduce them, because different groups may alter or crystallize their definitions of self-interest, establish new alliances, and enter into new political arrangements and compromises. Hence, the very process of political struggle can create opportunities for altering power dynamics and relations in the future through the re-evaluation of existing patterns and the establishment of new norms, regulatory frameworks, and institutional relationships.

THE POLITICAL TERRAIN OF THE BIOTECHNOLOGY MILLENNIUM

I close with three final observations about biotechnology, its meaning, and its future. First, many of the technological, social, and institutional developments that are occurring around biotechnology today are fundamentally ambiguous. As the most astute students of technology have argued, technologies embody emancipatory as well as oppressive potential; indeed, the meaning, consequences, and transformative potential of any particular technology depend upon how that technology is deployed, by whom and for what purposes and upon the meanings it is given by those who use it (Bijker, Hughes, and Pinch 1987; Bijker and Law 1992; Haraway 2002). In the context of the technologies that concerns us here—those involving the genetic engineering of plants, animals, and other living organisms—it is not hard to imagine liberatory and positive possibilities, as well as the more negative scenarios painted by biotechnology's critics.

A second and closely related observation is that social, historical, and environmental context matters. Who makes decisions about the development and deployment of a particular technology, where and how it is deployed, how much control various social groups have over these decisions, and how the nonhuman world acts and reacts—all these contextual factors matter enormously in determining the myriad consequences of technological change. This is the reason that it is so important to investigate and analyze the patterns of control and decision making in the case of contemporary agricultural and other related biotechnologies.

The final observation has to do with the broader political-economic developments that are taking place in the biotechnology field and that are poised to influence profoundly the contexts just described. On the one hand, we are clearly in the midst of a major restructuring of the agro-food system (Bonanno et al. 1994; McMichael 1994, 1995; Goodman and Watts 1997), a process to which biotechnology is an important contributor. Large corporations seem to be gaining greater control over many factors: the technologies used to produce food, fibers, and raw materials; the genetic material on which they are based; the labor, land, and production practices of farmers; and the food-distribution and food-marketing systems. On the other hand, and before we conclude that hegemonic corporate control over the agro-food system is the only possible future, we must recognize that no single set of actors—be they life sciences corporations, agro-industry, transnational elites, or powerful states—fully controls the agro-food system.

Even though the multinational life sciences corporations appear to have amassed unprecedented power during the last decade and half, that power is contested by a wide range of groups and actor networks (see Latour 1983). Indeed, the very process of moving specific biotechnologies from inception to commercialization has brought them into the public eye and given civil society access to them, in test plots and production practices as well as in the marketplace. These technologies' very presence in such public places makes them vulnerable to challenge and to alternative uses and interpretations. The politicization of biotechnology could have a highly democratizing effect on the agro-food system. Or at least these struggles will help to form the new political terrains of the biotechnology millennium.

NOTES

I am indebted to Michael Goldman, William Munro, and Dennis Kelso for their close reading of and useful feedback on this chapter.

1. In this book, we use the term *genetically engineered organisms* rather than *genetically modified organisms* to stress that our frame of reference is modern methods of genetic engineering rather than traditional plant-breeding techniques. Although farmers, crop and animal scientists, and others have been modifying the genetic makeup of plants and animals for centuries, only in recent decades has it become possible to broadly and routinely transfer genes *across* species in ways that are not likely to occur in nature. The techniques that form the basis for modern biotechnology— for example, tissue cell culture, protoplast fusion, the use of monoclonal antibodies, and embryo transfers—are often referred to as "the new biotechnologies," a convention that we uphold. A glossary of terms appears at the back of this book.

2. The term *agricultural biotechnology* is something of a misnomer here, in that the authors of this volume address the use of recombinant DNA techniques in plant and animal agriculture as well as in aquaculture, plantation forestry, and the pharmaceutical industry. We also use the terms *biotechnology* and *biotechnologies* interchangeably to reflect a wide range of related technologies and applications.

3. When we use the term *biotechnology* or *technological change*, we typically mean it in this broad sense of the word. Our aim is to avoid reifying (bio)technology or failing to recognize its multifaceted nature and the social and historical relations it signifies. See the discussion by Scott Prudham in this volume.

4. Most analysts locate the beginning of the biotechnology revolution in 1973, when Herbert Boyer of the University of California, San Francisco, and Stanley Cohen of Stanford University invented the technique of recombining DNA (rDNA). (For a fascinating history, see Wright 1994). In 1976, Boyer and an associate started the biotechnology firm Genentech, which two years later announced that it had successfully used recombinant DNA techniques to produce human insulin. From this point on, the industry aroused Wall Street's interest (see Kevles 1998).

5. We do not address human genetic engineering in this volume. There is a fascinating new literature on biotechnology and the human body that deals with this issue, however; see, for instance, the work of Emily Martin, Rayna Rapp, Lori Andrews, Dorothy Nelkin, and Charis Thompson Cussins.

6. A number of superb books on biotechnology have appeared in recent years, many of which were written by historians of science. See, for instance, Robert Bud's *The Uses of Life: A History of Biotechnology* (1993); Susan Wright's *Molecular Politics: Developing American and British Regulatory Policy for Genetic Engineering, 1972-1982* (1994); Arnold Thackray's edited collection *Private Science: Biotechnology and the Rise of the Molecular Sciences* (1998); Evelyn Fox Keller's *The Century of the Gene* (2000); and Lily Kay's *Who Wrote the Book of Life? A History of the Genetic Code* (2000). A useful primer for the nonbiologist is Richard Lewontin's *The Triple Helix: Gene, Organism, and Environment* (2000). The recent edited collections by Gerald Nelson (2001), Richard Hindmarsh, Geoffrey Lawrence, and Janet Norton (1998), and Brian Tokar (2001) provide useful analyses of the sector from a variety of viewpoints. Three popular books worth reading are *Lords of the Harvest: Biotech, Big Money, and the Future of Food*, by Daniel Charles (2001); *First Fruit: The Creation of the Flavr Savr Tomato and the Birth of Genetically Engineered Food*, by Belinda Martineau (2001); and *Dinner at the New Gene Café: How Genetic Engineering Is Changing What We Eat, How We Live, And the Global Politics of Food*, by Bill Lambrecht (2001).

7. As of July 2001, the U.S. Department of Agriculture had approved fifty-three varieties of genetically engineered crops, as well as several other agricultural applications (Shoemaker 2001, 18).

8. A major promoter of the technology is Clive James, chairman of the board of directors of the International Service for the Acquisition of Agri-biotech Applications (ISAAA), a "not-for-profit international organization co-sponsored by public and private sector institutions" based at Cornell University in Ithaca, New York. The ISAAA's self-proclaimed aim is to facilitate the acquisition and "trans[fer of] agri-biotech applications from industrial countries in the North, particularly proprietary technology from the private sector, to developing countries for their benefit" (ISAAA 2002). James is the author of the ISAAA's influential publication *Global Review of Commercialized Transgenic Crops*, which appears annually. As Frederick Buttel (2002) has noted, James's reviews are the primary (if not the only) source of data on the global diffusion of transgenic crops. They are also replete with remarkable boosterism, particularly for a publication that is, at least in name, clearly associated with a major and internationally renowned U.S. university. A look at the coverage and use these annual reports receive reveals that ISAAA is playing a critical (and sociologically fascinating) role in establishing the "fact" that agricultural biotechnology is an unstoppable juggernaut, hurtling its way around the world. We favor a more scholarly and nuanced interpretation of James's data, such as Buttel's.

9. This First World character of the technology is actually quite remarkable, given that the global spread of these crops has been actively pursued by the large life-sciences companies. In their global marketing efforts, these firms have been indirectly supported by multilateral trade agreements such as NAFTA, by the regulations of the WTO, and by the global embrace of neoliberal economic policies. All have helped to open up foreign markets for U.S. agricultural products.

10. Although the biotechnology applications mentioned here were recognized and, in some cases, developed as early as the plant biotechnologies discussed earlier, they have taken longer to come to fruition because of greater scientific and regulatory challenges. For instance, the first transgenic animal was the famous onco-

mouse created by Harvard university scientists in 1981 and patented in 1988. Transgenic pigs were developed as early as 1986 by USDA researchers, but these pigs still have not received government approval.

11. A good recent summary of the state of animal biotechnology is a report produced by Britain's Royal Society (Royal Society 2001).

12. According to John Matheson, a senior regulatory review scientist at the Food and Drug Administration's Office of Surveillance and Compliance in the Center for Veterinary Medicine, no bioengineered animals have been approved for any kind of commercial use in the United States (personal correspondence, e-mail, June 18, 2001). The one exception is the oncomouse mentioned earlier.

13. In economic terms, 80 to 90 percent of total biotechnology industry revenues in 1999 came from the pharmaceutical and human-health industries (Ernst & Young 2000, 1).

14. In 2001, for example, the University of Illinois committed forty new faculty positions to a new center for genomics research. Even for a major public university, this represents a huge commitment and symbolizes the profound shift in university science toward commodity-oriented research, a trend discussed by Scott Prudham in this volume.

15. See Fortun 1998 for a provocative analysis of the significance of speed in the context of the Human Genome Project.

16. We use the term "global South" to refer to the countries that used to be called the "Third World." We use the term "global North" to refer to the advanced industrialized countries.

17. Although Goodman concedes that these groups are not "devoid of anthropomorphism" (1999, 31) the contradictions embedded in their thinking may run deeper than he acknowledges. Donna Haraway (1997, 60-62) has offered a powerful critique of this activist position on the grounds that it assumes a static, pure, and ahistorical nature.

18. See, for instance, the divergent positions reflected in Gonzales and Kloppenburg 1993, Juma 1989, Kloppenburg and Rodríguez 1992, Rothschild 1997, and Brush and Stabinsky 1996.

19. Juanillo is an assistant professor in the Department of Human and Community Development at the University of Illinois.

20. Drawing on Law 1992, Goodman describes "black boxing" as the (temporary) stabilization of an actor network so that it is perceived as irreversible and can function as single node in another network. Another way to think of a black boxed network is one that has been successfully, if temporarily, institutionalized.

21. On the need for property rights see, for instance, Carl B. Feldbaum, president of BIO, Open Letter to President George Bush, January 16, 2002, retrieved November 23, 2002, from www.bio.org/issues/bush2002.asp. Genetic use restriction technologies (GURTs), also referred to as "terminator technologies," represent another attempt to circumvent the need for patents, by building sterility right into the seed. This is what Jack Kloppenburg (1988) called the "biological route" to commodification. At this point, however, it is still not clear that science is capable of delivering GURTs for a wide variety of crops or that social forces will allow GURTs to be deployed. The notion that farmers will not be able to save seed is offensive to many, and the issue has proved relatively easy to organize around.

22. Other global industries concerned about intellectual property rights are the telecommunications, publishing, and entertainment industries, all of which depend on the juridical system to establish and protect their rights to private property. Thus, biotechnology should be seen not as the sole catalyst for these changes but rather as an important part of a broad effort supported by a number of industries.

1

Wonderful Potencies?

Deep Structure and the Problem of Monopoly in Agricultural Biotechnology

William Boyd

The heredity values of specially bred strains of plants and animals are as real as the seemingly more concrete values of land or goods. Potent economic values run through generation after generation as persistently and as irresistibly as the river runs from its many springs to the sea. Unseen carriers of heredity determine whether the product shall be large or small, of high or low quality, lovely or homely. Their value to the nation is far above that of gold. Gladly we pay high prices for new "blood" in plants or animals because through the sure and potent agency of heredity the enhanced values continue during succeeding years. Heredity is a force more subtle and more marvelous than electricity. Once generated it needs no additional force to sustain it. Once new breeding values are created they continue as permanent economic forces.

"Heredity: Creative Energy," *American Breeders Magazine* I, 1910

In their opening editorial for the spring 1910 issue of *American Breeders Magazine,* Willet Hays and his staff offered a grand vision of heredity as a productive force. In their view, and presumably in the view of most members of the American Breeders Association, the new science of breeding and genetic improvement promised a sort of second industrial revolution for agriculture—a qualitative advance beyond efforts to improve productivity through mechanization and the application of fertilizers and other exogenous inputs. As breeding values were transformed into property rights, they became key vehicles for capital accumulation and, more broadly, for the industrialization of agricultural systems. At the beginning of the twenty-first century, more than one hundred years after the rediscovery of Mendel's work on inheritance, the application of the new biotechnologies promises to push this logic of intensification further than Hays and his colleagues likely ever imagined.

A professor of agriculture at the University of Minnesota and later undersecretary of agriculture, Hays was the founding secretary and guiding force behind the American Breeders Association (ABA). Founded in 1903 and composed of commercial breeders, scientists from agricultural colleges and experiment stations, U.S. Department of Agriculture (USDA) researchers, and other people interested in inheritance and breeding, the ABA proved to be an early force in the assimilation of Mendel's work into the practice of breeding (Kimmelman 1983; Rosenberg, 1997, 211-24; Paul and Kimmelman 1988). ABA members were among the first to appreciate the predictive value of Mendelian ratios, and they set to work on applying the "fundamental laws of breeding" to agricultural improvement. Here was an early illustration of the marriage of science and industry in an effort to press biology into the service of commercial gain. In the vision of Willet Hays, the ABA would bring together scientists and practical breeders "in a grand cooperative effort to improve those great staple crops and magnificent species of animals." Only on the basis of such cooperation between "the breeders and the students of heredity," Hays argued, could the "wonderful potencies of heredity be harnessed and placed under the control and direction of man as are the great physical forces of nature" (Hays 1905, 9-10).

One does not have to look far in today's politically charged debate over agricultural biotechnology to find boosterism that rivals that of Hays and the ABA. Americans and American business leaders have always had a remarkable enthusiasm for new technologies (Hughes 1989). Yet, whereas Hays spoke directly of harnessing heredity for economic and commercial gain, today's advocates tend to invoke a vision of a healthier and more environmentally friendly agriculture—often posed against a Malthusian backdrop of world famine. Lurking beneath the surface, of course, are the priorities of national competitiveness in strategic high-tech sectors and the power of large multinational corporations seeking to capitalize on the wave of innovations and proprietary technologies associated with recombinant DNA techniques (Wright 1998). In the process, the structure and practice of agriculture and agro-food systems are undergoing a substantial reorganization—the limits of which are not entirely clear.

The main stumbling block today, it seems, is not so much the science but the politics. Indeed, the politics surrounding agricultural biotechnology seem to be more potent than the breeding values themselves. As the public outcry against genetically engineered foods spreads from Europe to the United States and beyond, several of the first-movers in the field, most notably Monsanto, appear to be in trouble—their strategy for creating an integrated life-sciences complex very much on hold (Niiler 2000; Eichenwald, Kolata, and Petersen 2001). Some have even suggested that agricultural biotechnology may go the way of nuclear power in the United States—a pariah technology that never lived up to initial expectations (Loewenberg 1999). Although this reaction may be rather extreme, a number of serious legal and regulatory issues could severely dampen the enthusiasm of investors and consumers—without whom, of course, the technology does not have much of a chance.

Despite these lingering concerns and uncertainties, however, the commercial penetration of agricultural biotechnology in the United States and several other major crop-producing regions has been nothing short of astonishing. Since their introduction in 1996, the global area of the four principal transgenic crops (soybeans, canola, cotton, and corn) has increased to roughly 52.6 million hectares (130 million acres), constituting approximately 46 percent of global soybean acreage; 20 percent of global cotton acreage; 11 percent of global canola acreage; and 7 percent of global corn acreage (2001 figures). This represented an increase of 19 percent over 2000 acreages (James 2001).[1] Consequently, the value of the global market for transgenic seeds grew from a paltry $156 million in 1996 to more than $3 billion in 2000 (James 2001).

Not surprisingly, the United States has emerged as the leader in the adoption of agricultural biotechnology. By 2001, some 68 percent of the global area of transgenic crops was concentrated in the United States, but acreages continue to expand in a number of other grain- and oil-seed-producing regions around the world (James 2001). Moreover, despite considerable commentary in the press and elsewhere that the adoption of these transgenic crops would level off because of the public concerns regarding genetically engineered food products, U.S. farmers continue to embrace the technology. According to recently released USDA figures, for example, the total proportion of U.S. soybean acreage planted with transgenic varieties increased from 54 percent in 2000 to 63 percent in 2001 (Brasher 2001, B-3).

As of May 1999, U.S. regulators had approved some fifty-three different transgenic products for thirteen different crops, the vast majority of which are engineered for herbicide tolerance and insect resistance (Shoemaker 2001, 18). This first generation of "input-oriented" traits has focused exclusively on crop protection, with farmers being the target market. The next generation of "output-oriented" traits, which are just reaching commercialization, are focused on engineering qualities into crops that will produce enhanced food and feed products, such as feed grains with enhanced levels of amino acids, high-oil corn, beta-carotene-enhanced rice, field crops that produce vaccines and other specialty chemicals (Shoemaker 2001, 19). These products are focused more on consumers and other end users than on farmers and do not necessarily elicit the same sorts of health and environmental concerns that crop-protection traits do.

What has perhaps been most remarkable (yet least noticed) about the commercial success of agricultural biotechnology, however, is the massive industrial consolidation that has accompanied the spread of these technologies. As table 1 indicates, by 1999 the top three global seed companies were all chemical companies—each of which moved aggressively into the life sciences field during the 1990s. With its $7.7 billion purchase of

TABLE 1. Top 10 Global Seed Companies, 2000

Company	1999 Seed Sales (US$ millions)
DuPont/Pioneer (USA)	1,850
Monsanto (USA)	1,700
Syngenta (Novartis & AstraZeneca) (Switzerland/UK)	947
Groupe Limagrain (France)	700
Grupo Pulsar/Seminis (Mex.)	531
Advanta (UK/Netherlands)	416
Sakata (Japan)	396
KWS AG (Germany)	355
Dow (USA)	350
Delta Pine & Land (USA)	301

SOURCE: Rural Advancement Fund International.

TABLE 2. U.S. Corn Seed Market Shares, 2000

Company	Market Share (%)
DuPont/Pioneer	42
Monsanto	30
Syngenta	9
Dow	4
Cargill	3
Other	12

SOURCE: JP Morgan, Chemical Market Reporter.

Pioneer Hi-Bred in 1999, DuPont became the largest seed company in the world. Likewise, Monsanto spent close to $8 billion acquiring seed companies and other biotechnology firms during the second half of the 1990s. Novartis and Dow made similar moves. All told, between 1996 and 1999, roughly $15 billion worth of mergers occurred in the global seed industry (a remarkable figure given that the total value of the global seed market was only $25 billion), driven almost entirely by the desire to acquire high-quality germplasm to use as a vehicle for delivering proprietary traits.[2] By 2000, two companies, DuPont and Monsanto, controlled more than 70 percent of the market for U.S. corn seed (see table 2). Through its acquisition of major seed companies and its aggressive licensing program, Monsanto attained the number two market position in the U.S. corn seed market, the number one position in the Brazilian, Mexican, and Argentine corn seed markets, the number one position in the U.S. soybean seed market, and the number one position in the European wheat market (Monsanto Company 2000, 66-67). Viewed in the aggregate, these developments represent a profound restructuring in the ownership of and control over the germplasm resources for the major commercial crops, posing substantial implications for the structure, organization, and practice of agro-food systems.

As for the agricultural biotechnology market, Monsanto has clearly established itself as the early leader, commanding a market share of more than 80 percent by the late 1990s. In 1999, out of the total global acreage of 100 million acres of transgenic crops, Monsanto's agricultural biotechnology products were planted on some 86 million acres. Much of this success stems from the company's Roundup Ready soybeans, which have been genetically engineered to tolerate Roundup, Monsanto's glyphosate-based herbicide (Monsanto Company 2000, 65).[3]

Following Monsanto, leading firms have pursued a general strategy of building a vertically integrated structure that links research on and development of specific biotechnology products (traits) with seed-delivery systems (seed companies) in order to deliver to farmers a package of value-added inputs (seeds and chemicals). Figure 1 presents a schematic representation of the structure of the agricultural biotechnology complex circa 2002. This process of vertical and horizontal integration has resulted in consolidation of control over the basic transformation technologies used in the genetic modification of crops; control over proprietary traits; and control over the elite germplasm resources for many of the world's most important commercial crops. Patent rights, and the strategies these firms have deployed to capture the value associated with these rights, have been a driving force in this restructuring. Examining how and why these changes have occurred is the task of this essay.

The observation that motivates the essay is that there is a deep structure to the agricultural biotechnology complex that derives from the particular ways in which science, law, and business have come together in an effort to industrialize *agricultural* systems. Over the past several decades, and especially over the past ten years, key actors have been engaged in constructing a new industrial order that, if successful, promises to reshape large segments of the global agro-food system. Understanding how this industrial order came to be and the implications it raises for law and policy are the primary objectives of this essay.

The essay is divided into four sections. The first examines the transformation of agricultural breeding efforts under the influence of modern genetics and molecular biology, focusing on how the highly reductionist view of life that came to dominate breeding and genetic improvement

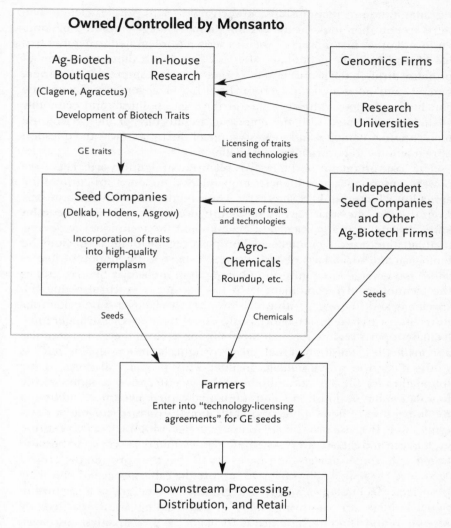

Figure 1. Ag-biotech firm structure (Monsanto), ca. 2002.

efforts following World War II has been accompanied by an accelerated shift in the locus of innovation from the public land-grant complex to private biotechnology companies, large life-sciences multinationals, and, more recently, small boutique genomics firms. The second section focuses on legal developments that have allowed both for the transformation of "novel" life forms and genetic sequences into new forms of property and for the reconfiguration of relationships between public and private science. The third section then looks at the organizational strategy employed by Monsanto and other first-movers to create a vertically integrated structure capable of capturing the economic value associated with these new forms of property through the acquisition of key germplasm resources, seed-delivery systems, and horizontal and vertical licensing arrangements. Finally, the concluding section addresses some of the legal, political, and economic challenges associated with the emerging architecture of the agricultural biotechnology complex and suggests some of the reasons why the question of regulation and governance is so challenging.

The basic argument of the essay is relatively straightforward: There are powerful monopolistic tendencies embedded in the deep structure of the agricultural biotechnology enterprise. These tendencies derive in large part from the synergies that have developed between the increased precision and calculability in the science of genetics and the techniques of genetic manipulation, a stronger intellectual-property regime for life forms, and the biological and social facts of agriculture. In short, as the notion of "life as code" has emerged as a governing paradigm in molecular biology, and as the technology of recombinant DNA has become a practical reality, the specificity and frequency with which proprietary claims can be made over novel life forms have grown enormously. The emergence of a stronger intellectual-property regime for such novel life forms since the early 1980s has also made the acquisition of such property rights far more valuable, adding to the incentives to consolidate an intellectual-property platform as the foundation for the agricultural biotechnology enterprise. Creating such a foundation has obviously entailed substantial capital investment, adding to the imperative of developing an organizational structure capable of delivering value. Because proprietary traits are useless without access to existing germplasm and seed-delivery systems for key commercial crops and because farmers (in some capacity) are necessary in that they provide the critical "grow-out" stage that allows firms to capture the value associated with their proprietary technologies, vertical integration has emerged as a key institutional vehicle for capturing value. Thus, leading firms, particularly Monsanto and DuPont, have acquired major seed companies and developed a system of contract farming tailored to the new biotech crops. In the long run, the hope is to integrate further downstream into the food-processing sector—linking the input and output segments of the agro-food chain into a coordinated industrial system. The result of these efforts, accomplished in less than a decade, is a global oligopoly of five firms that now controls large segments of the global agro-food complex. And it is this development—as much as labeling and biosafety—that begs attention from regulators, academics, and the public itself.

BREEDING AND BIOTECHNOLOGY: LIFE AS CODE

Heredity is described today in terms of information, messages and code. The reproduction of an organism has become that of its constituent molecules. This is not because each chemical species has the ability to produce copies of itself, but because the structure of the macromolecules is determined down to the last detail by sequences of the four chemical radicals contained in the genetic heritage. What are transmitted from generation to generation are the "instructions" specifying the molecular structures: the architectural plans of the future organism.

François Jacob, *The Logic of Life,* 1973

The metaphor of life as code has become second nature in the era of modern biotechnology. Drawing heavily on ideas from information theory and cybernetics, this "informationist" solution to some of the basic problems of molecular biology has come to provide much of the foundation for efforts to "improve" biological systems by intervening directly in the genetic program itself. Codes, as Lily Kay reminds us, can be cracked, programmed, and reprogrammed. The idea that the basic architecture of the organism is contained within its genetic code carries with it all sorts of interventionist possibilities (Kay 1998, 2000; Keller 1993).

The intellectual and institutional histories of molecular biology and, specifically, the story of how the structure and function of DNA were identified and elaborated are familiar enough (Allen 1978, ch. 7; Mayr 1982, chs. 18-19; Kay 1993; Morange 1998). As the "heroic" age of theoretical advance and synthesis gave way to what Thomas Kuhn (1969) called "normal" academic science, focused on refining and extending the key elements of the Watson-Crick model of the structure of DNA, the possibilities of practical application began to open up. The basic insight that all organisms employ the same rules for turning nucleotide sequences into amino acid sequences using three-letter nucleotide codons created the opportunity for the development of modern biotechnology. By the early 1970s, the demonstration by Stanley Cohen and Herbert Boyer that pieces of DNA could be taken from one organism and inserted into another in a manner that would lead to coding for particular proteins ushered in the recombinant era. For agricultural scientists and breeders, this technique provided the technical means for transcending the species barrier and moving genes that coded for desirable traits (assuming they could be found and isolated) between sexually incompatible organisms. The view of geneticists and molecular biologists as code breakers was conjoined with that of breeders as genetic engineers—architects capable of reconfiguring, rather than simply discovering and cultivating, genetic information in a manner that would generate new "breeding values."

When combined with the possibility of protecting these efforts through new forms of property (an issue taken up later in the chapter) and the presence of an infrastructure of financial and legal services, the commercialization of biotechnology seemed to be a foregone conclusion. Out of this institutional matrix emerged the new scientist-entrepreneur with one foot in the world of university research and the other in the world of high-tech start-ups. Following in the footsteps of the larger biomedical start-ups, notably Genentech, Amgen, and Chiron, agricultural biotechnology start-ups such as Agracetus, Calgene, and Mycogen promised to create new crops and techniques that represented a qualitative advance beyond previous agricultural improvement efforts (Kenney 1986, 1998). In addition to these start-up efforts, Monsanto and several other large chemical firms began to move into the area during the early 1980s—focusing on acquiring and developing the necessary science and the key enabling technologies (along with the associated intellectual property rights) in order to build an innovation pipeline.[4]

Progress in the lab came quickly. In 1983, California-based Calgene announced that it had discovered a mutant bacteria gene conferring resistance to the broad-spectrum herbicide known as glyphosate. Specifically, the gene coded for a mutant form of an enzyme that was immune to glyphosate. If the gene could be successfully inserted and expressed in crop plants, Calgene hypothesized, it might enable farmers to solve all their weed problems in a single herbicide application—a prospect that proved particularly interesting to Monsanto, given that glyphosate was the active ingredient in its best-selling herbicide, Roundup ("Monsanto, Calgene" 1983, 28). Spurred by this development, Monsanto unveiled a $150 million biotechnology research center the following year and announced that it had successfully expressed a mammalian protein in a plant. President and CEO Richard J. Mahoney also noted that the company would shift a third of its research efforts away from commodity petrochemicals toward agriculture, animal nutrition, and health care, hoping to commercialize its first biotech product by the end of the decade ("Monsanto Puts" 1984, 1). Other major chemical firms followed suit by establishing their own research initiatives, joining the race to develop and commercialize new biotech products.[5] In addition to expanding in-house research efforts, these companies also began developing research agreements and alliances with smaller biotech firms (Trewhitt and Bluestone 1985, 34).

The lure of biotechnology for these companies was not hard to understand. Until the 1950s, researchers could come up with one commercially useful pesticide compound for every two thousand screened. By the 1980s, largely because of increased resistance, researchers were screening twenty thousand or more compounds to come up with a single product. Developing a new crop-protection product and taking it to market took an average of seven years and cost roughly $30 million. Genetic engineering held out the promise of accelerated and more precise development of new products, speeding and expanding scientists' understanding of why certain chemicals affect plants in certain ways (Trewhitt and Bluestone 1985, 34). As one biotechnology researcher put it, "In the past we played roulette. We now have control over where the ball lands" (quoted in Rotman 1993, 33). Given the maturity of the agrochemical market, moreover, most of these firms were searching for new sources of revenue growth. Agricultural biotechnology, in short, held out the potential for both accelerated product cycles and new value-added products.

By 1985, initial investments began to bear fruit. In January, the biotechnology start-up Plant Genetic Systems announced that it had succeeded in inserting a *Bacillus thuringiensis* (Bt) gene into a tobacco plant, thus laying the groundwork for the development and commercialization of insect-resistant technology.[6] The following month, Calgene announced that it had successfully expressed its glyphosate-resistant gene in tobacco plants and had initiated glyphosate-tolerance projects in a wide range of other crops (Trewhitt and Bluestone 1985, 34). Not to be outdone, Monsanto followed several months later with an announcement that it had genetically engineered petunia, tobacco, and tomato plants to tolerate commercial sprayings of Roundup. In a sign of the impending competition in the sector, Monsanto also noted that Calgene's efforts to engineer glyphosate resistance were effective only against dilute concentrations of the herbicide and were thus not commercially viable ("Monsanto Unveils" 1985, 3). At the same time, various firms accelerated their efforts to develop new and more effective transformation techniques. In addition to the discovery and patenting of useful traits and new transgenic plant varieties, control over key transformation technologies held out the possibility of substantial competitive advantage. The gene wars had begun.[7]

As efforts in the lab progressed, attention shifted to field testing and regulatory approval. By the 1989 planting season, researchers were conducting some fifty-nine different field tests for genetically engineered plants—up from fewer than ten in 1988. If approval went smoothly, researchers hoped to commercialize the first transgenic crops by the early 1990s ("Plant Biotechnologists" 1989, 5). In 1992, the White House released guidelines promoting genetically altered foods, thereby lifting a cloud of uncertainty from the industry ("White House" 1992, 1).[8] Four years later, the first transgenic crops entered commercial production. Based on the technologies of herbicide tolerance and insect resistance developed during the previous decade, these new crops promised to revolutionize agriculture in the United States. After close to fifteen years of research and development, leading firms had successfully translated the notion of life as code, and the interventionist possibilities associated with recombinant DNA techniques, into commercial reality.

Notwithstanding their substantial investments in research and development, however, these firms proved unable to keep up with the rapid pace of innovation in the biotechnology sector. During the mid-1990s, as the first transgenic crops were being commercialized, the growing emphasis on genomics and bioinformatics forced Monsanto and other firms to develop strategic alliances with some of the leading companies in the genomics area and to invest heavily in their own genomics efforts (Ratner 1998, 810-11).[9] By the end of the decade, genomics had become the driving force of innovation in the industry—reshaping research agendas and stimulating intense competition to acquire key intellectual property rights.

Pioneer Hi-Bred kicked off the genomics race in 1996 through an alliance with Human Genome Sciences to sequence corn genes. As the largest seed company in the world, Pioneer was clearly "in the market" for genes and realized that sequencing offered a potential shortcut to the patent office (Fairley 1998g, 18).[10] Shortly after Pioneer's initial foray into genomics, Monsanto announced its own research collaboration with another leading genomics firm, Palo Alto-based Incyte Pharmaceuticals (Rotman 1997a; 1997b, 14). The following year, in 1997, Monsanto entered into a five-year, $218 million collaboration with the genomics powerhouse Millennium Pharmaceuticals of Cambridge, Massachusetts. Under the terms of that deal, Monsanto received exclusive access to Millennium's genomics technologies for all crop plants. At the same time, Monsanto also formed a wholly owned genomics subsidiary, Cereon, for the purposes of collaborating with Millennium in gene discovery (Marshall 1997). Such deals were intended to significantly increase Monsanto's expertise and capabilities in mapping and sequencing genes, complementing its efforts to put a seed-delivery organization in place and develop techniques for genetic modification. In the words of Steven Holtzman, Millennium's chief business officer, "Monsanto has all the tools necessary to deliver high-value genes in genetically engineered crops. Now it needs the genes" (quoted in Rotman 1997b, 14).[11]

Playing catch-up with Monsanto, DuPont and Novartis announced their own independent genomics investments in 1998—betting that genomics capabilities would be critical in the race to identify (and patent) novel traits for crop protection and crop enhancement. Witness the words of DuPont manager Forrest Chumley, "Very shortly all the genes that matter are going to be cloned [isolated for patent purposes]. There's a real race to get there first" (quoted in Fairley 1998d, 9). In July 1998 Novartis initiated a $600 million, ten-year plant genomics initiative, the centerpiece of which was a $250 million genomics center, the Novartis Agricultural Discovery Institute, in San Diego. In addition, Novartis developed strategic alliances with other genomics firms and universities, such as the University of California, Berkeley, giving the company right of first refusal on any patents produced through the initiative. Initial plans were to fund some 180 scientists working in fifty labs with a focus on generating databases tracing the relationships between genes, proteins, and specific traits (Welch 1998, 23; Fairley 1998d, 9).

By the late 1990s, with improved automation and increased capacity for sequencing and high-throughput screening, genomics became the primary locus of innovation in agricultural biotechnology, raising the stakes in plant biotech research. According to Monsanto, these new technologies drove the total cost of sequencing a gene from approximately $150 million in 1974 down to $150 by 1998 (Enriquez 2000, 7). By developing databases of genes and gene markers for major crops, the objective was to gain a deeper understanding of the entire genetic code of valuable crops in the hope of identifying valuable new traits and breeding strategies and, of course, locking up intellectual property as quickly as possible.[12]

Genomics promised the possibility of significant time compression in breeding efforts and the potential for acquiring new patent claims over the next generation of genetically engineered traits (Holmberg 2000, 1; Reichmann, Zhang, and Broun 1999, 12).[13] By February 2001, initial investments appeared to be bearing fruit when Syngenta (formerly Novartis) announced that its genomics research center had completed a map of the rice genome (the first complete genome sequence for a commercial plant), beating out a number of rivals, including Monsanto and the publicly financed International Rice Genome Sequencing Project. Although Syngenta promised to release the information without cost to research institutes that served developing countries as well as to academic scientists, the fact that a private entity produced the first genome map of such a commercially important crop reinforced fears that the genetic resources central to world agriculture were vulnerable to proprietary control (Smith 2001, 1; "University" 2000; Jacobs 2000).

In essence, the advent of genomics marks a further step in the ongoing transformation of biology into an information science. Although it is not entirely clear what the "product" of genomics is and where the ultimate payoff will be, the locus of innovation in the agricultural biotechnology industry has shifted decisively from attention to single-gene traits and gene transfer to genomics.[14] In some respects, the reductionism that has distinguished genetics and molecular biology since World War II has given way to a more holistic approach of mapping the entire genomes of particular organisms. The challenge, of course, lies not in determining the actual sequence of an organism's genome, but rather in interpreting it. The sequences of model organisms—yeast, the nematode *Caenorhabditis elegans,* and the fruit fly *Drosophila melanogaster*—are intended to provide a Rosetta stone of sorts for interpreting the genomes of more complex organisms. Genomics thus holds out the promise of a grand unification in biology, providing the key to the basic processes of gene function and protein synthesis common to all organisms (Lander and Weinberg 2000). For agriculture, genomics promises not only an acceleration of ongoing breeding efforts but also a greater precision in the understanding and control of critical metabolic pathways—a new stage in the effort to harness the power of heredity (Gura 2000).

This trend toward ever greater precision and calculability in the understanding of heredity and the transformation of that understanding into new "breeding values" derives in large part from the "informationist" approach to biology—the notion of life as code. As this trend has progressed, new possibilities for intervention and manipulation have opened up, allowing leading firms to develop an awesome array of capabilities.[15] At the same time, this trend has been accompanied by a tendency toward increasing proprietary control. Simply put, as the understanding of heredity has moved to the molecular level, the precision with which new breeding values can be represented has increased considerably, allowing for more specific legal claims and an improved ability to enforce such claims—all of which work to encourage privatization. In the context of the broad and hospitable intellectual-property system that has emerged in the United States, the new science of biotechnology has thus created a wealth of opportunities for new forms of property.

PATENTING LIFE: THE LEGAL ARCHITECTURE
OF A NEW ECONOMIC SPACE

Here, by contrast, the patentee has produced a new bacterium with markedly different characteristics from any found in nature and one having the potential for significant utility. His discovery is not nature's handiwork, but his own; accordingly it is patentable subject matter.
    Diamond v. Chakrabarty, 1980

The ability of genes derived from totally different biological classes to replicate and be expressed in a particular microorganism permits the attainment of interspecies genetic recombination. Thus, it becomes practical to introduce into a particular microorganism, genes specifying such metabolic or synthetic functions as nitrogen fixation, photosynthesis, antibiotic production, hormone synthesis, protein synthesis, e.g. enzymes or antibodies, or the like—functions which are indigenous to other classes of organisms—by linking the foreign genes to a particular plasmid or viral replication.
    First Cohen-Boyer patent, 1980

It is the policy and objective of the Congress to use the patent system to promote the utilization of inventions arising from federally supported research or development; [and] . . . to promote collaboration between commercial concerns and nonprofit organizations, including universities.
    Bayh-Dole Act of 1980

Three major legal developments in 1980—one judicial, one administrative, and one legislative—established much of the basic legal architecture that has structured the U.S. biotechnology industry. In June 1980, the Supreme Court handed down its famous *Chakrabarty* decision, overturning the U.S. Patent and Trademark Office's (PTO) denial of a utility patent for a newly engineered bacterium capable of metabolizing oil (*Diamond v. Chakrabarty*, 447 U.S. 303 [1980]). Six months later, the PTO issued the first Cohen-Boyer patent (the process patent), which gave Stanford and the University of California patent rights to the basic technique of genetic engineering (*Process for Producing Biologically Functional Molecular Chimeras*, U.S. Patent No. 4,237,224, December 2, 1980). And ten days after that, Congress passed the Bayh-Dole Act of 1980, allowing for the commercialization of federally sponsored research and ushering in a new era of university-industry collaboration and technology transfer between the public and private sectors (35 U.S.C. §200). Together these three developments created a new economic space in which the biotechnology industry could flourish.

The Chakrabarty Regime

Chakrabarty stood for the principle that human-engineered life forms were patentable subject matter under section 101 of the Patent Act (35 U.S.C. §100 et seq.).[16] The case involved a patent claim by General Electric scientist Ananda Chakrabarty on a microbe that he had developed for the purpose of degrading crude oil. In his patent application, Chakrabarty claimed the process of making the organism, a method for dispersing it, and the organism itself. The PTO accepted the first two claims but denied the third on the grounds that the microorganism itself was a "product of nature" and thus not patentable subject matter.[17] By a 5-4 decision, the Supreme Court rejected the arguments of the patent office, paving the way for a new and stronger intellectual-property regime governing living organisms and their constituent parts. As such, the decision was part of a more general trend in U.S. patent law that took shape during the early 1980s and resulted in stronger patent protections and extensions of patentability into new areas.[18]

Writing for the majority, Chief Justice Burger affirmed the Court's precedent that "laws of nature, physical phenomena, and abstract ideas have been held not patentable" (447 U.S. 303, 309 [1980]). In doing so, he distinguished the *Chakrabarty* facts from those of a 1948 case, *Funk Brothers Seed Co. v. Kalo Inoculant Co.* (333 U.S. 127 [1948]), that had explicitly rejected patent eligibility for a class of cultured root-nodule bacteria useful in stimulating nitrogen fixation in plants. In that case Justice Douglas noted that "patents cannot issue for the discovery of the phenomena of nature. The qualities of these bacteria, like the heat of the sun, electricity, or the qualities of metals, are part of the storehouse of knowledge of all men. They are manifestations of laws of nature, free to all men and reserved exclusively to none" (333 U.S. 127, 130).

But the *Chakrabarty* case was different precisely because of the nature and scope of human intervention necessary to engineer the new bacterium. In contrast to the bacteria involved in the *Funk Brothers* case, which represented "no more than the discovery of some of the handiwork of nature" (333 U.S.

127, 131), Chakrabarty's bacteria were not naturally occurring—raising the question of whether living organisms, natural or not, should be eligible for patent protection. In interpreting the relevant statutory language and legislative history of the various patent acts, Burger stressed that Congress "plainly contemplated that the patent laws would be given wide scope" (447 U.S. 303, 308-9). Quoting from the committee reports accompanying the 1952 Patent Act, Burger emphasized that Congress intended patentable subject matter to "include anything under the sun that is made by man" (303, 309). Thus, because Chakrabarty's new bacterium was "not nature's handiwork, but his own," it was patentable subject matter. The distinction between living and nonliving had no place in the patent law (310).

In a powerful dissent, Justice Brennan pointed out that Congress had previously addressed the issue of intellectual-property protection for certain life forms through two statutes, the Plant Patent Act of 1930 and the Plant Variety Protection Act of 1970 (35 U.S.C. §161 et seq.; 7 U.S.C. §2321 et. seq.). These acts, he argued, "strongly evidence a congressional limitation that excludes bacteria from patentability."[19] The fact that Congress found it necessary to enact specific legislation to extend patentlike protection to certain plant varieties demonstrated Congress's intent that living things were not covered under section 101 of the Patent Act. "If newly developed living organisms not naturally occurring had been patentable under §101," he pointed out, "the plants included in the scope of the 1930 and 1970 Acts could have been patented without new legislation." The majority's opinion thus rested on the shaky "assumption that Congress was engaged in either idle exercise or mere correction of the public record when it enacted the 1930 and 1970 Acts." But even if these acts did not dispose of the issue, Brennan maintained, the Court was exceeding its own institutional competence by extending patentability in such a radical manner. Congress alone was the appropriate entity for determining the scope of the patent laws in areas marked by uncertainty and substantial public concern (447 U.S. 303, 319, 320).

Although the *Chakrabarty* decision represented a victory for the proponents of biotechnology, the implications for agriculture, and specifically property rights over commercial plant varieties, were not immediately clear. The problem, suggested by both the majority and the dissenting opinions, was the potential overlap between the Patent Act as extended by *Chakrabarty* and the two statutes that specifically provided patentlike protection for certain plant varieties. Lacking judicial guidance on the issue and seeking to clear up the confusion, the PTO adopted a policy that gave the 1930 and 1970 acts preemptive status over the Patent Act. Subject matter that could be patented under either of those acts would not be eligible for protection under the general patent law. For the time being, *Chakrabarty* did not extend to the creation of new plant varieties, whatever the method (Kloppenburg 1988, 261-70).

Challenges to the PTO policy came quickly. Molecular Genetics, a small biotechnology firm from Minneapolis, contested the PTO's policy when it was denied utility patent protection for certain claims relating to maize seeds, tissue cultures, and whole plant lines that had been manipulated to produce increased levels of tryptophan. In a 1985 hearing before the Board of Patent Appeals and Interferences, the reviewing examiners rejected the PTO's arguments that the plant-specific acts provided exclusive protection for plant life covered under the acts. Based on the principles established in *Chakrabarty*, the board's decision, known as *Ex Parte Hibberd*, expressly allowed for the patenting of plants and their constituent parts under section 101 of U.S. patent law (*In re* Hibberd, 227 U.S.P.Q. 443 [Bd. Pat. App. & Interf. 1985]). This was an enormous step forward from the relatively weak intellectual-property regime that had previously governed plant-breeding efforts (Kloppenburg 1988, 130-51, 261-70; Bugos and Kevles 1992; Seay 1993). But it was only an administrative decision and thus had no power to bind a federal court.

Not until 1998 did the *Hibberd* ruling face its first judicial test. In a case brought by Pioneer Hi-Bred against a group of local seed suppliers for allegedly infringing Pioneer's utility patents on hybrid corn seed, an Iowa district court accepted the *Hibberd* ruling (*Pioneer Hi-Bred International Inc. v. J.E.M. Ag Supply*, U.S. Dist. LEXIS 21782 [N. D. Iowa, 1998]). On appeal, the Court of Appeals for the Federal Circuit affirmed, holding that seeds and seed-grown plants are patentable subject matter under section 101 of the Patent Act. In its opinion, the court noted that in the past plants had been ineligible for patent protection because they were "products of nature" and "could not be described with sufficient precision to satisfy the written description requirement of the patent statute" (*Pioneer Hi-Bred International, Inc. v. J.E.M. Ag Supply*, 200 F. 3d 1374 [Fed. Cir. 2000]). Owing to advances in breeding and biotechnology, both of these obstacles had been overcome:

> Now, however, mankind is learning how to modify plants in ways unknown to nature. In addition, precision of description is no longer an insurmountable obstacle. . . . The Court, cognizant of advances in science, has ratified the traversal of these past impediments to the compass of §101. Although there remain the traditional categories that have never been viewed as patentable subject matter, viz., laws of nature, natural phenomena, and abstract ideas, the policy underlying the patent system fosters its application to all areas of technology-based commerce. (200 F. 3d 1374, 1376)

In December 2001, the Supreme Court affirmed the court of appeals' decision, using the case as an opportunity to reinforce broad patent rights for plants and plant materials (*J.E.M. Ag Supply, Inc. v. Pioneer Hi-Bred Int'l, Inc.*, 122 S. Ct. 593 [2001]). Given the Court's precedent in the area and the massive growth of the agricultural biotechnology industry over the last two decades, the Court's holding that utility patents may be issued for plants under the patent statute did not come as a surprise.

By bringing plant materials under the domain of the general patent act, *Chakrabarty* and *Ex Parte Hibberd* thus opened the door for a proliferation of patent claims on plants and their constituent parts.[20] Whereas the prior regime of plant protection allowed for only a single claim over a new plant variety as an indivisible whole, utility patents allowed for multiple claims, including the plant itself and various constituent parts such as genes, cells, tissue cultures, and seeds.[21] Such protections reflected (and reinforced) the increased specificity and control made possible by the new biotechnologies and the view of life as code. Given their improved ability to describe, isolate, and manipulate various traits and organisms, plant breeders could make an increasingly compelling case for stronger intellectual-property protection.[22] At the same time, the lure of stronger patent protections created additional incentives for research and development.

In addition to patent protections for genetically engineered life forms, biotechnology also benefited from the extension of patent protection to cover DNA sequences. Unlike life forms, however, genes could be patented without posing any special problem for the subject matter requirements under section 101. Although genes qua genes, and DNA sequences in general, seemed to fall squarely within the patent law's prohibition on "naturally occurring phenomena," existing patent doctrine relating to chemical compounds provided an obvious solution. Assuming DNA sequences met the other requirements of patentability, they qualified as patentable subject matter as long as they were purified and isolated in a manner analogous to that used for chemical compounds. Under this standard, purified proteins, purified DNA transcripts, and even purified partial DNA transcripts would all be appropriate subject matter for patenting.[23]

The implications of this transition in intellectual-property protection for agriculture have only recently begun to emerge. The overall trend appears to be in the direction of increased concentration of economic power in the hands of large multinational firms, a situation that creates new risks and liabilities for actors all along the agro-food chain. To take one example, under the previous intellectual-property regime governed by the 1970 Plant Variety Protection Act, farmers could save seeds from their own crops to plant the following year.[24] Under the *Chakrabarty* regime, by contrast, utility patent holders can sue farmers who save seed. Over the last several years, Monsanto has done precisely that in enforcing the provisions of the technology-licensing arrangement it has developed with farmers who want access to the company's proprietary traits ("Monsanto Alleges" 2000).[25]

Chakrabarty and *Ex Parte Hibberd* thus created a much more formal and increasingly privatized system of intellectual-property protection for germplasm resources and new genetically engineered organisms. Incentive structures and revenue streams have shifted to favor private actors able to capitalize on the new technologies, facilitating a race to patent valuable resources and exploit first-mover advantages. Genomics simply reinforces this land-rush mentality, pushing private actors to expand the number and scope of their patent claims (Enriquez 1998).[26] By building up a broad portfolio of patent rights, firms seek to improve their bargaining position in relation to capital markets and competitors, create barriers to entry for new firms, and, if the property rights become commercialized, establish new entitlement lines that will allow them to capture value along the agricultural commodity chain.

Cohen-Boyer

Unlike *Chakrabarty,* the first Cohen-Boyer patent involved not an organism per se but rather a process for shifting bits of DNA sequence between sexually incompatible organisms. In many ways, this was the real technological foundation for the commercial biotechnology industry. As such, it fit perfectly within the new intellectual-property framework established by *Chakrabarty.* Not only the newly created organisms but also the processes used to create such organisms were patentable. Cohen-Boyer thus extended the incentives associated with privatization into the upstream reaches of the biotechnology complex. Almost all biotechnology research, to the extent that it involved a novel technique or produced a novel product, was now capable of being commercialized. The advantage to this, of course, was that it created substantial incentives for innovation. The disadvantage was that it had a potentially distorting effect on academic research, pushing researchers in directions that promised monetary reward and undermining incentives for collaboration.

The Cohen-Boyer patent also focused attention on the fact that universities could enrich themselves by licensing the inventions for their scientists. Stanford and the University of California, San Francisco, licensed the Cohen-Boyer patent widely, generating nearly $200 million in royalties before it expired in 1997 ("72 Firms" 1981, 4; Rauber 1997). This trend was a significant departure from the model of university research that prevailed after World War II. Indeed, because of restrictions associated with federal funding, much of the research carried out in universities was not amenable to commercialization. All of this changed in 1980 with passage of the Bayh-Dole Act, which allowed for the commercialization of federally funded research.

Bayh-Dole

The basic premise behind Bayh-Dole, that the patenting of such inventions was a public good, has stimulated significant debate. According to the thinking that guided the legislation, patent protection would provide incentives for researchers to develop products that would serve the very public whose tax dollars supported that research (although the public would essentially be paying twice for such research). In contrast to the "dead hand" effect of public ownership, by which valuable discoveries and inventions would atrophy in a public sphere that lacked entrepreneurial energy, the possibility of private appropriation would result in a more efficient utilization of public money (Eisenberg 1996).

As originally conceived, Bayh-Dole was intended to benefit mainly small businesses receiving federal funding, with the overall intention of stimulating industrial development, job growth, and international competitiveness. Universities and other nonprofit organizations were of secondary concern. Yet, Bayh-Dole had a substantial impact on university research because it opened the door for extensive university-industry collaboration. Moreover, although Bayh-Dole was not designed with biotechnology in mind, it had a tremendous influence on the biotechnology enterprise. Indeed, given the knowledge-intensive character of biotechnology (and the concomitant importance of university-based scientists) and the fact that patents are so important in the biotechnology area, the interchange between universities and industry facilitated under the Bayh-Dole framework has been far more intense in biotechnology than in almost any other field. The danger is that universities will be transformed from public goods into special interests intent on selling themselves as engines of economic growth.

What is important about Bayh-Dole for understanding the emergence and evolution of the agricultural biotechnology complex is that it created a whole new incentive structure for university scientists and forged new pathways between public and private science—critical elements of what Martin Kenney has termed the "university-industrial complex" (Kenney 1986). As such, the act complemented the intellectual property regime established under *Chakrabarty*, reinforcing the tendency toward privatization of biotechnology research and creating significant incentives for universities to develop their own intellectual-property portfolios and licensing strategies. Not surprisingly, many of the early biotechnology start-ups emerged directly from the university setting, and most of the major agricultural biotechnology firms have subsequently developed strong relationships with universities in their efforts to maintain an innovation pipeline for generating intellectual property.[27]

A New Legal Infrastructure

Taken together, *Chakrabarty*, Cohen-Boyer, and Bayh-Dole represented a new legal infrastructure for the agricultural biotechnology complex. When combined with the advances in molecular biology and genetics discussed in the previous section, these changes allowed for a major expansion in the nature and scope of proprietary claims over biological organisms and their

constituent parts. Given the increased precision and calculability made possible by the view of life as code, new legal claims could be made and
enforced more easily than in the past.

To take advantage of these opportunities, leading firms pursued a strategy of acquiring a portfolio of broad and fundamental patents relating to
key commercial crops and transformation technologies with the overall goal
of securing first-mover advantages and strengthening bargaining positions
vis-à-vis competitors. Using the new tools of biotechnology, these firms filed
increasing numbers of patent applications throughout the 1980s, not only
on specific genes and their application in particular plants but also on the
plants themselves (as well as their seeds and the progeny of those seeds) and
on the transformation technologies used to engineer new plant varieties. By
the early 1990s, as the first major agricultural biotechnology patents began
to issue, many observers expressed astonishment at the breadth of some of
the patent claims.

In 1992, for example, Agracetus received a patent that included a claim
covering all transgenic cotton (*Genetic Engineering of Cotton Plants and Lines*,
U.S. Patent No. 5,159,135, October 27, 1992). Using its proprietary "gene
gun" transformation technology to create the transgenic variety, the company won the broad claim on the grounds that it was the first to show that
cotton could be genetically engineered by any method.[28] Far exceeding the
scope of patents on particular genes, seed varieties, or transformation techniques, the claim thus covered all genetically engineered varieties of an
entire crop, effectively granting Agracetus the rights to any genetically engineered cotton produced by any method until 2008. The first of its kind, the
patent is still widely considered to be the broadest patent ever granted in
the field of plant biotechnology ("Patent" 1992, 5). Not surprisingly, it
stirred considerable controversy. Jerry E. Quisenberry, director of the
Cotton Systems Research Laboratory at the USDA, called the decision "very
unfortunate." "Rather than being able to release new genetically engineered cotton varieties directly to farmers, we are now forced to go to this
large company and enter into an agreement with them" (quoted in
Shulman 1994, 16).[29] Although Agracetus pledged to license its technology
widely, nothing in the law could compel it to do so. Indeed, early licenses
granted to Calgene and Monsanto were restricted to work focused on
improving the agronomic aspects of cotton. Licensees were explicitly barred
from attempting to alter the qualities and characteristics of cotton fibers, an
area that Agracetus wanted to preserve for itself ("Patent," 5). This kind of
licensing strategy simply reinforced the incentive to acquire strategic
patents to improve a company's position in future licensing negotiations. To
be a player in the arena of genetically engineered crops, having a sufficiently broad patent portfolio was the price of admission.

As more patents began to issue and as the first products approached commercialization, the industry saw a flurry of cross-licensing deals between leading firms. Many of these deals involved licenses for specific genes or traits, such as herbicide tolerance or insect resistance, whereas others involved specific transformation technologies.[30] Because many of the new patent claims were framed so broadly, particularly in the area of basic processes and inventions, it became increasingly difficult to develop new transgenic plants without infringing on patent rights of one sort or another (Barton 1998, 85-97). Cross-licensing obviously provided one way of sorting out these conflicting entitlement lines. Such agreements might be explicit or implicit (as in a tacit agreement not to sue for infringement), highlighting the strategic importance of acquiring patents likely to be infringed so as to enhance bargaining power (Barton 1998, 94).[31]

Licensing could only go so far, however. As firms raced to commercialize the new technologies, recently issued patents became increasingly valuable. Given that multiple firms were often working in the same area, and because the newly issued patent claims often overlapped, firms increasingly turned to litigation as a competitive tactic.[32] In one of the more heavily litigated areas—the case of the insect-resistance technology known as *Bacillus thuringiensis* (Bt)—a number of overlapping patents were awarded during the mid-1990s, including a patent to the first firm to clone the Bt gene; a patent to the first firm to put the gene in any plant; and a patent to the first firm to put the gene in a crop plant. Not surprisingly, as Bt products moved closer to commercialization, the breadth and overlap of the patent claims provided fertile ground for litigation and, in some cases, new incentives for consolidation (Barton 1998, 92-93; Barton 1999, 5; Neubar 1999).

Indeed, as leading firms such as Monsanto, Novartis, and DuPont have sought to develop and amass patent portfolios that are broad enough to bar entry by new players and deep enough in terms of their control over basic technologies to give them substantial economic power in key markets, litigation over the nature and scope of these patent claims has proliferated. Following a pattern typical of patent infringement actions, these firms often filed suit against their competitors as soon as they received a patent. Competitors usually responded with counterclaims of patent invalidity. In the case of Bt technology, for example, more than a dozen lawsuits were filed between 1995 and 1997, when the first Bt patents began to issue, involving most of the major players in the industry (Rotman 1995, 1996b; "Mycogen Stock" 1996; "Mycogen Proceeds" 1996; Lehrman 1996; "Dekalb" 1996; "Novartis" 1997). Although some of these suits have subsequently been dismissed, settled, or dropped as a result of mergers, several of the more important disputes have resulted in jury verdicts and appellate decisions.

In February 1998, for example, a federal jury in Wilmington, Delaware, rejected claims by Mycogen that Monsanto and its licensees had infringed

TABLE 3. Selected Ag-Biotech Patents by Assignee

(cumulative through March 2001)

Assignee	Maize or Corn Plants or Seeds	Soybean Plants or Seeds	Bacillus thurin- giensis	Plants or Seeds Generally
Monsanto (Dekalb, Agracetus, Calgene, Asgrow)	188	266	38	885
Syngenta (Novartis)	186	110	45	932
DuPont (Pioneer)	337	87	1	484
Aventis (Rhone Poulenc, Hoescht)	43	24	3	263
Dow (Mycogen)	43	19	130	275

SOURCE: LEXIS Patent Database, search by claim and assignee, March 31, 2001.

upon Mycogen's 1996 patents covering the use of Bt to create insect-resistant crops.[33] The jury's decision effectively invalidated the 1996 patents, depriving Mycogen of royalties and damages exceeding $70 million. Mycogen's stock subsequently dropped more than 20 percent (Fairley 1998b, 13). In March 2001, the Court of Appeals for the Federal Circuit upheld the lower court ruling (*Mycogen v. Monsanto,* 2001 U.S. App. LEXIS 3729 [Fed. Cir. 2001]). Four months after Monsanto received its favorable jury verdict against Mycogen, however, another federal jury in Delaware rejected a Monsanto action against Mycogen, Novartis, and others relating to a patent for synthetic Bt genes, invalidating the Monsanto patent on the grounds of prior invention.[34] But in November 1998, Monsanto prevailed again, receiving another favorable jury verdict in a Bt patent infringement action brought by Novartis (Rubenstein 1999).

To date, the litigation over the rights to Bt technology has invalidated patents held by Mycogen, Monsanto, and Novartis. These rulings have narrowed the respective portfolios of Bt patents held by these companies, suggesting that courts will likely not allow patents of very broad scope to stand. However, by early 2001, almost 400 patents had been issued with claims relating to Bt, and more are being issued all the time. As table 3 above indicates, Mycogen alone had 130 patents with claims relating to Bt. All the leading companies are also hard at work on developing the next generation of Bt technology. More important, they are also involved in cross-licensing agreements with one another. It may turn out that as the industry structure stabilizes, firms will find litigation less attractive and may seek out cross-licensing arrangements, explicit or implicit (Barton 1998, 94).

But licensing agreements have sometimes led to lawsuits as well, particularly in the wake of mergers. In 1998, for example, a California jury ordered Monsanto to pay $174.9 million in damages to Mycogen because Monsanto had refused to honor a gene-licensing agreement for Bt corn that Monsanto had negotiated with a company (Lubrizol Genetics) that was later acquired by Mycogen. In Mycogen's view, Monsanto's actions represented a deliberate attempt to lock Mycogen out of the Bt corn market (Kilman 1998).[35] Similarly, in February 2000, a federal judge in North Carolina upheld a jury award of $65 million to Aventis Crop Science against the Monsanto subsidiary Dekalb Genetics for misappropriation and fraud stemming from a 1994 licensing agreement for herbicide-tolerance technology ("Judge" 2000, 5; "Aventis" 2000, 10). And, in March 2000, DuPont filed suit against Monsanto, alleging that Monsanto stole the key technology used to create its herbicide-resistant soybeans when it acquired Asgrow Seed, a company that had worked with DuPont in the late 1980s to develop the technology ("DuPont Claims" 2000, 5).

Such lawsuits can protect firms against entry into particular product lines by others or, conversely, can open up new areas to competition. Through such litigation, the boundaries of economic power and the structure of the industry are being determined.[36] In effect, the courts are being used not only to clarify intellectual property rights but also to determine the boundaries between the handful of major firms that now dominate the industry. Litigation, in short, has become an important component of the strategies employed by these firms as they jockey for position in the emerging oligopoly.

Meanwhile, the rush to patent continues. As table 3 shows, the five major firms in the agricultural biotechnology industry have amassed considerable patent portfolios in key crops and technologies. Although the table captures only a portion of the total number of biotechnology-related patents held by these firms, it suggests the extent of these patent portfolios and the difficulties faced by new firms seeking to enter the industry. These overlapping patent portfolios have resulted in a veritable "patent thicket"—a densely overlapping matrix of entitlement lines that operate as a substantial barrier to entry (Shapiro 2000; Barton 1998). Any new firm seeking to enter one of these areas would face the daunting prospect of trying to patent around these portfolios or trying to negotiate a sufficient number of licensing agreements with the various patent holders to avoid infringement suits.[37] Not exactly an attractive set of options.

Genomics will likely strengthen these barriers to entry. Seeking to lock up as much intellectual property as quickly as possible, industry leaders such as Monsanto and DuPont have been pursuing patenting strategies based on expressed sequence tags, or ESTs (gene fragments that can be used to identify and ultimately isolate the gene itself), from the genomes of major commercial crops. Through their partnerships with elite genomics firms and on the basis of their own sequencing efforts, these large firms are developing libraries of ESTs (and genes) for the major crops and are filing patent applications as quickly as possible. Relying on a set of tools and techniques known broadly as bioinformatics (i.e., computer-assisted genetic analysis tools that infer gene functions from DNA sequences by comparing those sequences to well-known genes in other organisms), these firms are betting that inferred gene function will be enough to support patent claims. This prospect was reinforced in October 1998, when the PTO awarded an EST patent to Incyte Pharmaceuticals. But persistent confusion regarding the PTO's policy toward ESTs and the lack of any appellate-level decisions on these kinds of claims have made this strategy somewhat uncertain (Fairley 1998g, 18; Ratner 1998, 810-11).

Indeed, patent claims on DNA sequences derived from genomics and bioinformatics are of an altogether different nature than those derived from earlier techniques of isolating and purifying single genes. Because the new sequences are essentially computer-generated information, the chemical-compound analogy that provided the basis for granting gene patents in the past may no longer be appropriate (Eisenberg 2000).[38] In some respects, the uncertainties relating to the application of patent doctrine in this area simply reinforce incentives to file as many patent applications as possible. For these and other reasons, the avalanche of data derived from various sequencing efforts has translated into a flood of patent applications at the PTO.[39]

To deal with the flood, the PTO adopted new utility guidelines in January 2001 (U.S. PTO 2001). By requiring that a specific claim enable at least one credible use, the new rules, which have been around in draft form since December 1999, raise the bar for patentability of ESTs and other DNA sequences derived from genomics sequencing efforts.[40] Simply predicting or inferring gene function may not be enough under the new rules. But the policy has yet to be tested in court, and there is no guarantee that the Federal Circuit would follow it. Indeed, in a case decided in 1998, the Federal Circuit held that inventions involving the input, calculation, and storage of numerical data are patentable subject matter as long as they produce a "useful, concrete, and tangible result" (*State Street Bank & Trust v. Signature Financial Group*, 149 F. 3d 1368 [Fed. Cir. 1998]). Several commentators have suggested that this ruling, together with another 1999 Federal Circuit decision (*AT&T Corp. v. Excel Communications Inc.*, 172 F. 3d 1352 [Fed Cir. 1999]), may open the door to a variety of patenting strategies relating to bioinformatics and genome sequences (Alexander 1999, 395; Barton 2000, 805).

To the extent that patents do issue for genomics-derived sequences, the breadth and strength of the new patent claims will likely have a considerable impact on the structure of the industry and the relative positions of the major players. Given the stakes involved and the uncertainties associated with the attempt to develop a workable legal framework, the potential for conflicting intellectual-property claims will almost certainly increase. Yet, even if the genomics patent rush turns out to be a bust, the first-movers in the area, by virtue of their initial investments, will almost certainly find ways to use the technology to leverage their existing organizational capabilities and extend their control.

CAPTURING VALUE: BUSINESS ENTERPRISE AND INDUSTRIAL INTEGRATION

The cost of developing this technology is so high that companies want to capture as much of the value chain as they can to get the full margin. The trend is for companies to forward and backward integrate in this industry. I think the future is bleak for seed companies that do not have their own technology or germplasm to trade with other technology providers.

Col Seccombe, President of Garst Seeds, 1998

By the mid-1990s, as the first patents began to issue and as transgenic crops approached commercialization in the United States, the large agrochemical firms acquired the handful of agricultural biotechnology start-up companies that remained (i.e., those that had managed to acquire a sufficiently strong technology platform to stay in the business). In some instances cross-licensing arrangements evolved into controlling-interest purchases and then into full-blown acquisitions.[41] The overall objective was to consolidate a technology platform and the associated patent rights. By 1998, there were no major independent agricultural biotechnology start-ups left.

But developing and consolidating a technology platform (and the associated intellectual property rights) were merely the first steps in the effort to commercialize agricultural biotechnology. Leading firms also needed access to key germplasm resources and seed-distribution systems in order to get their new products into the hands (and fields) of farmers. Acquiring prominent seed companies solved both of these problems—giving first-movers such as Monsanto and DuPont access to a stock of high-quality germplasm and existing seed-distribution channels in the major agricultural regions. As one industry analyst put it: "The seed companies are the key to the whole world of biotech. How do you get your seeds to the farmer? You don't put them in an envelope and mail them. It's through seed companies" (quoted in Barboza 1999a, C-2). Thus, the late 1990s witnessed an extraordinary concentration in the North American seed industry, with the major biotechnology firms paying very high premiums for seed companies (Steyer 1998; Shimoda 1998, 62-63). In many respects, this willingness to pay such high premiums highlights the unique and seemingly irreducible "nature" of agriculture and the constraints that agriculture and farming place on the commercialization of agricultural biotechnology. Without a vehicle capable of getting these technologies out of the lab and into the ground, agricultural biotechnology would never generate any economic value for its proponents. Vertical integration via the downstream acquisition of seed companies provided the critical institutional vehicle for capturing value (Kalaitzandakes 1998, 40-42; Shimoda 1998; Olson 1998; Holmberg 1999, 31).

Monsanto again blazed the trail in the industry, gorging itself on an $8 billion buying spree between 1996 and 1999, a spree that included acquisition of major seed companies such as Asgrow, Dekalb, and Holden Seeds, as well as Cargill's international seed business (Smith 1998; Rotman 1996e, 1997a; Pezzella 1996; Fairley 1998c).[42] DuPont followed by completing its acquisition of Pioneer Hi-Bred, the world's largest seed company, in a transaction valued at $7.7 billion (Howie 1999). Novartis, which already controlled the former Northup King seed company, also pursued joint ventures with a number smaller seed companies (Olson 1998; Steyer 1998). By the late 1990s, only a handful of major players remained in the seed industry, leaving other biotechnology companies such as Aventis and AstraZeneca without a delivery system of their own—a lack that translated into far fewer opportunities for developing and pursuing their own commercial strategies. In response, these firms actively pursued technology-licensing pacts with seed companies, an increasingly risky strategy in light of the fact that such companies were either controlled by or dependent on Monsanto, DuPont, and Novartis.

As suggested in the previous section, such cross-licensing agreements are hardly new to the industry. Indeed, at the same time that leading biotechnology firms were acquiring the major seed companies, they were also developing licensing agreements with smaller independent seed companies and with their competitors.[43] Moreover, several of the seed companies that were acquired by major biotechnology companies had previously developed licensing arrangements with competitor companies. Pioneer, for example, has licensing agreements with Monsanto for both insect-resistance and herbicide-tolerance traits, agreements that supposedly last in perpetuity and are unaffected by any change in ownership or control of Pioneer ("Crop" 1999; Olson 1998).[44]

Litigation notwithstanding, the emerging pattern appears to be one of extensive cross-licensing among the major players in the industry. Such arrangements essentially allow companies to trade technologies. Firms such as Monsanto, Novartis, and DuPont, which control the lion's share of such technologies, can thus extend their market share and, in the context of licensing to independent seed companies, consolidate their hold over seed-distribution networks. Given the low margins associated with farming, and particularly with commodity crops such as soybeans and corn, capturing market share is obviously the key to recouping investment costs and generating profits.

The other major advantage of acquiring seed companies was the fact that they provided a system for delivering the new technologies to farmers. The challenges here were not insignificant. If these firms simply sold the seed to farmers through traditional channels, they might not get the full return from their intellectual property. Farmers often saved seed from year to year and sometimes exchanged seed with one another. These practices threatened to dilute the value of the proprietary traits in which the biotechnology firms had invested so heavily. The solution, it seemed, lay in contract farming, an institutional arrangement whereby farmers would be incorporated into the vertically integrated structure of agricultural biotechnology.[45]

Such an arrangement, under which farmers agree to grow certain crops under certain conditions in return for access to key inputs and, in some cases, downstream marketing channels, has a long history in American agriculture, from sharecropping to the modern production contracts that have come to dominate certain sectors, such as poultry.[46] In the world of biotech crops, the most prominent method of contracting to date is the "technology licensing fee" developed by Monsanto. In these contracts, a fee is attached to the sale of all seeds containing the technology. But the contracts also regulate the practices of those who purchase the seeds.[47] In the case of Monsanto's Roundup Ready soybeans, the licensing agreement mandates that the farmer must use only Monsanto's Roundup herbicide, despite the fact that other, cheaper herbicides containing the same active ingredients are available. The contract also prohibits the saving of seeds and includes harsh penalties for violation of the agreement: namely, payment of any legal fees that Monsanto incurs in enforcing the agreement, stipulated damages of 120 times the applicable technology fee, and forfeiture of any right to obtain genetically engineered seeds in the future. Finally, farmers are required to submit to inspections of their fields and records. Given the precision with which biotechnology companies can now identify and track their proprietary traits and technologies (that is, the specificity with which they can identify the specific genetic sequences involved), the mechanisms for surveillance and enforcement of these agreements are effectively built into the technology itself.[48]

Over the past several years, many U.S. farmers have willingly adopted Monsanto's approach, as evidenced by the rapid penetration of Roundup Ready soybeans (Brasher 2001). The reality of contracting, though, is that farmers will be more tightly integrated into vertically coordinated systems that are directed largely by the input suppliers. Moreover, as the number of input suppliers shrinks to only a handful of companies, all of whom control key technologies in various product lines, bargaining power clearly shifts in favor of off-farm actors.

Finally, besides acquiring seed companies and developing contractual relations with farmers, the leading agricultural biotechnology firms have also made some tentative efforts to move further downstream to establish linkages with food- and feed-processing operations. Such efforts have not met with the same success as previous efforts in other areas. Although the large grain companies are still accepting transgenic crops for processing, they are increasingly wary of the technology and its effects on the markets they serve. Food companies and food retailers, particularly those with lucrative brand-name labels at stake, are keeping an arm's-length relationship with agricultural biotechnology. Everybody, it seems, is waiting to see what happens. As agricultural commodity markets continue to differentiate, the various downstream actors are trying to determine which segments they want to be involved in and what the costs and benefits of embracing biotechnology will be for their businesses. Such uncertainty does not bode well for those who have invested so much in making biotechnology work.

Nonetheless, despite the ongoing uncertainty and the recent setbacks suffered by Monsanto and other proponents of agricultural biotechnology, the leading firms in the industry have already brought about a substantial restructuring of the agro-food system, a change that has resulted in a remarkable concentration of strategic assets among only a few major companies. During the late 1990s, some of these structural concerns became the subject of heightened government scrutiny, largely through congressional hearings and antitrust investigations by the Justice Department (Harl 1999; "Concurrent" 2000). At the same time, a number of private antitrust lawsuits were filed, directed almost exclusively at Monsanto. In 1998, for example, British biotechnology company Zeneca filed suit against Monsanto in U.S. federal court in Delaware. The suit alleged that Monsanto was using its control of glyphosate-tolerant crops to "effectively foreclose" Zeneca's sale of its own glyphosate-based herbicide ("Zeneca"1998, 6; Fairley 1998e). In December 1999, a group of high-profile plaintiffs' lawyers filed an international class-action lawsuit alleging that Monsanto and its "co-conspirators" had attempted to monopolize the transgenic corn and soybean markets and had conspired to restrain trade and fix prices in these markets (*Picket et al v. Monsanto,* complaint, filed December 14, 1999, U.S. District Court for the District of Columbia).[49]Finally, in March 2000, DuPont filed two antitrust lawsuits in two different federal courts alleging that Monsanto had "used a variety of illegal means to monopolize" the herbicide, soybean seed, and cottonseed markets.[50]

Of course, none of these lawsuits may turn out to have any merit. Still, the overarching fact of substantial concentration in the sector remains, raising a host of concerns about the desirable level of concentration and competition in a sector as important as agro-food. This is the problem of monopoly, and it has a long history in agriculture. What makes the contemporary context so challenging and so important is that the problem today derives not from estates in land, as in the past, but rather from proprietary control over the power of heredity.

CONCLUSION

We are learning about biology at a level and at a rate that is absolutely unprecedented in human history. There is an enormous potential space to be filled, and the stakes are very high. We want to be able to occupy and hold the most valuable territory.

   Robert Shapiro, CEO of Monsanto Co., 1998

We did proceed on the basis of our confidence in the technology. And we saw our products as great boons both to farmers and to the environment. I guess we naively thought that the rest of the world would look at the information and come to the same conclusion.

   Robert Shapiro, CEO of Monsanto Co., 1999

What a difference a year makes. For a company that seemed to be making all the right moves, at least as far as Wall Street was concerned, the turnaround in Monsanto's fortunes has been stunning. Facing increased consumer resistance to biotechnology and a mounting debt burden stemming from its three-year $8 billion acquisition spree, Monsanto saw its share price plunge in late 1998 and 1999, forcing the company to seek out a partner with deep pockets. The "merger of equals" with Pharmacia emphasized the company's pharmaceutical assets rather than its leadership position in agricultural biotechnology. Indeed, the agricultural side of Monsanto's business seemed to be more of a liability than an asset in the eyes of investors, forcing the newly merged company to propose a partial spin-off of the agricultural operations in an effort to liberate its share price (Deogun, Langreth, and Burton 1999).

These developments hardly spell the end of agricultural biotechnology, however. Companies may be changing hands, and agricultural units may be spun off. Research and development spending also appears to be leveling off. But the general structure of the industry is still in place, and efforts to commercialize the technology, particularly in the area of output-oriented traits, continue. Barring any major divestment of assets, a handful of companies now own many of the key property rights, most of the elite germplasm, and the basic seed-delivery systems that have supported the major oilseed, corn, and grain-producing regions in North America and elsewhere since World War II. In the end, the precise identity and ownership structure of these companies do not really matter as long as the strategic assets are concentrated in so few hands. This concentration obviously raises important governance questions that are quite distinct from those now dominating the public agenda (that is, labeling and biosafety).

As this essay has argued, such concentration derived from powerful monopolistic tendencies embedded in the structure of the agricultural biotechnology enterprise—specifically, the synergistic relationships between the increased precision and calculability in the science of genetics and the techniques of genetic manipulation, a stronger intellectual-property regime for life forms, and the biological and social facts of agriculture. Drawing on the metaphor of life as code and the interventionist possibilities associated with recombinant DNA techniques, leading agricultural biotechnology firms developed considerable capabilities for creating novel life forms during the 1980s. When combined with the stronger intellectual-property regime that took shape for such life forms in the early 1980s (largely in response to the scientific and technical advances associated with biotechnology), acquisition of property rights emerged as a central component of the overall strategy. Pursuing such a strategy obviously entailed substantial capital investment, adding to the imperative of developing an organizational structure capable of capturing the value associated with these new technologies. Because proprietary traits had little value without access to existing germplasm and seed-delivery systems for key commercial crops and because farmers were necessary to provide the critical "grow-out" stage in order for firms to capture the value associated with their proprietary technologies, vertical integration proved to be the key institutional vehicle for capturing value. Thus, leading firms, particularly Monsanto and DuPont, acquired major seed companies and developed a system of contract farming tailored to the new biotech crops.

In building such organizational capabilities around their proprietary technologies, however, these firms also found themselves confronting an increasingly dense patent thicket. As individual firms acquired vast numbers of patents in particular areas, competitors had little choice but to respond with similar strategies. This strategy of patent-portfolio racing seemed to derive less from the need to encourage innovation than from the defensive need to protect the company's own bargaining position. Because many of the basic patents issued in agricultural biotechnology contained overlapping and competing claims, firms often found themselves facing conflicting entitlement lines. In some cases, firms litigated to try to sort out these conflicting entitlement lines. In others, they pursued cross-licensing agreements or mergers. In the end, only those firms with substantial patent portfolios and sufficient organizational capabilities remained. The April 2002 agreement between Monsanto and DuPont, which drops all pending law-suits between the two companies and provides for extensive cross-licensing of technologies, suggests that this trend may have run its course, culmi-nating in what John Barton refers to as a closed cross-licensed oligopoly. ("Monsanto, DuPont" 2002; Barton 2002).

Looking back at the remarkable development of the industry over the last two decades, it is clear that the nature and scope of the patent rights involved in agricultural biotechnology have been instrumental in driving consolidation (vertical and horizontal) in the sector. Such a concentration of strategic assets in so few hands raises a number of important public-pol-icy issues. At the very least, these developments suggest the need for a rethinking of basic patent issues in the sector and the need for stronger antitrust oversight.

Economic concentration and the associated development of new legal protections in the agricultural input sector (notably seeds and chemicals) also have important implications for farmers. Facing a dwindling set of sup-pliers and finding themselves locked into more tightly controlled vertical production systems, farmers and their representatives have expressed con-cern over what they see as a loss of bargaining power and diminished auton-omy. Although such concerns have a long history in American agriculture, by extending the nature and scope of proprietary control over basic inputs and technologies, such as seeds, agricultural biotechnology appears to have created an altogether new set of contractual liabilities for farmers.

Finally, although these issues are well beyond the scope of this essay, agri-cultural biotechnology, together with the rapid consolidation of the sector over the last decade, poses a number of important issues for consumers. The notion that the food supply is controlled by a handful of multinational companies is profoundly unsettling to certain segments of the U.S. public. The world, it seems, is not ready for agricultural biotechnology. There can be little doubt that Monsanto, for example, severely underestimated the level of resistance it would face from consumers. In retrospect, it was a sig-nificant (perhaps colossal) miscalculation. Consumers are the critical link in the chain that allows the capital invested in the biotechnology enterprise to circulate and, ultimately, to generate profits. Blinded by its own technolog-ical enthusiasm and by ambitions of creating an agricultural biotechnology superpower, Monsanto failed to appreciate the deep cultural and political salience of food.

NOTES

Special thanks to John Barton, Tom Grey, Rachel Schurman, Michael Watts, and Gavin Wright for comments on this chapter. Earlier versions were presented at the MIT Workshop on Science, Technology, and Agrarian Change; the University of California, Berkeley, Workshop on Agricultural Biotechnology; and the Stanford Law School Legal Studies Colloquium.

1. Of the four principal transgenic crops planted in 2001, soybeans and corn accounted for about 82 percent of the total global acreage. In terms of traits, herbicide tolerance accounted for roughly 77 percent of global acreage; insect resistance accounted for 15 percent; and stacked traits of insect resistance and herbicide tolerance accounted for about 8 percent (James 2001).

2. *Germplasm* refers to the genetic material contained in a cell. In this essay, germplasm is more broadly understood as the total genetic stock of the commercially valuable crops—a product of centuries of selective breeding and improvement. These genetic resources are critical to the biotechnology companies because any traits that these companies own are essentially useless if they are not engineered into elite varieties that contain all the other valuable traits accumulated from prior breeding efforts.

3. Monsanto noted that in 1999 its Roundup Ready soybeans accounted for more than 50 percent of the total U.S. soybean crop and more than 80 percent of the Argentine crop (Monsanto Company 2000, 65).

4. In its first foray into the field, Monsanto purchased a $20 million interest in the Swiss-based biotechnology company Biogen NV in 1980 and announced plans to build its own biotechnology research center at company headquarters in St. Louis. At the same time, Dow Chemical announced a similar deal with United States-based Collaborative Genetics. The primary purpose of these deals was to train company scientists in newly emerging recombinant DNA techniques ("Dow" 1980, 17).

5. DuPont dedicated a $65 million agrochemicals facility in Wilmington and increased its annual life-sciences spending to roughly $250 million. Ciba-Geigy (which later merged with Sandoz to form Novartis) established a research facility in Research Triangle Park, North Carolina, to house its worldwide agricultural biotechnology effort (Trewhitt and Bluestone 1985, 34).

6. *Bacillus thuringiensis* (Bt) is a naturally occurring bacterium found in soil. Bt produces a protein that kills certain crop-destroying insects—such as the European corn borer (a pest that costs American farmers an estimated $1 billion a year in losses)—when it is ingested. Spraying crops with pesticides like the Bt protein, which farmers have been doing for years, is only partially effective. Inserting a Bt gene into a plant and thereby enabling the plant to produce its own pesticidal protein would effectively give the plant an endogenous, or built-in, defense against insects. For a discussion of Bt technology, see *Mycogen v. Monsanto,* 2001 U.S. App. LEXIS 3729, 7-10 (Fed. Cir. 2001).

7. In 1988, for example, two biotechnology companies, Agracetus and Biolistics, announced independently that they had developed a new gene-delivery technique known as the "gene gun." The technology used an electrical charge to blast minute metal particles coated with DNA directly into the cells of a plant. The technology promised to accelerate plant genetic engineering by allowing for more efficient gene insertion into plants. Over the next decade, the gene gun approach became the leading tool for developing transgenic plants. Both companies applied for patents on the guns, but Biolistics planned to make its gun widely available—signing ten-year licensing agreements with eight U.S. companies and universities. Agracetus, in contrast, kept its gun in-house and contracted to perform gene inser-

tion for other companies; that is, companies provided the plants and genes, and Agracetus did the insertion and returned the newly engineered plants to the companies (Spalding 1988, 16).

At the same time, all of the firms in the sector were racing to the Patent and Trademark Office to submit patent applications for these new inventions, but the first patents did not begin to issue until the early 1990s.

8. The guidelines focused on product characteristics rather than on process and stated that premarket review of any product was unnecessary if substantial equivalence to existing products could be demonstrated. In a preview of the political battles to come, environmental groups were angered by the decision, invoking consumers' right to know and calling for more extensive regulatory oversight and labeling ("White House" 1992a, 1).

9. *Genomics* refers to the study and sequencing of an organism's genome (that is, all the genetic material in the chromosomes of that particular organism) and the determination of the number and relative positions of individual genes on the chromosomes.

Bioinformatics refers to the use of computer-assisted genetic analysis tools to infer gene functions from DNA sequences (generated through genomics efforts) by comparing those sequences to well-known genes in other organisms.

10. The basic approach focused on identifying expressed sequence tags (ESTs)—snippets of DNA from active genes—which scientists could then use to identify genes and, with the tools of bioinformatics, infer gene function.

11. In addition to these collaborations, Monsanto has also developed smaller alliances with other genomics firms and university-based scientists. According to the company's SEC form S-1 prospectus filed on October 17, 2000, Monsanto has collaborative genomics arrangements with four principal companies (Millennium, Incyte, Mendel Biotechnology, and Paradigm Genetics). The company also notes, "Hundreds of agreements with universities provide us . . . with access to emerging genomics technologies and capabilities developed by top university scientists. Most of these agreements provide us with licenses or options to license developed technologies. Many of these licenses are exclusive" (Monsanto Company 2000, 69).

12. According to one 1998 estimate, Monsanto's library of genetic information doubles every twelve to twenty-four months (Feder 1998, B1). As of 1998, Pioneer and DuPont claimed to have a combined EST database representing more than 75 percent of corn's 80,000 genes, an interesting number given recent reports from the human genome project that humans have only 30,000 to 40,000 genes. According to Forest Chumley, DuPont's manager for technology partnerships and alliances, "We've built the capability to get all the genes in a bottle. Now the focus turns to choosing which ones to use" (quoted in Fairley 1998g, 18).

13. This time compression stems from the massive increases in computational capacity that have paved the way for high-throughput screening of plant and animal genomes. In theory, genomics allows for more rapid development of valuable transgenic traits, provides companies with expanded predictive ability in plant breeding, and thereby promises to speed up the entire process of isolating traits and transforming them into commercially valuable products. This is obviously true for traditional breeding efforts as well as for breeding efforts utilizing recombinant DNA techniques (Holmberg 2000).

14. Genomics is being used to identify genes for use not only in genetic engineering but also in traditional breeding programs—allowing selective breeding to proceed more precisely on the basis of genotype rather than phenotype. Through the use of genetic markers and screening technologies, breeders can ensure that their efforts transfer desirable traits. These techniques may provide a way to bypass many of the cultural and political hurdles associated with genetically engineered crops and may turn out to be the most valuable use of the technology (Fairley 1998g, 18).

15. Take the example of Monsanto. By 2000, with a staff of more than four hundred scientists, the company had the capability to conduct more than twenty thousand independent plant transformations (gene insertions) every year. With its in-house genomics staff of more than five hundred scientists, its collaborative arrangements with some two hundred additional scientists, its R&D budget of close to $700 million, Monsanto led the sector in genomics capability. The company's overall objective has been to discover new genes that will create commercially valuable traits (insect and disease resistance; tolerance for drought, heat, or cold; improved yield; and enhanced nutritional content). In addition to providing critical inputs into its genetic engineering efforts, genomics also enables Monsanto to accelerate and improve traditional plant breeding. In 1999, company scientists analyzed more than 2.5 million genetic characterizations of crop samples. When combined with the company's plant-breeding platform—one thousand people located at more than 150 breeding stations in more than fifteen countries managing more than 3.5 million test plots per year—the capabilities are truly awesome. Such comprehensive gene-to-seed capabilities, protected by a growing arsenal of patent rights, give Monsanto and the handful of companies that have acquired similar capabilities, considerable power to shape and direct the industry (Monsanto Company 2000, 67-70).

16. The Patent Act provides that "Whoever invents or discovers any new or useful process, machine, manufacture, or composition of matter or any new and useful improvement thereof, may obtain a patent therefor, subject to the conditions and requirements of this title." Prior to the *Chakrabarty* decision, numerous patents were issued on single-celled organisms that were part of an industrial process such as food processing, fermentation, and pharmaceutical development. By declaring that the newly engineered bacterium was patentable sui generis, however, the *Chakrabarty* decision represented a significant departure from past practice, giving the patent holder a much broader scope of legal protection. For a brief discussion of the history of patents on life forms, see Krimsky 1991, 45-49; and Kevles 1998.

17. The basic requirements for patentability are found in the Patent Act, at 35 U.S.C. §§100 et seq. Briefly, to obtain a patent, the inventor must demonstrate utility, that is, a "new and useful process, machine, manufacture, or composition of matter, or any new and useful improvement thereof" (§101), novelty (§102), and non-obviousness (§103) (as well as meeting a host of other statutory provisions under §102). The patent application must also fully describe (disclose) the invention (§112) so that the public receives the benefit of the new knowledge that the patented invention represents. If the Patent and Trademark Office agrees that these criteria have been met, it issues a patent giving the inventor, for a term of twenty years from the date on which the application was filed, "the right to exclude others from making, using, or selling the invention throughout the United States" (§154).

18. Adam Jaffe (1999) identifies four major policy changes that have strengthened and extended patent protection since the 1980s: (1) the 1982 creation of the Court of Appeals for the Federal Circuit to review patent cases; (2) the extension of patenting and licensing privileges to inventors in universities and government laboratories that use federal funding; (3) the extension and clarification of patentable subject matter into new areas, particularly software and gene research; and (4) international agreements under the framework of the General Agreement on Tariffs and Trade to extend and harmonize patent protection around the world.

19. The 1930 Plant Patent Act provided protection for asexually (clonally) propagated plants and thus applied only to fruit trees and nursery plants. The 1970 Plant Variety Protection Act allowed for slightly stronger intellectual-property protection for sexually reproduced plant varieties—protecting owners of novel seed varieties against unauthorized sales of their seed for replanting. As Justice Brennan pointed out, §2402(a) of the 1970 act specifically excluded bacteria from coverage (447 U.S. 303, 321).

20. Since the Board of Patent Appeals and Interferences's *Hibberd* ruling, the PTO has issued more than eighteen hundred utility patents for plants, plant parts, and seeds (*J.E.M. Ag Supply, Inc. v. Pioneer Hi-Bred Int'l, Inc.*, 122 S. Ct. 593, 596 [2001]). Note that this figure does not include patents on plant genes and DNA sequences.

21. Jack Kloppenburg (1988, 263-64) notes that "the ability to make multiple claims significantly broadens the protection afforded the invention. It also permits the licensing of particular components—e.g., a gene for herbicide tolerance—for use by third parties. Because genetic engineering in plants is geared to transformations at the cellular and molecular levels, utility patents provide a significant advantage over PVP [Plant Variety Protection] certificates, which can provide property rights only in the whole organism."

22. Glen Bugos and Daniel Kevles (1992, 76) argue that "the development of biological science has played a special role in the creation of intellectual property in plants. The quality of the property has turned on the intergenerational unity that breeders have been able to achieve; and the degree of protection that can be provided has depended heavily upon the specificity with which the property can be biologically described."

23. See *Amgen, Inc. v. Chugai Pharmaceutical Co.*, 927 F. 2d 1200 (Fed. Cir. 1991), in which the Court of Appeals for the Federal Circuit stated that

A gene is a chemical compound, albeit a complex one, and it is well established in our law that conception of a chemical compound requires that the inventor be able to define it so as to distinguish it from other materials, and to describe how to obtain it. . . . We hold that when an inventor is unable to envision the detailed constitution of a gene so as to distinguish it from other materials, as well as a method for obtaining it, conception has not been achieved until reduction to practice has occurred, i.e., until after the gene has been isolated.

To create "isolated and purified" (and therefore patentable) DNA sequences, scientists first isolate and clone the specific gene of interest. Because the naturally occurring gene contains DNA that is not essential to the gene's function in coding for a particular protein, scientists then remove these extraneous sequences (known as *introns*) to create a "new" stripped-down version of the gene. Because this new version—which is based on copy-DNA, or cDNA (i.e., a human-made copy of the gene's coding sequences)—is not found in nature, it is patentable as long as it meets the other requirements of the Patent Act.

The advent of genomics, however, has placed new strains on the patent system's approach to DNA sequences, undermining the applicability of the chemical-compound analogy. In short, as chemical specificity gives way to informational specificity, existing patent doctrine may not be able to adapt (Eisenberg, 2000).

24. In a 1995 decision concerning the ability of farmers to sell saved seed under the Plant Variety Protection Act, the Supreme Court held that §2543 of the act permitted a farmer to sell for reproductive purposes "only such seed as he has saved for the purpose of replanting his acreage" (*Asgrow Seed Company v. Winterboer,* 513 U.S. 179, 192 [1995]).

25. On March 29, 2001, a Canadian judge ordered a farmer to pay damages to Monsanto for patent infringement after canola plants containing the company's proprietary herbicide-tolerance trait were found growing in his field. The ruling was considered a major victory for Monsanto and other large agricultural biotechnology firms seeking to ensure that farmers continue to pay licensing fees to use their technology (Kaufman 2001b).

26. Juan Enriquez (1998) notes that the number of patent requests for nucleic acid sequences increased from 4,000 in 1991 to 500,000 in 1996, largely as a result of genomic sequencing efforts.

27. The recent agreement between Novartis and the University of California, Berkeley, is an example.

28. In 1994, Agracetus received a European patent of similar scope covering genetically engineered soybeans. As with its transgenic-cotton patent, Agracetus won the broad claim on the basis that its scientists were first to show that the species could be genetically engineered. In theory, the patent requires any company or researcher interested in genetically engineering soybeans to arrange licensing from Agracetus. In a rather odd affinity of interests, Monsanto and several public interest groups separately challenged the Agracetus patent. But whereas the activist groups argued that patent protection for major food crops was morally wrong, Monsanto, careful to note that it did not object to patents in the agricultural area, objected to the patent's excessively broad coverage ("Agracetus" 1994, 5).

29. In response to such criticism, the patent office agreed in 1994 to a formal reexamination of the patent. The USDA also mounted a legal challenge to the patent on the grounds that it was overly broad. Meanwhile, Agracetus began pursuing patents similar to the one granted in the United States in other major cotton-producing regions, including Brazil, China, and India (Shulman 1994, 16). In December 1994, the PTO suspended the patent, and the issue is now in appeal.

30. In 1993, for example, Monsanto and Calgene signed a series of cross-licensing deals to head off potential patent conflicts involving Monsanto's Bt technology and Calgene's antisense RNA technology. According to Calgene, the deal would allow both firms to "focus on commercializing products rather than engaging in costly litigation" ("Monsanto, Calgene" 1983, 30). Although determining the actual extent of licensing in the industry is difficult, litigation and SEC filings clearly indicate that most of the key technologies—herbicide tolerance, insect resistance, and

gene-insertion techniques—have been the subject of extensive licensing among various companies.

In 1996, for example, Dekalb and DuPont entered into a cross-licensing arrangement whereby each was granted access to the other's proprietary transformation technologies. According to Bruce P. Bickner, Dekalb's chairman and CEO, "A license to DuPont's gene gun, which complements Dekalb's proprietary transformation technology, is an important step toward ensuring freedom to commercialize Dekalb's pipeline of transgenic seed products" ("DuPont Licenses" 1996).

31. John Barton describes explicit cross-licenses as situations in which "each firm permits its cross-licensee to use certain of its own basic technologies in return for the right to use the cross-licensee's basic technology" and implicit cross-licenses as situations in which "the possibility of a suit is countered by the threat of a counter suit, leaving each party relatively free to use the other's technology." In light of these practices, Barton concludes that "it may be as important for a firm to obtain patents that others are likely to infringe as to obtain patents to protect its own proprietary position" to bolster its bargaining power in the cross-licensing context (Barton 1998, 94).

32. Barton identified more than twenty disputes involving almost thirty different patents occurring between 1991 and 1997 (Barton 1998, 88-91, tables 8-1 and 8-2 and pp. 88-91).

33. The jury verdict that the patent was invalid by virtue of prior invention was upheld by the district court in September 1999 (*Mycogen v. Monsanto,* 61 F. Supp. 2d 199 [D. Del. 1999]).

34. The jury found that although the patent was literally infringed by the defendants Novartis, Mycogen, and Agrigenetics, it was not enforceable, owing to a finding of prior invention. In September 1999, the district court affirmed the jury's verdict. (*Monsanto v Mycogen,* 61 F. Supp. 2d 133 [D. Del., 1999]). The matter is currently on appeal before the Court of Appeals for the Federal Circuit.

35. In June 2000, an appeals court reversed the California jury's verdict, and in November 2000, the California Supreme Court agreed to hear Mycogen's appeal (Sissell 2000a, 2000b).

36. Barton (1999, 5) notes that some of the mergers in the industry have also been driven by the need to settle or avoid patent litigation.

37. Although such a firm could also try to challenge such patents on the grounds of invalidity, this tactic would be time-consuming and expensive.

38. Rebecca Eisenberg (2000) distinguishes between patents on DNA molecules and patents on DNA sequence information stored in computer-readable media, concluding that in the genomics era the chemical analogy used to justify patents on isolated and purified DNA sequences no longer applies.

39. According to Enriquez (2000, 11), the PTO received patent applications for four thousand DNA sequences in 1991. By 1996, with the advent of genomics, the number had soared to half a million. He goes on to note that in 1998, GenBank, the public gene-sequence depository at the National Institutes of Health that receives sequence information for all organisms, was receiving as much data every ten days as it did during its first decade of existence.

40. Credible uses might include a probe for a particular gene, a marker for a particular genetic trait, a diagnostic, or a sequence that encodes for a protein having a

particular function (Crane, Kelber, and Labgold 2000, 39; Barton 2000, 805; Doll 1998, 689; Gold 2000, 1319; and Grisham 2000, 921).

41. For example, in 1995 Monsanto paid $150 million for a 49.9 percent stake in Calgene—giving it more secure access to Calgene's technology ("Plant Biotech" 1995, 25). In April 1996, Monsanto's purchase of W. R. Grace subsidiary Agracetus gave it control over Agracetus's important technology for genetically modifying plants—including its "gene gun" technology (which Monsanto had been licensing since 1991)—as well as over the broad Agracetus patents on transgenic cotton and soybeans. The deal also resolved a long-running patent dispute between the two companies regarding an Agracetus patent covering disease protection in plants (Rotman 1996c, 8). In June 1996, Monsanto strengthened its cross-licensing arrangements with Calgene, which gave it access to Calgene's technology for increasing the oil content in corn, soybeans, and sunflowers (Rotman 1996d, 10). Two months later, Monsanto took a controlling interest in Calgene—boosting its stake from 49.9 percent to 54.6 percent—for $50 million ("Monsanto Takes" 1996, 5). And in April 1997, Monsanto acquired the remaining 46 percent of Calgene for $240 million ("Monsanto to Acquire" 1997, 2).

Likewise, beginning in 1996, Dow Chemical began acquiring an ownership interest in Mycogen. In July of that year, DowElanco, the agricultural chemicals joint venture between Dow Chemical and Eli Lilly, took a 46 percent stake in Mycogen for $126 million ("DowElanco" 1996a, 9). The following February, Dow took a controlling share of Mycogen—increasing its stake from 46 percent to 52 percent—thereby securing control over one of the most coveted patent portfolios in the plant biotech business (Stringer 1997, 55). In January 1998, four days before jury selection began in the Monsanto versus Mycogen Bt patent litigation in Delaware, Dow increased its stake in Mycogen to 63 percent (Fairley 1998a, 10).

42. Monsanto also attempted to make a $1.8 billion stock deal for the Delta Pine and Land Co. in 1998, the leading U.S. cottonseed company and owner of the infamous "terminator technology." By combining Delta Pine's cottonseed operations with Monsanto's own, the deal would have given the company control over some 80 percent of the market for cottonseed. Because of antitrust concerns, the deal was never consummated (Kilman 1999; Guidera 1999). Antitrust concerns were also raised in connection with the Dekalb acquisition. In December 1998, the Department of Justice (DOJ) approved the deal on two conditions. First, Monsanto agreed to donate the rights to agro-bacterium-mediated genetic transformation in corn to the University of California, Berkeley. This emerging technology for placing new genes in plants generated antitrust concerns because of the strong patent rights held by Dekalb and Monsanto over other transformation technologies. Second, Monsanto guaranteed continued access to corn germplasm, via licensing, for 150 seed companies that were customers of Holden's Foundation Seeds, a Monsanto subsidiary. According to Joel Klein, head of the DOJ antitrust division, "The spin-off of the transformation technology and the wide licensing of corn germplasm will preserve competition in this newly emerging market for corn with transgenic improvement. Competition in biotechnology ensures that American farmers have access to the latest innovations in seed technology" (Fairley 1998f, 12; "DOJ Approves" 1998).

43. Monsanto, for example, licenses its proprietary traits to more than three hundred small seed companies in North America (Monsanto Company 2000, 72).

44. In March 2001, however, a federal district judge in St. Louis ruled that certain license agreements between Monsanto and Pioneer relating to Roundup Ready soybeans and Roundup Ready canola did not survive the acquisition of Pioneer by DuPont in October 1999. DuPont appealed and promised to continue marketing the technologies during the appeal process ("DuPont Says" 2001).

45. The other method of capturing value associated with these transgenic seeds, of course, is simply to charge a premium for the seed. Companies generally use a mix of these strategies (Wood and Fairley 1998, 27).

46. On contract farming generally, see Harris and Massey 1968. For a more theoretically informed perspective, see Watts 1994. For a specific discussion of contracting in the context of grain crops, see Hamilton 1994.

47. All purchasers of Roundup Ready soybeans sign an invoice stating that "if a herbicide containing the same active ingredient as Roundup Ultra herbicide (or one with a similar mode of action) is used over the top of Roundup Ready soybeans, the Grower agrees to use only Roundup branded herbicides" (cited in Fairley 1998d, 8).

48. By the end of the 1990s, Monsanto had brought a number of "seed piracy" enforcement actions against farmers, primarily for saving seeds. These suits signal the changing balance of power in the agricultural biotechnology complex (Weiss, 1999).

49. Among other things, the complaint charged that "Monsanto's unlawful conduct in aggregating the power to control all aspects of the production of corn and soy appears to be motivated by its desire to control the basic means of production of the global food supply."

50. In the first lawsuit, filed on March 27 in U.S. District Court in Florence, South Carolina, DuPont alleged "a complex scheme of economic coercion through which Monsanto has tried to monopolize cottonseed and herbicide markets." Echoing the earlier charges made by Zeneca, DuPont claimed that Monsanto forced growers into technology-licensing agreements that made it "virtually impossible to buy competing brands of glyphosate." In the second lawsuit, filed on March 30 in federal court in Wilmington, Delaware, against Monsanto and its Asgrow subsidiary, DuPont alleged that Monsanto had appropriated trade secrets for producing Roundup Ready soybeans, technology developed in a joint venture between DuPont and Asgrow before Monsanto acquired Asgrow in 1997. As a result, DuPont claimed, Monsanto was able to introduce its Roundup Ready soybean two years ahead of schedule, thereby destroying DuPont's own herbicide-resistant soybean. Monsanto dismissed the lawsuits as baseless, suggesting that they were filed in retaliation for a suit Monsanto had recently filed to terminate a 1995 licensing agreement on Roundup Ready seed technology with DuPont subsidiary Pioneer Hi-Bred ("DuPont Files" 2000, 9). In April 2002, however, DuPont and Monsanto agreed to drop all pending lawsuits between the two companies and engage in extensive cross-licensing of technologies, illustrating the increasingly closed nature of the emerging oligopoly ("Monsanto, DuPont" 2002).

2

Building a Better Tree

Genetic Engineering and Fiber Farming in Oregon and Washington

W. Scott Prudham

The development of technology, and thus the social development it implies, is as much determined by the breadth of vision that informs it, and the particular notions of social order to which it is bound, as by the mechanical relations between things and the physical laws of nature.
David Noble, *America by Design*, 1977

On the arid plains of eastern Washington and Oregon, next to the placid Columbia River, tens of thousands of acres of hybrid cottonwoods grow in even rows, supplying fiber to nearby paper mills. Grown on a seven-year rotation, hand planted in blocks of six hundred clones per acre, watered by drip irrigation, and cultivated under chemical control, the plantations are among the most intensively managed anywhere in the world. Two hundred and fifty miles down river, in Corvallis, researchers at Oregon State University's Tree Genetic Engineering Research Cooperative (TGERC) have been developing genetically engineered (GE) trees for use in the plantations since 1995. Several varieties are now in field trials. Should they be approved for commercial deployment and planted on the banks of the Columbia, they would become the first GE trees to be used in commercial forestry in the United States.

Though less contentious in the public eye than GE food crops have become, commercial GE trees also raise numerous concerns. These include the risk of gene transfer to wild trees and other species; the potential for consolidation of industrial and scientific forestry; and the political and ethical issues raised by proprietary control over life forms (Kenney 1998; Kevles 1998; May 1998; Mullin and Bertrand 1998). These concerns cast in relief the potential importance of commercial GE tree cultivation and the sense that by embracing the new biotechnology, industrial forestry is on the brink of a socially and environmentally significant transition.

To assess this transition, we must consider the social origins of commercial forest biotechnology. Where does technological change come from? How is science politically and economically harnessed to industrial innovation? Is biotechnology—specifically genetic engineering—to be understood as an "event," a discontinuity, or as part of an unfolding process, representing both continuity and change? I suggest the latter. Those who view biotechnology as a source of new social relationships get it partly right, but this view says nothing about how commercial forest biotechnology, and the social and ecological changes that accompany biotechnology, can be understood as socially produced and socially embedded.[1]

I examine Oregon State's TGERC as a nexus between two threads in the history of the institutions involved in science-based forest intensification in the United States. The first thread is the prevalence of public involvement and cooperative institutions, both of which are exemplified by the TGERC. For the better part of a hundred years, scientific forestry has been heavily supported by public-sector efforts, channeled through federal research stations, as well as by federal and state funding for forestry research at public universities. In more recent years—coincident with the transition from old-growth, extractive forestry to young-growth, plantation management—industrial cooperation and public-sector support have converged in a proliferation of forestry research and development (R&D) cooperatives that bring together private firms, state agencies, and academic researchers. Oregon State's TGERC is one of these co-ops.

The second thread involves models of "academic capitalism" (Slaughter and Leslie 1997) and "academic enclosure" (Harvie 2000) surrounding the commercial development of biotechnology. The TGERC reflects and reinforces these new models of academic-industrial relations, which emphasize more-formal management of research as intellectual property in the realms of patenting and technology transfer and licensing, and are thus characterized by more-exclusive relationships, public and private. The TGERC specifically embodies these tendencies with its emphasis on formal patent protections for and licensing of discoveries.

These two threads, intersecting in the political economy of forestry research, are far from disparate phenomena. Rather, they constitute an unfolding dialectical relation between the social and the biological in the intensification of industrial forest cultivation. Understanding the TGERC at the nexus of both change and continuity within this dialectic requires consideration of the ways in which commercial imperatives to intensify forest growth over approximately the last century have confronted a series of biology-based challenges. These challenges include the slow rates at which trees grow to commercial maturity (that is, turnover time), geographic fragmentation in commercial tree-breeding programs, and problems in achieving asexual reproduction on a mass scale. Collectively, these issues indicate how the industrial intensification of forest growth confronts biological challenges and, in turn, how these challenges have deterred more proprietary and exclusively private forms of industrial intensification. Cooperative institutions and the public sector have undertaken what individual firms would not do on their own. Yet, as new technological and new institutional possibilities define the development of forestry biotechnology, many of these challenges are confronted and transformed. As this transformation occurs, more exclusive and proprietary forms of private forest intensification, including more complete commodification of life, become desirable to firms.

Thus, on the one hand, the TGERC emerges from the history of industrial cooperation and public-sector efforts that have been hallmarks of commercially driven forestry science in the United States. On the other hand, by practicing more exclusive forms of intellectual-property management and drawing on wider commercial interests than is typical of other co-ops, the TGERC also highlights how significant changes in academic-industrial relations reflect and reinforce the commercial potential of biotechnology, both in forestry and more broadly. Drawing from several observers of the long-term industrialization of agriculture (Goodman and Redclift 1991; Goodman, Sorj, and Wilkinson 1987), I highlight the institutional fragmentation of efforts to rationalize forest cultivation for commercial purposes as a reflection of specific biological challenges to those efforts, and at the same time, as a reflection of the ways in which new strategies coalesce around biotechnology. In this manner, reproductive biology acts historically as both obstacle to and opportunity for the commodification of life (Boyd, Prudham, and Schurman 2001; Kloppenburg 1988). My goal is to situate the emergence of forestry biotechnology in this longer-term process, representing it as significant but not entirely novel, and hardly without identifiable social origins.

In what follows, I first outline the basic architecture of TGERC research. I then elaborate by discussing the two institutional influences on the TGERC: (1) the tradition of public and cooperative scientific approaches to rationalizing forest growth in the United States in general and Oregon in particular and (2) shifts in industry-academic relations. Subsequently, I explore the ways in which the TGERC must confront tensions between these two traditions. In particular, I discuss some of the implications of the commodification of life for the public sector and cooperative forestry research. I close by discussing ongoing regulatory review of transgenic trees and the very recent outbreak of open political opposition to TGERC research. I argue that developments in these arenas highlight the important and contingent role of social sanction in determining the fate of commercial forest biotechnology. Yet I insist that contemporary political scrutiny of GE trees—and biotechnology more generally—must also include appraisal of the social origins of the technologies. Failure to do so will result in what

Les Levidow (1998) calls "technology as reification," a tendency to focus on biotechnologies as events or things rather than as the outcome of historical processes with distinct social underpinnings.

THE TREE GENETIC ENGINEERING RESEARCH COOPERATIVE

At present, several varieties of engineered hybrid cottonwood—specifically a hybrid of eastern cottonwood (*Populus deltoides*) and black cottonwood (*P. trichocarpa*)—produced by the TGERC are in field trials intended to evaluate their biosafety as well their biological and commercial viability (Strauss, DiFazio, and Meilan 2001; Strauss, Knowe, and Jenkins 1997). Should any of these varieties be approved, they are likely to find an immediate commercial demand in the region's established hybrid cottonwood plantations and thus to place TGERC research at the forefront of integrating biotechnology into intensive forestry.

The TGERC was formed in 1994 after a series of discussions, beginning in 1990, concerning the need for a biotechnology research program to service the growing acreage of cottonwood plantations in Oregon and Washington. Currently led by the Oregon State University (OSU) forest scientist Dr. Steven Strauss, the organization includes private firms and public agencies as members. It operates by means of financial and in-kind contributions from member firms, heavily supplemented with public money and institutional support. Between 1994 and 1999, the TGERC was funded by $1.5 million from member contributions, $1.3 million from competitive grants, and $1.0 million from OSU (Tree Genetic Engineering Research Cooperative 1999). However, the largest sources of competitive grants are the Department of Agriculture, the Environmental Protection Agency, the Forest Service, and the National Science Foundation, all public sources; and money from OSU, a land grant university, is also largely public in origin.

The TGERC offers a good deal for firms whose resources would be strained if they attempted similar research on their own. In exchange for their dues, members gain control over the research, as well as access to researchers, equipment, and results. Research priorities are established through negotiations among members in consultation with the research team (including Strauss, assistants, and graduate students), as well as through periodic voting. Members gain access to silvicultural expertise— including that of university scientists and graduate students whose research is included under the cooperative's umbrella—that is largely paid for by the state and by tuition fees.[2] Members also gain access, through the researchers, to sophisticated and expensive equipment paid for by the university, again largely from state funds and tuition fees. Moreover, the co-op structure allows firms to share the risks of their research investments in the face of scientific and economic uncertainties surrounding the commercial potential of the research. This distribution of risk accounts for the histori-cally prominent role of public-sector support and cooperative institutional organization in U.S. forestry research more generally.

In recent years, TGERC researchers have pursued three main avenues of development, all of which involve the production of genetically engineered varieties of the cottonwood hybrids used in the Oregon and Washington plantations: genetic engineering of insect resistance, engineered sexual sterility, and engineered herbicide resistance.

In 1997, TGERC researchers first reported the successful introduction of *Bacillus thuringiensis* (Bt) toxicity into hybrid cottonwoods as part of the TGERC's research into insect resistance. This technique, which uses genetic material taken from a common soil bacterium, represents one of several efforts to manufacture insect-resistant varieties of tree species, in *Populus* and other genera (R. R. James 1997, table 1). This research is directly anal-ogous to and draws on extensive work on engineered Bt toxicity in agricul-tural crops (see Krimsky and Wrubel 1996). The major commercial advan-tage of the technology is that it induces trees to produce their own insecticide, which reduces or eliminates the costs of labor, machinery, and chemicals for external pesticide applications (Strauss, Howe, and Goldfarb 1991).[3] The Mycogen Corporation, a biotechnology company that has been involved in developing several Bt crops, provided the gene construct in question. Monsanto has also provided the co-op with Bt genes to support this research, and efforts are under way to introduce Monsanto's genes into cottonwoods (Tree Genetic Engineering Research Cooperative 1997).

TGERC researchers are also pursuing genetically engineered sexual sterility in hybrid cottonwoods. This emphasis emerged in direct response to concerns about the implications of genetically engineered trees flowering in plantations and crossing with wild, nontransgenic poplars (Strauss, Rottmann, and Sheppard 1995). Genetically engineered sterility might combat this problem if it prevents trees from flowering. According to a for-est geneticist, this issue is the single greatest constraint on the commercial deployment of transgenic cottonwoods: "Right now it is the limiting factor. If you ask 'Why aren't there commercial transgenic trees in use now?' that is the reason. We don't have a means for sterilizing them yet."[4] Another potential commercial appeal of sterilization technology is that it strengthens and diversifies options for enforcing intellectual property rights. That is, engineered sterility offers a protection against illegal propagation of pro-prietary varieties (Brunner et al. 1998). It therefore allows firms with pro-prietary breeding and genetic-engineering programs to protect their advanced varieties of trees while bypassing disclosure of sensitive informa-tion during the patent application process (Busch et al. 1991).

As their third major focus, TGERC researchers have produced geneti-cally engineered varieties of herbicide-resistant cottonwoods. Many herbicides not only suppress weeds but also have a debilitating effect on commercial species, precluding the use of the herbicide altogether or constraining use to particular periods in the crop life cycle. Genetically engineered herbicide resistance thus has obvious commercial appeal and represents by far the most commonly introduced trait in GE crops.[5] At the TGERC, researchers have successfully engineered resistance to the chemical herbicide glyphosate—known commonly as Roundup, the brand produced by the Monsanto Corporation. The resulting Roundup Ready cottonwoods (Strauss, Knowe, and Jenkins 1997) have entered field trials (Tree Genetic Engineering Research Cooperative 1997). The development of these trees and their commercial potential have significant implications for the intensive cultivation of hybrid cottonwoods and also for Monsanto, given that conventional varieties are quite susceptible to glyphosate. Moreover, weed control is a major challenge in existing plantations, and herbicide application is a large expense for plantation operators. Herbicide-resistant trees would be of immediate interest to plantation managers.

The TGERC is a significant presence in all three areas of research. The commercial deployment of TGERC-engineered varieties could represent the first use of genetic engineering in commercial forestry. In this context, the institutional structure of the TGERC—involving multiple private firms, state agencies and funds, and academic researchers and facilities—is significant. This structure is not anomalous: rather, the TGERC is an example of the substantial contributions of public-sector efforts and cooperative institutions to the development of more intensive, rationalized forest cultivation. At the same time, the TGERC belongs in the context of recent changes in academic-industrial relations, a relationship that has moved in the direction of proprietary public research and that is coalescing in many ways around biotechnology. These traditions come together in the TGERC and comprise twin, albeit conflicting, avenues of the social production of biotechnological change.

PUBLIC SCIENCE AND COOPERATIVE SILVICULTURE

Public support and cooperative institutions have long been crucial to the scientific rationalization of forest growth because private industry has tended to eschew these activities. Industry has instead relied upon and pushed for public support, largely because investments in growing trees have historically been plagued by uncertainties, long payback periods, and challenges related to the biological basis of intensive forestry.

Despite the obvious importance of growing trees, the industry is generally on the low end of the scale in R&D investment and is particularly loath to invest in forestry. According to the National Science Foundation (1996), private R&D expenditures in the lumber, wood products, and furniture industries averaged 0.7 percent of sales from 1984 through 1994, and expenditures in the paper and allied products industry averaged 0.9 percent of sales. By contrast, manufacturing industries on average invested 3.1 percent of sales during the same period. Private R&D expenditures in the forest products sector are heavily skewed toward investment in forest products research rather than in forestry per se: Paul Ellefson (1995) estimates that four or five companies dominate private investment in forestry and that, overall, more than 90 percent of private investment in the forest sector is oriented toward forest products research.

Tepid enthusiasm for private, proprietary industrial forestry research is manifest not only in the particularly high profile of public support and public institutions but also in the cooperative institutional tradition. Specifically, since World War II, silvicultural co-ops much like the TGERC have proliferated at U.S. universities in forested regions throughout the country. According to the American Forest Council, fifty-one universities hosted such cooperatives as of 1987. North Carolina State and OSU have the most extensive cooperative programs; other important host institutions include the University of Washington, the University of Florida, the University of Maine, Texas A&M, and Virginia Polytechnic Institute and State University (American Forest Council 1987; Ellefson 1995). In appraising the significance of these co-ops, it bears noting that their research focuses predominantly on biological intensification.

To what can the peculiar political economy of forestry research in the United States, characterized by a high profile for public sector and cooperative institutions such as the TGERC, be attributed? Ellefson (1995, 134) notes rather casually that "industrial forestry research efforts . . . must face the realities of long pay-back periods for investments in forestry research, high risks and uncertain consequences of research investments," but he does not dwell on the underlying reasons for these realities. I argue that the division of labor between public and private sectors in forestry R&D has long been shaped by a set of biological challenges or obstacles to proprietary investment in forestry. As Marx (1967a, 248) noted long ago, "The long production time . . . and the great length of the periods of turnover entailed make forestry an industry of little attraction to private and therefore capitalist enterprise." Although the need to rationalize the forest resource has long been recognized, industry has been loath to undertake this project alone because of the biological peculiarities of trees as a form of capital.[6]

Chief among the biological obstacles to R&D investment is the slow maturation rate of forest trees (Cheliak and Rogers 1990), which makes trees a particular *kind* of fixed capital.[7] Such natural delays can limit the response of commodity systems to shifts in markets in other spheres of cultivation as well, (Mann 1990), as in the establishment of orchard trees and grapevines

(Henderson 1998), but forest trees present an extreme example of the problem. For example, in western Oregon, the rotation age of Douglas-fir (used to manufacture lumber and plywood) is sixty to eighty years. This is a long-term investment by the standards of private capital markets and carries with it risks of loss from fire, disease, and storms. That Douglas-fir takes about twelve years to reach sexual maturity also introduces delays in tree-improvement breeding programs.[8] At the same time, like most trees (and indeed most organisms), Douglas-fir exhibits growth dynamics that depend not only on genetic variation but also on adaptation to local environmental conditions. Thus, the uneven topography of the Cascade and Coast Ranges translates into highly fragmented breeding zones, and this fragmentation is exacerbated by a patchwork of property ownerships. This in turn limits economies of scale in breeding programs. Douglas-fir is also difficult to propagate through shoots or cuttings or in the laboratory via tissue cultures. This resistance represents a further biological limit to economies of scale in breeding. Consequently, advanced varieties have so far not proved amenable to mass production.

The significance of these aspects of forestry's biological basis is reflected in the political economy of national and regional traditions of forestry research and development.

Public Science and Forest Rationalization

The division of labor between private and public in forestry research in the Northwest was forged during early-twentieth-century political struggles over control and regulation of American forests. On one hand, industry actively opposed both federal land retention and regulation of private forest practices. On the other hand, a number of problems, including destructive fires, pest infestation, and concerns about a possible timber famine brought on by rapid liquidation of forested lands led industry to press for public support of scientific forest management, including reforestation (Demeritt 2001; Robbins 1982; Williams 1989). At the time, there was no clear policy for managing the burgeoning network of federally owned forests established in the wake of the Forest Reserve Act of 1891 (Dana and Fairfax 1980), and this policy vacuum created an additional justification for public forestry. Although important figures such as Gifford Pinchot advocated for a more confrontational approach to the private sector, industry figures with close ties to and prominent roles in key federal agencies established a more cooperative relationship emphasizing federal support for scientific forestry on public and private lands (Rajala 1998).

During the first half of the twentieth century, this cooperative approach gave rise to a series of federal programs supporting projects such as forest inventories, fire prevention, and reforestation of cutover lands (Dana and Fairfax 1980; Robbins 1982). This approach also underpinned the creation of the U.S. Forest Service's network of regional forest experiment stations, the first of which was established in 1908 in Fort Valley, Arizona. This station was followed in 1910 by the Forest Products Laboratory at the University of Wisconsin, Madison. In each case, the federal government committed staff and resources to research on improved forest-management techniques—improved, that is, by the application of forest science to rationalizing forest growth. This tradition has been maintained: there are seven federal forestry research stations, including the Pacific Northwest Research Station—with facilities in both Portland and Corvallis (Oregon)—and the Pacific Southwest Research Station in Albany, California. These key institutions in U.S. forestry undertake research on a broad range of forest-management issues and on the application of scientific forestry to public and private lands. They constitute the principal direct federal presence in scientific forestry.

The federal research stations were augmented following World War II by federal support for scientific forestry channeled through the land grant universities. Although consistent with established federal support for scientific forestry, the growth of federal funding for university-based scientific forestry also reflected and reinforced massive increases in state patronage for academic research during the postwar period—much of it targeting biology (Wright 1994). Modeled after the Hatch Act, which provided for federal support for agricultural research and development, the McIntire-Stennis Cooperative Forestry Research Act of 1962 consolidated a formal alliance between the federal government and public universities in forestry. McIntire-Stennis created a system of federal and matching state grants to public universities for forestry research; in addition to directly supporting research through the Forest Service, McIntire-Stennis funds account for approximately 80 percent of all federal funds specifically designated for forestry research (National Research Council 1990).

In a further parallel with agriculture, federal money has also been used to support forestry extension, which the National Research Council (1990) identifies as the most important avenue for technology transfer in forestry. Extension moneys come in part from federal appropriations under the Smith-Lever Act of 1914 (formula money for extension efforts) and under the Renewable Resources Extension Act, which allocates money for all renewable resource-related extension.[9]

Public-sector support for scientific forestry has traditionally drawn not only on federal programs and institutions but also on those of the states. In fact, an estimated two-thirds of all public-sector funding for forestry comes from the states (National Research Council 1990; Ellefson 1995). In Oregon, this tradition dates to the 1941 Oregon Forest Conservation Act. Aside from establishing the first regulations on state forest practices in the nation, the act created the Oregon Forest Products Research Laboratory as a joint venture between the Oregon Board of Forestry and OSU's College of Forestry. The lab was specifically established to provide research in support of industry and improved industrial reforestation. The Oregon Department of Forestry's in-house research program became the first comprehensive state forest-research program in the nation.[10]

Although Oregon intervened directly, local state support for scientific forestry has increasingly been channeled through land grant universities as well. Reflecting and reinforcing this institutional model, the Oregon State Forest and Experiment Station was established at Oregon State University in 1954, and the Forest Products Research Lab was merged in 1957 with the state's in-house silvicultural research initiative at OSU and renamed the Oregon State Forest Research Laboratory (FRL). Today, the FRL remains the principal site for state-funded forestry research within Oregon and also acts as an umbrella organization for forestry research at OSU.[11]

These developments helped to establish OSU as one of the leading institutions for forestry research, with a worldwide reputation. Despite stagnating levels of support from the state of Oregon in recent years and a marked shift in the FRL's funding from federal and state appropriations to competitive grants and contracts,[12] OSU continues to be a central site for scientific forestry research. According to data compiled by the OSU College of Forestry, although Oregon ranked fourteenth in the country in state appropriations for forestry research, OSU ranks first in drawing both federal and nonfederal grants for research in this area (personal communication, August 1997). One reason is that the campus is an incredibly dense node of expertise in scientific forestry, home not only to the FRL but also to the Forest Science Laboratory (FSL) of the Forest Service's Pacific Northwest Research Station. The FSL staff supervise Oregon State graduate students and collaborate with faculty, and the lab's facilities are also used by university faculty. This concentration of facilities and researchers underpins OSU's position as a key location for scientific forestry research.

Cooperative Silviculture

Just as the TGERC's location on the OSU campus—supported in various ways by public funds and facilities—attests to the high profile of public-sector forestry research, so too the TGERC's cooperative structure reflects an institutional tradition in public-private collaboration. In fact, during the late 1950s and early 1960s, cooperative silviculture emerged as an important avenue for science-based innovation in plantation forestry in the Pacific Northwest, as well as in other parts of the country. In the face of the biological challenges to proprietary silvicultural intensification, the formation of such cooperatives has become a key strategy for confronting the challenges, risks, and uncertainties that impede more-intensive forest tree cultivation.

The first silvicultural cooperative in the Pacific Northwest was a tree-improvement cooperative. Regional cooperative tree improvement emerged amid a climate of declining inventories of old-growth timber, increasing pressure from the public and the state to more adequately reforest land, and a growing understanding of genetics' role in increasing yields from cultivated forests. In 1954, a coalition of Northwest forest-products firms called the Industrial Forestry Association established the first regional tree-improvement program on an experimental basis (Hagenstein 1973). Twelve years later, the region's first operational tree-improvement initiative was established in Vernonia, Oregon.

From the outset, a range of biological challenges—including slow growth rates in the trees, uncertainty in selection and breeding methods, pollen drift in seed orchards, impediments to clonal propagation, and fragmented breeding zones—confronted industrial tree-improvement efforts in the region (Adams et al. 1997; Bordelon 1988; Hagenstein 1973). Cooperative from the outset, these efforts were spearheaded by the Oregon State Department of Forestry, the Crown Zellerbach Corporation, Longview Fiber, and International Paper. The Vernonia Co-op also received extensive technical guidance from Dr. Roy Silen of the Forest Service Forest Sciences Laboratory at OSU, adopting Silen's "Progressive System" (Silen 1966, 1978) of tree improvement.

The Vernonia cooperative became the basis for the Northwest Tree Improvement Cooperative (NWTIC), an umbrella group for what is now a network of twenty-two local tree-improvement cooperatives in western Oregon and Washington. These local co-ops bring together landowners whose holdings are in close proximity to one another so that the landowners can share superior parent trees as sources of genetic material, as well as seeds from the resulting crosses. This sharing includes numerous jointly operated seed orchards that generate superior crosses from selected parent trees. Co-op members are now able to meet at least 75 percent of their reforestation needs in western Oregon and Washington using improved seeds from this program (Bordelon 1988). The NWTIC is serving as the primary avenue for the production of genetically improved seed for member firms. Indeed, Weyerhaeuser is the only firm in the region that has undertaken a proprietary model of tree improvement as part of its High Yield Forestry program, launched in 1966 (Hee 1992; Morgan 1969). As the region's largest landowner by far, Weyerhaeuser is the exception that proves the rule, able to overcome biological impediments to proprietary tree-improvement with massive, contiguous landholdings.[13]

Never formally affiliated with Oregon State University, the NWTIC is the exception among regional silvicultural co-ops. Beginning in the early 1980s, the NWTIC was supplemented by a proliferation of research cooperatives based at public universities in the Northwest, particularly the University of

Washington in Seattle and OSU in Corvallis. Since the first such research cooperative was established at OSU in 1979,[14] many have followed, all designed to tackle specific aspects of intensive plantation silviculture. In tree improvement, the largest, oldest, and most important of these cooperatives is the Pacific Northwest Tree Improvement Research Cooperative (PNWTIRC). This co-op was established in 1983 by Dr. Tom Adams, who still leads it. PNWTIRC research emphasizes early selection of Douglas-fir for cold- and drought-resistance and determination of the genetic basis of these traits and the relationship between these traits and traits that have more-direct commercial advantages (for example, wood density) (Pacific Northwest 1996). The ultimate goals of this research are to breed trees across wider geographic ranges, to increase the economic efficiency of tree improvement, and to capture greater genetic gains in each successive generation of improved trees. In addition, PNWTIRC researchers are looking for ways to improve current practices in operational Douglas-fir breeding by attacking, for example, the problem of contamination of seed orchards by wind-blown pollen from surrounding "natural" forests and the problems associated with self-pollination (Adams et al. 1997).

Genetic engineering has had no role in regional conifer tree-improvement programs, though this may soon change. Quantitative trait loci (QTL) marker techniques (used to map the association between performance and specific DNA regions on a species' genome) are being used on Douglas-fir and other conifer species to identify DNA loci that control commercially important traits, including under the auspices of cooperative research at the University of Washington, as well as research being carried out by the Forest Service at the Institute of Forest Genetics. Yet, here again, specific obstacles to or restrictions on genetic manipulation are related not only to fundamental characteristics of the species but also to the interaction between biological characteristics and commercial imperatives. Since Douglas-fir has proved resistant to clonal propagation on a commercial scale, techniques for inserting genes into single cells and then producing entire organisms from these cells are not commercially feasible. According to one regional forest geneticist, "Producing a transgenic plant with Douglas-fir is technically very possible; [but] clonally propagating that [plant] and using it on a broad scale is much more expensive and technically challenging than it is in poplar, for instance."[15]

The success of the silvicultural co-ops relies on a high degree of sharing and on relatively informal intellectual-property regimes. For example, the success of the Northwest Tree Improvement Cooperative (along with its research affiliate, the PNWTIRC) relies on the fluid transfer of plant genetic material between firms, without formal property protections over plant varieties. Within breeding zones, genetic material is essentially treated as common property, while seed and seedling orchards are paid not for the genetic material per se but for their services. This arrangement stands in strong contrast to the formal intellectual-property protections that have increasingly marked the breeding of crops and orchard trees during the twentieth century and that have emerged as a significant facet of the TGERC's operations.

PUBLIC SCIENCE AND THE CHANGING LANDSCAPE OF RESEARCH AS PROPERTY

Beginning with the Vernonia co-op, intensive silvicultural R&D in the Pacific Northwest has involved widespread cooperation among firms and has increasingly been supported by contributions from public science. This is one line of the TGERC lineage. However, the TGERC must also be understood in reference to a second, more recent institutional phenomenon: the restructuring of industry-academic relations during the last two decades, much of it coincident with and indeed constitutive of the emergence of commercial biotechnology. On the one hand, this restructuring is one of the key processes by which commercial biotechnology has been socially produced. On the other hand, the maturation of commercial possibilities from biotechnology, accompanied by developments in intellectual-property law and regulation, continue to open what Martin Kenney (1998) refers to as new economic spaces (cf. Schumpeter 1950). The TGERC exists within this matrix, representing both continuity and change in the political economy of intensive forestry.

To understand the origins of this second line of biotechnology's social production under the TGERC, it is necessary to refer to a climate of economic uncertainty and turmoil in the United States and other advanced industrial nations during the 1970s. Stagnating industrial productivity and declining economic competitiveness created a sense of crisis among the countries of the Organization for Economic Co-operation and Development (Harvey 1989). In response to this crisis, neoliberal economic orthodoxy became ascendant in numerous countries, most prominently the United States. This orthodoxy informed a new approach to science policy, wherein universities were viewed as both a potential target of fiscal retrenchment and a potential source of renewed economic competitiveness and innovation. Thus, after several decades of expanding state support for science, the U.S. government began restricting appropriations to universities while pursuing regulatory and institutional reforms aimed at encouraging industrially oriented research (Wright 1994). Pushed by diminished public appropriations and pulled by enhanced opportunities for private-sector alliances, industry-academic relations underwent a shift that has been referred to as the rise of "academic capitalism" (Slaughter and Leslie 1997).

Central among the institutional reforms were new approaches to the commodification of academic discoveries. One of these new approaches was the Bayh-Dole Act of 1980, which encouraged university and government researchers to patent their discoveries. This legislation was ostensibly intended to protect the intellectual property of academic researchers. Yet Bayh-Dole also clearly facilitates the development of innovations into commercial technologies, encouraging the creation of clear and excludable property forms and thereby facilitating the sale and licensing of these new commodities by academia to industry. The academic-industrial restructuring included a series of changes in federal technology-transfer policy during the 1980s, changes that further facilitated technology transfer from the public sector (including universities). Examples include the Federal Technology Transfer Act of 1986 and the National Cooperative Research Act of 1984 (PL 98-462), which exempted joint industry-university R&D from antitrust regulations (see Slaughter and Leslie 1997).

Biotechnology has been central to this project. Biotechnology—along with information sciences and technology development more generally—was a focus of attempts to reinvigorate the U.S. economy (Castells 1996; Wright 1994). In fact, the Bayh-Dole model of intellectual-property management as it applies to academic institutions was pioneered by Harvard University (Kevles 1998), which in 1975 established a new patent policy in direct response to emerging possibilities in biotechnology development: Harvard, in a shift from its historic stance against patenting the discoveries of university researchers, allowed the practice for the purposes of licensing or selling those patents to private firms. The change was largely propelled by the university's concurrent agreement with Monsanto to undertake biomedical research and to grant Monsanto the exclusive right to license patentable discoveries. Around the same time, the National Institutes of Health decided to allow Stanford University and the University of California, San Francisco, to patent the Cohen-Boyer process. Together, these shifts initiated a debate about whether universities should hold patents (Kevles 1998), a debate that led eventually to Bayh-Dole. In the aftermath of Bayh-Dole, biotechnology has remained central to more tightly integrated industrial and academic relations in the innovation process. By 1991, the congressional Office of Technology Assessment (1991) was reporting that fully 45 percent of the funding for academic research in biotechnology was being supplied by corporate contributions.

TOWARD A VERTICALLY INTEGRATED SILVICULTURE

Within the TGERC, the tradition of extensive public and cooperative contributions to forest intensification intersects with the more exclusive forms of public-private partnerships in the post-Bayh-Dole era of academic industrial alliances. Thus, one reason for the TGERC's significance is that it presents a possible institutional path toward greater upstream proprietary interventions by forest product firms into forestry R&D and toward more exclusive (i.e., noncooperative) partnerships between firms and universities in research, partnerships along the lines of the 1999 research arrangement between the University of California, Berkeley, and Novartis.[16] In short, the TGERC is at the intersection of past and present in the political economy of commercial biotechnology, as a tradition of public and cooperative institutions confronts new property regimes and commercial possibilities through the industrial appropriation of genes and life forms as commodities.

The balancing point between continuity and change lies in the realm of intellectual-property controls over genetic material as a mechanism for industrial appropriation in forestry and for the commodification of life.[17] By supplanting conventional breeding techniques via the introduction of "industrially produced" genetic constructs, genetic engineering offers an avenue of appropriation that ties the use of engineered varieties to specific companies through their control over genes as property. Unlike the use of herbicides and other industrial inputs, this avenue of appropriation accelerates the commodification of the organism per se. That is, when accompanied by strong legal protections, such as those in the United States, for engineered organisms as patentable inventions, appropriation via genetic engineering makes the plants themselves into commodities. In this respect, genetic engineering represents a distinct form of appropriation, one in which capital increasingly circulates not only through techniques of cultivation but also through living organisms (Kloppenburg 1988).

The TGERC's pursuit of patent protections over several engineered varieties contrasts markedly with the fluid and informal internal management of plants as property in other regional co-ops. The TGERC's patent claims include gene sequences related to cottonwood sterility, as well as filings for insect-resistant Bt cottonwoods and glyphosate-resistant cottonwoods. At the same time, as noted above, the research on genetically engineered cottonwoods has proceeded on the basis of formal technology licenses obtained from Mycogen and Monsanto covering genetic material. Any commercial deployment of genetically engineered Bt-producing or herbicide-resistant trees produced by the TGERC will require negotiated license agreements or outright sales of ownership, involving the university as well as the original owners of inserted genes, as laid out in the memorandum of agreement signed by all members of the TGERC upon joining.

These tendencies toward formalism suggest that commercial genetic engineering may lead to a significant realignment in industrial forestry—in parallel with the realignment in agriculture (see Boyd, this volume)—and specifically to a more vertically integrated silviculture (Sagoff 1991). Consider, for instance, the TGERC membership itself. Among the founding members are not only Boise Cascade, Fort James, and Potlatch—the three forest-products firms with the largest cottonwood acreage in the region— but also International Paper, Georgia Pacific, and Weyerhaeuser, forest giants all, none of which has investments in cottonwood plantations. Westvaco and Union Camp have also participated as members in the TGERC, even though they have no lands or facilities of any kind in the Pacific Northwest. This remarkable diversity of the firms that have an interest in the TGERC, as compared to other regional co-operations, reflects leading forest-products companies' desire to monitor the potential of biotechnology in forest tree-improvement programs. But what is most telling is that the TGERC claims Monsanto and Mycogen as associate members, and their interest in shaping TGERC research is not hard to discern: they own and license important genetic material being used in the research. Monsanto, for example, may gain by locking in Roundup as the herbicide of choice for chemical weed-control in the cottonwood plantations and by securing license fees associated with the deployment of Roundup Ready cottonwoods as proprietary technologies.

POLITICAL AND REGULATORY SANCTION

No matter what commercial interests accompany the deployment of genetically engineered trees (or other organisms) and no matter what social arrangements surround such deployment, the commercial success of genetic engineering is contingent on social sanction. This sanction has two dimensions, the more formal and institutional dimension of regulatory review of ecological risks and the less formal dimension of the politics of GE trees. The increasing controversy over biotechnology highlights the fact that neither of these forms of social sanction can be assumed.

Although biotechnology in general and genetic engineering in particular have been introduced in forestry research on numerous fronts,[18] the TGERC research on genetically engineered trees is significant because it is likely to provide the first opportunity for regulatory review of GE forest trees intended for commercial use in the United States. The genetically engineered cottonwood varieties generated by the TGERC are being evaluated in trial plantings near Corvallis, not only for information about their performance but also for information about their potential risks. Prior to their approval, the trees will be evaluated both by the Animal and Plant Health Inspection Service (APHIS) of the Department of Agriculture (USDA) and by the Environmental Protection Agency (EPA). APHIS assesses the risk that the plants will become pests, and the EPA evaluates the possibility that the plants will release potentially harmful substances, for example, plant-produced pesticides, into the environment (R. R. James 1997; R. R. James et al. 1998). These risks are far from trivial, not least because forest trees are at most only a handful of generations removed from wild trees and can typically interbreed freely with wild populations. Moreover, forest trees grow for longer periods than are agricultural crops, which may increase the risk that engineered gene constructs will transfer to nontarget populations. Certainly the ongoing public scrutiny of GE crops in agriculture, when combined with the genuine ecological risks of GE tree deployment, indicates that regulatory approval cannot be assumed.

Yet, even if TGERC GE varieties are approved, their ultimate acceptance is by no means guaranteed. Public resistance to commercial genetic engineering has been concentrated in the agro-food sector but is also relevant to forestry, as protests targeting TGERC prototype trees have recently revealed. In a reflection of the TGERC's place at the leading edge of biotechnology development in forestry, activists opposed to genetic engineering attacked test plots of transgenic cottonwoods in March 2001. "Concerned OSU students and alumni" destroyed approximately twelve hundred genetically engineered TGERC prototypes and other hybrid cottonwoods at testing sites near Corvallis and Klamath Falls, Oregon. In an open letter to TGERC's research director, Steven Strauss, the group described the attack:

> During mid-March, three of your genetically engineered (GE) tree research sites were visited by night. The test plots of Populus genus trees (poplars and cottonwoods) at these places were independently assessed and found to be a dangerous experiment of unknown genetic consequences. Therefore, we ring-barked or cut down 90% of your trees at OSU's site at the Peavey Arboretum on Arboretum Rd. . . . At OSU's tract near Half Moon Bend of the Willamette River . . . , we eliminated 60% of the trees. Lastly, every tree was cut down in one test plot at OSU's Agricultural Experiment Station in Klamath Falls, Oregon.[19]

This first direct action specifically targeting genetic engineering in forestry in the United States highlights both continued public apprehension about and opposition to genetic engineering.[20] To become the next wave of industrial appropriation and technological innovation in intensive forestry, genetic engineering will have to address these public concerns, and the social acceptance of forestry biotechnology cannot be considered in isolation from broader debates about biotechnology both in the United States and abroad. The necessity of achieving social sanction is in fact one more illustration that technological innovation must be understood as socially produced, that is, politically enabled not only by the historical political economy of scientific forestry and institutions such as the TGERC but also by the contemporary politics of nature. In the context of building coalitional politics in support of both socially acceptable uses of genetic engineering and a broader scientific (particularly public scientific) accountability, it is significant that the communiqué by the OSU activists, although it focused on the ecological risks of genetically engineered forest trees, made no significant mention of the role of public science in supporting the research.[21]

CONCLUSION: CONTINUITY AND CHANGE

Those who emphasize the novelty of genetic engineering and the new biotechnology, whether in economic, ethical, political, or environmental terms, have the story partly right. However, in attempting to embed in history the emergence of forestry biotechnology R&D in the Pacific Northwest, my aim has also been to understand the social origins of these technologies and the science that underpins them. This goal is a vital project in critical evaluations of biotechnology. Popular and academic critiques that treat biotechnology as though it emerged from the ether will necessarily miss the fact that innovations such as GE trees result from longstanding trajectories of technological change propelled by efforts to rationalize and intensify forest-growth processes in the service of more efficient commodity production. Biotechnology and genetic engineering do not simply happen but are instead called forth by particular cultural and institutional processes.[22]

The significance of this perspective is both analytical and political. Embedding biotechnology in political-economic histories is critical to understanding the character and significance of particular technologies and technological change. There is no history of technology that is not also social history. At the same time, in expressing concern about the implications of technologies such as genetic engineering, it is essential to make transparent the avenues—including the links between public science and academic science—by which these technologies are called into being. This project is vital to rendering technologies and technological innovation more accessible to democratic politics (Haraway 1991); by exploring the political and institutional origins of the present, we may discover ways to shape the future. By addressing the institutional history of intensive silviculture as it is reflected in the emergence of the TGERC and its research agenda, I hope to have forged a better understanding of the social production of biotechnology and genetic engineering, contributing thereby to critical appraisals of both the technologies and the social processes that have brought them into being.

NOTES

I thank William Boyd, Julie Guthman, Anne Kapuscinski, Denny Takahashi Kelso, Kathy McAfee, Astrid Scholz, and Rachel Schurman for comments on an earlier draft. I take full responsibility for any shortcomings of the completed version. I also acknowledge the support of the John D. and Catherine T. MacArthur Foundation and the Social Science and Humanities Research Council of Canada.

1. The terms *socially produced* and *socially embedded* are drawn from distinct literatures. Many geographers working in a Marxist or neo-Marxist tradition have emphasized the need to consider environmental change and environmental politics in the context of nature's increasingly socially produced character, particularly under expanding networks of capitalist production and commodity circulation. That is, both nature and its politics increasingly "arise from the relations between local social formation, international political economy, and profit driven ecological transformation" (Castree 1995, 20). At the same time, the notion that technological innovation has a social context—and a specifically geographical one—has been crucial to the resurgence of regional industrial geography and to the study of so-called innovative regions (see, e.g., Gertler and Barnes 1999; Saxenian 1994; Storpor 1997). This perspective is in keeping with a neo-Polanyian emphasis on the social embeddedness of economic institutions, including markets—that is, an emphasis on positing these institutions as dependent on crucial but often overlooked issues of social and cultural context (Evans 1995; Granovetter 1985; Hollingsworth and Boyer 1997; Martin 2000). In emphasizing that commercial forest biotechnology is embedded within a history of science-based innovation in forestry, I also draw on students of technology and technological change, students who emphasize the interactive or dialectical relationship between society (including culture) and technology (see, e.g., Noble 1977, 1984; Vanderburg 2000).

2. The significance of graduate student involvement should not be overlooked. Graduate students constitute one of the best deals available in skilled scientific labor and are often able to raise additional funds from grants and fellowships—for example, NSF grants to doctoral students—funds that do not show up in the TGERC budget.

3. The endogenous production of Bt toxin promises to preempt the need to apply Bt dust to control insect predation. In addition to offering potential cost savings, genetically engineered Bt toxicity may be more targeted than standard pesticide applications, although Bt is relatively short lived in the environment because it quickly breaks down. One potential disadvantage of endogenous Bt toxin is that it is present in plant materials at all times. Engineered Bt toxicity may therefore increase selection pressure on resistant strains of insects exposed to the toxin (James et al. 1998; Krimsky and Wrubel 1996).

4. Interview by author, Corvallis, Ore., September 3, 1997.

5. For example, of the fifty GE crops approved for environmental release in the United States as of March 2002, thirty-two had been engineered for herbicide tolerance. In Canada, the analogous figure is twenty-two of thirty-two (GMO Database, Agriculture and Biotechnology Strategies (Canada) Inc. Web site, data retrieved March 11, 2002, from www.agbios.com/default.asp).

6. I do not dwell on determining what ideological and political factors explain public-sector willingness to assist in these endeavors. However, I believe that a modernist impulse to subject nature to rational manipulation—what James Scott (1998) refers to as making nature more "legible" to social control—is relevant and not altogether ontologically subordinate to capitalist ethos and politics per se. Thus, my focus on firms' reluctance to invest in the project themselves instead of "seeing like a state" should not be confused with a narrow, functionalist perspective on state actions and institutions. Reality is, I realize, much messier.

7. Determination of the rotation age occurs in combination with commercial imperatives, of course. For example, the fact that Douglas-fir in Oregon takes on average about eighty years to reach maturity is not only biologically determined by growth rates but also socially determined by the criteria for a commercially mature tree.

8. Tree improvement is directly analogous to crop breeding in agriculture, but the former is a more recent phenomenon than the latter (Morgenstern 1996; Zobel 1974, 1981). As Jess Daniels (1984, 164) writes, "Through the technology of tree improvement, we seek to direct and accelerate the evolutionary process toward the utilitarian goals of forestry—to create trees that are inherently better suited to our specific needs and purposes than any presently available to us." Tree improvement by means of conventional plant-breeding techniques is thus the immediate techno-logical precursor to genetic engineering. Typically, traits—such as growth rate, number of branches, branch angle, and wood specific gravity—that translate directly into superior commodity production have been of most interest to firms pursuing tree improvement.

9. Although similar in design and intent, the forestry extension program does not rival the agriculture program in size: in 1988 federal allocations for natural resource extension programs totaled $9.7 million out of $345 million for all exten-sion programs.

10. R. M. Kallander, administrator of Oregon's Forest Protection and Conserva-tion Committee, to George J. Annula, chairman of the Oregon House Committee on Forestry and Mining, January 22, 1957, Oregon State Archives, Salem, Oregon.

11. Interview by author, Corvallis, Ore., July 17, 1997; interview by author, Cor-vallis, Ore., July 22, 1997.

12. In the early 1970s, competitive grants and outside contracts made up only about 30 percent of FRL income. By the 1995-96 fiscal year, this figure had risen to 76 percent. Most of this money comes from competitive federal grants, but about 7 percent of all FRL funds now come from private contracts (Oregon State University 1995, 1997). The shift to competitive grants and contracts is to some extent a reflec-tion of stagnation in Oregon's support for research needs but also reflects a wider trend in academia (Slaughter and Leslie 1997).

13. Other things being equal, large areas of timberlands provide a greater area from which to recoup investments in all kinds of forestry research and development, particularly when investments are aimed at strategies that can be applied across these areas. That is, by reducing the costs of these investments per tree planted, Weyer-haueser's large land base justifies greater investments in forest intensification. How-ever, equally if not more important is that Weyerhaeuser's lands are in large, con-tiguous blocks, particularly in western Washington. This configuration eliminates some of the fragmentation in tree breeding encountered by other firms when patchy landholdings are overlaid with seed zones. In short, Weyerhaeuser can achieve greater economies of scale in tree improvement than can its regional competitors.

14. The first co-op was the Co-ordinated Research on Alternative Forestry Treat-ments and Systems co-op (CRAFTS), which has since been renamed the Vegetation Management Research Cooperative.

15. Interview by author, Corvallis, Ore., September 3, 1997.

16. In November 1998, the Swiss pharmaceutical, agrochemical, and biotech-

nology company Novartis signed an agreement with the Department of Plant and Microbial Biology at the University of California, Berkeley (a deal brokered by administration of the College of Natural Resources). The deal provided the department with $25 million in funding from Novartis and access to the company's gene-sequencing and DNA resources. In return, Novartis received right of first refusal over patent rights from research conducted using the funds and also gained two seats on a five-member departmental panel established to allocate funds to research projects. The deal was and remains highly controversial at Berkeley, and in wider circles, because of the degree to which it transfers governance over research in the department to a single firm, and is part of a more widespread turn toward exclusive partnerships between universities (public and private) and private companies in research funding and control over and dissemination of research results. The salient issue is not the role of private money in public and academic research, nor necessarily the commodification of academic and public research, although some do argue these points. Rather it is the degree to which private money comes in the form of exclusive alliances, thereby privileging certain private-sector actors in the conduct of the research itself (not least via corporate governance over research funding), while at the same time radically intervening in peer review and academic publishing as traditional avenues for the dissemination of research findings in academia.

17. I draw here on the work of David Goodman, Bernardo Sorj, and John Wilkinson (1987), who define industrial appropriation as the tendency for industrially produced inputs to gradually offset discrete aspects of on-farm production while leaving the farm in place as the basic unit of production in agriculture. The substitution of synthetic organic fertilizers for manure is an example. Farming and forestry differ in important ways, but by making increasing use of industrial inputs such as synthetic chemicals and artificial irrigation systems, thereby expanding capital circulation in forest cultivation, the intensification of forest cultivation systems has proceeded in a fashion somewhat similar to that of farming.

18. In the western United States, for example, considerable work on the development of transgenic varieties of commercial conifer species has been undertaken at the Institute of Forest Genetics (Institute of Forest Genetics 2002).

19. Concerned OSU students and alumni to Steve Strauss, March 23, 2001. E-mail message (subject heading: "GE Trees Destroyed at Oregon State University") posted to Transgenic Trees electronic mailing list, March 26, 2001. List archives available at www.iatp.org (as of January 11, 2003).

20. A similar attack against research plots of GE trees in the U.K. in 1999 targeted AstraZeneca research. AstraZeneca subsequently discontinued this line of research, citing the attack as one reason.

21. Concerned OSU students and alumni to Steve Strauss, March 23, 2001

22. Although Manuel Castells's (1996, 10) view of "society's autonomous innovative energy to create and apply technology" is problematic, his discussion of the way that technological innovation must be embedded within networks of social relationships is useful.

3

The Migration of Salmon from Nature to Biotechnology

Dennis Doyle Takahashi Kelso

The president of A/F Protein Inc., which owns the patent on transgenic growth hormone-enhanced Atlantic salmon, switches on the slide projector to show a photograph of three fish. "These three fish are the same age," he explains to an audience of business people at the San Francisco Seafood Show. "The two fish on the right are what a salmon farmer expects to see roughly . . . 14 or 15 months post-hatch. The fish on the left, if you can detect a slight difference, is its transgenic sibling." The audience laughs, then murmurs. The transgenic fish, an AquAdvantage salmon, is several times the size of the two normal fish combined.

> That fish . . . now weighs about three and a half kilos, and basically is ready for market. The bottom line is that using this technology . . . roughly a year and a half has been cut off the development time. So that instead of taking approximately three years or slightly less to develop a fish for the marketplace, we can do that twice in the same time span that it takes farmers to do it once. (Entis 1999)

Commercial salmon aquaculture, unlike wild-capture fisheries, uses technology to minimize unpredictable natural factors in raising fish. Salmon farmers fertilize, incubate, and hatch eggs in a controlled hatchery environment. There the juvenile fish develop into smolts, which are ready to live in saltwater.[1] The smolts are then moved to net pens or cages suspended in coastal marine waters, where they grow to market size and where the salmon farmer harvests them before they reach sexual maturity. Salmon farmers attempt to shorten production times by using a variety of technologies and husbandry techniques—for example, manipulating photoperiod and water temperature in the hatchery, feeding diets formulated for specific life stages, and breeding selectively to reproduce desired performance characteristics.

These techniques produce only incremental improvements. In contrast, genetic engineering, which enhances growth hormone levels through manipulation of chromosomal DNA, produces growth rates in the laboratory that are four to six times as fast as those of A/F Protein's control group (Entis 1997). If confirmed under commercial production conditions, this increase may mean not only more market-ready fish per year but also cost savings per unit of production through better conversion of feed, which is the single largest cost in salmon grow-out (Penman, Woodwark, and McAndrew 1995). By cutting in half the time during which capital is tied up in the production cycle, salmon-farming companies could also trim financing costs.

With an enthusiasm tempered only by uncertainty about public acceptance, the developers of the new technology claim that it will transform the industry: "It's very clear then that the economics of this kind of development are extremely powerful. It allows for us to create an aquaculture industry which is far more efficient than anybody had ever conceived of before" (Entis 1999).

If approved by the U.S. Food and Drug Administration (FDA) and deployed in salmon-farming operations, AquAdvantage salmon would likely be the first transgenic food animal in commercial production. With this biotechnology as the key, A/F Protein envisions aquaculture's "blue revolution"—the equivalent of agriculture's technology-mediated "green revolution" (Entis 1997, 1999).

Because they promise faster growth and more efficient production, transgenic fish would seem to be nearly irresistible to the salmon-farming industry. However, far from being preordained, commercial adoption of transgenic salmon is an uncertain outcome that will be shaped by social agency and struggle as well as by the technology's actual performance under the environmental and other conditions of intensive production. In the case of transgenic fish, both the public and the existing aquaculture industry may prove to be sources of social resistance. The public—including some scientists, consumers, and antibiotech activists—has concerns about whether foods made from genetically engineered animals are safe, whether these organisms will harm the environment, and whether commercialization of transgenic fish will concentrate control over the food supply. The public's food-safety and environmental concerns are shaped, in part, by technical information, but they are fundamentally political questions about what risks are acceptable and under what conditions. In addition, these concerns are fueled by scientific uncertainty, expressed as disagreements among scientists, that derives from the novelty of the organisms and from our limited understanding of aquatic ecosystems. That is, regardless of the actual magnitude of the risks, the public's perception of those risks will be an important factor in determining the degree of social resistance. The perceptions of the North American public about risk are also influenced by related controversies in Europe over genetically engineered foods.

The salmon aquaculture industry's resistance is based upon three concerns. First, salmon-farming-company officials worry that consumers will reject not only transgenic fish but also selectively bred (non-transgenic) farmed salmon because of confusion about what is genetically engineered and what is not. Second, salmon aquaculture firms fear that public perception of transgenic fish as environmentally risky would add to the social conflict surrounding the salmon aquaculture industry's operations in North America and would make the industry's expansion more difficult. Third, these firms have invested heavily in conventional technologies such as selective-breeding programs, and the danger is that successful adoption of transgenic fish by some firms could not only erase the gains from existing technologies but also lead to a competitive scramble that would restructure the industry to the disadvantage of companies that are now in strong positions.

The classical Marxian view holds that the existence of efficiency-enhancing technology will compel adoption because capitalism continuously revolutionizes the forces of production, and those who do not adapt are invariably left behind. In contrast, my analysis supports theories that recognize the role of social struggle in the development of new technological commodities, a struggle in which the trajectory is neither predetermined nor inevitable (see Kloppenburg 1988). In other words, despite the opportunities for faster and more efficient production, deployment of transgenic fish in commercial aquaculture is not assured.[2]

Social forces, along with the "agency" of nonhuman nature, have the potential to determine whether, where, and how this technology is used and, ultimately, whether the technology is profitable. I contend that social agency and struggle will prove vital to both the process and the direction of change. To explore the reasons for this uncertain dynamic, I begin with the technology itself and then examine the marketing of the patented AquAdvantage salmon—particularly the promoters' evolving positions on controlling risks of harm to ecosystems—and the current resistance from within the salmon aquaculture industry. I consider the competitive pressures favoring adoption of this technology and the countervailing forces that act as a brake on the technology treadmill, and I discuss scientific uncertainties, public perceptions, and competing discourses about transgenic salmon. I conclude with observations about regulation-centered conflicts that will likely be the focus of social resistance, which is facilitated by the aquaculture industry's reluctance to embrace commercial production of transgenic salmon at this time.

BUILDING THE TRANSGENIC SALMON

The attractiveness of transgenic salmon for commercial aquaculture depends on the enhancement of commercially valuable traits under production conditions. The developers of transgenic salmon have tailored their fish primarily to grow faster. Although there is disagreement about how commercially significant the increases might be in practice, there is little doubt that fish with these growth characteristics are extremely unlikely to occur in nature. These performance differences lie at the root not only of the marketing claims made by proponents but also of the environmental objections raised by opponents.

To create transgenic fish, scientists introduce millions of copies of novel gene constructs into the chromosomal DNA of the newly fertilized developing egg (Kapuscinski and Hallerman 1991). These spliced genes comprise structural genes (which encode a specific protein product) linked to regulatory DNA sequences necessary for successful expression of the structural gene.

A/F Protein's scientists developed AquAdvantage fish by linking growth-hormone structural genes from chinook salmon (*Oncorhynchus tshawytscha*) to an antifreeze protein gene promoter from the ocean pout (*Macrozoarces americanus*). This gene construct increases growth rates by encouraging year-round production of growth hormone, primarily in the liver of the transgenic fish (Entis 1997; Hew and Fletcher 1996). In nontransgenic salmon, growth hormone genes are expressed in the pituitary gland, and hormone secretion varies seasonally and is interrupted by a winter shutdown.

This growth-rate enhancement is most dramatic during the early life cycle stages (Penman, Woodwark, and McAndrew 1995; Devlin et al. 1994), and A/F Protein reports that its transgenic Atlantic salmon and their nontransgenic counterparts begin to grow at approximately the same rates by about sixteen months after first feeding (Entis 1997). Nevertheless, the early growth-rate differential is sufficient to produce a much larger transgenic smolt. For example, laboratory experiments with growth hormone-enhanced transgenic coho salmon at the West Vancouver Laboratory of Canada's Department of Fisheries and Oceans produced a portion of transgenic first-generation juveniles that were, on average, eleven times as heavy as same-age nontransgenic controls and that matured in two years instead of the normal three or four (Devlin et al. 1994). Both A/F Protein's transgenic Atlantic salmon and the West Vancouver Laboratory's transgenic cohos developed smolt characteristics early. Early smoltification may offer advantages to salmon farmers because commercial aquaculturists now either conduct the juvenile rearing phase in cold freshwater, which results in slower growth rates, or in heated freshwater, which results in faster growth but additional expense (Devlin 1997). All three consequences of growth-rate increases—earlier smoltification, larger smolts, and shorter time to market size—may provide competitive advantages if they are realized under production conditions.

The actual cost savings to growers depend upon the licensing fees for the patented grow-out stock, the environmental conditions under which the fish are raised, and the containment measures required for deployment (interview by author, 1999).[3] For example, possible restrictions demanded by A/F Protein (to protect property rights embodied in their patented fish) or by government regulators (to control risks from commercial production) might impose costs that would make transgenic fish less advantageous. The performance of a particular transgenic individual is unpredictable because the expression of a trait or traits depends on the interactions between genetic factors and environmental influences (Kapuscinski and Hallerman 1991). It is not simply a matter of plugging in the requisite gene constructs. Some salmon farmers argue that if all production factors are taken into account, the efficiency gains from the use of selectively bred smolts,[4] high-performance feeds, and improved feed-delivery systems may be competitive with the efficiency advantages actually achieved by transgenic fish (interview by author, 1998). For example, too much concentration on growth rate could detract from other characteristics (e.g., delayed sexual maturity and disease resistance) that are also important to commercial success. A fast-growing Atlantic salmon with poor survival rates or unacceptably high rates of precocious sexual maturation is not necessarily an advantage.

Despite uncertainties about the significance of the potential gain, the four- to six-fold growth rate increase remains a strong selling point for A/F Protein's patented salmon. As an aquaculture trade association official put it, "There's no doubt that transgenic fish grow faster"; the question is whether these salmon will be acceptable to regulatory agencies, salmon farmers, and consumers (interview by author, 1999). Consequently, A/F Protein has attempted to market its salmon with an eye toward neutralizing criticisms about the risks posed by its fish.

"A SOLUTION WITHOUT A PROBLEM"?

A/F Protein's advertising initially emphasized that its patented transgenic fish would be safe for the environment because they would be raised in tanks on land. In a letter submitting its official position to the North Atlantic Salmon Conservation Organization, the company wrote:

> The ability to grow fish very rapidly improves the economics of our industry so that land-based grow-out systems are economically viable and can become even more efficient than pen systems placed in natural waters. This is particularly true when we take into account the unique economic risks associated

with outdoor aquaculture—storms, disease, predation, and the cost of conforming to regulatory controls designed to protect the environment.

In addition, since our technology now appears to increase existing food conversion rates—by as much as 20%—the economics of matching AquAdvantage technology with land-based systems will become even more attractive. Thus, we are committed to the principle that our licensees will grow AquAdvantage salmon in land-based systems, or, if they must grow in ocean sites, to use only sterile animals in the grow-out pens. (A/F Protein 1997, 3)

This approach was originally part of the company's argument for support and approval of its transgenic fish in commercial aquaculture. However, although raising salmon in tanks is technically feasible, many aquaculture producers scoff at the idea because of the high capital and operating costs, even for fast-growing transgenic salmon. Consequently, the company soon moderated its enthusiasm for tanks and moved instead toward the use of sterile fish in saltwater net pens. Writing in an aquaculture industry journal, Elliot Entis, the president of A/F Protein, foreshadowed this shift: "The issue that requires most attention is that of accidental escape. Aqua Bounty Farms believes that initial approvals to grow AquAdvantage fish commercially will be for land-based facilities where escape into the oceans is not an issue, or in seaside pens with fish that are sterilized, as is often done now, thus eliminating the environmental issues" (Entis 1997).

Marine cage culture provides important advantages, including lower capital costs, a mechanism for waste removal, and an oxygenated water supply. In addition, salmon farmers have doubts about the performance of land-based, recirculation facilities. As a former aquaculture industry association official put it: "Even a transgenic salmon is not going to perform well in a re-circ system. They are prone to get diseases. They are prone to get oxygen deficiencies. They are prone to crowding. . . . The other thing . . . is, think about how big a re-circ operation is going to have to be to begin producing at [economies of] scale" (interview by author, 1998).

To increase the acceptability of its fish to farmers, A/F Protein has abandoned the idea of raising salmon in tanks on land and now favors grow-out of sterile fish in marine waters (interview by author, 1999). This change also reflects the company's recognition that it must produce sterile fish in order to protect its intellectual property. In the words of an A/F Protein official: "Don't look at us and say, 'Well you're doing this because you're protecting the environment.' We're protecting a property. . . . Protecting a property is our business. . . . But on the other hand, we are completely convinced it should be sterile fish in the environment anyway" (interview by author, 1999).

If fertile transgenic fish were deployed commercially, A/F Protein would have difficulty preventing reproduction of its patented fish from grow-out stock. Consequently, it is imperative that A/F Protein distribute only sterile fish or at least fish that the buyers believe to be sterile. The most feasible way of sterilizing transgenics is to produce all-female triploids (Donaldson et al. 1996).[5] Because triploidy arrests the process of egg development, female triploids are more reliably sterile than male triploids, which have the potential to achieve sexual maturity (Devlin and Donaldson 1992; Kapuscinski 1995). According to company officials and outside scientists, A/F Protein has begun producing triploid all-female AquAdvantage fish (interviews by author, 1999).

Because the company will have to incur the costs of making triploid all-female salmon anyway, reliance on reproductive containment rather than physical containment in tanks makes business sense. However, the use of triploid fish poses a problem for A/F Protein because salmon farmers insist that triploid fish do not perform well. Among the problems associated with nontransgenic triploid salmon are slow growth, structural deformities (e.g., larger than normal heads), and sensitivity to environmental stresses (lower survival rates) (interviews by author, 1998, 1999). Research scientists have also observed that triploid transgenic salmon exhibit lower growth and survival rates than do diploid transgenic fish (interviews by author, 1999).

A/F Protein must address salmon farmers' concerns both about efficiency reductions due to triploidy and about the costs of licensing and other expenses. If salmon farmers further discount the predicted growth-rate advantages in light of the efficiency gains they can achieve with conventional technologies, the industry will have less incentive to adopt transgenic fish and to incur the risk of public resistance. Largely because of the salmon aquaculture industry's fears about that resistance, the debate within the industry has focused on the social and political questions posed by the use of transgenic fish. In addition, resistance to transgenic salmon within the aquaculture industry reflects concern about how this technology will affect the industry's structure.

Joseph McGonigle, former executive director of the Maine Aquaculture Association, has called transgenic salmon "a solution without a problem" (Stoll 1999). A veteran salmon-farm manager in Cobscook Bay, Maine, echoed this view: "There's just no need for it right now. . . . The market is pretty well saturated. That's why the price is down. . . . Why bother making a more efficient, streamlined fish?" (interview by author, 1999). With lower costs of production and more salmon in the market, salmon farmers contend, prices will fall; and many existing salmon-farming companies will be unable to compete.

The salmon aquaculture industry has enjoyed a rapid climb in production rates and success in its competition with wild-salmon products. The industry annually produces about 1.2 million metric tons of salmon worldwide, most of it Atlantic salmon. Global aquacultural production of salmon first exceeded the total wild-salmon catch in 1997 (B. C. Salmon Farmers Association

2002b). North American commercial salmon aquaculture produces primarily Atlantic salmon (*Salmo salar*) on both coasts. The North American industry also grows three species of Pacific salmon—chinook/king (*O. tshawytscha*), coho/silver (*O. kisutch*), and steelhead (*O. mykiss*)—on the Pacific Coast. Industry insiders argue that the growing maturity of the salmon-aquaculture sector is reflected in greater concentration of production capacity in fewer companies, vertical integration, and stability (interviews by author, 1998).

If genetically engineered fish are deployed in commercial salmon aquaculture, however, salmon farmers fear loss of control at several levels. Patented transgenic fish would be available only to those producers licensed by the owner of the patent. If the competitive advantage is of the magnitude claimed by A/F Protein, the industry's current structure could unravel as some producers gain access to the technology while others do not. In addition, companies could lose the competitive advantages they have obtained by investing in the development of fast-growing fish through artificial-selection programs. In areas, such as North America's east Coast, that compete in markets also supplied by regions with lower production costs (e.g., Chile), producers who did not (or could not) adopt the technology would be subject to intense price pressure from competitors who did deploy transgenic fish. In the words of a Maine industry advocate, "It will put my industry in the same position as the rise of salmon aquaculture put the wild salmon capture fishery in" (interview by author, 1999).

THE BATTLE FOR PUBLIC PERCEPTION

An overwhelming number of aquaculture industry organizations have said that transgenic fish are a bad idea for the industry at this time. Producers fear that the controversy about genetically engineered fish as food would lead the public to reject not only the transgenic product but also farmed salmon generally, whether conventional or transgenic. In its review of salmon aquaculture, British Columbia's Environmental Assessment Office expressly recognized this concern: "Currently, there are no transgenic salmon being farmed commercially in B.C., nor has there been any interest expressed for doing so. This is primarily related to the negative public perception of transgenics, and the potential for this to affect all farmed salmon sales" (Environmental Assessment Office 1997, 1:81).

The industry has achieved profitability by using technologies to control natural production processes and has enjoyed substantial consumer acceptance of those technologies. Without a compelling reason, salmon-farming companies do not want to adopt an innovation that is likely to trigger objections and perhaps raise additional questions in the minds of consumers.

The industry's concern about consumer reaction is underscored by the readiness of some wild-salmon fishing interests to attack farmed fish as either unhealthy (e.g., by calling attention to the use of pharmaceuticals in the production process) or environmentally harmful (e.g., by calling attention to waste discharges and other practices at grow-out sites). One Seattle-based commercial fisherman, who also processes and markets his fish, laid out the strategy he would follow if transgenic salmon became a commercial reality:

> If the wild industry doesn't go in the direction of stressing its organic characteristics and pointing out that there are a lot of unintended consequences of socio and genetic engineering, then we'll be in big trouble, because this will just accelerate the undermining of the wild fish industry. And so it's just more reason to stress the ways in which wild fish go with the grain of nature rather than going against it. We have to really focus on that organic and health aspect of it and get aggressive. (interview by author, 1999)

A British Columbia aquaculture scientist described the likely effects of transgenic salmon production: "This polarization, where one's good and one's bad—[genetically engineered salmon] would just enshrine that, I'm afraid. . . . So, it could be a good technology; and it could have a real price tag on it in terms of public support for the industry" (interview by author, 1999). Both men agree with the farmed-salmon industry that the battle for public perception is critical.

The strength of the industry's resistance to transgenic fish will depend substantially on its level of concern about adverse public perceptions as well as its evaluation of possible effects on the structure of the industry. At the same time, salmon-farming companies will continue to assess this particular technology as a possible efficiency advantage in their intensely competitive business—a business that depends on technology to shape natural processes of production.

Social Forces and the Technology Treadmill

The aquaculture industry's assumption that technological innovation is inevitable is consistent with much of classical Marxian thought and with theories of agrarian transition that pay little attention to the influence of social resistance and agency on the processes of technological change. With respect to transgenic fish, however, the salmon-farming industry's actual conduct points away from inevitability, suggesting that there are uncertain processes that depend fundamentally on social agency and struggle as well as on nature's "agency."

Commercial salmon farming depends on technologies to modify natural processes. Access to and development of such technologies are critical to reducing costs and maintaining a competitive position in the industry. Vertical integration has become an increasingly common strategy, in part because it ensures the availability of essential technologies (Churchill 1996; Environmental Assessment Office 1997; interviews by author, 1998). As long as the resulting commodities are acceptable in the marketplace, adoption of production technologies that save money or improve quality may strengthen the innovator's short-term competitive position in relation to salmon farmers who have not implemented those technologies.

Theories of technological change in agriculture offer insight into the dynamics of this competition. In general, classical Marxian theorists have asserted that the adoption of efficiency-improving technology is part of a competitive spiral at the heart of the interaction between industrial capitalism and natural factors of production. The literature suggests a logic of production that should make new, efficient technology virtually irresistible to capitalist aquaculture. This deterministic view maintains that if the innovation is advantageous, it compels adoption by the producer and reshapes production for the industry as a whole.[6] Successful innovations in production methods, including adoption of new technologies, may thus enable the innovator to achieve greater profitability through cost or quality advantages and to outdistance (and ultimately force out of business) competitors who do not innovate.[7] This view downplays or overlooks the influence of social agency and resistance on technological change.

David Harvey takes up Marx's contention that "competition impels capitalism towards perpetual revolutions in the productive forces" but notes that technological innovation is only one of the possible responses to heightened competition. However, the social consequence of this competition is "continuous leap-frogging in the adoption of new technologies and new organizational forms independent of the will of any particular entrepreneur." Interaction of technological developments in one sphere with those in others leads to "a spiral of multiplier effects" in which "technological change appears to assume an autonomous dynamic." That is, the prevailing ideology of technological progress presumes the necessity and inevitability of technological innovation; and the striving for change becomes an end in itself (Harvey 1982, 120, 121, 122).

In the context of agriculture, David Goodman, Bernardo Sorj, and John Wilkinson (1987) argue that the need to adopt new technologies arises from "the central constraint" on industrial capitalism: "the inability to eliminate the risks, uncertainties and discontinuities intrinsic to a natural or biological production process" (156). Application of technology enables industry to reduce the importance of nature in production and thereby increases industry's control over natural uncertainties.[8] As advances in science and technology make elements of nature-based production processes "amenable to industrial reproduction, they are appropriated . . . and reincorporated . . . as inputs or produced means of production" (7). Technological advances create new opportunities for control that enable appropriationism to occur "within the changing limits defined by technical progress" (2).

The Goodman, Sorj, and Wilkinson framework is useful for understanding how commercial aquaculture has reduced, but not eliminated, the industry's dependence on nature. In their analysis, however, the available technology determines the scope of "appropriationism." Other analysts rightfully criticize this lack of attention to "social events and forces" that may "foster or obstruct technological innovations" (Mann 1990, 45).

Social forces that challenge the transitions to new technological commodities are central to Jack Kloppenburg's (1988) analysis of agricultural technologies (particularly the biotechnology of hybrid seeds)—even as he acknowledges the power of competitive pressures that favor innovation. Kloppenburg describes a "technology treadmill" that enforces adoption of process changes: "New technologies offer a means of reducing . . . [unit] costs [of production]. Early adopters of new technologies enjoy windfall innovators' rents, but these disappear as adoption spreads and the cost curves for all operations converge. Because the adoption of new technologies results in increased production, there is a tendency for prices to fall. This merely sets the stage for another round of innovation" (35). This treadmill not only speeds the producer toward adoption of technology but also impels the system toward "cannibalistic centralization," as marginal producers—those unable to adopt new technologies—either are absorbed by other operators or disappear entirely. Like Goodman, Sorj, and Wilkinson, Kloppenburg observes that the technology is itself an industrially produced commodity—a production input that may reduce the unit cost of producing other commodities.

For Kloppenburg, however, the transition from knowledge to technological commodity is a crucial moment at which the technology becomes an arena for social struggle. In writing about the development of hybrid seeds, the changing role of state-supported agricultural science, and the diffusion of seed technology, Kloppenburg argues that "to extend the imposition of the commodity-form to new areas is to expand the system" (1988, 24). Social struggle accompanies these expansions. Consistent with Kloppenburg's analysis, the advent of patented transgenic fish extends the commodity form to include genetic materials and the transgenic organisms created with these new genetic commodities.

The salmon aquaculture industry's adoption or rejection of existing production technologies illustrates both the explanatory value of appropriationism as developed by Goodman, Sorj, and Wilkinson, and the limitations of technological determinism. Obstacles in the path to adoption of certain chemical treatments demonstrate that the social struggle and agency suggested by Kloppenburg are potent for salmon aquaculture. That is, salmon farmers report and historical events demonstrate that social forces strongly influence the industry's choices of technologies. In particular, because of possible adverse effects on public perceptions about the wholesomeness of farmed salmon, the industry has chosen not to implement certain technologies.

For example, hormone treatments can prevent or modify the timing of sexual maturation and can increase growth rates in farmed salmon (Donaldson et al. 1996). Developers of the treatment techniques acknowledge that they are unattractive simply because of potential consumer resistance (interviews by author, 1999). The aquaculture trade press has characterized these technologies as "the marine equivalent of bovine growth hormone used to induce cows to grow faster and produce more milk" ("UM Researcher" 1994, 6). In light of the controversy about this form of milk production, salmon farmers say that the risk of consumer resistance makes these chemical techniques unacceptable for aquaculture (interviews by author, 1998).

Resistance is effective, in part, because farmed salmon face competition from well-established protein sources such as chicken and pork (see generally Economic Research Service 1999; Forster 1999a). In addition, some producers of wild salmon are eager to differentiate their products from aquaculture commodities and to raise questions for consumers about the desirability of farmed fish (interviews by author, 1998, 1999). For salmon aquaculture, public perception is reality, and negative perceptions may outweigh the advantages of certain available technologies, regardless of their promise to extend control over nature.

Social struggle has also shaped the conditions for continued use of pharmaceutical treatments for farmed salmon, a technology that the aquaculture industry has already adopted. In March 1997, immediately after the World Aquaculture Society meetings, a billboard appeared in downtown Seattle showing a salmon with a hypodermic needle protruding from its side; the caption read "Wild Salmon Don't Do Drugs—Learn the Truth about Farmed Salmon" ("Let Them," 1997, 14). Despite the industry's complaints that the billboard distorted the reality of pharmaceutical applications in salmon farming, the news media quickly picked up the theme of hazards to the environment and to human health. One reporter noted the importance of public perception in the dispute: "The claims and denials by the industry and its critics . . . indicate the debate will be based as much on emotion as on science" (Howard 1996, A5). British Columbia's 1997 review of salmon aquaculture called for a "proactive policy of prevention" rather than the reactive use of therapeutants, in part to avoid "greater exposure to negative public sentiment" with regard to the use of drugs in salmon farming (Environmental Assessment Office 1997, 1:95). The B.C. Salmon Farmers Association was left trying to reassure the public that the industry was already reducing its reliance on antibiotics by using other techniques instead (see, e.g., Kenney 1997; see also B.C. Salmon Farmers Association undated-b). Both the antibiotics example and the hormone example illustrate the important roles of social resistance and agency in influencing the choices of technologies and in conditioning their uses.

Nevertheless, salmon farmers are under a great deal of pressure to stay abreast of technological changes. Salmon farmers describe a powerful momentum that is pushing producers from technology to technology, raising anxiety about the possibility of being left behind in the competition to lower production costs and reduce prices. In the words of a British Columbia aquaculture trade association representative: "Nobody can resist lower cost production. . . . Certainly if somebody comes up with a way of doing it and . . . you sell it for a dollar a pound less than conventionally reared salmon, . . . either the rest of the places in the world will have to meet that or they'll go out of business" (interview by author, 1999).

Salmon farmers expect, and fear, that once a salmon aquaculture company successfully uses transgenic fish somewhere in the world, others will adopt the technology to avoid being left behind. The combination of improvements in production efficiency, opportunities for competitive advantage, and expectations of spiraling adoption pressures seem to support the conventional wisdom that a transgenic treadmill and consequent structural change may be compulsory for this industry.

However, this assumption is undercut by the escalating social struggle that has accompanied the development of the new transgenic commodities. Much of this conflict addresses organisms and products other than transgenic salmon, and social resistance has focused initially on consumer concerns about the safety of genetically engineered foods and on the concentration of corporate power that would be furthered by transgenic food production. These controversies are well developed in Europe and are increasing in North America (see, e.g., Schurman and Munro, this volume). In light of the salmon industry's keen awareness of these public perceptions, A/F Protein faces a severe challenge: promoting its technology in the context of growing objections to transgenic foods.

"A Slight Juggling of the Genes"

Food-safety issues have been the most prominent European point of attack against the use of transgenic organisms (see, e.g., Mistiaen and Boucq 1999; Petersen 1999). Widely publicized incidents of disease and contamination have raised questions about the safety of foods and the trustworthiness of industrial food producers (Cohen 1999). A/F Protein has recognized this resistance to transgenic salmon:

> Unlike the United States, many European countries—particularly Norway and Germany—are still wrestling with the fundamental aspects of biotech foods. Norway and Germany have doubts about when and how to introduce transgenic foods into their societies. Norwegians, in particular, are publicly averse to any application of biotechnology to fish production, both because they fear the

environmental implications and because they are afraid of consumer rejection of a product which is so important to their economy. (Entis 1997, 15)

The European opposition has also raised issues about control over food production and about retention of national and cultural identity. Linked to the dominance of U.S. agro-food companies, controversies over genetically engineered foods may reflect "the specter of nature being rendered more uniform by scientists in America . . . meshed with a wider fear of an increasingly undifferentiated planet where national distinctions fade" (Cohen 1999, 1).

This conflict over the cultural content of genetically engineered organisms reflects the fundamentally political nature of the struggle over the use of this technology. Whether couched in terms of national identity, food safety, or environmental risk, the underlying conflict is about whether deployment will occur, under what conditions these technologies will operate, and who will control the decisions about use. In attempting to influence these outcomes, the contending interests mobilize arguments ranging from the results of scientific studies to symbolic images.

Sheldon Krimsky describes a battle between those who characterize genetic technologies as natural and those who characterize them as unnatural: "By advancing the thesis that biotechnology uses nature's own methods . . . its advocates hope to give biotechnology a more favorable image while disassociating biological agents from the negative image often ascribed to chemicals." Krimsky argues that "control over the symbolic meaning of biotechnology" is the fundamental issue in the emergent social conflict and that the struggle over deployment and regulation of the technology is its superficial manifestation (1998, 145). In the case of transgenic salmon, however, the debate about deployment and regulation is the crux of the contest over the technology's symbolic meaning. Rather than being merely the surface outcropping of controversy over an individual biotechnology, the battle over deployment and regulation is where the struggle over symbolic content is being fought.

By painting transgenic salmon as "natural," its proponents are attempting to contain within familiar, established forms the conditions that will govern use of the technology. If AquAdvantage fish are but a minor extension of familiar natural organisms, then proponents can more easily argue that existing regulatory forms are adequate. But if the public perceives this technology as "unnatural," then it may demand more scrutiny and perhaps new regulatory forms. Consequently, social resistance and agency have focused on symbolic content in order to influence the adoption outcome.

The claim of naturalness is apparent in A/F Protein's promotion of AquAdvantage salmon as "using the salmon's own growth protein production system more efficiently than before." "Aqua Bounty Salmon are no different from standard salmon" (A/F Protein [1998], 4). According to Elliot Entis of A/F Protein, the application of this biotechnology is merely an extension of the "green revolution" in terrestrial agriculture—"the result of skilled plant breeders learning how to move important genes into modern varieties of wheat, rice, and corn." "Right now in aquaculture, we are where crop breeders were in the early 1950s. . . . The ability to transfer desirable traits from one food source to another through biotechnology innovations allows aquaculturists to create beneficial changes much more rapidly than through traditional breeding techniques" (Entis 1997, 12). "When you're eating our transgenic fish, you're not eating anything new, it's just a slight juggling of the genes" (Entis, quoted in Stoll 1999, 3). Some salmon farmers, such as Jeff Stevens, also share this view: "Selective breeding goes back a long way. Genetic engineering isn't that different from what we're already doing" (quoted in Stoll 1999, 2).

By contrast, critics of genetically engineered foods attempt to "stigmatize" them by emphasizing their unnaturalness and their riskiness (Krimsky 1998, 146). Opponents present images of a degraded, hazardous environment—for example, protesters in England wore "decontamination suits" during attacks on experimental plots of genetically engineered grain (Mistiaen and Boucq 1999, A1). News media accounts of the conflicts often refer to transgenic salmon as "Frankenfish" (see, e.g., Golden 2000; Schmidt 1999). Wild-salmon fishermen and other opponents of these fish describe them as unnatural and unsafe (Knutson 1999).

Aware of these conflicts and of the wild-salmon sector's eagerness to portray its product as "naturally organic," salmon farmers and their representatives overwhelmingly express concern about the reactions of consumers (interviews by author, 1998, 1999; Loy 2000). Recalling the controversies over genetically engineered foods in Europe, some describe their industry's market share as potentially vulnerable because public controversy over transgenic fish in salmon aquaculture might deter consumers from choosing any form of farmed salmon (interviews by author, 1998, 1999).

Although farmed-salmon producers describe negative public perceptions as a serious problem, some believe that concerns may subside as the public becomes more familiar with engineered food. A marketing report prepared for the International Salmon Farmers Association captures this ambivalence: "Though there are serious questions about environmental impact and consumer perception still unresolved, it is inevitable that the pressure to use such techniques will increase and that the technology itself will improve. Genetically modified foods are likely to become a fact of life in the twenty-first century and, subject to satisfactory resolution of the questions, farmed salmon may be among them" (ISFA 1998, 44). For the present, however, salmon aquaculture trade organizations have publicly rejected the use of transgenic fish, primarily because of uncertainties about consumer acceptance (interviews by author, 1998, 1999; see also Schmidt 1999).

From this technology's inception, scientists have tried to anticipate potential consumer objections to genetically engineered salmon:

> Since the main reason for producing transgenic fish is to improve the economics of fish production for food it seems unwise to use gene constructs from organisms other than fish (human, bovine, mice, bacteria, viruses, etc.) because they are likely to be rejected at the market place. For this reason we have isolated the promoter region from one of our fish antifreeze protein genes and linked it to a full-sized chinook salmon cDNA clone. (Du et al. 1992, 177)

In their patent application for A/F Protein's AquAdvantage fish, the inventors noted their concern that "transgenic fish using mammalian GH [growth hormone] genes may not be suitable or acceptable for human consumption" (Hew and Fletcher 1996, 5). Consequently, the all-fish gene construct for growth hormone was useful in terms of market acceptability.[9] Scientists at the West Vancouver Laboratory took the all-fish gene construct one step further, acknowledging "public concern over the use of DNA from non-homologous sources" (Devlin et al. 1994, 209), and developed instead a gene construct for transgenic coho salmon in which all the genetic elements came from sockeye salmon.

Despite this concern about consumer acceptance and the prominence of consumer-safety controversies in both the trade press and the news media, wild- and farmed-salmon producers agree that food safety will ultimately not be the most serious problem (interviews by author, 1998). Although activists have raised questions about food safety in order to demand additional analysis and labeling, the salmon industry seems generally agreed that food safety is only the tip of a much broader wedge of resistance.

In the conflicts over genetically engineered foods, issues of control over both food supply and food producers are important subtexts. As a British Columbia activist explains:

> I'm unclear as to what the risks [of transgenic salmon] are . . . , but it offends me that this source of protein that we've got—the last source of protein from the wild—is being taken over by big business. . . . There are huge social implications of this privatization of what was a wild resource. . . . Now, socially, what this means is that little fishermen in Ucluelet [B.C.] could be having to work for A/F Protein rather than being independent. Somebody in a little coastal community is now the serf in the corporate kingdom. (interview by author, 1999)

The public is hearing more-frequent allegations that transgenic organisms may harm the environment and is becoming more concerned about how serious the risks may be (see, e.g., Schurman and Munro, this volume).

The public's perception of ecological risk is partly due to scientists' uncertainty about what will happen if transgenic organisms escape or are released intentionally into natural ecosystems. Also contributing to the controversy is the documented, persistent problem of farmed fish that escape from floating net pens into surrounding waters and then travel long distances. For salmon farmers, the issue of escaped fish is the most prominent and difficult in a suite of claims by the industry's opponents about environmental harms caused by salmon aquaculture.[10] If genetically engineered salmon are deployed, escapes of these fish will be the most important factor in their potential to cause ecological harm.

Scientific Uncertainty and Public Perceptions of Environmental Risk

Salmon frequently escape from net pens. Canada's Department of Fisheries and Oceans and Washington's Department of Fish and Wildlife have documented the escape of at least 850,000 salmon from marine aquaculture facilities in British Columbia and Washington between 1991 and 1999 (Atlantic Salmon Watch Program 2002; Washington Department of Fish and Wildlife 1999; McKinnell and Thomson 1997). Washington salmon farms lost about 100,000 fish in 1996, another 370,000 in 1997, and 115,000 in 1999 (Washington Department of Fish and Wildlife 1999; see also "Extreme Tides" 1999). The industry concedes that escapes are inevitable as long as the fish are raised in net pens (Forster 1999b). However, there is no evidence, salmon farmers insist, that wild populations have been harmed in areas where Atlantic salmon are native (McGonigle 1998) or that self-sustaining populations of feral Atlantic salmon have been established in Pacific waters (B.C. Salmon Farmers Association 2002a; interviews by author, 1998, 1999; see also Pollution Control Hearings Board 1997).[11] Nevertheless, some aquaculture industry representatives do envision risks to both the industry and the environment if *transgenic* fish escape (interviews by author, 1999).

Salmon farmers identify two dangers to the industry posed by environmental concerns about transgenic fish. First, they fear that the public perception of environmental risk could fuel additional opposition to all forms of salmon farming, regardless of how serious the risks from transgenic fish really are (interviews by author, 1998). Second, some aquaculture advocates suggest that the release of transgenic fish might pose ecological risks different in kind or degree from those posed by selectively bred Atlantic salmon (interviews by author, 1998, 1999). As one British Columbia industry official noted, biologists have decades of experience with Atlantic salmon—an exotic organism in Pacific waters—including experience with previous efforts to establish wild populations of Atlantics on the Pacific Coast:

> Over a hundred years and over 30 countries trying to stock [Atlantic salmon] in their rivers, there's never been one successful sustaining run of Atlantic

salmon outside of their home range. . . . And so we've got that kind of information. . . . We don't know that with this [transgenic] thing . . . The unknowns
are just not worth the risk, particularly with something like this. You can do laboratory tests and you can put it with other species and things like that and see
what happens. There's still going to be unknowns there. So I never see this
being a part of net-pen or ocean-raised fish. . . . Now if you can have completely
escape-proof facilities, that's a different topic. (interview by author, 1999)

Although scientists point out that introduction of any exotic organism—
transgenic or not—may pose risks,[12] the primary environmental concerns
about transgenic salmon stem from possible ecological effects associated with escaped fish that have novel life-cycle traits (Kapuscinski and
Hallerman 1991; Regal 1994; Skaala 1995).

Environmental safety questions raised by scientists are important for two
reasons. First, government regulatory processes—the FDA's review, in the
case of AquAdvantage salmon—rely on the information submitted by A/F
Protein and on the analyses available in the scientific literature. That is, science frames the regulatory discussion and helps shape its outcome. Second,
the debate among scientists about potential environmental effects of transgenic fish contributes to an atmosphere of uncertainty that influences the
public's perception of environmental risk; and the public's perception may
ultimately be more important than the details of the scientific debate. This
interaction of uncertainty and perception is reflected in British Columbia's
1997 salmon aquaculture review: "In view of the uncertain potential risks,
and the serious public concern that has been expressed, it is recommended
that the farming of transgenics continue to be prohibited in marine netcage systems" (Environmental Assessment Office 1997, 1:81).

Scientific uncertainty may also provide opponents the grounds to mobilize public opinion against the technology. Even if regulatory agencies
approve the deployment of transgenic fish on the basis of scientific analysis, approval does not necessarily resolve the issues that underlie public
resistance. Consider, for example, the FDA's approval of recombinant
bovine growth hormone (rBGH), also known as recombinant bovine somatotropin (rBST). The agency's application of its scientific protocols did not
overcome the perception that rBGH was a bad idea. Nor did it resolve all
the technical disputes. Continuing disagreements between scientists are
illustrated by the rejection of rBGH by Canada's drug-regulatory agency
and by the international food-regulatory agency (Codex Alimentarius
Commission) decision upholding the European Union moratorium on use
of rBGH. With that controversy in mind, a British Columbia aquaculture
scientist extended the issue to genetically engineered fish: "Just looking at
it pragmatically, [bovine growth hormone] hasn't been a very smooth
technology to introduce to the public. There's a lot of reaction. And so, I
don't have a good feeling for what would happen with transgenic fish on
farms, in terms of public perception. Certainly, the critics of salmon farm-

ing would leap on that, and it would become a huge issue" (interview by author, 1999).

The arguments about risks from escaped genetically engineered fish illustrate the depth of the scientific uncertainties associated with deployment of transgenic salmon. These risks arise from the possibility that transgenic fish may reproduce or maintain relatively long-lived populations in natural ecosystems (Kapuscinski 1995).[13] Potential problems include gene flow from cultured populations to wild populations, flow that changes the ecological fitness or life-history characteristics of the wild fish. This issue is particularly important for salmon populations that are adapted to a complex, constantly changing series of specific environmental conditions. Skeptics and proponents of transgenic fish disagree sharply about the degree of risk and the appropriate protective measures.

The environmental issues posed by escapes of transgenic fish are fundamentally questions about risk rather than certainty of harm. According to Anne Kapuscinski and Eric Hallerman (1991), two leading commentators on environmental risks from transgenic aquatic organisms, we cannot rule out the possibility that transgenic fish will pose greater ecological risks than fish with endogenous genes recombined through artificial selection or hybridization of closely related species. The use of triploid salmon, with their high incidence of sterility, would reduce but not eliminate the risk that escapees could mate with wild fish or establish feral populations. Although the percentage of fish that are successfully made triploid may exceed 99 percent (Donaldson et al. 1993), some fraction of the treated fish will likely achieve sexual maturity (interviews by author, 1999).[14]

Proponents of transgenic fish acknowledge that environmental concerns must be considered, but they suggest that too much is being made of unlikely harms. They argue that the residual risk from the small percentage of fertile transgenic fish remaining after triploidy induction would be no different from the risks posed by many other low-probability events, risks that our society considers acceptable. In the words of an A/F Protein official, "There's no such thing as 100 percent certainty out there" (interview by author, 1999). From this perspective, the issue is not elimination of risk but risk management—that is, applying industrial quality-control techniques to the process used to create triploids rather than testing each fish: "It could be completely auditable, like in any manufacturing process, because you're only going to say, 'Okay here's an agreed-upon sub-sample' " (interview by author, 1999).

Other scientists argue that a statistically finite risk is unacceptable when permanent environmental harm may result. As one researcher who works with transgenic fish put it:

> At the moment, the only sure way . . . that exists for containing them is to verify the triploid condition by flow cytometry of every animal, not: 'I'll test 30 out of this batch of 10,000, and yeah, they were all triploid.' That's not good

enough because we just don't know. Unless one knows what risks are associated with that fertile individual, then I couldn't predict. . . . So I would say 100
percent triploid is required, 100 percent sterile is required. (interview by
author, 1999)

That is, complete reproductive containment is necessary because any release of fertile transgenic salmon could lead to irreversible ecological
changes: "There may be no going back here. . . . If you get one fish that
has a sufficient fitness advantage that is not eliminated by stochastic variables . . . it may take off" (interview by author, 1999).

Proponents of AquAdvantage salmon object that requiring the company to ensure that there is absolutely no environmental harm is unreasonable. They argue that A/F Protein should not be subjected to the "precautionary principle" and should not have to "prove a negative" (interview
by author, 1999). In the view of company officials, there is no realistic risk
that escaped transgenic fish will survive and reproduce: "What we're
breeding here is cows that are not particularly fit [for natural ecosystems]"
(interview by author, 1999). This lack of ecological fitness, they contend,
reduces the need for proving 100 percent reproductive containment. An
A/F Protein scientist complained that the company is caught in a bind
because opponents of transgenic fish claim that the risk is too high
regardless of whether AquAdvantage salmon are less fit to survive in natural ecosystems:

> Are your fish more fit or less fit? If they're more fit, then some people would
> say, 'They're actually going to out-compete the fish out there.' Well, . . . it's
> unlikely to be happening. The trouble is, if you quote the other side of the
> coin and say that they're now less fit, you know they're a problem, as all the
> ecologists say to you—they're going to interbreed and make the general pop-
> ulation less fit. So there's not a winning argument on this modeling. And it
> will take proper modeling with maybe some realistic data to come to some
> level of risk management here. If [there is] one fish in 10,000 or one fish in
> 100,000 that's reproductively capable, what's its probability of actually making
> a match? Because survival is low in the wild. (interview by author, 1999)

Advocates of AquAdvantage salmon also argue that natural ecosystems
would resist harm from introductions of these fish because the DNA in wild
fish would swamp any new genetic material that entered the ecosystem. The
influence of the introduced DNA would attenuate rapidly as a "diminishing
sum," thereby eliminating long-term ecological risk: "What breeds itself out
of existence isn't the animal that's more fit, but the crossbred strain which
is not fit and while it might slightly reduce the total number of animals for
a very brief period of time, it will have absolutely no effect on the surviv-
ability of that species. . . . Two divided infinitely by a greater number will
always be smaller in the succeeding number, the succeeding result" (interview by author, 1999).

Therefore, fears about genetic harm to wild populations and the establishment of feral transgenic fish in natural ecosystems are exaggerated. Implicit in this argument is a conception of nature as a set of stable, balanced ecological systems that return to near equilibrium following disturbance, so that introduction of a few transgenic fish poses little danger to the underlying stability. On this point, too, scientists disagree.

The science of ecology has moved toward emphasizing instability and contingency rather than equilibrium (Kapuscinski, Nega, and Hallerman 1999; see generally Pimm 1991). In addition, ecologists have attacked generic claims about the ecological unfitness of transgenic organisms and have argued that a small number of ecologically fit organisms may be enough to change the state of an ecosystem if conditions are favorable (Regal 1993, 1994). Consequently, neither the small percentage of fertile transgenic organisms nor the diminishing amount of the genetic construct in the population eliminates the risk of ecological impact. Recent research has strengthened this position by suggesting that traits of transgenic fish may simultaneously promote spread of the gene into a wild population and reduce the viability of the offspring of matings between the two populations (Muir and Howard 1999; *cf.* Devlin et al. 2001).[15]

This clash of viewpoints about the potential risks posed by transgenic fish and the adequacy of triploidy as a reproductive containment measure demonstrates that substantial questions remain about the environmental effects of transgenic organisms. These issues are not likely to be resolved before the regulatory and political decisions about deployment are made. Although scientific research will help frame the debate, decisions about uncertain risks are fundamentally political—the domain of public perception and social agency—and cannot be resolved solely by science.

CONFLUENCE AND CONFLICT AHEAD

Adoption of transgenic fish by the North American salmon aquaculture industry is not preordained. Much of the literature on analogous changes in agriculture understates the importance of social resistance and agency. In commercial salmon farming—my model for examining more general issues of transgenic technology adoption in aquaculture—companies' survival and profitability depend on public acceptance of their commodities and methods, as well as on production efficiencies. The idea that cost-saving technologies are irresistible in this particular form of capitalist production, because of an innovation treadmill or the technology-enabled appropriation of natural production processes, is inconsistent with the behavior of salmon aquaculture firms and with the growth of social resistance to some biotechnologies. Salmon farmers' concerns about public perception and social resistance—especially consumer objections—have already shaped the adoption and use of chemical technologies in this industry. These concerns have also influenced the industry's reluctance to embrace genetically engineered salmon. Consequently, this technology will be contested, not only by opponents of biotechnology but also by established participants in the aquaculture industry. Its trajectory will be determined by the interrelationships between public perception (mobilized as social resistance), natural processes, regulatory standards and procedures, scientific uncertainties, and unpredictable coincident events.

Nature's role will likely be significant in two ways. First, environmental conditions and natural processes will affect the degree of aquaculture industry resistance by influencing how much relative advantage, if any, is realized by transgenic fish compared with the industry's existing proprietary, selectively bred salmon stocks. Fast growth is not the only characteristic that determines whether fish can be produced profitably in salmon farms. Net cages in coastal waters typically have high population densities as well as variations in temperatures, dissolved oxygen, and other environmental factors. Farmed transgenic salmon may also be exposed to extreme weather conditions, pathogens, predators, and other dangers that may interfere with their survival and growth. These variables affect the performance of nontransgenic fish, too. However, it is not yet clear whether nature's constraints on commercial production will favor transgenics, will provide an advantage to selectively bred salmon, or will generate some combination of relative advantages for different traits. Second, nature's interactions with other genetically engineered organisms may contribute to changes in public awareness of environmental risk and in levels of social resistance. The discovery that other genetically engineered organisms can have unintended and unanticipated effects on nature—such as the appearance of volunteer transgenic corn in Mexico or transgenic canola in Canada—will likely influence the public perception of both risk and uncertainty. If these events are frequent and dramatic, public awareness of the risks and concern about the uncertainties will likely increase; and along with that awareness, the potential for social resistance may grow.

Resistance on the part of the aquaculture industry and a critical public are only two of the forces that are moving the biotechnology industry and its opponents rapidly toward conflict. The third stream in this confluence includes the regulatory process and its environmental protection standards. Although not all the elements have yet emerged, the confrontation will likely develop along the following lines. In the United States, the Food and Drug Administration has already taken the lead for premarket review of food-safety and environmental data on AquAdvantage Atlantic salmon. The agency claims jurisdiction because the transgenic manipulation of the fish's growth hormone constitutes a "new animal drug" under the Federal Food, Drug, and Cosmetic Act (FFDCA, 21 U.S.C. §§301-360bbb-2, 321(g),

321(v); Matheson 1999). However, there are no substantive standards to guide the FDA's consideration of potential environmental impacts from introduction of these transgenic organisms. The FDA has indicated that the safety and efficacy requirements for premarket approval as a new animal drug are broad enough to include impacts on wild fish and other organisms that may be affected by the introduction of transgenic salmon (CEQ/OSTP 2001). At best, that construction of the law is strained. The FFDCA addresses the health of animals in which the transgenic manipulation operates or the health of human consumers who use those animals as food, not the environmental risks or harms that may result (see 21 U.S.C. §§321(u), 355). Nor does the rest of the statute seem to cover ecological functions that might be changed by harming wild populations.

The National Research Council's (2002a) Committee on Defining Science-Based Concerns Associated with Products of Animal Biotechnology has questioned how the FDA's asserted statutory authority would actually work (112) and whether the FFDCA's safety standard for animal drugs is adequate "to sustain FDA's regulatory authority over broad, systemic effects of animal biotechnology on ecosystems" (116). The council also underscored the risks from escape or inadvertent release of transgenic fish because they easily become feral, are highly mobile, and have historically caused substantial harm (83). Consequently, the FDA is exploring its new regulatory terrain at a time when public scrutiny is high and concern is rising.

Amid this controversy, A/F Protein continues to publicize its patented fish, attempting to promote AquAdvantage salmon to potential customers, to ease public concerns, and to encourage early completion of the FDA review process. However, the controversy puts salmon-farming companies in an awkward position: the industry must respond not only to assertions by A/F Protein that salmon farmers are ready to adopt transgenic fish but also to objections by the technology's opponents, some of whom are eager to use this issue in their arguments against commercial aquaculture generally. Regardless of any ambivalence it may have about future uses of the technology, the global aquaculture industry—with an eye toward European, North American, and Japanese markets—publicly rejects the use of transgenic fish.[16] This policy not only undercuts A/F Protein in the regulatory process (by suggesting that there is no real demand for AquAdvantage salmon) but also silences a potentially powerful supporter of the technology. With the aquaculture industry either sitting out the debate or actively resisting deployment of genetically engineered fish, other sources of social resistance can gather momentum. The first hints of that resistance, in the context of the FDA process, are already apparent. Ultimately, the regulatory process itself will be the target of efforts to effect change.

The stakes are huge, both for A/F Protein and for opponents of the technology. If the FDA does not give its approval, there will be no U.S. market for AquAdvantage salmon, either as a production technology or as a food commodity. If the FDA approves the use of these fish as food but imposes expensive restrictions on their deployment in the United States, A/F Protein may move its fish into another production venue, such as Chile, and then return the finished food commodities to North American or other markets. That scenario is a nightmare for North American producers of farmed salmon unless the domestic market turns against foods made from transgenic fish. Activist groups opposing this biotechnology (see Schurman and Munro, this volume) are committed to neutralizing the value of FDA approval by raising consumer doubts, in the United States and in other major markets, about transgenic foods in general and genetically engineered fish in particular. Consequently, the battle for public perception and regulatory precedent will continue to escalate.

Even if the FDA approves the use of these transgenic fish, the contest over this technology will not likely end soon. In North America, for example, the social struggle will shift from the national level to that of the state and provincial agencies that control tidelands and coastal waters.[17] Because salmon can travel across national borders, there may be additional pressure for action under the Cartagena Protocol on Biosafety or other international agreements. This debate over how society should handle genetically engineered fish will contribute substantially to the construction of the symbolic meanings of broader genetic engineering technologies. As a result, the current debate over whether, or under what conditions, these technologies should be deployed may produce fundamental changes in our approach to weighing the risks and benefits of genetically engineered food organisms. In the course of that discussion, we will necessarily make choices about who holds the power to decide.

NOTES

This chapter draws on data gathered during a larger study of transitions from wild-salmon fishing to farmed-salmon production on the Pacific Coast and policy implications of the potential introduction of transgenic salmon into natural ecosystems. The study area included Alaska, British Columbia, and Washington; Maine provided a comparative case for aquaculture. The larger study included one hundred in-depth semistructured interviews conducted between June 1998 and December 2002. To maintain informant anonymity, I cite the interviews by year in this book. Interview data used in this chapter and in the conclusion come from thirty-two interviews conducted in Alaska, British Columbia, Washington, California, Maine, Maryland, and Washington, D.C. Generous support for this work came from the MacArthur Foundation, the Switzer Foundation, the National Science Foundation, and the University of California, Berkeley. The author wishes to acknowledge the generous substantive assistance of Rachel Schurman and Anne Kapuscinski.

    1. *Aquaculture* refers to the rearing of aquatic organisms under controlled or

semicontrolled conditions. "More simply, aquaculture is underwater agriculture" (Stickney 1994, 1). *Smoltification,* or *parr-smolt transformation,* refers to the physiological, biochemical, morphological, and behavioral transformations that enable young salmon to make the transition from freshwater, where they hatch and develop as juveniles, to saltwater, where they grow to adult size and sexual maturity.

2. Diverse species of transgenic fish are the subject of research in many laboratories, and salmon are not the only species with the potential for commercial production. On the basis of anecdotal evidence, research scientists and government regulators believe that China is already raising transgenic warm water food fish (interviews by author, 1999). A/F Protein is investigating transgenic Arctic charr, trout, tilapia, turbot, and halibut (A/F Protein 1999); and California-based Kent Sea Tech Corp. is developing transgenic striped bass for use in its inland aquaculture operations but has not yet proposed commercial deployment (Carlberg 1999).

3. The term *grow-out stock* refers to a salmon farm's stock of fish that have reached the smolt stage during hatchery culture and have subsequently been transferred to salt water aquaculture facilities, in which they grow to market-size adults. By contrast, *broodstock* refers to the stock of fish raised to sexual maturity in order to provide eggs or sperm (milt) for hatchery reproduction (including artificial selection), which produces subsequent generations of suitable grow-out stock.

Some salmon breeders suggest that additional performance gains may be realized if transgenic fish are selectively bred to maximize the expression of the desired characteristic (interview by author, 1999). However, recent research questions whether transgenic fish will provide the dramatic growth-rate gains observed in the transgenesis of wild salmonid strains if the transgenic lines are developed instead from domesticated strains that have already been selectively bred for growth (see Devlin et al. 2001).

4. Aquaculturists artificially select commercial salmon broodstocks to increase growth rate and to enhance other characteristics of commercial interest (Isaksson 1991). Vertically integrated salmon-farming companies and specialty suppliers of smolts have invested heavily in broodstocks that exhibit substantial increases in growth rates (as well as other performance characteristics) compared to wild fish of the same species (interview by author, 1998; Isaksson 1991). Salmon growers obtain hybrid vigor from out-crossing pure strains of their broodstocks with fish from other populations (interviews by author, 1998).

5. Triploid cells or organisms bear three haploid sets of chromosomes instead of the usual two sets (diploid) (King and Stansfield 1997, 397; see the glossary for the definition of *ploidy*). Triploid organisms are usually sterile because their fertilized eggs contain chromosomes that remain unpaired. Triploids vary among species in the degree to which reproductive structures, reproductive behaviors, and gamete production occur (Devlin and Donaldson 1992). The main method of inducing triploidy in diploid organisms is through application of temperature or pressure shock soon after egg fertilization (Kapuscinski and Hallerman 1994).

6. David Harvey argues that technological determinism is a misinterpretation of Marx. That is, when Marx speaks of "technology," he means the concrete form taken by the labor process through which use value is created. The labor process includes the embodiment of social relations of production and productive forces, "the sheer power to transform nature." Harvey also notes the difficulty of explaining the

dynamism of technological change "in a way that locates its origins in society rather than treating it as some external force with its own autonomous dynamic" (Harvey 1982, 99, 119-120).

7. Joseph Schumpeter's (1950) "perennial gale of creative destruction" refers to the sporadic but continuing process by which capitalism "incessantly revolutionizes the economic structure *from within*" (83, emphasis in original). Schumpeter argues that new combinations of the means of production, including innovations in technology, lead to competition that "strikes . . . at [the] foundations and . . . very lives" of non-innovating, existing firms (84). Michael Storper and Richard Walker (1989) criticize Schumpeter's emphasis on the role of science and invention because of his failure to consider adequately the social and institutional structures in which science and invention are embedded.

8. Goodman, Sorj, and Wilkinson (1987, 2) use the term "appropriation" to identify this process of using technology to modify natural factors of production, transforming them into industrial activities, and reincorporating them as "inputs."

9. In addition, experiments using gene constructs from organisms other than fish had not produced the performance gains obtained with the gene construct comprising ocean pout promoter and termination signal combined with chinook growth-hormone gene (Hew and Fletcher 1996; cf. Devlin 1997).

10. Environmental groups, fishermen, neighboring landowners, and some of Canada's First Nations have criticized pollutant discharges in the vicinity of pens and other conditions that have resulted from salmon-farming practices, and they have expressed concern about potential harms from escaped fish (see, e.g., Ellis and Associates 1996; Goldburg and Triplett 1997). Aquaculture industry advocates reject these charges and insist that they are based on conjecture rather than on evidence (see, e.g., B.C. Salmon Farmers' Association, undated-a and -b; Kenney 1997; McGonigle 1998).

11. Scientists offer diverse perspectives on the colonization risks. Research in British Columbia has identified twelve juvenile Atlantic salmon from two different year classes that were taken in 1998 from a river on the northeast coast of Vancouver Island, indicating repeated successful spawning (minimum of two years) by Atlantic salmon. The authors suggest that these findings indicate "the potential for colonization" and that Atlantic salmon "may constitute an invading species" (Volpe et al. 2000, 902). However, reviews of potential impacts of Atlantic salmon in Puget Sound have found low risk of colonization by escaped Atlantics in Pacific salmon habitats (Nash 2001; Waknitz et al. 2002).

12. Ecologically competent "exotic" fish, whether Atlantic salmon in Pacific waters or transgenic fish with traits for which there is not currently heritability, may pose substantial risks (interview by author, 1999; Kapuscinski, Nega, and Hallerman 1999).

13. Uses of recombinant DNA and other biotechnologies to modify the genetic structure of fish for traits such as faster growth and larger size may lead to changes in the fitness of the transgenic fish and consequent impacts on ecosystems in which these fish are introduced (see, e.g., Devlin and Donaldson 1992; Devlin et al. 1994; Hallerman and Kapuscinski 1992; Kapuscinski 1995). Although artificial selection and hybridization may also pose genetic risks (see, e.g., Devlin and Donaldson 1992), transgenic fish have the potential to contain new genetic information "that

would not be easily acquired . . . during the course of evolution" (233). Nor, depending on the source of the transferred genes, would these genotypes be likely to occur through hybridization of closely related species. The expression of this genetic information in novel phenotypes influences the ecological impact of the information (Kapuscinski and Hallerman 1991; Regal 1994). In addition, the "evolutionary potential" of released transgenic fish may produce new genetic configurations with potentially surprising ecological effects (Kapuscinski, Nega, and Hallerman 1999, 13).

14. Raising only females could further reduce the risk of self-sustaining feral populations.

Even with triploid fish, potential ecological impacts may result, for example, from interference with wild fish spawning (e.g., interference by infertile but sexually active males) (Devlin and Donaldson 1992; Kapuscinski 1995; Utter, Hindar, and Ryman 1993). This issue would be of particular concern if populations of wild fish were already in decline; any reduction in reproductive success could exacerbate the downward trend.

15. William Muir and Richard Howard (1999) used transgenic Japanese medaka (*Oryzias latipes*) as a model organism and applied deterministic equations to empirical life-history data. In computer simulations, after release of a few transgenic fish into a natural population of the same species, one trait of the transgenic fish (larger males) increased mating success, thereby spreading the transgene in the wild-type population. Although the introduced transgene provided a mating advantage, it also reduced the viability of the offspring. Consequently, the experiment predicted that the transgene would drive the mixed population of transgenic and wild fish to local extinction.

In another experiment, Robert Devlin and his colleagues injected a salmon gene construct "overexpressing growth hormone" into the eggs of two rainbow trout (*Oncorhynchus mykiss*) strains: one relatively slow-growing wild fish and the other a fast-growing domesticated, artificially selected fish. The researchers observed that transgenesis can affect the final size of the transgenic wild strain at sexual maturity ("an observation that warrants concern"), that the viability of both the transgenic domesticated strain and the wild strain was reduced, and that all the fish in the transgenic domesticated strain died before sexual maturation (2001, 781).

16. The industry's position is apparent from the policies articulated by many of the major (national) salmon aquaculture trade associations, the recommendations of industry consultants, and the comments of industry officials.

17. In 2001, Maryland enacted a five-year moratorium on the release of transgenic fish into any state waters that connect to other waters (Maryland Natural Resources Code Annotated Section 4-11A-02 (2002)). The Washington Fish and Wildlife Commission adopted regulations effective July 1, 2003, that prohibit the use of transgenic fish in marine aquaculture (Washington Marine Administrative Code Section 220-76-100). In February 2003, the California Fish and Game Commission adopted regulations that require closed containment for holding, rearing, or transporting transgenic aquatic animals (14 California Code of Regulations Sections 671.1(a)(9) [effective upon filing with the Secretary of State]; see www.dfg.ca.gov/news/news03/ 03016.html, accessed on April 5, 2003.

4

Making Biotech History

Social Resistance to Agricultural Biotechnology and the Future of the Biotechnology Industry

Rachel A. Schurman and William A. Munro

In retrospect, it seems incredibly naive, but it's the truth. We had real leadership; we had worked hard to do it. We had shown faith in this science when others were dubious, and it all seemed to be working. So we painted a big bull's-eye on our chest, and we went over the top of the hill.
Robert Shapiro, CEO of Monsanto, 2000

Over the last two decades, the life sciences industry has made enormous investments in biotechnology research and development; thrown tremendous energy into getting its genetically engineered (GE) crops approved, patented, and commercialized; and lobbied U.S. farmers and food producers to use them. For their part, the U.S., British, and other governments that envision the biotechnology sector as the wave of the future, and as a means of augmenting their national competitiveness, have strongly supported the industry and its efforts to commercialize (and normalize) these new technologies. They have devoted considerable sums of money to biotechnology research (Gottweis 1998; Kenney 1986), taken significant strides to deregulate the industry (Wright 1994; Kelso, this volume), and sought to promote the spread of U.S.-style intellectual property rights in the World Trade Organization (see the introduction to this volume). The U.S. government in particular has also promoted the dissemination of agricultural biotechnology in developing countries through the U.S. Agency for International Development (U.S. AID).[1]

With so much economic and political muscle propelling them, it is not surprising that GE crops hit the ground running when they came onto the scene in the mid-1990s. But what is surprising is that the rapid growth in GE crop deployment has been matched by an equally remarkable (and perhaps historically unprecedented) proliferation of citizens' voices challenging the biotechnology industry on economic, environmental, cultural, and moral grounds. Indeed, long before transgenic crops made their way to the market, individuals and groups concerned about the dissemination of these new technologies were already questioning their safety, utility, and necessity.[2]

In this chapter, we explore the character and impact of the new social movement against genetic engineering in agriculture (hereafter, the "anti-biotech movement"),[3] as it is unfolding in the North, which is the heart of the agricultural biotechnology industry and the main arena in which these technologies have thus far been deployed. We analyze the strategies social activists have employed in efforts to limit the deployment of biotechnology in food and agricultural production, and their effectiveness in achieving this goal. This antibiotechnology activism, we contend, has turned what until recently looked like a done deal in the trajectory of agricultural indus-trialization—the shift from farming to biotechnology, as David Goodman and his colleagues have put it (Goodman, Sorj, and Wilkinson 1987)—into a moment of uncertainty and openness. Activism has created this uncer-tainty, we argue, by affecting the fortunes of the biotechnology industry and the political environment in which it is developing in three substantial ways. First, activism has forced states to reconsider their liberal regulatory approaches to agricultural biotechnology, and to take steps to regulate the industry more seriously. Although pushing recalcitrant states toward stronger regulatory oversight remains difficult, there are signs that more-stringent national-level regulation will be forthcoming in many countries, including the United States. Second, antibiotech activism is helping to spawn new global regulatory regimes for genetically engineered organisms, such as the Cartagena Protocol on Biosafety and new Codex Alimentarius Commission standards on bioengineered foods. Although social activists are not the main actors negotiating these regimes, they have helped ensure that their content moves the world toward more substantive regulation of these organisms. Third, the antibiotechnology movement has imposed important direct and indirect costs on the firms developing this technology. In addi-tion, organized social activism has moved the issue of agricultural biotech-nology out of relative obscurity, and out of the hands of a small number of corporate and state actors, into the public arena, where it is being debated by a broader spectrum of society.

In making this argument, we want to emphasize two points with respect to the recent sociological (as well as popular) literature on the industrial-ization of agriculture, of which biotechnology can be seen as the latest man-ifestation (Doyle 1985; Goodman, Sorj, and Wilkinson 1987; Kloppenburg 1988). First, in contrast to those who suggest that the events of the past sev-eral decades have provided transnational corporations with virtually unchal-lenged power to determine the future of world agriculture (Bonanno et al. 1994; Greider 2000; Heffernan and Constance 1994; McMichael 1999; McMichael and Myhre 1991; Pritchard and Fagan 1999), we argue that social activists and their organizations are critical actors that have been overlooked by analysts of world-food-system restructuring. Without exaggerating their power with respect to large corporations and powerful states, we argue that social activists are playing an underappreciated role in shaping patterns of food production, consumption, and distribution. In the case considered here, antibiotechnology activists have placed new demands on biotechnology firms and, even more significantly, on states, demands that have forced them to abandon certain paths and move in new directions.

Second, we want to distinguish ourselves from those who see consumer resistance as the primary basis for the recent change in the political and economic climate surrounding agricultural biotechnology ("Of Greens" 1997; Moore 2001). Although we do not mean to ignore the influence of consumer opposition, we hold that it is social-movement mobilization that has made consumers aware of genetic engineering of the food supply and that has motivated consumers to take a stance. Even in Europe, where consumer opposition has been energized by food and health scares such as mad cow disease in Britain, AIDS-tainted blood in France, and a dioxin scare in Belgium, it is activist nongovernmental organizations (NGOs) that have made agricultural genetic engineering into a social issue.

We begin by providing a sketch of what the antibiotech movement looks like and who it comprises.[4] We then discuss the three main arenas in which the movement has concentrated its efforts in the North—the domestic regulatory sphere, the international regulatory sphere, and the corporate sphere—and evaluate its effectiveness. Finally, we consider the strengths and limitations of this type of activism.

FLUTTERING BENEATH THE MONARCH SUITS

In the mainstream U.S. media, one is most likely to encounter three rather different representations of antibiotechnology activism. One projects an image of playful public protest, such as the piece of street theater outside the Food and Drug Administration's (FDA) 1999 public GE hearing in Chicago, which featured a human fish-tomato, a grotesque cow that was shot up with genetically engineered bovine growth hormone by a mad scientist, and eight children dressed as monarch butterflies who were symbolically killed by genetically engineered mutant corn pollen (Burns and Chiem 1999). This sort of action has created a distinctive iconography for the antibiotechnology movement, in which the monarch butterfly has become a prominent symbol. Thus, in the popular street politics that has become commonplace in Northern countries since the 1999 WTO protest in Seattle, the antibiotechnology movement has a discrete recognizable presence that is not reducible to the antiglobalization sensibility into which many observers lump this politics. In fact, many movement participants are associated with local food-safety organizations or are organized in local or regional activist networks, such as the U.S. RAGE (Resistance against Genetic Engineering) and British GenetiX Snowball networks. They mobilize for specific campaigns and have played a major role in grassroots civic and protest activities such as "raiding" supermarkets and labeling GE products.

The second representation is less forgiving. It depicts "special interest terrorists" and "eco-warriors" who clandestinely try to derail the biotechnology industry by vandalizing research facilities and destroying seed trials. Such actions are generally undertaken by local grassroots groups (some with rudimentary organizational bases) that often sport rebellious names, such as the Dusty Desperadoes and Strawberry Liberation Front in northern California, and GrainRage and the "elves" of the Earth Liberation Front in Minnesota. By some accounts these groups represent no more than an alternative youth culture with anarchist leanings (Knickerbocker 2000). They have fueled an image of nocturnal sabotage, illegality, and antisocial mayhem that has led legislatures in several U.S. states to press for tougher law-enforcement penalties in property-destruction cases. Indeed, in February 2002, the Federal Bureau of Investigation singled out the Earth Liberation Front as a particularly dangerous domestic organization, one that poses a serious terrorist threat to the United States (Federal Bureau of Investigation 2002). They are, in fact, a fringe element in the movement, though they have been expensive to the industry and, in some people's opinions, to the movement as well.

The third image is one of antiscience, antiprogress Luddites, an image that to some observers also connotes a mysticist sensibility. This image is frequently invoked, especially by scientists, who express anger at the critics of biotechnology. A good example is Norman Borlaug's characterization of the "antiscience zealotry" that drives antibiotech activists (Borlaug 2000). To many scientists, the extraordinary risk-aversion of biotech's critics and their insistence that we should step back from the potentials of scientific discovery simply because they fear there is a genie in the bottle are irrational, non- or antimodern, and selfish. Yet those who frame the issue in this way fail to recognize that a significant segment of the antibiotech movement also comprises intellectuals, researchers, social scientists, and natural scientists working in established institutional settings on a range of issues. Many antibiotech activists are scientific experts in their own right, such as Rebecca Goldburg at Environmental Defense, Jane Rissler and Margaret Mellon at the Union of Concerned Scientists, and Michael Hansen from Consumer Policy Institute. The movement also maintains connections with university scientists. The importance of this small but crucial group of activist-experts is that they are able to engage in the politics of expertise, framing their claims to authoritative knowledge in the terms used by industry scientists but presenting the issues from the perspective of the public interest (Purdue 2000).

All these images of antibiotech activism, taken separately or together, are at best partial, and even misleading. What the images do indicate is that the movement is, both strategically and organizationally, diverse and complex. Strategically, the movement works in a rather loosely connected bricolage pattern of action: there are campaigns, labeling drives, protests, trial-crop destructions, and also serious research and knowledge-generation efforts to counter science with science. Organizationally, the movement comprises an extensive web of activist networks that engage a wide array of civil-society organizations connected not only across the world but also across a variety of issues, social concerns, and interest groups. This network mobilizes the resources of both mainstream and radical environmental NGOs, running the gamut from the Sierra Club and the British Soil Association to Greenpeace and Friends of the Earth International. It includes science-based groups, such as the Council for Responsible Genetics in the United States; the Research Foundation for Science, Technology and Ecology in India; and the Institute for Science in Society in the United Kingdom. It links the lobbying capacity of food policy NGOs such as the Institute for Development Policy ("Food First") and the Institute for Agriculture and Trade Policy in the United States with Southern activist groups such as the Tamil Nadu Women's Forum in India, BioWatch South Africa, and MASI-PAG in the Philippines. It engages farmers' organizations in the North as well as the South, such as the Confédération Paysanne in France and the New Agriculture Movement in Bangladesh. In short, the network nodes of antibiotechnology mobilization extend across local, national, regional, and transnational organizational structures.

In a movement of this kind, organizational leadership and unity give way to coordination and decentralization. This means that local-level activism has cultural and political dynamics that go beyond street theater, mass protest, and the illegal destruction of trial plots. In Britain, the United States, and Canada, activists have been arrested inside supermarkets for affixing warning labels to products containing GE ingredients. In Ecuador and Brazil, activist groups have prevented ships carrying GE grain from docking. In the United States, local lobbying campaigns have persuaded city councils in Austin, Boston, Boulder, Ann Arbor, and other places to require GE food labeling. Moreover, local actions are hooked into a larger panoply of activities facilitated by the network structure. In particular, activist organizations have used communication networks and the Internet to advertise protests and other actions, to generate petitions, and to solicit letters of protest against governments and firms around the world. Internet sites such as Resistance is Fertile and GenetiX Alert were established exclusively as clearinghouses of news and information about antibiotechnology actions.

Such informational networks have facilitated creative collaborations between NGOs and local activists across the North and South. The United

States-based Institute for Agriculture and Trade Policy, for instance, supported a long march for sustainable agriculture in Thailand; and Greenpeace has been a ubiquitous campaigner, assisting local actions from Boston to Bombay. In addition, these networks have enhanced the ability of NGOs and advocacy groups in the North to coalesce and share resources. In July 2000, for instance, seven major public-interest NGOs in the United States formed the Genetically Engineered Food Alert to press for a moratorium on genetically engineered foods until they are safety-tested and labeled and until biotechnology companies accept liability for any harm to human health or the environment.[5] The coalition's strength is its ability to coordinate the resources and skills of the different organizations while moving information rapidly between them in order to build public support and sustain pressure on the biotechnology industry.

As with any social movement, the prospects of the antibiotech movement depend on its ability to maintain its momentum. Although the future is hazy, activists have become a real force, and this complex, multifaceted movement has real institutional strengths. These strengths are manifested particularly in the ability of organizations to coalesce and to apply the weight of their resources and capacities—finance, human power, professional skills and training, infrastructure—synergistically to the pressure points of regulation and profitability in the deployment of agricultural genetically engineered organisms (GEOs). In so doing, these organizations engage two core principles of a democratic polity: accountability and choice.

"THE BATTLE ROYALE OF TWENTY-FIRST CENTURY AGRICULTURE": ARENAS OF ACTION AND ACTIVISM

In trying to limit the production and trade of GEOs, antibiotechnology activists have focused their efforts in three broad arenas. One is the domestic regulatory arena, where activists are pressuring the state to become a more serious regulator of biotechnology; the second is the international arena, where activists are working to create new supranational regulatory regimes for the global deployment of GEOs; and the third is the economic arena, where activists have sought to pressure biotechnology firms and consumers of their products to change their behavior. In each of these arenas, antibiotechnology activists have developed carefully thought-out strategies and achieved significant successes.

Holding the State Accountable

Although some of the globalization literature claims that states have been rendered powerless by globalization, this is clearly not true with respect to the regulation of biotechnology. States continue to exert significant leverage over the biotechnology industry and its behavior at the national level, particularly in the advanced industrialized countries where biotechnology has been most aggressively developed and deployed. It is true that governments in some advanced capitalist countries—especially the United States, Canada, and Britain—have chosen to regulate the agricultural biotechnology industry only minimally and to encourage its growth.[6] In this context, antibiotech activism has concentrated on exposing the dangers inherent in such a liberal regulatory approach and on pushing governments to adopt more comprehensive and responsible regulatory policies.

On both sides of the Atlantic, activists have revealed the weaknesses of existing regulatory structures by making embarrassing public revelations of government practices. In May 2000, for instance, activists in the United Kingdom seized on the fact that a Canadian company had inadvertently (and illegally) sold conventional rapeseed (canola) contaminated with Monsanto's Roundup Ready rapeseed to British farmers, who unknowingly planted it on more than ten thousand acres. Activists used the incident to claim that the technology is effectively uncontrollable and that the government was overly complacent in providing no oversight. (The problem had, in fact, been discovered not in Britain but in German field tests.) In an effort to minimize the seriousness of this event, government politicians initially insisted that the contaminated seed was effectively sterile and unlikely to cross-pollinate. But activists' ability to expose the government's low level of knowledge, its weak regulation, and its tendency to take industry claims at face value severely undermined its popular credibility.

Just four months later, antibiotech organizations in the United States made similar hay of the StarLink taco debacle, described in the introduction to this volume. In this case, activists pioneered the use of a new tactic: paying for independent testing of food products to see whether they contain genetically engineered ingredients. Indeed, it was the antibiotechnology coalition Genetic Engineering Food Alert that hired an Iowa-based genetics-testing firm, headed by a sympathetic scientist, to test whether several commercial brands of tacos shells contained StarLink. After determining that the taco shells did indeed contain the unapproved corn, the coalition shared this information with the press and took the U.S. government to task for creating a regulatory system that could allow a bioengineered product to be approved for one type of use (animal consumption) but not another (human consumption), with no effective means of keeping the two separate. In addition to the tremendous economic costs that the StarLink debacle imposed on the industry, retailers, farmers, and grain traders, the incident pushed the issue of agricultural biotechnology—and the weakness of government oversight—squarely into the public eye.

In both the rapeseed and taco cases, antibiotechnology activists stressed the difficulty of controlling this technology (especially under a free-market system) and highlighted the responsibility of the state to do so. They have complemented this strategy with sustained litigation. Court action is a powerful instrument for raising the stakes of public accountability in the food-regulation regime because it enables activists to frame specific and sometimes technical questions in terms of the state's responsibility to the public. For instance, in 1999, a coalition of activist organizations and citizens filed suit against the FDA, seeking to overturn its 1992 policy of neither labeling GE foods nor subjecting them to special testing. The litigants claimed that the FDA's decision violated the Federal Food, Drug, and Cosmetic Act, the agency's principal regulatory instrument. The point of the lawsuit was to show that the FDA had failed to ensure the safety of consumers regarding GE foods because the available scientific knowledge did not sustain the assumption of "substantial equivalence" and because safety tests carried out by the industry were tailored to meet government criteria that were designed to favor the industry.[7] Thus, the suit was not about the safety of GE foods per se, but about the adequacy and accountability of government regulatory procedures. One consequence of the suit was that it forced the government to place in the public domain a vast amount of information about internal disagreements, decision-making procedures, and the bases of scientific findings, information that compromised the confident tone of its regulatory pronouncements.

Activists have also pressed for public accountability with respect to the environmental impact of the new agricultural biotechnologies. In 1997, seventy nonprofit organizations filed a petition against the U.S. Environmental Protection Agency (EPA) in an effort to stop the release of crops modified with the bacterium *Bacillus thuringiensis*, or Bt crops. Supporters of the technology argue that Bt is a boon to the environment because its built-in resistance to pests enables farmers to use much less insecticide. Opponents argue that there is a good chance that pests will become tolerant to the Bt toxin, thereby reducing its effectiveness and its utility in organic farming. An additional concern is the potentially harmful effects on other species, such as the monarch butterfly larvae, that were indicated by a study at Cornell university.[8] The petition called on the EPA to withdraw all current registrations and deny future approvals of Bt crops, pending appropriate evaluation of environmental risks and economic impacts on organic growers.

This petition was unsuccessful. But it demonstrates how such actions can increase public pressure on government agencies to exercise stronger oversight. As part of the petition, Greenpeace commissioned a review of the impact of transgenic Bt plants on nontarget organisms. The review, carried out by an independent group of Swiss scientists, was highly critical of the industry's scientific tests, which provided the basis for the EPA's approval for insect-resistant crops. Though the EPA continues to insist that its regulatory process ensures that these products are safe for human health and the environment (partly through a controversial and costly "refuge" requirement),[9] the agency was forced onto the defensive and agreed to undertake a comprehensive review of its policies in 2000-2001. The FDA and the U.S. Department of Agriculture (USDA) also reviewed their agencies' regulatory procedures during this same period, largely in response to activist scrutiny and pressure.

In tandem with these "risk and procedure" cases, activists have also pushed "risk and rights" cases against state regulatory agencies. In particular, activists have argued that clear labeling of GE and non-GE foods would allow consumers to make informed choices about their own level of acceptable risk. Activists have pushed hard on this front because the political logic is inexorable: that citizens should have the right to know what they are ingesting is so obvious that almost any argument for curtailment advanced by the industry or by the government seems suspicious. Indeed, repeated polls have indicated a widespread public preference for labeling. In March 2000, the Center for Food Safety (CFS) spearheaded a large coalition of organizations that filed a legal petition with the FDA demanding the development of a thorough premarket environmental-testing regime and mandatory labeling for GE foods. The CFS built its argument on consumers' right to know which foods have been genetically engineered and their right to make an informed choice. This tactic aimed to inject citizens' rights into the struggle over regulation as part of a broader strategy to force government agencies to articulate their responsibilities to citizens in the authoritative arena of the court and to pressure retailers to treat their consumers with respect.

How effective have such actions been? In Europe, activist-inspired public pressure virtually forced the fifteen governments of the European Union to stop approving new GE crops in 1998 (Moore 2001)—a de facto moratorium that effectively persists today (Clapp and Romero Melchor 2001). And in the United States, some fifty thousand public comments to the FDA (many of them the result of organized petition drives) and three heated public meetings in 1999 pushed that agency to develop a more stringent policy proposal for approving genetically engineered plants.[10] In 2000, then secretary of agriculture Dan Glickman initiated a review of the USDA's GE-related policies and procedures by the National Research Council of the National Academy of Sciences. The review was critical of current regulatory procedures, specifically calling for greater public participation and interdepartmental scientific review in the regulatory process. Though it is still too early to discern the actual impact of the independent review, it might lead to some policy changes.[11]

Given the power and authority of the organizations involved in the development of biotechnology, these shifts are important markers of political struggles over the deployment of GEOs, especially in the United States, where industry strategists have relied on high levels of public inertia. To be sure, part of the motivation for reconsidering regulation has been the rising outcry against GEOs in Europe, the threats to trade, and the falling sales faced by biotechnology companies. But these developments have been greatly advanced by the actions of public advocacy and environmental activist groups. In effect, activist initiatives have forced government regulatory agencies to respond to their efforts to shape a critical public consciousness of biotechnology's social impact and their efforts to force the state into a tighter regulatory role.

Regulating beyond the Nation-State

Activists have also sought to slow the biotechnology train by helping to create supranational regulatory regimes that govern the international deployment of GEOs in food and agriculture production. This strategy is reflected in the movement's efforts to create an international protocol (known as the Cartagena Protocol on Biosafety) regulating trade in transgenic organisms, as well as in its ongoing efforts to influence the work of the Codex Alimentarius Commission, the UN organization that sets international standards for food health and safety.

The idea for an international biosafety protocol was born during the negotiation of the UN Convention on Biological Diversity in 1992. During these negotiations, participants from the global South pointed out that their rich stores of biological diversity were uniquely vulnerable to the introduction of genetically engineered organisms. For this reason, Southern participants saw an urgent need for a protocol to oversee international trade in GEOs, which threatened to increase dramatically in the coming years. But the United States and a handful of its allies (known collectively as the Miami Group) perceived such a protocol as a threat to the "right" of Northern farmers and corporations to produce and sell their goods, including genetically engineered agricultural commodities, worldwide and without prejudice. The group thus did its best to prevent the negotiation of such an agreement.[12]

Ultimately, the powerful Miami Group lost. Although the final agreement was not as strong or comprehensive as most of the South wanted, it was broadly perceived by Southern negotiators and the antibiotech movement as a victory, since both groups had been seeking at least some form of control over GEO trade. Moreover, the fact that the regulatory regime would operate under the auspices of the relatively inclusive and democratic UN was perceived as a significant achievement, as the Miami Group had made a preemptive move to shift the onus of regulation to the clearly undemocratic World Trade Organization (WTO).

Although many factors contributed to the successful negotiation of the

Cartagena Protocol in February 2000, the role of social activists was crucial. Prior to the negotiations, European activists and publics had put tremendous pressure on their governments to take genetic engineering seriously and to adhere to the "precautionary principle" (Buttel, this volume). This pressure induced the European Union to dispatch a number of high-level ministers to the negotiations, sending a clear signal to other parties (including the United States) that Europe intended to be responsive to its citizens. Representatives from a wide range of NGOs, from the North and South, also attended the meetings in person and used a variety of tactics to pressure delegates to reach a meaningful agreement. The NGOs engaged in a division of labor, sending some members into the meetings as formal observers and spokespersons and others onto the streets to demonstrate. Activist groups organized all-night vigils in the freezing Montreal weather, trotting out one colorful image after another to keep the media's attention. (One reporter for a Montreal newspaper noted that the activists "played the media like a Stradivarius" [Abley 2000].)

Activists on the inside also worked around the clock, lobbying delegates and disseminating up-to-the-minute economic, legal, and scientific information. Shortly after the negotiations began, the activist network released a position statement, signed by twenty-five influential NGOs from around the world, that demanded a strong biosafety protocol and admonished the Miami Group for obstructing the negotiations. Activist organizations also sought to shore up the power of Southern delegations. Once it became clear that the United States had no interest in listening to the activists' position, they focused their efforts on forming a transnational alliance with state actors from the main negotiating bloc for the South, known as the Like-Minded Group. The activists supplied these Southern delegates with information, helped them assess proposed text, and made concrete recommendations about accepting, rejecting, or changing specific language. They also brought environmental scientists to the meetings to give public presentations, and invited the delegates to attend.[13]

Reflecting on the negotiations, Tewolde Egziabher, the chief negotiator from the South, highlighted the importance of the activists' support when he explained how the Like-Minded Group, composed largely of African countries, managed to achieve anything against foes as powerful as the United States and its allies. "We had friends," Egziabher wrote.

> Africa is financially so poor that the African Group would not have functioned . . . without friends. But we soon made friends who filled in our gaps. . . . the Third World Network gave us critically needed assistance, and facilitated critically needed interactions, both South-South and South-North. African telecommunications are so poor that had it not been for the Gaia Foundation of London acting as an information relay station, we could not have been effective. And had our many, many other friends all over the world

not helped, we would not have managed to stay as informed and as effective as we did. (Egziabher 2000)

As one observer put it, the activists "were the eyes watching for society at large, calling delegates on the carpet if they didn't remember that they have citizens back home who might not be happy if they do certain things. . . . They were the watchdogs."[14]

Many of the same organizations are playing a similar watchdog role in the context of the Codex Alimentarius Commission. In 1999, the Ad Hoc Intergovernmental Task Force on Foods Derived from Biotechnology was set up within the Codex to develop standards and guidelines for foods derived from biotechnology. The definition of these standards and guidelines—which include risk-assessment criteria and labeling requirements and which recognize the role of the precautionary principle in food safety standard setting—lies at the heart of the political struggles over the task force's work. Activists have followed the committee's deliberations closely, studying and critiquing the official positions taken by governments and their representatives and pressuring governments and the task force itself to try to influence its decisions. A central goal of these activist groups is to ensure that task force decisions do not contradict or override the biosafety protocol's provisions.

Activists are of course not the only ones trying to affect these decisions; every group with a strong interest in the Codex's decisions has sought to get its voice heard. In fact, one could argue that the activists' efforts are simply aimed at counteracting the influence of far more powerful Northern agribusiness interests. Generally speaking, however, activists' efforts to establish and shape new international regulatory regimes for genetically engineered foodstuffs have helped to make decision making about agricultural biotechnology more democratic by ensuring that decisions about the deployment of biotechnology are not left entirely up to those with the most to gain from promoting these products and the least to lose if the products have negative economic or environmental consequences in importing nations.

Nuns, Farmers, and Frito-Lay: Putting the Industry on the Defensive

Getting a new biotechnology crop approved is probably high on the list of dumb things to do for your stock price right now. It amounts to sticking your chin out and saying we're going forward with this stuff regardless.

Alex Hittle, industry analyst with A. G. Edwards and Sons Inc., 2000

Social activism has not only forced the issue of biotechnology firmly on to the regulatory agenda but also complicated the economic lives of the biotechnology corporations. In recent years, church groups, consumers, farmers and farmers' associations, chefs, food processors, food retailers, and professional environmental and food-policy activists have all put direct pressure on these corporations, forcing them to rethink their strategies and, in some cases, to change their behavior.

Perhaps most striking about the experience of the biotechnology industry in the 1990s is how unprepared it was for the strong reaction to its new attempts to "improve" nature. As one economist dryly observed, "Monsanto didn't even know a train was *coming* before it got run over."[15] This may explain in part why the industry was so slow to react to the barrage of criticisms, consumer campaigns, lawsuits, and other actions that have thrown this techno-scientific project into question. But another part of the explanation surely resides in the divergent character—and preparation—of the two adversaries in this intense struggle for public opinion. On one side is a group of scrappy and diverse activist organizations who can punch and jab faster than you can say "genetic engineering," and on the other side is an elephant tethered to a post by its size, its enormous and sunk costs, and its competitive character. Moreover, activist organizations have spent the last twenty years in basic training for just such a battle, one that requires particular political, organizing, and issue-framing skills and occurs on many different fields simultaneously. By contrast, many life sciences corporations were so preoccupied with building up their strategic positions in this long-lead-time, capital-intensive, and risky industry (Goldsmith 2001; Boyd, this volume) and with trying to control the regulatory agenda that they barely knew they had an adversary in the making.[16]

From this position of strategic if not economic advantage, antibiotechnology activists and other concerned groups have launched an all-out offensive against firms situated at virtually every point along the commodity chain. They have instigated shareholder actions against publicly owned corporations, demanding that they disavow the use of genetically engineered inputs.[17] Activists have also exerted pressure through lawsuits, such as one filed in 1999 by several prominent antitrust lawyers against Monsanto on behalf of small farmers and farm groups. The suit, inspired by a coalition of environmental groups, accused the biotechnology giant of being at the center of an international conspiracy to control a large part of the world's seed supply and of giving farmers "false and fraudulent guarantees about the safety and marketability of a new breed of bioengineered seeds" (Barboza 1999c, C1).

Activists have also organized consumer campaigns to convince food processors, retailers, and restaurant chains to stop selling genetically engineered foods, under the assumption that the market signals would quickly travel back up the supply chain to exporters, farmers, and, ultimately, the life sciences companies. In response to consumer activism, a number of major supermarket chains, particularly in Europe, started to remove GE products from their shelves as early as 1998, and some North American and Canadian chains are now following suit.[18] The Organic Consumers Association and the BioDemocracy Campaign have also targeted fifteen food companies and distributors—dubbed the "Frankenfoods Fifteen"— to get them to stop using GE crops in their products (Belsie 2000).[19] In general, these campaigns have been surprisingly successful. Since 1998, some of the world's major food processors, including H. J. Heinz, Gerber, Bestfoods, Frito-Lay, Unilever, Seagram's, and Nestlé, have publicly declared their products to be GE-free in some or all their markets. And in August 2000, a major biotechnology producer, Novartis (now part of Syngenta), declared that it was eliminating GE ingredients from all of its consumer food products—in effect refusing to buy its own products (Cummins 2000).

Consumer pressure—or the fear of it—has affected the whole food system. In 1999, McDonald's, fearing a threatened boycott, decided not to use genetically engineered potatoes in its French fries. After similar decisions were taken by Wendy's and Burger King, three major potato processors— J. R. Simplot, McCain Foods, and Lamb-Weston—advised farmers they would not be buying Monsanto's genetically engineered NewLeaf potatoes the following year (Bernton 2000). In consequence, Monsanto closed the research lab in Maine where the NewLeaf was developed ("Monsanto Lab" 2000; Bernton 2000) and ultimately, pulled the potato from the market.[20]

In Europe, these campaigns have succeeded in part because they tap into a smoldering anger about U.S. food imperialism. This anger was graphically depicted in 1999 when activist farmers dumped four tons of GE grain in downtown London from a truck bearing a large sign that read "Tony, Don't Swallow Bill [Clinton]'s Seed." When the French farmer José Bové, who trashed several McDonald's restaurants in his country and became a kind of folk hero, was asked what motivated his extreme actions, he replied, "To fight against globalization and advance the right of people to eat as they see fit." (quoted in Klee 1999, 33). In the United States, activists have gathered support for their corporate campaigns by appealing to people's health concerns. One poster printed up by Greenpeace depicts a Kellogg's cereal box, with a caption reading "Kellogg's Frosted Fakes." The Kellogg's mascot Tony the Tiger also appears, saying "Frankenfood BAD!" In general, activists have portrayed the industry as greedy and irresponsible, more concerned with profits than with public health, the environment, or poor countries' food security.

U.S. markets in Europe, Japan, and other countries have been significantly affected by the negative reaction to GEOs in the food supply. Between crop years 1997-98 and 1998-99, for instance, European imports of U.S. corn fell precipitously, from 2 million to 137,000 tons (Goldberg 2000).[21] Worried about losing their export markets, some farmers are adopting a more cautious attitude toward new GE crop varieties, such as GE wheat (Kilman 2002; Lang 2002). Gary Goldberg, CEO of the American Corn Growers Association, argues that farmers' reactions are motivated by their economic concerns: "For agricultural producers, this debate over GEOs is not a safety, environmental or health issue. It is an economic issue. . . . Simply put, can farmers afford to grow a crop that they may not have a market for?" (Goldberg 2000, 2).

These pressures have made it difficult for biotechnology firms to proceed with business as usual. Evidence that the biotechnology industry has been hurt is apparent both in the defensive moves the big firms have made in the last few years and in the industry's all-out effort to redeem itself in the eyes of the public, its direct customers (farmers), and its investors. For years, the industry kept a low profile, quietly developing and commercializing its new gene technologies, but that strategy has become impossible. The industry effectively admitted as much in November 1999, when seven of the largest life sciences firms formed a new industry alliance, the Council for Biotechnology Information (CBI), to counter criticism from antibiotechnology organizations.[22] "The protest industry has gone too far," Edward Shonsey, a chief executive at Novartis Seed, told a *New York Times* reporter in November 1999. "They've crossed the boundaries of reasonableness, and now it's up to us to protect and defend biotechnology" (quoted in Barboza 1999b). Through the CBI, the industry launched a $50 million advertising campaign to win back control of the discourse about agricultural biotechnology. Running the ad campaign are several high-powered public relations firms (Barboza 1999b, 2000a).

Individually and collectively, the life sciences firms are seeking to depict themselves as firmly committed to improving the social condition. One DuPont television commercial identifies one of its future tasks as "find[ing] food to fight breast cancer." Another portrays a poor old woman carrying a cooking pot in an unnamed Southern country; the caption proclaims that biotechnology will be able to "make food grow where food can't" (Barboza 1999b). The health and nutrition page of the CBI's Web site highlights four areas in which the industry is poised to improve the human condition: by producing foods that will deliver oral vaccines, reduce or eliminate allergies, be more nutritious, and last longer and taste better (see www. whybiotech.com). In addition, the life sciences firms are undertaking highly publicized goodwill efforts in the battle to remake their image. In early April 2000, Monsanto announced that it had a complete sequencing of the first crop-plant genome (rice) and then made this information publicly available by donating it to the International Rice Genome Sequencing Project, a consortium of ten publicly funded genome centers based in Japan. A month later, AstraZeneca announced that it would help make a genetically engineered strain of "golden rice" freely available to the developing world (Barboza 2000b). (Golden rice is fortified with beta-carotene, which converts into vitamin A.)

But perhaps the most significant evidence that social activism and consumer concerns are hurting the biotechnology industry financially is the shake-ups that have occurred in the biotechnology stock market and the fortunes of individual companies. Monsanto's stock price fell by half in 1999 because of the company's troubles in the agricultural biotechnology arena. In March 2000, Monsanto was compelled to merge with Pharmacia & Upjohn, which then hived off the agricultural part of its operation and put it on the market. Before it was sold, however, the new Monsanto Co. was radically restructured, its agricultural research budget was cut by 15 percent and narrowed to work on the four major crops, and the business was subjected to a stringent cost-cutting regime (Barrett 2000). As one Monsanto employee put it, "It went from a time when everything was possible and there were no limits to one where priorities matter and costs matter. [It's] a very different place" (quoted in Barrett 2000). Another one of the "big five" companies in the industry, Aventis, sold off its agricultural division, Aventis CropScience, to Bayer AG, a move that was presumably related to its debacle with StarLink corn.

CONCLUSION: THE POWER OF ACTIVISM

In recent years, the literature on agro-food system restructuring has made much of the growing power of transnational corporations to determine the future of world agriculture. As states and firms have integrated themselves ever more tightly into the global economy and as private corporations have grown in size and economic power, large agribusiness firms have indeed augmented their reach and control over the agro-food system. But the power exerted by these transnational corporations is not absolute, unitary, or uncontested. In fact, a significant social movement has arisen to challenge this power and to try to alter the course of agricultural industrialization. The antibiotechnology movement has certainly not stopped the biotechnology train in its tracks. But it has reduced its velocity, possibly altered its trajectory, and created a great deal of uncertainty for the life sciences firms by means of a vigorous and sustained political engagement with both the industry and governing agencies. Antibiotechnology activists have challenged the dominant discourse surrounding the promise of agricultural biotechnology and have offered an alternative framing of its potential social, economic, and environmental effects. They have tried to make states more accountable to their citizens by questioning the adequacy of national regulatory policy. They have supported supranational regulatory regimes that strengthen the hand of governments desiring to regulate imports of GEOs. And they have altered the economic calculus of the technology's developers.

Yet the power of the antibiotechnology movement should not be overestimated. Antibiotech activism has stimulated the emergence of a significant countermovement comprised of biotechnology firms, industry associations, and other proponents of the technology, including scientists, NGOs, and other nonprofit institutions. Depending on the strategic behavior of this countermovement and how influential it becomes, the impact of anti-biotech movement activism may be attenuated. The movement has far more limited access to financial, political, and public relations resources than do its adversaries. In addition, it is operating in a political context in which democratic participation in social issues is at an all-time low; and other political issues are considered more pressing than the food issue. Furthermore, the discourses of neoliberalism, deregulation, and market competition now carry the day in policymaking. States and politicians feel a pressing need to support industries and undertake policies that foster national competitiveness in a rapidly globalizing economy (Kelso, this volume). High-technology industries such as biotechnology clearly fall into this category.

Precisely who the movement represents and what democratic promise it holds are questions that require closer attention. Although we firmly believe that this new social movement has enhanced democracy by publicizing the biotechnology issue and bringing critical new voices into the biotechnology debate, it still behooves us to ask what the movement's relationship is to the larger societies in which it is embedded. Does it stand to be dominated by a few large organizations pursuing their own agendas, or will it remain diverse and participatory and closely connected to its grassroots? Does the movement mainly address the concerns and fears of a group of highly educated, upper-middle-class, mainly white consumers, or does it reflect the interests of a broad range of citizens, including those for whom basic food security and the cost of food may rank much higher than preserving the right not to buy GE food? Indeed, is the movement committed to addressing the concerns of those whose primary worry is where their family's next meal is coming from rather than whether that meal is GE-free? These questions cannot be answered here, but it is clear that they need to be addressed seriously, both by the movement's leadership and by its silent supporters.

Finally, we need to determine the extent to which the movement can challenge the highly unequal power relations, both within specific countries and between them, that characterize the current agro-food system. This question of course focuses our attention on the movement's tactics and strategies, their potential for producing change, and their limitations. A good example, as Julie Guthman suggests in this volume, is the strategy of supporting labeling, which can have the perverse effect (from the viewpoint of the activists) of legitimizing the use of agricultural biotechnology. Although such tactical and strategic decisions necessarily reflect the political realities of the environment in which any social movement operates (as well as its strategic resources and capacity), these choices invariably shape and constrain the political impact of social movement organization. The antibiotechnology movement at the beginning of the millennium is no exception.

NOTES

We thank the other contributors to this volume, as well as Michael Goldman and Gerald Nelson, for their insightful comments on an earlier version of this chapter. We also gratefully acknowledge the support of the University of Illinois Campus Research Board and the Institute for International Studies at University of California, Berkeley.

1. U.S. AID seeks to promote the spread of biotechnology both directly, through agricultural programs and project assistance, and indirectly, through the support of such organizations as the International Service for the Acquisition of Agri-biotech Applications, based at Cornell University.

2. In North America, among the first to express concern, in the late 1970s and early 1980s, were Jeremy Rifkin and his nongovernmental organization, the Foundation on Economic Trends; the Cambridge-based Coalition for Responsible Genetics (later renamed the Council for Responsible Genetics); Pat Mooney, Cary Fowler, and Hope Shand from the Rural Advancement Fund International (RAFI), based in both Canada and North Carolina; and Jack Doyle, at the Environmental Policy Institute in Washington, D.C. Jane Rissler and Margaret Mellon (originally at the National Wildlife Federation and now at the Union of Concerned Scientists), Rebecca Goldburg at Environmental Defense, and Michael Hansen at the Consumer Policy Institute were also involved from early on.

3. The term *antibiotech* is something of a misnomer in that not all of the groups involved officially oppose the use of *any* genetic engineering in agriculture. Although some groups and individuals fiercely oppose any use of the technology ("not on planet Earth"), others do not reject the technology out of hand but stress the importance of tighter regulation, more research, and a more precautionary approach to the technology. Virtually all insist on the need for democratic discussion and debate. We urge the reader to keep this diversity of opinions in mind.

4. Although activism in the South is also widespread and important to the future of biotechnology, our primary focus here is on the North.

5. The coalition includes the Center for Food Safety, Friends of the Earth, the Institute for Agriculture and Trade Policy, the National Environmental Trust, the Organic Consumers Association, Pesticide Action Network North America, and the state public interest research groups (PIRGs).

6. For a fascinating historical account of biotechnology regulatory politics in the United States and Britain, see Wright 1994.

7. In 1992, the president's Office of Science and Technology Policy under the first Bush administration decided that products produced with genetic engineering were phenotypically similar to traditionally bred organisms and therefore did not warrant any special consideration for precautionary regulatory oversight. This pol-

icy, or the assumption on which it is based, is referred to as "substantial equivalence' (Kelso, conclusion to this volume).

8. The study, by John Losey, on which the monarch findings were based, has generated tremendous scientific debate. Several other researchers have done follow-up studies and come to different conclusions.

9. Refuges are areas that are set aside to be planted with non-genetically engineered seed. They are required as part of a strategy for managing the growth of insect resistance to Bt.

10. By the end of October 2001, the agency had already received 96,000 comments from the public, 76,000 of which were form letters (Kahn 2001).

11. The National Research Council's (2002b) report, entitled *Environmental Effects of Transgenic Plants: The Scope and Adequacy of Regulation,* is available on the Web at www.nap.edu.

12. The Miami Group comprised the United States, Canada, Argentina, Australia, Uruguay, and Chile. For a comprehensive history of the convention negotiations, see the Earth Negotiations Bulletins (ENB) published by the International Institute for Sustainable Development (as of October 2002, the ENB archives were available online at www.iisd.ca/voltoc.html). For useful summaries and political analyses, see Cosbey and Burgiel 2000; Dawkins 2000; Lim 2000; and Ling 2000a, 2000b.

13. Kristin Dawkins, interview by author, June 2000, Minneapolis, Minnesota; Dr. Philip Bereano, personal communication with author, August 2001.

14. Anonymous academic observer, interview by author, June 2000.

15. Dr. Gerald C. Nelson, personal communication with author, 2000.

16. This myopia was greater among U.S. corporations, and particularly of Monsanto, than it was of the biotechnology industry in Europe. See Charles 2001, especially chapter 11, for an interesting discussion of differences in corporate approaches.

17. As of May 2000, concerned groups had put anti-GE resolutions on the shareholder agendas of some two dozen firms, including life sciences corporations, food companies, supermarkets, and even restaurants; this figure represented an increase from zero the previous year (Friedlin 2000; Gonzales 2000; Organic Consumers Association 2000).

18. These European supermarket chains include Carrefour, Sainsbury, and Iceland. In the United States, Whole Foods, Genuardi's Family Markets, and, most recently, Trader Joe's either have gone or are going GE-free.

19. Greenpeace has been a major force behind these consumer campaigns.

20. Monsanto executive, personal communication with author, October 30, 2001.

21. Soybean exports were less affected because certain GE soybeans had been approved in Europe before the moratorium was enacted. However, the moratorium makes approval of new GE varieties in Europe highly unlikely, at least in the near future.

22. Aventis Crop Science, BASF, Dow Chemical, DuPont, Monsanto, Novartis, and Zeneca AG were among the founding members. For more information about the organization, see the CBI's Web site at www.whybiotech.com (available as of January 11, 2003).

5

Eating Risk

The Politics of Labeling Genetically Engineered Foods

Julie Guthman

The commercial release of genetically engineered agricultural products has been synchronic with the rising tide of public concern about the risks and failures of industrialized agriculture. Whether an unfortunate coincidence for the biotechnology industry or another addition to a mountain of evidence, the degree to which the battle over agricultural biotechnology has corresponded with other food scares—such as meat poisoned by *E. coli* O157:H7 or bovine spongiform encephalopathy (mad cow disease)—is surely striking. Because organic agriculture is often regarded as the antidote to agro-food industrialization, the movement for organic agriculture has intersected with this latest round of food fights in interesting ways. As but one example, antibiotech activists were able to build on the outpouring of opposition that occurred when the U.S. Department of Agriculture (USDA) released its first proposed rules for organic agriculture in 1997 (rules that have since been modified and finalized). The USDA's ill-timed inclusion of genetically engineered organisms (GEOs) within definitions of what constitutes "organic" contributed to public awareness of the extent to which GEOs are already part of the nation's food supply. Fallout from this incident stepped up the call for broader government oversight, even before the more recent wave of regulatory embarrassments, including the StarLink corn incident (see the introduction to this volume) and cases of contamination of organic fields and products with GE organisms.[1]

Labeling, a mode of regulation that has defined the organic industry, is one of the vehicles being debated for government oversight of GEOs. Yet, in 1992, the U.S. Food and Drug Administration (FDA) temporarily foreclosed mandatory labeling by ruling that food made with genetically altered crops was substantially equivalent to conventionally grown food, thereby dismissing the need for informational labels. When Vermont voters passed a

1996 referendum requiring that dairy products derived from cows treated with recombinant bovine growth hormone (rBGH) be labeled, an appellate court struck down this law as well, on the basis of the assertion of a First Amendment right not to speak filed by Monsanto and the dairy industry (Lappé and Bailey 1998). Some manufacturers had voluntarily labeled their products as free of GEOs, only to be told that they must include a disclaimer on such labels. For example, when the ice cream manufacturer Ben & Jerry's (along with three other companies) sued the state of Illinois for prohibiting voluntary labeling, the 1997 settlement in their favor still fundamentally circumscribed what could be said: the labels had to be worded so as not to disparage food produced from GEOs. Such labels were thus reduced to statements about the companies' practices and views: for example, "Our suppliers pledge not to use rBGH" or "We oppose rBGH."[2]

Perhaps the FDA's failure to exercise caution is the reason that labeling has become a primary, though not uncontested, focus of public action to curb the premature release of GEOs. In November 1999, a bipartisan group of forty-eight members of Congress called on the FDA to enforce the labeling provisions of the Federal Food, Drug, and Cosmetic Act that are intended to ensure that consumers are thoroughly informed and not misled about the characteristics of their food. Shortly thereafter, twenty members sponsored the Genetically Engineered Food Right to Know Act, which called for mandatory labeling of all genetically engineered foods on the market ("Rep. Kucinich" 1999). Thousands of people appeared at three FDA public hearings in December 1999, and many of the public comments involved demands for labeling. And in ABC News poll in 2001, 93 percent of those polled said that the federal government should require labels for genetically engineered food.

For all the furor, it is not clear that the use of labeling to enforce consumers' right to know will stave off further encroachment of GEOs into basic food production. On the one hand, labeling can force food manufacturers to be more selective in sourcing ingredients and can pressure suppliers to abandon genetic-engineering technologies completely. On the other hand, labeling makes risk management a matter of consumer choice and effectively privatizes what should be social decisions. So, although labeling may be a credible tactic for reversing the gung-ho commercialization of genetically engineered crops, by itself it is insufficient and may well have unforeseen consequences.

Drawing on lessons from the regulation of organically grown food and so-called eco-labeling more generally, this chapter problematizes labeling as a strategy for confronting the potential risks of the new agricultural biotechnologies. The development of organic regulation is particularly relevant. Despite organic farming's countercultural genesis, its growth was contingent on the establishment of marketable definitions of "organically grown" food. The effectiveness of this strategy set a precedent for other social causes to promote their agendas through the market. Growing and buying organic became vehicles for proactively addressing environmental risk and food safety, particularly in the context of what many felt was insufficient regulation of agricultural pesticides and fertility enhancements. Yet, as a regulatory vehicle, the "organic" label effectively created a price premium and hence a niche market for products bearing the label—what Ulrich Beck (1992) calls an "escape option" for those who feel they can afford to purchase relative safety. Organic producers came to vehemently defend such an approach as they grew dependent on the price premiums that such eco-labels are *designed* to create.[3]

Thus, the larger purpose of this chapter is to further an understanding of how the politics of consumption can both enliven and eviscerate broad public participation in technological decision-making. Is *any* sort of privatized regulation appropriate when potentially widespread risks are involved and when technologies are brought to fruition just because they are scientifically possible? To answer this question, I begin with a look at current U.S. regulation of GEOs by discussing the discursive terrain on which the battles are being fought and then providing a brief history of the existing regulatory impasse. I then take a more focused look at labeling and finally narrow to the lessons to be learned from the regulation of organic products.

NATURE, NOVELTY, AND RISK: THE DISCURSIVE TERRAIN OF REGULATION

Three interrelated debates have become central to the politics of biotechnology and thus to its regulation, or lack thereof. All are simultaneously technical, moral, and political, although usually the proponents of biotechnology have taken a technical stand and the opponents a moral one.[4] So, although the biotechnology debate could be framed in terms of a political economy of risk (i.e., how risk is created and distributed), much of the rhetoric rests on abstractions of nature, novelty, and acceptable risk, abstractions that are framed in technical terms in one camp and in moral terms in the other. It is arguable that the opposition's failure, until recently, to put these debates in explicitly political terms has contributed to the regulatory impasse.

The questions about novelty and nature are particularly intertwined. Do these technologies make food commodities substantially different from those extracted from nature? Is that alone a meaningful basis for regulation? Proponents of agricultural biotechnology claim that genetically engineered plants are virtually the same as conventionally bred plants and, moreover, that novelty cannot necessarily be equated to risk (see, e.g., Miller 1997).[5] On the other side, opponents claim that genetically engineered plants (and animals) differ substantially from their forebears, even those that have been substantially domesticated and thereby altered. That is, opponents assert that transgenic technologies cross barriers between species, which is both unnatural and likely to create unexpected consequences. In this way, novel is a gloss for unnatural; GEOs are risky because they are de-natured.

To rest the case on nature, and specifically the sacred bounds of species, is surely problematic. Jeremy Rifkin, one prominent, if controversial, spokesperson for the opposition, ultimately argues that each organism has its own set of attributes and is not just a system of information flows. Henry Miller (1997), representing the ultraconservative Hoover Institute, counters this by emphasizing flows, noting that genes and biochemical pathways are shared among many different species and that this sharing is part of evolution. Donna Haraway (1997) also made this point, albeit on the basis of different politics. Although the echo is undoubtedly unintentional, Miller's rhetoric resonates with Michel Foucault's discussion of the social construction of species and genus in *The Order of Things* (1994), in which Foucault shows how the development of such taxonomies depended both on emphasizing difference over continuum and on privileging certain attributes (particularly visible, structural features) over others.

Haraway's (1997) fascinating discussion of the parallels between transuranic elements and transgenic organisms is particularly relevant here. (These two technologies are often compared—with good reason—although the biotechnology industry prefers to compare itself with the computer industry.) Uranium, like genes, is found in nature, there to be discovered and extracted. Like the development of genetic engineering, the discovery of plutonium was an "ordinary, natural offspring of the experimental way of life." At the same time, the transuranic elements, lethal as they are, "have changed who we are fundamentally and permanently" (55). "Like the transuranic elements, transgenic creatures, which carry genes from 'unrelated' organisms, simultaneously fit into well-established taxonomic and evolutionary discourses and also blast widely understood senses of natural limit" (56).

It is hard to win this game, and the use of nature as a discursive anchor has been subject to a barrage of critiques about its social and cultural construction.[6] This problematic is one reason that protesters in East Anglia, under the guise of "Captain Chromosome," reject the nature-versus-artifice debate and go along with their business of sabotaging genetically engineered crops, not because those crops do violence to nature but because they are an assault on the commons (Boal 2001). Indeed, privatization may be the core ethical issue here (Lappé, 1998; Boyd, this volume) and a hook for bringing the debate back to politics. Nevertheless, the nature and novelty standards—often conflated—are the bases of the existing regulatory context for genetically engineered foods. The 1993 FDA guidelines state that the insertion of a foreign gene does not by itself make a crop either unnatural or different from foods derived by other methods of plant breeding. Consequently, genetically engineered foods are not regulated in the same way that foods that have been mixed with synthetic chemicals are. Genetically engineered plants are considered no less natural than those that have been bred selectively (Krimsky and Wrubel 1996, 216).

The symbolic importance of nature in these debates may disappear once risk is managed (Krimsky and Wrubel 1996, 219). Yet the debate over risk is itself problematic. From the perspective of biotechnology's proponents, neo-Luddite scaremongers such as Rifkin are exacerbating the fears of a gullible public, which is already too risk-averse and fails to appreciate the benefits that come with the risk. To counter this argument on its own terms, some contend that these technologies have been allowed on the market solely because of their agronomic promise (e.g., higher yields through more efficacious crop protection) and that they have not actually been submitted to the rigorous cost-benefit analysis and comparative risk assessment that are claimed to justify their use (see, e.g., Scientists' Working Group on Biosafety 1998; Regal 1994; Kapuscinski and Hallerman 1994).[7]

Yet calling for more risk assessment is also a perilous strategy for opposing these technologies. Comparative risk assessment assumes that risks, once reduced to a common measure, are "sufficiently fungible to be compared, traded off, or otherwise aggregated by analysts" (Hornstein 1992, 354). Even case-by-case risk assessment reinforces a pretense that risk choices are analytical choices when, in fact, they are political choices. But mostly, as Donald Hornstein points out, risk assessment assumes a limited menu of choices. Because risk analysis does not require engaging with the underlying cause of any given risk, it belies consideration of whether the technology involved is necessary in the first place. Those who call for more risk assessment thus circumscribe the debate to a trade-off of least desirable risks.[8]

Many of the food and biosafety risks involved are not only immeasurable but also deeply socialized (Beck 1992). They are also rendered doubly inaccessible to public control in that science—broadly understood—is integrally involved in creating not only the technologies themselves but also the ability to understand and evaluate them (also Crook 1998). These features alone should force a rethinking of the politics of regulating risk. In Beck's terms, such risks create conflict between those who produce risk definitions and those who consume them, between those who profit from risk and those who are afflicted by it (46); such risks create new antagonisms of interest. This conflict cannot merely be "weighed" away in the technical arena of risk assessment. Disagreement between "experts" who find a particular risk acceptable and members of the public who do not should not to be dismissed; such disagreements must remain at the center of regulatory politics—and at the center of the discursive struggle that shapes those "real" politics.

FROM REGULATORY IMPASSE TO RIGHT-TO-KNOW

The wholesale vindication of biotechnology did not always exist, nor is it shared across all relevant regulatory agencies. At an international conference at Asilomar in 1975, for instance, the risks of recombinant technologies were emphasized far more than the benefits (Bud 1998; *cf.* Wright 1998). The regulatory impasse that ensued in the United States was due in part to a felt imperative to be globally competitive. It does not seem accidental that the appearance of commercial possibilities for these technologies coincided with the economic crises of the 1970s and early 1980s, which were partially attributed to the United States' failure to keep pace with technological innovation in other countries, particularly in electronics (Castells 1996). Both the Carter and Reagan administrations were strongly committed to rapid technological development as a vehicle for economic recovery, and they provided substantial tax incentives for investment in biotechnology. As Susan Wright says, "the real risk was now defined as that of losing out on a novel field with immense commercial impact" (91).

The Reagan administration pushed hard to convince the populace that regulation had caused economic slowdown. During Reagan's presidency, there was a notable shift in the United States from what Marc Eisner (1993) calls a societal regime of regulation to an efficiency regime. Whereas the societal regime sought to prevent hazards to health and environment, the efficiency regime sought to eliminate policies that interfered with market mechanisms or imposed large compliance costs. And whereas the societal regime imposed mandates and timetables (i.e., "command and control"), the efficiency regime required formal cost-benefit analysis of regulation and, in some cases, outright deregulation.

So it is not surprising that the regulatory climate for biotechnology abruptly shifted in the years following Asilomar. The emerging debate was about whether genetic engineering techniques or the products of those techniques should be uniquely regulated (Miller 1997). The process-versus-product debate ended with the decision that only the product would count; if an organism was phenotypically identical to an organism found in nature, that would be deemed sufficient.[9] Because the product definition gained the upper hand, the burden of proving safety shifted from those who wished to pursue genetic engineering to those who wished to control it (Wright 1998). As Sheldon Krimsky and Walter Wrubel put it, "a minimalist, cost-effective, priority-driven approach" was chosen (1996, 250).

No new laws were passed, and no agency was created to specifically address biotechnology. The 1986 "biotechnology regulatory framework" failed to provide a coherent way to regulate the new technologies; instead it spread responsibility among existing agencies—primarily the EPA, FDA, and USDA, all of which carry different mandates—and allowed much oversight to fall between the cracks altogether (Ferrara 1998). Although the EPA interpreted the Toxic Substances Control Act of 1976, which requires premanufacture notices for all new chemicals and nonnatural substances, as including genetically engineered organisms (Krimsky and Wrubel 1996), the agency's record of toxic-release prevention has been notably spotty. Its effectiveness has been limited by the backlog of substances under review, the historically narrow definitions of risk, and the high permissible tolerances (Steingraber 1997). In fact, as one of its first rulings on biotechnology, the EPA modified residue tolerances to allow greater forage use of herbicide-resistant crops (Lappé and Bailey 1998).

In effect, the FDA became the doorkeeper to the proliferation of genetically engineered plant products for food. That fact alone excluded issues other than food safety from regulatory oversight because the FDA, unlike the EPA or the Animal and Plant Health Inspection Service of the USDA, has no power to review the potential ecological risks of agricultural biotechnology. An FDA policy statement released in 1992 indicated that labeling was required if food derived from a new plant variety differed from its traditional counterpart or if a safety or usage issue required consumers to be alerted. Safety issues would include increased toxicity, the presence of allergens, or changes in nutrient levels (Miller 1997, 98); the fact that a food source has been genetically engineered had no bearing. As long as genes came from an approved food source, the FDA treated new or altered genes as natural, not novel, additives (Ferrara 1998). This, then, was the justification for not requiring mandatory labeling and for treating voluntary labeling as only an advertising claim, with the requisite caveats. At the same time, the 1992 policy also exempted corporations from having to test bioengineered crops for food safety before putting them on the market, giving them the option of voluntary "consultation" with agency representatives.

Anti-GEO activists have construed the FDA's position as a failure to respect consumers' right to know. Without mandatory labels, it is argued, consumers cannot be made aware of the extent of genetic engineering, much less make informed decisions about what goes into their bodies. By making this argument, activists, perhaps unintentionally, have reinforced a market approach to regulation. The right to know does create opportunities for resistance and gives citizens an informational basis on which to demand greater state regulation. Yet, it also plays into the idea that rational (and now knowledgeable) self-interested individuals, operating through the market, can regulate more efficiently than the state by giving citizens the ability to "vote" for their environmental preferences with their dollars (Power 1997).

The problem is not that this strategy is unsuccessful. The fact that several multinational food conglomerates—including the baby-food giants Gerber, Heinz, and Mead-Johnson (which makes infant formula); the pet food purveyor Iam's; the corn chip king Frito-Lay; the European agro-food giant Unilever; and several sizable supermarket chains—have gone "GEO free" is no doubt related to increased consumer knowledge and pressure. But often the right to know becomes consumer choice, not citizen choice. When that is the case, it creates a niche market, especially when labeling plays a part in enabling those choices. That Gerber is a subsidiary of leading biotechnology firm Novartis points to the trenchant contradiction at work here. Moreover, in the case of GEOs, labeling could take the sights off direct state regulatory action, such as a moratorium or an outright ban, thus making a labeling law a Pyrrhic victory.

FROM RIGHT-TO-KNOW TO ECO-LABELING

As food labeling has progressed from pure advertising to a means of imparting important *science-based* information to consumers, regulatory efforts have shifted from trying to assure the contents of products to monitoring the truthfulness of labeling claims about contents and attributes. With the Nutrition Labeling and Education Act of 1990, the FDA started requiring all packaged food products to have labels that uniformly detailed not only a list of ingredients in order by volume but also an accounting of calories, macronutrients (e.g., proteins and carbohydrates), certain vitamins, and other elements felt to be important for dietary decision-making, such as sugar, cholesterol, dietary fiber, and sodium. By requiring a uniform presentation of information on all food labels, this law opened up a can of worms by compelling the inclusion of theretofore undisclosed information on the contents of the food. Yet these new labels are at least as interesting for what they do not require—for example, the geographical source of the product its constituents (other than nation of origin of the final product), the processes employed in its manufacture, or the purposes of the many microingredients. As a result, the labels fetishize the commodity insofar as they reinforce the idea that any given commodity is the sum of its ingredients and nutritional constituents rather than the idea that it comes from a particular place and is manufactured under particular social and ecological conditions. The product, not the process, is paramount.

Mandatory labeling of potentially harmful substances is also required by the FDA and is increasingly used to regulate substances with high market demand but controversial effects. Labeling's key role is to encourage consumer choice, or market preference, as a regulatory vehicle. This is exactly the sort of regulation that allows Olestra, a nonfat fat substitute that causes intestinal pain and perhaps more long-lasting health problems, to nevertheless be included in products, to be purchased at the buyer's discretion. In other words, the assumption behind most mandatory labeling is "buyer beware"—that is, it is up to the consumer to decide whether to ingest products with known risks.

Any additional information about food items, particularly about how they are made, is voluntary and therefore treated as advertisement; although it is not wholly unregulated in so far as it must comply with truth-in-labeling laws or, in some cases, be verified by a third-party. Because voluntary labeling is explicitly designed to entice, it includes information that the producer expects consumers to perceive as a benefit. Increasingly, beneficial product attributes are constructed on the basis of the processes by which products are made.

Such is the case with eco-labeling, a form of labeling that is also in some sense advertisement but is simultaneously purported to defetishize the commodity because it imparts information about the conditions under which the commodity was produced. With eco-labeling, these tend to be ecological conditions more than the social conditions to which the strictly Marxist conception of commodity fetishism applies (see Allen and Kovach 2000). Yet what sets these labels a sea apart from, say, the Good Housekeeping Seal of Approval is that they erase the line between social movement and business. The labels describe product attributes as being part of a social cause, but they are also designed to capture economic rents.[10] The labels encourage increased "environmental consciousness" at the same time that they try to make money from that consciousness. They assert a politics of consumption, and they allow the consumption of politics. They are, in other words, deeply contradictory.

As voluntary labeling is increasingly used to differentiate products with social content, the industry has responded with a rash of antidisparagement complaints, many of which have been supported by government rulings and legislation. As early as 1975, the FDA issued label regulations prohibiting claims that natural, unprocessed, and organically grown foods are superior to or more nutritious than conventionally grown foods (a proposal to ban the terms altogether was seriously considered). More recently, specific antidisparagement laws have been passed in thirteen states, and more are on the way. Coming as a reaction to the 1989 Alar pesticide scare, which seriously hurt the apple industry, these laws essentially give producers the right to sue anyone who disparages their product unless the claim can be backed up with scientific evidence (Fox 1997). The most famous antidisparagement action to date has been the beef industry's decision to sue Oprah Winfrey for discussing on her television show the potential dangers to humans associated with mad cow disease. This trial was a test case for a new legal standard that greatly lightens the burden of proof in libel cases (Center for Media and Democracy 1997). Although the court ruled in favor on Winfrey, it did so because statements made on her show were based on facts and therefore did not qualify as disparagement.

So what are the implications of these labeling conventions and laws for GEOs? As evident in the December 1999 public hearings held by the FDA, many activists are calling for mandatory labeling of products containing genetically engineered organisms. In response, the FDA continues to reiterate its position that it *might* consider a mandatory label only if an organism contains known allergens or if a convincing case is made that genetic engineering is directly harmful to human health. It bears repetition that the FDA can consider GEOs' safety as food only.

Voluntary labeling is a compromise approach that some activists feel is better than nothing and one that regulators could conceivably support as a face-saving measure.[11] Indeed, those who support voluntary labeling say that voluntary labeling allows consumers to make a choice but does not put a cost burden on everyone (Powell and Leiss 1997). Yet, this sort of peaceful coexistence between the alternative product and the criticized one reflects the logic of the niche market and arguably undermines serious questioning of the necessity for and risks of the product or process under scrutiny. This same reasoning enabled the USDA to come up with a rule for organic production without offending the vast majority of farmers it ostensibly serves. A further testament to the irony is that former secretary of agriculture Dan Glickman, who originally supported a weak federal rule for organic production that did not exclude GEOs, later said that there was no need to label genetically engineered food, because consumers could be sure that their food was free of genetic engineering by buying organic food produced in the United States ("Organic" 1999).[12]

If the FDA did decide to require mandatory labeling, the least costly way for producers to meet such a requirement would be a label that said something like "this product may contain ingredients produced with genetically engineered organisms." To be sure, this was the language that was agreed on for unverified shipments of food to countries that agreed to the terms of the Montreal Biosafety Protocol adopted (but not by the United States) in January 2000. In other words, the onus of proof and segregation would still fall on producers who do not use GEOs. In effect, GEO labeling, whether voluntary or mandatory, could suffer many of the problems that have confounded the organic movement.

LESSONS FROM ORGANIC REGULATION

The "organic" label is the most evolved (and therefore baroque) of all eco-labels. Although critiques of industrialized food production continue to provide the nominal justification for organic agriculture, organic definitions themselves are quite narrow. In essence, for a crop to be labeled "organically grown," production practices must, for the most part, exclude the use of synthetic compounds. Organic growers may incorporate practices such as crop rotations, biological pest control, and composting, but these practices are not necessarily regulated. Hence, the crux of organic regulation is the so-called materials list, which itemizes and differentiates between allowable, restricted, and prohibited inputs for organic farming.

This state of affairs reflects the particular evolution of the organic movement. Over time, it has come to be led by third-party certifying agencies and producers associations, who defined "organically grown" specifically as a production standard for farmers (and later processors), not as a food safety standard for consumers and certainly not as an alternative system of food production and distribution. The movement thereafter evolved into a drive for institutional legitimacy and regulation of the term "organically grown" in the interest of trade. Consequently, the right to claim that any product was organically produced became contingent on compliance with legal definitions enforced through an unusual configuration of private and state institutions.[13] And although codification arose from multiple intentions, its greatest success was to open up markets.

Furthermore, although there was always a tension between the movement and business interests within the organic community, there were aspects, both practical and political, of the rule making itself that facilitated the shift from critique to marketing label. One aspect was that rule making was to define enforceable standards; the players involved faced the enormous difficulties of including often contested and sometimes contradictory imperatives in a standardization process and sufficiently delimiting the issues to be addressed. A second aspect of rule making was the need to ensure adequate enforcement mechanisms, especially in the absence of comprehensive state involvement. Private third-party certification became the primary mode of regulation and evolved into a form of self-regulation.[14] The third aspect follows directly from the second: there were contradictory imperatives to define standards in ways that were clear and attainable but at the same time protected existing participants. Consequently, many of the rules were formulated as barriers to entry, which, in turn, helped make organic products a niche market.

GEO labeling has the potential to replicate many of the pitfalls of organic regulation. But there are three important caveats that could suggest divergent trajectories. The first is that organic regulation's original goal was codification of production processes rather than product attributes, although the former became increasingly difficult as the organic industry became involved in food processing and as the industry itself was challenged by those wanting to sell commodities identified as free of pesticide residues. Although anti-GEO forces may want to highlight that it is the process of creating GEOs that creates the need for regulation, the goal of labeling nevertheless reinforces a focus on product attributes. Second, "organically grown" and now "organically processed" are much broader claims than "GEO-free," which is just one of the claims of organic production. Consequently, defining "organic" is much more complicated than defining "GEO-free." Third, the organically label is, and always has been, a voluntary label. It was never conceived of as a way to pressure conventional agricultural producers, which is the idea behind mandatory GEO labeling, no matter where the burden of proof ultimately falls.

Creating Standards

Regulatory standards must be based on a clear definition of what is being regulated. In keeping with the organic movement's philosophical roots, the original idea behind a production standard for organic products was to codify processes that replicate those found in nature. Accordingly, the first legal definition of "organically grown" allowed only the use of materials found in nature and thus proscribed synthetically produced inputs, including fertilizers and pesticides.

This seemingly straightforward definition was hardly airtight. For one thing, it raised the question whether some botanical pesticides (such as pyrethrum), which are found in nature but create the same sort of "pesticide treadmills" that chemically derived pesticides do, should be considered organic. It also raised the more fundamental problem that the use of "natural" or "found in nature" as the basis of acceptability relied on clearly problematic assumptions about the essential goodness of nature and made all decisions subject to the determination of where the line between nature and artifice falls. In practice, materials started being assessed on a case-by-case basis, but in the process, standard-setters have often lost a sense that it might be industrialized agriculture in general that people are protesting.

Similarly, any claim that a product is free of GEOs requires a clear and relatively durable definition of what constitutes a GEO. Because the underlying justifications for rejecting GEOs are so closely entwined with those for supporting organic agriculture, many of these same sorts of questions are likely to arise. As in the case of the organic label, the object of regulation (and hence labeling) will have to be determined. Is it the processes of genetic engineering or the products (i.e., the seeds, hormones, and so on) that are to be regulated? Efforts to delimit the two will surely necessitate that thorny issues like nature and novelty be revisited. Precise definitions of how the seeds or processes in question differ from those stemming from classic breeding or hybridization will be required if we are to specify exactly which processes and seeds are acceptable and which are not. And although the process of regulation requires simple definitions, such definitions (e.g., no transgenes) are unlikely to be acceptable, either because these definitions will be too narrow or because they will be too broad. Moreover, because these definitions are so entangled with science, they will always call for more fundamental questions about, for instance, the nature of gene exchange. At best, potentially prohibited technologies will need to be assessed individually and then reassessed as the technology changes—which is not necessarily a problem until the politics come into play.

As if delimiting the substances in question was not difficult enough, determining what it means to be "free" of something is even more complicated. Given the assumption that there will always be trace amounts of any environmental pollutant, the determination requires specific standards regarding the permissibility of trace amounts of prohibited substances. Attention to geographic and temporal bounding is also necessary. For example, the current federal rule for organic production holds a crop can be considered organic only if three years have passed since the last prohibited substance was applied to the land from which it was harvested. The problem is that any designated transition period is clearly arbitrary because different substances have different half-lives: DDT remains in the soil for decades, but Roundup dissipates fairly quickly. Likewise, the rules generally stipulate that the boundary between organic fields and adjacent conventional fields must be marked by unambiguous, permanent physical objects and be buffered by zones of a certain width. This requirement is particularly artificial because pesticide drift cannot be controlled with that sort of exactitude, especially when the pesticides are applied from airplanes. Consequently, the standards make provisions for unavoidable drift and residues. The organic rule says that crops that have pesticide residues greater than 5 percent of allowable EPA standards cannot be sold as organic even if the drift was unintentional. That the first USDA proposal was much more lax here under the aegis of "unavoidable environmental contaminants" illustrates how efforts to assess the intent of the grower can also come into play.

There exist all sorts of rules requiring adequate segregation and traceability in processing and handing, so that organic product is not contaminated by conventional product. But again, it is not just a matter of absolute prohibition. As the organic industry has moved more into food processing, some of those involved have pushed to allow the use of more additives and ingredients in processing. Accordingly, the rule says that a processed product can be called organic if 95 percent of the product was made from organically grown ingredients. Although the ostensible purpose of this rule is to allow processors to use microingredients that are difficult to source organically, it enables a good deal of slippage as to what is considered organic.

Again, several of the boundary problems encountered in the debate over the organic label are likely to be replicated in efforts to define labeling standards for GEOs. For example, to allow for the possibility that genetically engineered varieties might appear as residual weeds, crop production standards would need to specify the length of time since a particular parcel last saw a genetically engineered seed, as well as the size of the spatial bound-aries and buffers. These specifications would presumably need to have a scientific basis, which is notoriously difficult to establish. Standards would have to stipulate an acceptable amount of trace weeds, given the already existing evidence of widespread pollen contamination from GEOs to organic fields. Clear standards for segregation in food processing and han-dling would also be required; but, again, there might be reasons to allow for trace amounts of GEOs; and those reasons would have to be specified and justified. And because a large proportion of genetically engineered crops are going into animal feed (corn, soy, and cotton by-products), reg-ulators would have to develop standards for livestock, in terms of feed, seg-regation of herds, and so forth. Finally, there would be verification issues. For instance, would standards privilege monitoring of practices, such as seed purchases, or monitoring of results, such as sample testing? Although these may seem to be mere details, such details must be included in any standard precisely because, as we have seen with organic regulations, the very existence of standards creates incentives to push the limits of those standards.

Enforcing Standards

If labeling claims are to have any bite, they must be verifiable. Given the FDA's reluctance so far to allow any substantive labeling claims, the burden would likely fall to non-GEO users to prove that their products are GEO-free, thus relieving the state of much of its regulatory burden. Although there will certainly be some state oversight if the FDA changes its tune, pro-ducers might nevertheless be asked to validate their claims with third-party certification.

Third-party certification has coevolved with voluntary labeling, with its privileging of the politics of consumption through regulatory privatization. As a process of external verification that organically produced foods are grown in accordance with established rules, organic certification thus assumes both well-defined rules and effective enforcement. Certification exists both to protect consumers from fraudulent claims and to reward pro-ducers who play by the rules; it has become a virtual necessity for interstate commerce. Before the enactment of the new federal rule for organic pro-duction, which significantly altered and harmonized the practices of certi-fication, most certification was done through private agencies with little state oversight. Now these agencies are accredited by the USDA but remain primarily responsible for verification.

Before the enactment of the new rule, growers who wanted to be certi-fied had to fill out extensive paperwork, including a farm plan; agree to ini-tial, annual, and perhaps spot inspections; fulfill requirements for crop or soil sampling; pay various dues, fees, and assessments; and, of course, agree to abide by the practices and input restrictions designated by the certifying agency and any existing state laws for organic production. Before the federal rule, certifiers had significant discretion in how they enforced standards. Certification presented a legal standard that could be enforced by civil codes, which have less exacting standards of proof than do criminal codes. In fact, most enforcement was extralegal. It usually involved action taken by the certifier: from prohibition of the sale of a certain crop as certified organic (in the case of drift violations) to fines to decertification. In all these cases, the burden of proof rested almost entirely on the alleged violator, and the degrees of due process in bearing that burden varied widely.

Furthermore, most of the older certification agencies were nonprofit organizations that had developed as part of the movement and thus tended to be advocacy-oriented as well. Although the style of decision-making varied in these organizations, they tended toward self-regulation in that growers made decisions, set standards, and reviewed one another's operations. Thus, standards tended to be set according to what represented growers wanted and needed rather than defined in some wider public sense. Nevertheless, as trade organizations, these certifiers had a stake in upholding the integrity of the organic label, so enforcement actions were strong and tended to make the label harder to get.

In the late 1980s, another type of private certifier came on the scene: private for-profit organizations that treated certification as a business, which made them less beholden to the organic movement than the trade organizations above. They traded on making it easier to be organic; they tended to require less paperwork, to limit their inspections, and to certify within a week of two of application. They also tended to be less transparent in their practices: some (but not all) did not make their standards or list of certified-grower clients publicly available.

Several of both types of certifiers are already poised to provide certification for GEO-free labeling, without the strictures of federal oversight now intrinsic to organic regulation (a few are already doing so on an international level).[15] Although the exclusion of GEOs has been a part of organic regulation all along, it has until recently been a minor part of the certification process, mainly because there were few commercial applications of agricultural biotechnology and the existing applications were obvious. With the advent of more widespread and less conspicuous applications, verification will require much more attention, especially as the standards for verification become better defined themselves.

If the FDA reverses its current position or Congress passes a law to allow labeling, the certification industry will mushroom, given the volume of crops and livestock that will be affected. As a result, many of the strengths and weaknesses of organic certification are likely to reappear and even

amplify with GEO labeling. For instance, insofar as existing grower-led certification agencies get involved (or as new ones are formed), there will be
pressure to define claims more in growers' interests than in consumers'
interests, despite the fact that consumers are leading the charge for labeling.[16] It is not hard to imagine a debate over buffer zones being divided
along producer-consumer lines. If organic labeling debates are any indication, consumers are also more likely to take tougher stances than producers
on the use of microingredients in processing and on all livestock issues. Yet,
if certification is left to those agencies that do it solely as a business service,
the political content of the issue could be eroded. No matter what happens,
the most significant effect of following the organic-certification model will
be the creation of rents and market niches, which will thwart the politics of
consumption that labeling is designed to enable.

Barriers, Rents, Niches

One of the many ways to create barriers to entry in an industry is to use regulations themselves as barriers (Eisner 1993, 179). The organic industry, in
many ways a product of its unique evolution and lack of mainstream political legitimacy, took this tack. Growers are keenly aware of these entry barriers, and often try to fortify them, once the growers are under the organic
umbrella. The grower-led certification agencies in particular gave certain
organic growers tremendous power in shaping the rules for entry into the
sector, and many argue that organic standards became tougher over the
years precisely because of this phenomenon.

   The most unmistakable barriers to entry are associated with certification
itself. Fees and compliance costs can be imposing; bureaucratic hassle and
unusual levels of surveillance also act as disincentives to entry. The key barrier to the organic label, however, has been the required transition period:
crops cannot be harvested and sold as organic unless three years have
passed since the last disallowed substance was applied to the land on which
they are grown. During these three years, yields generally decline because
prohibited substances have been abruptly withdrawn but biological controls
have not had time to become established. Because the product must be sold
at conventional prices, the grower bears substantial opportunity costs.
Although the ostensible purpose of the transition is minimization of toxic
residues in the soil, it is widely understood that preventing rapid entry into
the organic market by those who seek only to make a fast killing is the
underlying reason for the transition period. It also potentially reduces
fraud: many rule violations are made by people who quickly enter and exit
and thus are never fully inculcated with the meaning of organic.

   These entry barriers are important in that they create economic rents,
which effectively structure participation within the sector for producers and
consumers alike. If the certification costs only realized prices that covered

these direct costs, along with the cost of amortizing the three-year transition, there would be no strictly economic reason to enter into organic production. Entering the market would be a marginal proposition even if prices also covered the incremental costs and yield shortfalls, insofar as they exist, of farming in accordance with organic standards. The underlying purpose of delineating organic growers in this way is to create and uphold a price premium: an additional return above and beyond the minimum required to cover costs and to deliver a "normal" rate of return. Those who defend the barriers claim they are needed to ensure the integrity of organic product, at the same time recognizing that one of the purposes of these barriers is to prop up the price premium, which is, by definition, an economic rent.

These sorts of economic rents depend on maintaining quasi-monopolistic conditions through the vehicle of regulation. Regulations must restrict supply not only by maintaining barriers to entry but also by prohibiting substitutes, which is why organic regulations restrict the use of terms such as "ecologically grown." Regulations also must convince buyers that the product they receive is valuable. Organic agriculture's entry barriers are clearly somewhat permeable; the real success of organic regulation lies in its valorization of the product. Consumers believe not only that organic food may be safer and environmentally protective but also that it does the very things that it in fact does not do, from "saving" the family farm to providing so-called whole food. Organic, in other words, has the added advantage of having a "movement" behind it, which ultimately bestows it with much more meaning and durability than a brand name might.

There are two major problems here for widespread participation in the sector. The first is the Schumpeterian problem that economic rents—or super-profits—characteristically attract more entrants into the sector and threaten to erode the profitability that makes participation attractive in the first place. Indeed, with the increased price competition that has plagued organic markets in certain commodities over the past several years, some organic growers are looking for new ways to uphold the rents, by looking to go "beyond organic" in areas such as wildlife habitat, local food distribution, and farm labor conditions. Yet, these embellishments of organic standards allow farmers "to commodify intangibles such as 'trust' and 'rurality'" and in a certain sense privatize environmental reforms (DeLind 1993, 9). There is a more than palpable tension between the goal of retaining a premium and the goal of encouraging broader participation in organic production for its ecological benefits.

The second problem is that economic rents structure participation on the consumption end. Affluent consumers disproportionately purchase organic food. Even as wholesale prices come down, retailers play on this knowledge and are able to retain large surpluses. This knowledge thus "co-opts the reform potential to be found within alternative agriculture" by suggesting that good food and meaningful food choices are available only to the well-off (DeLind 1993, 7). Such positioning does some other work too. The marketing of organic products as a specialty or niche market allows them to stand side-by-side with conventional products without disparaging the latter (Clunies-Ross 1990, 262). But again, positioning organic food this way thwarts the potential for real expansion, which necessarily does away with the premium.

GEO labeling may have similar effects. There will surely be the costs of certification and inspections, and perhaps there will be transition periods. There will also be the incremental costs of segregating genetically engineered commodities along the entire chain of provision, which will especially affect processors and handlers. If the biotechnology industry fulfills its promise that genetically engineered crops will have better yields (a claim that for now remains dubious), traditional crops will effectively cost more to grow per acre, as per-acre sales drop in comparison. Dairies that use rBGH are already seeing yield differentials, which contribute to an overproduction crisis (Kingsnorth 1998). Because such incremental costs are likely to be passed on to the consumer, at the very least, prices for non-GEO food will be marginally higher.

The question of whether economic rents will be created through certification and labeling is more speculative, and in large part the answer depends on some unanswered empirical questions. If, indeed, GE growers start to consistently receive more value per unit, as the dairy industry has, the cost of not using GEOs will become much higher, which actually has the potential to make GEO-free products a vanity good. If, however, producers' economic returns with GEOs are marginal, or if they fear that consumer backlash will decrease demand, the cost of being GEO-free will seem less daunting. This may lead them to stay with or revert to non-genetically engineered varieties and products, without the incentive of a price premium.

Ultimately, the question of economic rents rests on the nature of the standards, if any, that will be used to prove that commodities are GEO-free. Basically, more stringent standards increase the likelihood that a rent will be created, because of the cost of meeting that standard. Yet, positioning the "GEO-free" label as precious is more challenging than doing the same for the organic label because, at least theoretically, producers have only to do what they were already doing; they do not have to fundamentally change their production practices. Nonetheless, producers who are already GEO-free will have strong incentives to build a mystique around the label. They could construct rules so that growers who have planted GE crops could not be certified until some specified time period had passed, or so that those who had the bad luck of being too close to a field planted to a GE crop, and thus found their non-GEO crop contaminated by wind-blown pollen, would be ineligible.

The most obvious problem is that the focus on the label itself, as the embodiment of consumer desire and politics, plays into the notion of political choice as taste. Under these conditions, GEO-free food comes to be yet another "option for the rich and neurotic," as Laura DeLind puts it, and another niche market to make a few farmers happy for a while. The paradox is that the expression of consumer sentiment holds the best possibility for curbing the proliferation of what remain controversial technologies, but one of the mechanisms for expressing these sentiments—that is, labeling— could undermine these very politics of consumption.

RIGHT-TO-KNOW OR RIGHT-TO-BUY?

As the political economy of organic agriculture has evolved, so have the meanings that animate it. Although disclosure, or consumer right-to-know, is by no means a done deal, it is fast becoming a proxy for delimiting what it means to be organic, in the absence of the simple measures that the natural versus synthetic divide once seemed to offer. The rise of disclosure, however, represents an important shift in the politics of organic regulation. Disclosure privileges consumer interests for the first time. This is not a bad idea, considering that debate over the federal rule proved that the strength of the movement lies in consumers. But disclosure also privatizes regulation in the strongest sense, as if a private purchasing decision were an adequate means for regulating what are clearly socialized risks. This form of regulation sits a bit too easily with the USDA's goals for the Organic Foods Production Act. The USDA had to be careful not to imply that the non-organic food supply was unsafe or to disparage it in any other way for that matter. So the department couched its grudging support in terms of providing farmers a niche and, as Secretary Glickman said upon the release of the federal rule in 1997, offering consumers "freedom of choice." This, no doubt, is the same language that will be used to justify any changes in the law for labeling GEOs.

There are other possible parallels between GEO and organic labeling. In a new twist on commodity fetishism, GEO labeling could reduce both the strongly voiced ethical concerns about and the less salient social critiques of GEOs to another product attribute, as with nutritional labels. Insofar as a food label must address the content of the food to which it is affixed, it will be read as a food-safety claim, no matter what its broader purpose. Moreover, to the extent that labeling and certification will make a product more costly, they could make this attribute of GEO-free a choice only for those who believe they can afford it. Beck (1992) notes that risks strengthen rather than abolish class society, especially when the wealthy can purchase safety and freedom from risk. Donna Haraway (1997) also notes that safety and right-to-know issues are strongly shaped by class and race formations. In these ways, labeling leads to another form of NIMBYism, this time re-phrased as "not in my baby's belly" (see also DuPuis 2000, regarding "not in my body").

Even if the risks of agricultural biotechnologies are understood more broadly as including biosafety risks as well as food-safety risks, the principle of right-to-know is not without problems. Disclosure of such risks as a risk-management strategy puts tremendous responsibility on the consumer-buyer, who is effectively asked to make a risk decision with every purchase. Even more important, such a privatized risk-management strategy does not address the social nature of the risks involved, especially in the absence of complementary regulatory mechanisms at the site of production.

It is easy to confuse consumer right-to-know with consumer right-to-buy, to conflate important notions of liberal transparency with shallow ideas of purchasing freedom. A regulatory focus on consumption fits all too well with neoliberal approaches to regulation, approaches in which command-and-control regulation has lost legitimacy and state services are reduced to "the provision of information and expert advice to 'responsible' individuals and industries" (Crook 1998, 138). Ultimately, public health and safety, environmental quality, and fair labor practices—what were once the clear purview of the state—may become regulated by consumer "choice." Even as consumers are confronted with too many choices—what brand to buy, whether to buy low-fat, low-sodium, or GEO-free—they are also confronted with a limited choice, an industrial food system that plays on the concern of the day.

Just like the obsession with the "novelty" of GEOs as a regulatory hook, or the ontologically limited calculus of risk assessment, labeling thwarts a more fundamental critique of the technology. Genetic engineering technologies do not exist in a vacuum but reflect deeper tendencies in the industrialization of agriculture itself. To focus on the technologies themselves is to minimize the social relations and historical conditions that created these technologies (see Prudham, this volume). A similarly technical focus is exactly why the organic label has been so comfortably incorporated into existing agro-food conventions. As Haraway (1997) says, "it is very hard to ask directly if new technologies and ways of doing science are instruments for increasing social equality and democratically distributing well-being. Those questions are readily made to seem merely ideological, while issues of safety and labeling can be cast as themselves technical. . . . The power to define what counts as technical or political is very much at the heart of techno-science." The goal then "is to help put the boundary between the technical and the political back into permanent question" (89). Such boundary smashing is an important component of what I see as an emerging political economy of risk. But the point is not to throw out the right to know with neoliberal understandings of consumer choice. The question is how to build an effective politics of consumption, of which labeling may be a part, in an era when at best the state supports privatized regulation and at worst is thoroughly incapacitated by its interest in fostering international competitiveness.

NOTES

The author thanks William Boyd, Anne Kapuscinski, Dennis Kelso, Kathy McAfee, Scott Prudham, Astrid Scholz, and Rachel Schurman, for their comments on this manuscript as well as for ongoing engagement with and discussions on biotechnology. The research on organic certification has been supported by grants from the National Science Foundation (SBR-9711262), by the University of California's Sustainable Agriculture Research and Education Program, and by the Association of American Geographers.

1. For example, in 1999 PrimaTerra, an organic corn chip producer, was forced to destroy eighty thousand bags of corn chips after they tested positive for traces of genetically engineered corn.

2. *Ben & Jerry's Homemade, Inc. v. John Lumpkin et al.,* U.S. D. Ct. N. Dist. Illinois, No. 96 C2748, August 27, 1996.

3. The portions of this chapter that specifically address organic production and regulation derive from the author's dissertation research (Guthman 2000). The study included more than 150 semistructured interviews with both all-organic and mixed (i.e., both conventional and organic) growers that took place in 1998 and 1999 in California. Data on organic regulation were also collected through in-depth interviews with representatives from several of the certifying agencies, which operate within California, along with public officials, advocates, and technical experts. In addition, the study included textual analysis of legislative and certifier archives, industry conferences, and online discussions.

4. Within the field of biology, there is fierce debate the scientific merits of agricultural biotechnology. Unfortunately, the nuances of this more technical debate have not become a part of the public discourse, as evidenced, for instance, by the public hearings held by the FDA in late 1999.

5. Of course, in another breath proponents are quick to boast about how they are reconfiguring nature in unprecedented ways. See, for instance, the advertisement for Operon showing both an applorange (spliced apple and orange) and a zucchana (spliced zucchini and banana) (Haraway 1997). Moreover, as Andrew Kimbrell of the International Center for Technology Assessment points out, if these technologies are not novel, then the U.S. Patent Office should withdraw the patent protections that many of them enjoy (FDA hearings on food biotechnology, Oakland, California, December 1999).

6. The public, too, can be fickle about appeals to nature. As Melanie Dupuis (2000, 293) argues, the meteoric rise of organic milk in response to the rBGH controversy is enmeshed in the discourse of milk as a cultural staple. Would consumers care if the biotech industry could make a more nutritious, delicious strawberry with rDNA techniques, especially if the industry stopped using methyl bromide as a result?

7. Phillip Regal, though, refutes any generic arguments about safety, saying that

technologies must be assessed and tested systematically on a case-by-case basis. More recently, Kapuscinski has suggested that there may be a strategic importance to risk assessment in that it forces policymakers to work through a decision tree, and by doing so they may find that information lacunae will prevent premature marketing (personal communication, 1998).

8. Peter Wills, in contrast, notes that the goal of these endeavors is defined by the means by which to accomplish them—a solution looking for a problem. "In this sense it is pointless to look for 'alternatives' to genetic engineering because the technology is by-and-large irrelevant to solving problems that have not already been defined as being amenable to a genetic 'fix'" (1998, 79). In effect, he reinforces Hornstein's point.

9. Interestingly, the product orientation reinforced an emphasis on visible and structural attributes.

10. Economic rents are the additional return to producers above and beyond that required to cover costs and deliver a "normal" rate of return. They are often referred to as price premiums.

11. The courts have taken the position that even a voluntary label creates a negative connotation and effectively stigmatizes the unlabeled product (*Ben & Jerry's Homemade, Inc. et al. v. John Lumpkin et al.*).

12. The Clinton administration's stance on GEOs turned out to be a boon for organic products because the "organic" designation provides the only existing assurance (in the United States) that a food is free of GEOs. The reason that the first USDA-proposed rule for organic production did not prohibit GEOs is that Secretary Glickman did not want to send a message to trading partners that there existed doubts about the safety of genetically engineered crops. Glickman's motivation was divulged in an internal USDA memo discovered and published by *Mother Jones* magazine (Broydo 1998).

13. Under the 2002 federal rule, there is a single definition of "organically grown" within the United States. Heretofore, organic rules and standards differed depending on state law (or lack thereof) and the many private and state certification agencies that put those laws into operation. That said, 1990s harmonization efforts brought their respective definitions into much closer alignment—and most of the differences between them remained in the nature and level of enforcement.

14. Although they call themselves third-party certifiers, in truth, the trade associations that did most organic certification offered only second-party certification, with third-party status reserved for organizations that are completely independent of the industry they certify (Caldwell 1998).

15. One such firm is Genetic ID, a privately held fee-for-service organization. The founder has been a vocal advocate for mandatory labeling of GE foods, which has caused those in the biotech industry to quip that he is manufacturing interest for his own company's services (FDA hearings on food biotechnology, Oakland, California, December 1999).

16. Consumers were given lots of lip service in organic certification and were key in forcing the USDA to revise its proposed rule, as most of the 280,000 comments posted to the *Federal Register* were from consumers. Nevertheless, although consumers sat on state advisory boards responsible for the creation and enforcement of organic laws, they usually did not sit at the tables of the certifiers themselves.

6

The Global Politics of GEOs

The Achilles' Heel of the Globalization Regime?

Frederick H. Buttel

In early 1999, agricultural biotechnology seemed to be on a roll. Three years earlier, the World Trade Organization (WTO) had been established by the Uruguay Round of the General Agreement on Tariffs and Trade (GATT). The Uruguay Round Agreement on Agriculture (URAA) and the larger WTO agreement contained a number of provisions favorable to the private biotechnology industry. The Agreement on Trade Related Intellectual Property Rights (TRIPS), for example, set forth the global intellectual property rights framework desired by multinational biotechnology firms. The Agreement on the Application of Sanitary and Phytosanitary Measures (SPS) stipulated that although member states could set their own standards for sanitary protection, the standards and measures had to be based on scientific evidence and could not be unjustified barriers to trade. The WTO Agreement on Technical Barriers to Trade also made it possible to challenge labeling practices on the grounds that they were technical barriers to trade (see Dunkley 2000 for a general overview of the provisions of the WTO agreement and von Schomberg 2000 for a discussion of how WTO provisions have affected the biotechnology industry and the prospects for genetically engineered crops).[1] In addition, the recombinant bovine growth hormone (rBGH) controversy in the United States had largely blown over by 1999, and even the successful attempts at labeling milk as BGH-free had largely ended (Buttel 1999).

From 1996 through the summer of 1999, herbicide-resistant soybeans were adopted in the United States more rapidly than any other agricultural technology in history. In the same period, Bt cotton and Bt corn in the United States and transgenic canola in Canada were not far behind. In the 1999 growing season, about 50 percent of U.S. soybean acreage and nearly 30 percent of U.S. corn acreage were devoted to genetically engineered

(GE) varieties.[2] Nearly forty GE crop varieties had been approved for sale in the United States by 1999. Adoption of GE soybeans and corn increased even further in 1999, and by that time GE varieties had also made major inroads into the potato and canola sectors (James 1998, 1999, 2000). The likelihood that herbicide-tolerant wheat would be commercialized by 2003 portended a future in which GE crops would be grown from coast to coast and from Texas to North Dakota. Though the public did not widely recognize it at the time, perhaps more than a third of manufactured food products in grocery stores already contained GE ingredients.[3]

By the late summer of 1999, however, GE crops had become highly contested. In this chapter, I explore the recent history of the controversy over genetically engineered organisms (GEOs). I particularly emphasize the global context of the controversy, since active resistance to GEOs appears to have originated in northern and northwestern Europe and then extended to the United States through trade rules and resistance to them. I suggest that in agriculture, and in the life sciences industries more generally, "trade liberalization," as defined by WTO proponents, requires "harmonization" of a range of practices, including not only trade rules themselves but also regulatory and intellectual-property practices. Although the WTO nominally reflected harmonization of each of these practices, the implementation of the WTO, URAA, SPS, and TRIPS agreements has exacerbated rather than resolved national disagreements about regulatory practices. These disagreements have been manifested as conflicts over trade and environmental-protection policies. Accordingly, what led to the abrupt change of political climate with respect to GEOs was, first, the fact that the WTO's track record of overruling national environmental policies had led virtually all major environmental nongovernmental organizations (NGOs) to oppose the WTO and, second, the fact that for a combination of reasons the GEO issue became "environmentalized." Indeed, what galvanized the opposition to GEOs in the United States was the protest against the WTO at the Seattle Ministerial Conference in late November and early December 1999. In addition, opposition to GEOs was critical in the mobilization of the coalition that was organized for the protest. This fact has led many observers, such as Jill McCluskey (2000), to suggest that the GEO controversy might be the Achilles' heel of the WTO. However, I contend that the opposite is more likely to be true; that is, that globalization and the WTO may prove to be the Achilles' heel of GEOs and the agricultural-biotechnology industry.

THE GLOBALIZATION REGIME

The range of interpretations of "globalization" is extraordinary, and virtually all of them make significant reference to the role of trade liberalization and the WTO in the globalization process (Held and McGrew 2000; Hirst and Thompson 1999). For present purposes, however, it is not necessary to claim fidelity to any one of these interpretations. I merely suggest that the terminology of the "globalization regime" is useful here as a general framework (McMichael 1996, 2000).

This terminology originated from Harriet Friedmann and Philip McMichael's (1989) work on (global) "food regimes," by which they mean political-economic governance structures that shape the conditions of food production and of cross-border movements of agricultural commodities. For Friedmann and McMichael, the first food regime emerged during the era of British imperialism and was constituted by Britain's role as the "workshop of the world" and by the related politics of building and maintaining a global food system consistent with this role (especially the process of accessing wage foods imported from the white settler colonies and obtaining industrial foods and other agricultural raw materials from the colonial possessions). This regime also involved a global trading system consistent with this division of industrial and agricultural labor across space and social units. With the demise of British hegemony and in the aftermath of the two world wars, an aid-based food regime rapidly supplanted the first one. The second regime—the post-World War II food-aid regime—was based on the politics of disposal of overproduced foods in the United States and other countries of the Organization for Economic Cooperation and Development (OECD) (chiefly by way of foreign food-aid), and on the diffusion of U.S. agricultural institutions, technologies, and foods to the global South.

McMichael (2000) asserts that we are now well into a successor global regime that has followed the decline of American hegemony, the breakup of the Bretton Woods system of fixed exchange rates, and the decline of the national type of economy and of social Keynesianism in the early 1970s. The emerging "globalization project" is anchored in a coincidence of interests among dominant states and influential capitals and in a set of institutions— the GATT and the WTO, globalization of finance and capital mobility, "structural adjustment," export-oriented production within a "liberal" comparative advantage framework—derived from the system of "floating" exchange rates that emerged in the context of international economic disorder during the early and mid-1970s (see McMichael 2000 for a recent statement).[4]

The globalization regime, then, consists of a set of institutions and regulations that govern the profitable movement of financial and industrial capital, as well as goods and services, across world borders. The intellectual basis of the coincidence of interests underlying the globalization regime is partly a neoclassical adherence to notions of the mutual benefits of trade through the economics of comparative advantage. But despite the considerable consensus on the mutual benefits of comparative advantage through more liberal trade that has existed for more than a century, the impulse

toward radical liberalization of world trade and movements of money capital has been quite recent, essentially dating from the global economic
slump that began in the mid-1970s. Indeed, the impetus behind the globalization regime was a fairly recent coincidence of interests among developed industrial states, international financial institutions, and multinational
corporations. This coincidence of interests led to the establishment of the
WTO as well as regional trade blocs such as the signatories to the North
American Free Trade Agreement (NAFTA) and Mercosur. These coincident
interests include the interests of international development finance institutions in maintaining the integrity of the global financial system (which
includes preventing massive loan defaults by the nations of the South); the
interests of multinational firms in establishing global-scale markets and
global recognition of intellectual property rights; the interests of dominant
states in ensuring their economic dominance into the future; and the interests of Northern states and firms in ensuring that the countries of the South
remain within the world trading sphere and in preventing the establishment
of trade barriers that would threaten the overall trend toward liberalization
of trade.

Interestingly, although the WTO is the direct descendant of the GATT,
and although in the first round of GATT negotiations, the United States
participated only with the agreement that agriculture would be exempted
from coverage, agriculture was in some sense the pivot of the Uruguay
Round. The United States and its allies valued agricultural trade liberalization not only because it was in their own interests but also because it was a
carrot that could be offered to Southern countries to induce them to ratify
the WTO (and thus to remain within the dominant world trading system
and avoid defaulting on loans). Agricultural trade liberalization, including
(a promised) expansion of the South's access to agro-food markets in the
North, was a critical provision of the Uruguay Round; the prospect of
expanded export revenues from the North was crucial in convincing governments of the South that there were better alternatives to defaulting on
loans and agitating for more favorable terms from the World Bank and the
International Finance Corporation (IFC). The WTO thus involved provisions for deregulating agriculture, mainly by reducing import quotas and
tariffs, nontariff restrictions on trade, and export subsidies and rolling back
agricultural commodity programs, all of which ostensibly increase the
South's access to Northern markets in agricultural goods. In exchange for
these URAA provisions, the multinational firms and states of the North
negotiated new GATT/WTO provisions to facilitate agricultural biotechnology, which was held out as vital to the future of the world's food supply.
Industrial states and their firms also achieved liberalization of trade in services, reduction of tariff and nontariff barriers to trade, and significantly
more protection of intellectual property.

Although agricultural trade liberalization was advanced as being particularly beneficial to developing countries, several of the world's leading agro-exporters saw the 1990s globalization regime as a means of solidifying their positions as the breadbaskets of the world.[5] The United States, Canada, and Australia have been integral to both developing countries and agro-exporters, but both blocs have also included major agro-exporters from the South (e.g., Argentina, Brazil, Costa Rica, Chile, Indonesia, Malaysia, Paraguay, the Philippines, Thailand, and Uruguay).

However, the Seattle WTO protests demonstrated that although there has been powerful momentum behind the globalization regime, serious weaknesses threaten its future. Many of these weaknesses pertain to agriculture and agricultural biotechnology. We are now nearly a half decade into a global farm crisis, and the U.S. government has had to violate the spirit of the URAA to keep its producers of basic food and feed-grain commodities in business. Thus, in the federal government's 2001 fiscal year, farmers received a total of more than $25 billion in direct payments, despite the Freedom to Farm Act (FAIR) enacted by the U.S. Congress to comply with the WTO. This level of farm outlays was the largest in U.S. history. The lingering profitability crisis in U.S. agriculture has led to huge emergency programs every year since 1998 ($4.6 billion in 2001). The unresolved farm crisis (which was probably induced in large part by the liberalizing provisions of the URAA) now makes it unlikely that the Millennial Round of the WTO will involve significant further agricultural trade liberalization.

While the U.S. government's simultaneous embrace of FAIR and of record-setting farm subsidies seems absurd and hypocritical, activist opposition to the WTO centers more on GEOs, biotechnology, food safety and risk, and proprietary protection of agricultural and life-science innovations.[6] The last three years have witnessed multiple instances of resistance to the agricultural components of the globalization regime.

Although the dynamics of globalization tend to circumscribe the abilities of states and social movements to contest the prerogatives of capital, globalization of regulatory processes may also open up new opportunities. The Convention on Biological Diversity (CBD) has provided a forum far more conducive than the WTO for achieving the goals of activist NGOs and of a number of governments in the South (see McAfee, this volume). The CBD was originally drafted in the negotiations leading up to the 1992 Rio de Janeiro United Nations Conference on Environment and Development (the so-called Earth Summit). In January 2000 the Cartagena Protocol on Biosafety was approved at the Montreal negotiating round of the CBD. Not only did the protocol include a number of GEO regulatory provisions favored by activist groups, but the language of the protocol endorsed the "principle of precautionary action" (the precautionary principle), a set of regulatory conventions that most environmentalists and opponents of GEOs strongly favor.

WHAT CHANGED THE MOMENTUM BEHIND AGRICULTURAL BIOTECHNOLOGY?

The repoliticization of agricultural biotechnology in 1999 was due to several interrelated factors. One is that for a number of years, and well before the establishment of the WTO, there had been numerous agriculture-related trade conflicts between the United States and the European Union (EU). But the establishment of the WTO intensified these conflicts because the WTO provided an expanded forum for trade complaints and appeared to be a more decisive mechanism for dispute resolution and enforcement of rulings. In 1993, prior to the establishment of the WTO, the EU had adopted a tariff quota system for bananas that favored banana imports from former European colonies and thus had the effect of discriminating against bananas produced by U.S.-based multinationals in Latin America. The WTO ruled against the EU on banana imports, but the EU did little to comply with the WTO ruling. This noncompliance resulted in a $191 million annual tariff retaliation by the United States against a rotating group of EU exports, beginning in March 1999. Note that even the U.S. tariff retaliation was contested by the EU; ultimately the WTO ruled in favor of the EU, declaring that the United States had jumped the gun on implementing retaliatory tariffs by forty-six days ("Still Bananas" 2000)

Even more long-standing are the EU sanctions against hormone-treated beef. Since the mid-1980s the EU has banned imports of all live animals and products from animals treated with growth hormones. The United States ultimately received two favorable WTO rulings in hormone-treated beef cases (in 1997 and 1998), but the EU ban essentially remained in effect through 2000 (Pollack and Shaffer 2000). The EU delayed complying with these WTO rulings until early 2001 because, first, European publics and consumers overwhelming oppose hormone-treated beef and because, second, the EU maintains staunchly that there remain major gaps in the scientific evidence on the safety of the beef.

Best known are the EU's de facto bans or restrictions on imports of genetically engineered foods (including not only raw food and feed but also seed and consumer products). The struggle is focused primarily on Bt and other GE corn varieties, some of which were approved by the EU in the late 1990s. The EU has also resisted imports of (largely GE) soybeans and soy products from the United States. European consumer resistance and EU (as well as Asian) import restrictions on GE soybeans have led to a substantial decline in U.S. soy exports to Europe. As a result, Brazil—still the only GEO-free country in the Western Hemisphere—has picked up some exclusive clients in Europe and Asia.[7] Although Europe is heavily dependent on imported soy, particularly imported U.S. soybeans and soy products, it is less dependent on imported corn, because Europe is a major corn producer. As a result, farmer and consumer opposition to Bt corn in Europe has been strong, even though some Bt corn varieties have been approved by the EU.

The U.S.-EU GEO trade dispute has escalated with increasing evidence that non-GEO grain and seed (particularly corn and canola) can be contaminated by pollen from GEO varieties, making segregating and labeling GEO crops even more difficult than previously thought. Contamination concerns culminated in the StarLink controversy of 2000-2001: a large share of the U.S. corn supply became contaminated with a Bt gene sequence that had been approved by the U.S. Environmental Protection Agency for animal but not human consumption (see Schurman's introduction to this volume). More recently, there has been a highly politicized conflict over Bt gene contamination in peasant maize landraces and in the maize gene bank of the Center for Wheat and Maize Improvement (CIM-MYT) in Mexico.

Although the United States has tended to prevail over the EU in trade disputes brought before WTO dispute-resolution panels, it considered the EU's responses to the WTO rulings to be inadequate and in contempt of the spirit of the WTO agreement. Thus, considerable tension over trade in general—and agricultural trade in particular—has emerged as a result of the United States' having forced the EU's hand at the WTO. Furthermore, by early 1999 it was becoming apparent that the United States would threaten WTO dispute-resolution action against the EU with regard to GE corn.

Because European public opinion is strongly against GE crops, even if the EU caves in to U.S. pressure to resume GEO-product approvals and to facilitate imports of U.S. GE grains, opposition to GEOs is likely to persist in most of Europe. Opposition is particularly intense in the three most powerful EU states: Germany, France, and the United Kingdom. During 1999 the shift in public sentiment against GEOs was particularly rapid in the United Kingdom and France, two countries whose governments had actively promoted biotechnology from 1996 to 1998 (Marris 2000). Accordingly, on July 17, 2000, owing in substantial measure to the French leadership, the EU decided to maintain its moratorium on new GE product approvals indefinitely.[8] Six months later, in February 2001, the European Parliament agreed to end its three-year de facto moratorium on new GE crop approvals. In October 2002, the EU member states agreed on the rules for implementing the GE crop approval process, which will be implemented in the EU countries by the end of 2003. The lifting of the product approval moratorium, however, was only a partial victory for pro-GE interests because in April 2001, the European Parliament also approved a resolution to impose tough labeling and traceability requirements on GE products. In July 2001, the European Commission adopted the labeling and traceability proposal. As of this writing, the rules for implementing the labeling and traceability directive are being debated, but it seems quite likely that there will be a mandatory GE labeling and traceability directive in the EU by 2003.

A second factor leading to the repoliticization of agricultural biotechnology was the steady accumulation of scientific evidence about the potentially negative ecological effects of GEOs and other agricultural-biotechnology products. Bt resistance among insects had been demonstrated under laboratory conditions before 1999, though evidence under field conditions had not yet emerged. There had, however, been evidence of herbicide-resistance genes spreading to wild and weedy relatives of canola in Canada. The John Losey, Linda Rayer, and Maureen Carter (1999) study at Cornell University raised the further possibility that Bt toxin in corn pollen could kill monarch butterflies—the Bambi of the insect world—though again there is no evidence of this under field conditions thus far, and the study has been criticized by many mainstream entomologists sympathetic to biotechnology. In addition, in February 1999 Canada's drug regulatory agency barred the use of rBGH. Even more significant, in August 1999, the Codex Alimentarius Commission, the FAO food-regulatory agency given standing under WTO's SPS Agreement to develop global health and safety standards for agricultural products in international commerce, upheld the EU's 1993 moratorium on the use of rBGH. The commission's decision was the first scientifically based repudiation of a major biotechnology product by an international regulatory agency. The accumulation of scientific evidence and speculations regarding various GEO products led many formerly neutral groups to come out against GEOs on environmental health and safety grounds, or at least to take the position that more careful and independent testing procedures for GEOs should be required. Perhaps the best U.S. example is the shift in the views of two relatively centrist environmental groups, the Worldwatch Institute and the National Wildlife Federation, during 1999. The fact that there is now nearly universal opposition to GEOs by mainstream transatlantic environmental groups has no doubt reinforced public opposition to GEOs in most European countries.

A third factor contributing to the reversal of views on GEOs during 1999 was the fact that most major European grocery chains (e.g., Sainsbury and Marks and Spencer) and food manufacturers (Nestlé, Cadbury Schweppes, and Unilever) responded to consumer and NGO resistance to GEOs by declaring their intention to make their product lines GEO-free. There were, to be sure, a good many firms that were reluctant to go GEO-free or who wanted it both ways. For instance, Novartis (now part of Syngenta) is one of the world's major players in the agricultural-biotechnology industry; yet in July 2000, Novartis's food division declared all of its food product lines (beginning with its Gerber baby foods division in 1999) to be GEO-free. Most European agribusiness firms would prefer to have no trade restrictions on GEOs. Nonetheless, the fact that these firms took the lead in declaring their products GEO-free and have continued to do so has forced many U.S.-based firms to follow suit—sometimes only in Europe (e.g., fast food chains such as McDonald's) but occasionally worldwide (e.g., Heinz).[9] In addition, in 1999 several U.S. firms (e.g., Archer Daniels Midland) announced that they were preparing to ask their farmer suppliers to refrain from using GEOs.[10] These events not only began to raise the possibility that U.S. farmers might not be able to sell GE products but also legitimated the anti-GEO movement.

The GEO Politics of Seattle

The fourth factor that decisively reduced the forward momentum of agricultural biotechnology was the buildup to and demonstration at the Seattle Ministerial Conference in November and December 1999. It is worth noting here that it was essentially because of the arrogance and hubris of the WTO and U.S. government officialdoms that the ministerial meeting was held in such a public manner and that the coalition of NGOs was handed such an extraordinary opportunity to campaign against WTO. Trade economists, international lawyers, and CEOs of multinational corporations have had difficulty accommodating themselves not only to the formidable opposition to trade liberalization among NGOs and both left- and right-wing politicians and intellectuals but also to the considerable ambivalence about liberalization among wide swaths of the U.S. public.[11] The arrogant assumption by the U.S. government and the WTO that the successful establishment of the WTO effectively represented a victory over resistance to trade liberalization was a major tactical error. The Seattle Ministerial provided not only an extraordinary mobilization opportunity for civil-society groups but also ideal conditions for bringing together an impressively and unprecedentedly broad coalition of groups (Danaher and Burbach 2000).

The mobilization at the Seattle Ministerial was galvanized not by the GEO issue but by three other issues: the actual and potential threats that the WTO's practices posed to national environmental regulations; the threat that the WTO might undermine the position of trade unions and reduce industrial wages in the United States; and the dissatisfaction of many Southern governments and NGOs with the implementation of the WTO. The focal point of mobilization was perhaps the steady accumulation of rulings by GATT and WTO dispute-resolution panels rulings that effectively negated some national environmental protections (e.g., the U.S. tuna-fishing regulations protecting dolphins). Occasional WTO vetoes of national environmental protections had already induced most major national and international environmental groups, including some that had been neutral or positive toward NAFTA and the WTO, to join the anti-WTO coalition

(Dunkley 2000; Jaffee 1999). These circumstances led to the "environmentalization" of the WTO opposition. Environmental claims played an increasingly important role in arguments against trade liberalization in general and against WTO procedures in particular (Jaffee 1999). As Daniel Jaffee has noted, the most important shift in the coalition was the decisive change in environmental organization positions on trade liberalization policies since the 1993 NAFTA vote. In 1993, only a minority of major environmental groups opposed NAFTA, and roughly half publicly supported approval of NAFTA. By late 1999, however, not a single major U.S. environmental NGO publicly supported the WTO, and most (including Environmental Defense, the World Wildlife Fund, the National Wildlife Federation, Friends of the Earth, the Sierra Club, Greenpeace, Public Citizen, and Defenders of Wildlife) were actively opposed. Among the major U.S. environmental NGOs, only the Nature Conservancy, the Natural Resources Defense Council, and the Audubon Society remained neutral and refrained from publicly criticizing the WTO. The second mobilizing factor was that to most Southern governments and NGOs, the WTO, and globalization more generally, appeared have led to increased international inequality and to few benefits for the South. These two blocs joined forces with organized labor, the most enduring base of opposition to the WTO.

However, several factors magnified the importance of the GEO issue in galvanizing the Seattle coalition. As noted earlier, one was the emergence of tentative evidence about the adverse environmental and safety effects of some GEO products. Some activists and others also claimed that the GEO regulatory system in the United States (and, by extension, the types of evidence that the Codex Alimentarius and WTO dispute-resolution panels would call on) was inadequate. The inadequate regulation of GEOs and the international regulatory system's tendency to ignore environmental concerns about GEOs reinforced environmental criticism of the WTO. In addition, growing resistance to GEOs reinforced anti-WTO sentiments among some farm groups, sustainable agriculture organizations, anti-hunger groups, and development action groups that would not otherwise have become involved in such a protest. Thus, Seattle witnessed an impressive coalition among labor organizations, antiglobalization groups, peace groups, disarmament groups, human rights groups, consumer groups, environmental groups, farm groups, sustainable agriculture organizations, and the anti-hunger community.[12]

Just before Seattle, too, an important farm crisis emerged, one that many groups, particularly farm groups, attributed to the dismantling of much of the agricultural protectionism structure within the provisions of the URAA. This farm crisis cemented the role of farm groups in the Seattle coalition. The U.S. National Farmers Union—which both opposes GEOs and favors a restructuring of farm programs for the benefit of small producers, a restructuring that would be inconsistent with the URAA—played a particularly important role. Finally, the growing momentum toward enshrining the precautionary principle within the Convention on Biological Diversity's Cartagena Protocol had generated growing confidence that contesting the WTO was a realistic option. In particular, the possibility of success in the CBD negotiations made it seem plausible that the precautionary principle could become a counterweight to Article III of the WTO SPS Agreement, which effectively rules out precautionary regulations of trade in GE foods.

Even so, GEOs were an unexpectedly important issue at Seattle—a bridging issue. A Washington State University agricultural economist (McCluskey 2000, 39) may have exaggerated when she wrote in the American Agricultural Economics Association's journal *Choices* that "GMO labeling was the most controversial and talked about topic at the World Trade Organization meetings in Seattle." But her analysis makes clear that WTO opponents repeatedly employed the example of GEO crop varieties to demonstrate how WTO practices, if they continued to be implemented, would expose citizens and consumers around the world to potentially problematic new technologies and products.

UPPING THE ANTE: THE CARTAGENA PROTOCOL

A decade or so hence, observers will likely regard the passage of the Cartagena Protocol on Biosafety as one of the most critical decisions regarding the globalization regime and the commercialization of agricultural-biotechnology products. Although GEOs might seem to have little to do with biodiversity—given that biodiversity seems to pertain mainly to tropical rainforests and sensitive eco-zones in the South—in practice the CBD has focused to a surprising degree on biotechnology (see McAfee, this volume). In part, this focus reflects the importance of the biotechnology sector and of the social biology of genetic engineering. The groups that wrote and debated the original provisions of the CBD made biotechnology an integral part of the convention for several interrelated reasons. Genetic-engineering techniques magnify plant breeders' ability to make varieties genetically homogenous (Busch et al. 1991; Krimsky and Wrubel 1996). Thus, genetic engineering—not only of crops but also of trees, fish, and other species—is seen by many biodiversity activists as a singular threat to biological diversity. The essence of genetic engineering of crop plants is that a very few genes or gene sequences would become incorporated in a large range of crop varieties across the globe. These increasingly more uniform transgenic varieties would tend to displace traditional peasant cultivars. There has been concern for over a decade and a half that genetically engineered crops might lead to ecological disruptions of one sort or another, and such disruptions would be an additional threat to biodiversity (Krimsky and Wrubel 1996).[13]

Although the global biodiversity community had definite reasons for concerning itself with biotechnology in the CBD negotiations, perhaps even more fundamental to the biotechnology emphasis of the CBD and its biosafety provisions was the fact that the CBD represented a forum for environmental and related NGOs to contest some of the major provisions of the evolving globalization regime. Thus, although the Uruguay Round GATT negotiations took a considerable amount of time and had to surmount strong opposition, they were ultimately brought to closure because, in part, civil-society groups were excluded from the process. The structure of the CBD negotiations, which occurred under the auspices of the United Nations, was much more conducive to NGO input. Owing to input from the NGOs and their appeal to countries that had originally signed the CBD in Rio,[14] the CBD negotiations were protracted and bitter. Though analysis of the dynamics of the CBD negotiations is beyond the scope of this chapter, there emerged surprisingly broad national-governmental sentiment in favor of applying the precautionary principle (PP) to biosafety regulation.

The PP, which had been widely recognized as the guiding principle for regulation of chemicals and potentially hazardous practices in the EU for several years before the Cartagena agreement, has two major components. One is a shift in the burden of proof from government regulatory agencies to private firms: the government is not obligated to prove that a new product or production practice is harmful; instead private firms are obligated to prove that it is safe. The second component is that the scientific standard for implementing the PP in regulatory decision-making is a more encompassing one than that employed in the U.S. regulatory environment. Products or practices can be rejected if there is evidence of any harm or if there is a plausible scientific rationale that approval could lead to negative health or environmental effects.

Despite the tremendous influence the Miami Group (a small but powerful bloc of countries comprising the United States, Argentina, Australia, Canada, Chile, and Uruguay) in the negotiations, the opposing group (the Like-Minded Group, consisting of the G77 plus China and minus Chile, Uruguay, and Argentina) was far more numerous and was supported by the NGO community.[15] Faced with the risk that a strongly worded agreement endorsing the PP and directly contradicting the WTO could pass, the Miami Group remained in the negotiations and secured the most favorable compromise that it could.[16]

The Cartagena Protocol compromise must be seen in two quite different aspects. On one hand, the protocol essentially allows countries to refuse to import GEOs, on the basis of the PP. Exporters must register new GEO products with a database to be administered by the UN in conjunction with the protocol. The filing with the database must include information on how the GEO product was developed and tested. To ship new products for the first time, exporters must seek permission from importing countries. Commodities that are not specifically labeled "GEO-free" must be labeled "May contain GMOs." On the other hand, elsewhere in the treaty, language was added to appease the Miami Group. The protocol states that any national rejection of an imported GEO product must be based on credible scientific evidence and that the agreement is not intended to supersede the WTO agreement. Nonetheless, it is generally agreed that the specification of the PP in the Cartagena Protocol is largely inconsistent with WTO rules.

The enduring significance of the protocol is not simply its institutionalization of the PP in international law (presuming the required fifty countries ratify the treaty so that it can be implemented). Even more than this, Cartagena has legitimated the precautionary principle—which, prior to Cartagena, was essentially sneered at by U.S. regulatory and trade officials. Cartagena has also emboldened governments and groups elsewhere to stand behind the PP and behind the notion that precautionary action is the best approach to preventing environmental harm of from new products and technologies.

GEOs beyond Seattle

The EU is hardly against international trade or even trade liberalization. After all, the EU is an outgrowth of a customs union, the European Economic Union. European states and European capital are by no means seeking to employ the GEO issue to reverse the Uruguay Round. Most European observers—state officials, academics, and even NGOs—do not see the GEO issue as being primarily a trade issue, as tends to be the case in the United States and most of the Western Hemisphere. The dispute between the EU and the United States over GEOs has largely been a "trade irritant" rather than a full-blown trade crisis (von Schomberg 2000).[17] Indeed, the impulse behind the EU's disposition of GEO issues seems to have little to do with the desire to reintroduce protectionism.

The GEO issue is ultimately about the significant global differences in the social institutions underlying regulation of life sciences innovations, and different beliefs and institutional histories relating to agricultural protection, rural livelihood, and culture. EU regulation of life sciences technologies and products includes not only the standard health, public safety, and risk criteria but also political and precautionary principles. The EU regulatory process has an intrinsic political component, namely that the "fourth criterion"—social impacts, broadly conceived—is a significant factor because regulations must be ratified by national ministers.[18] Most important, the PP is now formally enshrined as a critical parameter of regulatory decision-making (von Schomberg 2000). The regulatory process for life sciences products in the EU is by no means fully trusted by European publics, but this lack of trust apparently has little to do with the fact that the political nature of the process can include consideration of social or environmental impacts. The inclusion of social impacts in regulatory decision-making may well be valued by a good many European citizens and NGOs. Indeed, it is frequently stressed that technological calamities and mishaps in Europe (e.g., mad cow disease and nuclear accidents) have caused Europeans to be more risk averse than North Americans (von Schomberg 2000).

In the United States, by contrast, the regulatory process is conducted by regulatory agencies (FDA, EPA, USDA) that are difficult for civil-society groups to penetrate. U.S. regulatory agencies pride themselves on being isolated from anything or anyone other than scientific data and researchers. The regulatory process is in principle "science-driven" in that sociopolitical considerations are supposed to have no standing (though substantial pressure is often placed on regulatory agencies by corporations and the executive branch of the federal government). Essentially all the data in the regulatory process are those provided by private corporations, according to protocols laid out by the relevant regulatory agency. The U.S. regulatory process contradicts the essence of the PP in that in a PP regime the burden of proof lies entirely on the corporation, and the absence of adverse environmental impacts is not a primary evidentiary requirement.

To a considerable extent, then, the GEO controversy is a struggle over regulatory styles—and ultimately over the principles and institutional structures of regulation. Trade comes into play only insofar as the WTO agreement involves superimposing some of the major principles of the U.S. product-regulation process on other nations by defining major departures from U.S. procedures relating to global commerce as technical barriers to trade.[19] Thus, although the precautionary principle appears to enjoy strong adherence across Europe as the basic principle that should undergird regulation, it does not play a major role in policymaking in the United States, particularly in the regulation of the life sciences industry. WTO proponents will have great difficulty inducing the EU bloc to back away from this principle, which has so much public support (von Schomberg 2000).

A number of observers believe that a solution to the GEO controversy will be forthcoming when the U.S. government overcomes its unwillingness to proceed with a labeling regime (Runge and Jackson 2000). In Europe, labeling is widely seen as the obvious way out of the year-old trade conflict, and since 2001 a draft GEO-labeling policy has been on the table at the Codex Alimentarius. But will the United States agree to segregate or "identity preserve" GEO grains? Would such a concession lead to a consensus solution to the global GEO conflict? Corporations fiercely oppose labeling, and grain-exporting and food-manufacturing companies are engaged in an ongoing campaign to dramatize—and, arguably, exaggerate—the costs of segregation and labeling. This reluctance to segregate GE and non-GE foods is undoubtedly due in substantial measure to the large sunk investments in high-volume grain-handling facilities, as well as to the fact that widespread segregation (other than for niche products) would render these facilities essentially obsolete. But beyond the interests attached to maintaining the value of high-volume bulk-grain-handling facilities, there are other corporate and public-policy concerns about labeling. Chief among these are the complications that would arise in testing, certification, and labeling and the corporate desire to avoid the obstacles to multiple sourcing that segregation would entail. It is also becoming increasingly apparent that transgenic contamination (particularly in corn) is now so widespread that segregation and labeling might not, in fact, ensure the existence of GEO-free foods—even among those that meet the standards for organic certification (Barboza 2001b).

Although an agreement between the EU and the United States on segregation and labeling could reduce the tension over GEOs (because it would permit the two regulatory styles and institutions to coexist), there is an important reason for skepticism about the feasibility of segregation and labeling. These practices are premised on the existence of substantial privately appropriated (or appropriable) rents derived from the productivity increase involved in the use of GEO technology. If segregation and labeling are to be feasible, grain firms must be able to appropriate some of the GEO rent from farmers, consumers, and others across the food chain to mitigate the costs involved. Part of this rent could conceivably come from the value-added in GEO-free products, but there is little evidence that this surplus will be large (McCluskey 2000; Nelson 1999). Anecdotal evidence suggests that the economic surpluses from GEOs accruing to farmers are modest. Our own research group at the University of Wisconsin, for example, has found that more than 40 percent of the users of corn and soybean GEOs in 1998 and 1999 reported that their per-acre profits did not improve as a result of using these varieties. We have also found that GEO "dis-adopters" have discontinued use of Bt corn and herbicide-tolerant soybeans more because of performance shortcomings than because of worries about finding buyers for their grain (Chen and Buttel 2000). There may be surpluses to be appropriated from segregated and labeled grains being exported to Europe, though European importers would no doubt prefer to continue buying GEO-free Brazilian grains (especially soybeans) and pay no price premium. In any event, the economic rents from GEO varieties (price premiums for GEO-free product and the on-farm profitability premium that can be captured by farmers) may simply not be large enough to justify investments in new plant and equipment for handling large quantities of identity-preserved non-GE grains.

There is also the possibility that the United States and its Miami Group allies have in mind a de-escalation of the GEO trade skirmish for the future to avoid jeopardizing the gains already made within the WTO. Although there is no formal admission of the point, there is widespread speculation that although the U.S. government knows it would succeed in several possible complaint actions against the EU, the government has elected not to pursue these complaints. European-based biotechnology companies are also known to oppose U.S. complaint actions because of concerns that such actions would inflame European public opinion and ignite even more formidable NGO activism. The United States is also probably refraining from bringing actions because it suspects that the EU would not comply with the WTO rulings or be intimidated by sanctions.

The reasons for this conclusion are twofold. One is that the WTO clearly has a structural weakness that reduces its ability to enforce its decisions,[20] and as more WTO rulings are ignored by the EU at the implementation stage, this weakness becomes more apparent. Because the U.S. government is strongly committed to the success of the WTO—and, even more important, to the success of the Millennial Round of WTO negotiations—tilting at GEO windmills is not likely at this point. In addition, the United States is aware that the legitimacy of the EU among European publics (with some exceptions, such as in Spain) is low and that even further erosion of EU authority would result if the EU lost at the WTO and elected to comply with a WTO ruling on GEO imports (Levidow and Maris, 2001). Because of the significant possibility of public anger against the EU, there is essentially no prospect of inducing the EU to move substantially toward the U.S. position on policies regarding the importation and regulation of GEOs.

The future of agricultural biotechnology and trade will be strongly shaped by the degree to which the EU feels pressure to contest the Miami Group's position in the Millennial Round negotiations. At stake are not simply the trade rules that will govern GEOs but virtually the entire scope of the WTO's procedures and enforcement capabilities. EU (and, to some extent, Japanese and Korean) reluctance to comply with the SPS Agreement and the Technical Barriers Agreement (and also with the URAA on subsidies) has already circumscribed the WTO's authority by exposing the weaknesses of its present enforcement powers. The Miami Group's agenda for the Millennial Round will include a number of measures aimed at bolstering these enforcement powers and at trying to bring the EU and some East Asian countries to heel on trade barriers and agricultural protectionism. But it is doubtful whether the global community is prepared for a Millennial Round that would involve either significant strengthening of WTO enforcement powers or a move toward institutionalizing the U.S. regulatory style around the world.

CONCLUSION

Are GEOs the Achilles' heel of the globalization regime, or is globalization the Achilles' heel of biotechnology? One way to answer this question is to say that there is probably a consensus among the OECD countries and the

Southern members of the Miami and Cairns Groups that permitting an issue such as GEOs—or even the larger arena of environmental policy (Steinberg 2002)—to scuttle the Doha Round WTO agreement would not make sense. And EU (and East Asian) resistance to GEO imports clearly does not reflect the fact that nation-states are ambivalent toward trade liberalization. But it is also true that the abruptness of the imposition of WTO rules relating to GEOs on European societies and their publics, who were already wary about GEOs, has elevated the issue to such prominence in European (and East Asian) politics that the GEO issue will necessarily be one of the key parameters in EU strategy during the next round of negotiations. The EU negotiators will probably not be at liberty to move very far toward the U.S. position, at least without some major concessions in the agriculture agreement—such as some endorsement of "multifunctionality" in agricultural policy (OECD 2001)—that would appeal to European states and publics. EU negotiators may be particularly constrained if the political-cultural differences between the United States and Europe continue to widen as the George W. Bush administration continues to spurn the Kyoto Protocol of the Framework Convention on Climate Change, pursues selective protectionism (e.g., for the benefit of the U.S. steel industry), and moves aggressively to promote its antiterrorist agenda.

Another important point is that although the architects of the WTO in the early 1990s clearly knew how important agriculture would be to a successful Uruguay Round, deregulating agriculture and promoting biotechnology were hardly the most important items on their agenda. The Uruguay Round architects were mainly concerned with liberalizing trade in services, enforcing patents across international borders, ensuring security of international investments, and reducing trade barriers—while simultaneously keeping the bulk of the South within the global financial and trading system. But it turns out that each of these critical components of the WTO involves biotechnology in some way. Thus, the Miami Group's ability to make concessions in the GEO area is limited because most of the concessions the group might consider would undermine the WTO's underlying principles. GEOs would thus appear to be the Achilles' heel of the globalization regime.

There are several additional uncertainties in the relationship between the GEO issue and the WTO. It is conceivable, for example, that in several years the GEO issue will have blown over to some degree and thus have been removed from the list of knotty issues to be dealt with in the Millennial Round. My own conjecture is that there are sufficient primordial sentiments relating to agriculture and food, especially in northwest Europe, to keep GEOs on the agenda for an indefinite period.

Another wildcard, of course, concerns the factors that have driven opposition by environmental and labor groups to the WTO. The nub is that if the negotiating posture of the United States and its allies with respect to WTO is changed to appease environmental and labor protesters, this prospective Millennial Round version of the WTO will not appeal to most governments in the South. Most countries in the South have received few benefits from the WTO—at least relative to what was promised in the Uruguay Round— in part because widespread opening of markets to primary agricultural exports from the South has not occurred and because global capital mobility has favored industrial countries over low-income countries. Thus, governments of the South are not going to be interested in a new WTO agreement that essentially forces on them unwanted protections for workers' rights and the environment. The two main groups of WTO opponents— environmental, social issue, and labor opponents, mainly in the North, and critics from the South who want even more liberalized access to Northern markets—thus catch the OECD countries in general and the aggressive Northern liberalizers in particular in a crossfire. The two groups of demands are largely contradictory. It is hard to know how the aggressiveness of the two types of WTO critics will balance out, but that balance will likely be critical in shaping the Millennial Round.

Another wildcard is the question of whether the GEO conflict will lead the major agricultural biotechnology and agribusiness firms to refrain voluntarily from pushing the envelope in ways that offend the publics and officials of Europe and Asia. Whether this occurs will no doubt depend strongly on the short-term economics of the situation. The agricultural-biotechnology industry is widely recognized as being in a difficult period owing to low stock valuations, the likelihood of slow sales growth over the short to medium term, and the adverse public relations that their advocacy of GEOs has caused. Many of the powerhouse biotechnology firms have either been forced to merge with other multinationals (e.g., Monsanto with Pharmacia & Upjohn), have been bought out (Pioneer Hi-Bred by DuPont), or are being hived off to preserve corporate profitability (e.g., the agricultural-biotechnology divisions of Novartis and AstraZeneca have recently been combined under the corporate name Syngenta, with the understanding that the two firms will seek a third-party buyer). Will the OECD country governments sacrifice the aspirations of their biotechnology firms to obtain a Millennial Round agreement? Will a significantly weakened agricultural-biotechnology sector back off from controversy and from reliance on high-stakes negotiations by the U.S. government and Cairns-Miami-type allies? Or will its weaknesses lead it to defend its interests even more aggressively? The latter appears to be happening in the United States: the Biotechnology Industry Organization has initiated a $50 million public relations effort on behalf of agricultural-biotechnology interests. Although this strategy is understandable, it is not without risk, and this fact is recognized by European biotechnology firms that are generally more comfortable with a low-key approach. Thus, although it may be that GEOs will be the Achilles' heel of the globalization regime, in some sense the globalization regime has been the Achilles' heel of GEOs, or of the agricultural biotechnology agricultural-biotechnology industry. If the plans sketched out for the industry nearly two decades ago are to be realized, deregulation (harmonization of regulation along the U.S. pattern) and reregulation (placing more authoritative regulatory control in the hands of international regulatory agencies that cannot be readily affected by civil-society action) are necessary. These changes, which were largely achieved in the URAA, have focused a great deal of unwanted scrutiny on the major transnational firms in the biotechnology industry. The changes have also galvanized a movement that seems as committed to direct civil-society action now as it was in December 1999.

The increasing Third World tilt of corporate and state policy strategies in support of genetically engineered crops and foods could signal another plausible direction for GEO politics. In some sense this strategy might seem unexpected, since as of 2001 there were scarcely more than 2 million hectares of GE crops in the entire developing world outside Brazil (where illegal GE crops are used clandestinely) and Argentina (Buttel 2002). But although there are virtually no GE crops in the South, there has been a growing tendency to promote GE regulatory approvals and GE crop adoption by offering the prospects of alleviating hunger in the Third World and of giving developing countries access to biotechnology products. Rhetoric stressing the benefits that "golden rice" would bring to the hungry and malnourished in the South is the most visible example of this discursive shift. Other examples include rhetorical pronouncements that there is an ethical and moral imperative to encourage the use of GE crops in the developing world now that data on the rice genome sequence have been published in *Science* (vol. 296, April 5, 2002). It is also apparent that the U.S. trade representative and some private firms such as Monsanto are trying out a new strategy to actively encourage—and, if necessary, pressure—selected developing countries to approve GE crop varieties and to endorse the U.S. position on GE crops and on trade and regulatory policy. The focal point of efforts to enlist Third World support for GE crops and U.S. GE food policy is, interestingly enough, cotton. There have been widespread efforts to encourage use of Bt cotton (e.g., in China, Brazil, and much of Southeast Asia), with some surprising successes (e.g., the Indian government's approval of GE cotton in March 2002). GE cotton is certainly a logical focal point because it is a nonfood crop and its use does not involve major trade concerns. But the fact that cotton—an industrial input rather than a major staple food crop—has been chosen as the leading edge of a campaign to encourage support in the South suggests that the discourse of alleviating hunger in the developing country is fragile.

The unresolved farm crisis makes it seem unlikely that the Millennial Round of the WTO will involve significant further deregulation of agricultural programs. The WTO has not had much impact on agricultural subsidies over the past five years and perhaps never will. At present only the political and intellectual ideologues of trade liberalization see that the gains would be sufficient to override the tremendous opposition and inertia that now stand in the way of further liberalization of agricultural trade. It will be difficult enough for the Miami Group to fight the GEO wars with the EU and East Asia without adding the goal of simultaneously achieving liberalization of farm programs. A new WTO agreement could likely be made with no significant further agricultural liberalization. And the future of WTO probably no longer depends on horse-trading with the nations of the South by offering them decreased OECD subsidization of agriculture and agrofood market access in the North in exchange for agreements on intellectual property, services, and so on. Now that the WTO is in place as the only game in town, it is almost certain that virtually all the South will sign on to the Millennial Round to maintain their positions in the world trading environment. Thus, contradictory regulatory styles, the precautionary principle, and GEO issues could very well continue to be the most critical barrier to a new agreement.

NOTES

An earlier version of this chapter was presented at the annual meeting of the Rural Sociological Society, Washington, D.C., August 2000. I am grateful for Rachel Schurman's useful comments on the earlier version.

1. I use *GE crops* and *GEOs* (genetically engineered organisms) synonymously.

2. The adoption of GE soybeans has continued to increase since 1998. GE soybean varieties were estimated to account for about 70 percent of U.S. soybean acreage in 2001. GE corn adoption has actually decreased since 1998, with GE corn varieties (both Bt varieties and herbicide-tolerant varieties) accounting for a little less than a quarter of U.S. corn acreage in 2001 (Buttel 2002).

3. In a front-page article in the *New York Times,* David Barboza (2001b) suggests that officials at biotechnology corporations not only have been aware for several years of the extent to which manufactured food products contained GEOs but also were aware that transgenic varieties would cause widespread contamination of non-GE crops. The facts that widespread genetic proliferation would occur, and that it would be difficult and costly to ameliorate contamination, were apparently seen by some corporations as a strategy to prompt acceptance of GE crops in Europe and among GE opponents elsewhere.

4. Thus, the "globalization regime" is not only a "food regime" but also a more general regime of accumulation.

5. The Cairns Group in the Uruguay Round GATT negotiations consisted of a set of trade-oriented, agro-exporting countries from both North and South as well as from the former Eastern European state-socialist bloc (Argentina, Australia, Brazil,

Canada, Chile, Colombia, Fiji, Hungary, Indonesia, Malaysia, the Philippines, New Zealand, Thailand, and Uruguay). The Cairns Group overlapped closely with the Miami Group in the Convention on Biological Diversity negotiations, which sought to restrict precautionary principle-type restrictions on imports of GEO products.

6. Activist groups whose concerns center on the South are also likely to criticize the WTO because it has had little effect in opening up Northern markets for the major developing countries' agricultural exports, such as sugar, tobacco, and bananas.

7. At least 10 percent—and perhaps much more—of the Brazilian soy crop comes from contraband GEO varieties, mostly smuggled from Argentina. The use of smuggled GE (largely Monsanto) soy varieties in Brazil (in Brazil, the smuggled varieties cost only a fraction what they cost in neighboring Argentina) has led to complaints from American soy farmers because foreign competitors can obtain the seed far more cheaply than Americans can.

8. Also of considerable significance for the long term is the fact that U.S.-EU trade disputes are not confined to agriculture. Over the last year there have been major disputes regarding EU tariffs on imported U.S. audiovisual products (i.e., films and recorded music). In addition, the United States is agitated about the extent to which the British, French, and German governments are providing large subsidized loans to the companies in the Airbus consortium, Boeing's major competitor for overseas sales of passenger aircraft. The Office of the U.S. Trade Representative is pushing these three governments hard to comply with the U.S. interpretation of a U.S.-EU trade pact that preceded the establishment of the WTO.

9. Perhaps the most dramatic synchronization of opposition to GEOs across national borders involves the decisions by Frito Lay, Simplot, and other potato-product manufacturers to advise their producers to refrain from using Bt potatoes (Monsanto's NewLeaf variety). Though I am not aware of hard data as to adoption rates over time, the actions by the potato producer manufacturers appear to have led to a decisive rollback of Bt potato adoption in the United States. In global terms, Bt potato adoption as late as 2002 has been minuscule (Buttel 2002).

10. In 2000, however, Archer Daniels Midland backed away from its earlier intention to stop purchasing GE grain and decided instead to work toward segregation of GE and non-GE grains and products.

11. For example, a frequently cited set of surveys conducted by University of Washington researchers (Keith Stamm and his graduate students at the School of Communications) immediately before and after the Seattle demonstration showed that respondents tended to be ambivalent about trade and skeptical of the WTO and its policies. Both before and after the protest, a majority of the respondents disagreed that consumers benefited from free trade through reduced consumer prices, and a significant minority of respondents (about a third in each survey) agreed that free trade destroys well-paying jobs. But although attitudes toward trade in general were not greatly affected by the Seattle protests, the protest did increase sharply the percentage of respondents who felt that the WTO is harmful (from 39 to 54 percent), and the percentage who agreed that the WTO does not care what the public thinks (from 53 percent to 68 percent) (survey information retrieved August 2000 from seattlep-i.nwsource.com/business/surv04.html and "How Puget Sound Citizens Perceive the WTO and Global Trade," survey conducted November 8-14, 1999, www.washington.edu/wto/study.html). Although skepticism about such sur-

veys is always warranted, the point remains that the general public is ambivalent about free trade.

12. Among the pillars of opposition to the WTO were Southern governments and NGOs who maintained that it had led to increased international inequality. Although many NGOs from the South opposed WTO policies on grounds similar to those brought forward by the NGO coalition from the North, much of the opposition to the WTO from the South came from developing-country governments that opposed WTO leaders' gestures to incorporate labor and environmental protections. Thus, the two main factions of the Seattle resistance to the WTO had a significant difference of interest that, although papered over at Seattle, could very well divide them during the Millennial Round.

13. Technically, the CBD negotiations were to turn on struggles over Article 19 (3) of the 1992 Convention on Biodiversity, which involves the issue of prior informed consent to consume transgenic products. This "advanced informed agreement" procedure would "oblige countries to ensure that its exporters give prior notification to importing countries to enable them to make a risk assessment of the GM product before import is approved" (Martinez-Alier, 2000, 31).

14. The United States was among the few nations present at the Earth Summit that did not sign the CBD. Nevertheless, the U.S. government was the most important actor during the CBD negotiating rounds, particularly the January 2000 round in Montreal.

15. The EU was another major bloc; it supported the PP but did not generally adopt an anti-GEO stance. The Central and Eastern European countries, and a bloc known as the Compromise Group (Mexico, Japan, Norway, Singapore, Korea, and New Zealand), were also influential in the negotiations.

16. See Dawkins 2000 for a useful overview of the negotiations in Montreal and Cosbey 2000 for a helpful summary of the current status of international negotiations involving trade and environment.

17. The major East Asian market countries (especially Japan and Korea) now take roughly the same position on GEO trade and labeling that the EU does. It is not clear, however, whether these positions are anchored in public views and concerns about genetic engineering or in regulatory cultures and institutions. Although Australia was active in the Miami Group during the Cartagena Protocol negotiations, the strong public opposition to GEOs in Australia could result in lengthy moratoriums on GEO-product approvals and restrictions on GEO-product imports. In New Zealand, too, now a quintessential neoliberal political economy, the strong opposition to GEOs is not entirely out of character. Though New Zealand is the world's largest dairy-product exporter, rBGH has not been employed there, out of concern that its use could prejudice foreign markets against New Zealand cheese and other dairy products.

18. Thus, for example, GEO product approvals must be ratified by national environment ministers, whose decisions can be expected to include a political component, such as public opinion (Carr and Levidow 1999).

19. Note that the SPS Agreement already permits member states to consider market impacts when making decisions about animal and plant health.

20. WTO sanctions are confined to retaliatory tariffs. The retaliatory tariffs in the cases of the hormone-treated beef were clearly not the reason that the EU changed its policy to comply with the WTO ruling in 2001.

7

Biotech Battles

*Plants, Power, and Intellectual Property
in the New Global Governance Regimes*

Kathleen McAfee

Biotechnology, along with closely related issues of food, farming, and intellectual property rights, has become a flashpoint in multilateral trade and environmental negotiations between developing nations, the United States, and Europe. Sharp disagreements about trade in genetically engineered products and about the patenting of living things have sparked disputes about the powers and scope of emerging institutions of global governance. Central to these controversies are tensions between the principles and jurisdictions of the World Trade Organization (WTO) and those of the international Convention on Biological Diversity (CBD) and the new Cartagena Protocol on Biosafety. In addition, there are contradictions within the biodiversity convention itself. The WTO, established in 1994, fosters market-based regulation of biotechnology and genetic resources. The CBD, which was ratified in 1993, does this as well but also invokes environmental and social criteria for management of biodiversity and biotechnology.

Contrasting understandings of biotechnology's effects are pivotal in these disputes. New agricultural biotechnologies promise control over the traits and reproduction of food crops and livestock. Advocates of crop genetic engineering argue that transgenic crops can increase world food production while limiting environmental damage from agriculture. Their critics contend that claims about the precision and power of genetic engineering are dangerously exaggerated (McAfee 2003). Widespread adoption of transgenic crops would at best permit only temporary food-production increases, they say, and would endanger agricultural genetic diversity, the livelihoods of farmers, and the food security of countries that depend on food imports (compare, e.g., Altieri and Rosset 1999 and McGloughlin 1999).

Genomic mapping and molecular bioengineering have opened new opportunities for capital accumulation in agricultural research and development, technology licensing, and sales of seed, food, and pesticides. These new profit opportunities have speeded the mergers of agribusiness, pharmaceutical, and chemical corporations and takeovers by these firms of seed and biotechnology research companies (Busch et al. 1991; EU Directorate-General for Agriculture 2000; Boyd, this volume). One result is the consolidation of technological and genetic resources, economic clout, and political influence in a handful of transnational corporations. These firms are in a position to dominate international markets in agrochemicals, germplasm (seeds and varietal breeding lines) of major commercial crops, and biotechnology itself (equipment, expertise, genome databases, and other proprietary information).

Facilitating this trend is the expansion of intellectual property rights (IPRs). In some countries, those who discover or devise new types of plants, animals, microbes, or genes; novel uses for them; or processes for altering them at the molecular level may be granted patents or other private-ownership rights to such inventions.[1] These "life patents" are controversial in part because they enable patent holders, which are primarily corporations based in the global North, to profit from products they have developed from crop varieties and medicinal materials obtained from the biodiversity-rich global South, sometimes by means of only minor modifications.[2] Because such patents restrict the rights of farmers to save or exchange seeds, critics contend, they may undermine food security. In addition, many indigenous peoples' groups and some governments object on moral or political grounds to the private ownership of living things.

Meanwhile, public institutions have become dependent on private-sector partnerships for access to privately owned materials and techniques. As a result, for-profit companies are gaining growing influence over the research agendas of universities and the priorities of public agricultural research and extension services around the world. Moreover, the trend toward intellectual enclosure—the use of IPRs to restrict what scholars and research organizations may publish or share with students, colleagues, and the public—has begun to impede access to new technologies and the exchange of scientific knowledge (Pollack 2001; Press and Washburn 2000).

Such concerns have raised the stakes in long-simmering international controversies about food, farming, and trade policies and intellectual property rights. These debates have grown more heated as many governments and social movements have begun to question the benefits of economic globalization and the terms on which it is taking place. In the 1990s, concerns about the growing power of the multinational "gene giants" added fuel to this fire. New global environmental institutions, particularly the Convention on Biological Diversity and its Cartagena Protocol on Biosafety, have become staging grounds for resistance to WTO rules and to the market-based management of genetic resources that the WTO supports. This resistance is rooted in preexisting patterns of inequitable resource flows and the resulting inequality, mainly between the gene-rich global South and the technology-strong North.

During the past two decades, developing countries have fought to include in international environmental accords provisions that offer opportunities to redress—or at least not replicate—the exploitative relations of the past. As a result, the new environmental treaties provide openings for the inclusion of social equity and environmental justice as principles of international governance. Nevertheless, these new institutions contain their own contradictions. The CBD embodies a deep tension between market-oriented and alternative or pluralist approaches to biotechnology regulation and resource management, a tension reflected in ongoing disputes about the role of intellectual property and biotechnology in the treaty's implementation.

Southern governments and activist nongovernmental organizations (NGOs) have represented the CBD as counterbalancing the more narrowly economic principles of the WTO. However, the United States is determined to make the WTO the primary, overarching regime for regulation of biotechnology trade and food and environmental standards, and to limit the purview of the CBD and its offspring, the biosafety protocol. This agenda is linked to U.S. agricultural and technology export goals. The continuing repercussions of these disputes are evident in the WTO and other multilateral forums, particularly with regard to intellectual property rights to the raw materials and products of biotechnology. These disputes have contributed to shifts in the pattern of alliances between major grain-exporting industrial countries, especially the United States and its former European allies, as well as the developing countries of South and Southeast Asia, Africa, and much of Latin America.

CONFLICTING MODES OF ENVIRONMENTAL-ECONOMIC GOVERNANCE

At stake in the conflict between the WTO and the CBD is a model of global economic governance that subordinates social, environmental, and ethical concerns to the overriding objectives of economic growth and trade liberalization. U.S. delegates to the biosafety protocol and WTO talks insist that the genetic-resource inputs to and the genetically altered products of biotechnology are ordinary commodities, subject to standard rules of transnational commerce and to the jurisdiction of the WTO and its Agreement on Trade Related Intellectual Property Rights (TRIPS) (Khor 1999a; Lourie 1998; World Trade Organization 2001). Biotechnology's raw materials (seeds and plant and animal samples), its technological tools and related knowledge (genetic information, databases, and product formulas), and its products, according to this view, should be managed as private property, freely bought and sold, with minimal labeling requirements or restrictions on their import, export, and use. Any benefits from the commercial sales of genetically engineered products ought to be allocated strictly under the terms of standard, two-party business contracts (World Trade Organization 1998, 1999a, 2001).

The theoretical rationale implicit in this approach is a neoliberal version of environmental economics (McAfee 1999c). It assesses the values of genetic and other natural resources in terms of their world-market prices or the dollar costs of replacing them, regardless of the fact that lack of hard currency leaves the world's majority with no purchasing power in global-resource markets. Neoliberal environmental economics takes scant account of nonmonetary and long-term values of ecosystems and their components, or of the place-specific values of nature to local communities. Instead, this economics constructs food, ecosystems, and organisms as stocks of industrial raw materials, fungible units of natural capital and genetic information for sale to the highest bidders (Lutz and Serafy 1988; Munasinghe 1993; Aylward and Barbier 1996).

Yet agro-biotechnology and related food-security and environmental issues are proving difficult to subsume under this economic reductionist paradigm. The conceptualization of biodiversity as an export commodity and a technological input is contested by some governments and by networks of indigenous peoples and other NGOs. In WTO negotiations, Southern-country coalitions have attempted to delay implementation of the TRIPS Agreement and to widen TRIPS loopholes that permit the use of social and moral criteria in national policies on intellectual property. These TRIPS critics argue that uniform application of WTO rules will foster even greater North-South inequality and that the TRIPS Agreement in particular conflicts with the CBD. In the words of Cameroon's ambassador to the European Union, Philomenon Yang, speaking on behalf of the African Group of CBD delegations, "The TRIPS Agreement creates potential for disastrous conflicts between the technologically advanced and the less technologically advanced countries. It will endanger the traditional rights of farmers and of local communities all over the world . . . [and] greatly jeopardize the application of the [Biodiversity] Convention."[3]

The WTO TRIPS Agreement: Origins, Limitations, and Conflicts

The U.S. government wants to strengthen WTO TRIPS rules that make it illegal under most circumstances for local citizens, businesses, or government agencies to duplicate or use proprietary medicines, plant varieties, gene sequences, therapeutic techniques, or research technologies. The U.S. goal of obtaining stronger TRIPS rules for crop varieties is supported by Australia, Canada, a few Latin American food-exporting states, and, with reservations, by some European governments and Japan. Against these economic powerhouses stands a large group of developing countries that are opposed to the strengthening of TRIPS. In the period leading up to the Seattle Ministerial Conference, more than one hundred developing countries endorsed proposals to roll back the 1993 TRIPS accord (International Centre 1999; Stillwell 1999; "U.S. Wants" 1999). Conflicting efforts to amend TRIPS have continued in the WTO's Council for TRIPS.

The U.S. position is that "unimproved" genetic materials taken from crops developed by informal breeding or from wild organisms belong to whoever would make use of them, as part of humankind's "common heritage." As such, the United States recognizes, these genetic-resource inputs of biotechnology are covered by the CBD, which requires that its member governments make their genetic resources accessible to others. In contrast, access to and regulation of biotechnology industry outputs—genetically engineered products, their genetic recipes, and the tools and know-how for producing them—fall outside the CBD mandate, in the U.S. view, because they are private, tradable commodities and thus subject to WTO rules and to intellectual property rights (World Trade Organization 1999a, 2001).[4]

While the CBD was being negotiated from 1989 to 1992, the United States pressed this position forcefully in the Uruguay Round of the General Agreement on Tariffs and Trade (GATT IV). These negotiations transformed the GATT into the WTO, expanded its purview to include trade in agriculture and services as well as in goods, and added the TRIPS Agreement (Purdue 1995; World Trade Organization 1996). The United States, the main force in the WTO, wanted member governments to open their markets to foreign exports and investments, especially in industries where the United States is relatively strong, such as agriculture, financial services, computer electronics, entertainment media, and biotechnology. The TRIPS accord, initiated and pushed by a coalition of European, Japanese, and U.S. multinational corporations (Drahos 1999), stipulates that WTO parties must adopt laws to enforce patents "in all fields of technology" (TRIPS, Sec. 6, Art. 27.1). It requires WTO member countries to recognize the proprietary rights of local or foreign citizens or enterprises to crop varieties, whether conventional or genetically engineered, and to genetically altered microorganisms and other biotechnological innovations.

During the GATT IV talks, developing countries were able to obtain small but significant exceptions to the blanket requirement for IPR coverage of living organisms and related technologies. Section 5, Article 27, Section 3(b) of the TRIPS Agreement allows WTO member governments to exclude from patentability "plants and animals other than microorganisms, and essentially biological processes for the production of plants or animals other than non-biological and microbiological processes. However, Members shall provide for the protection of plant varieties either by patents or by an effective *sui generis* system or by any combination thereof."

The TRIPS accord also permits states to adapt their IPR regimes in ways necessary to safeguard the environment, morality, or *ordre publique* (TRIPS, Sec. 5, Art. 27.2). As a further concession to developing countries, TRIPS was slated for review in 2000-2001. As the ramifications of IPRs in crop and medical biotechnology have become more apparent, developing-country WTO members have requested reconsideration of the application of TRIPS rules to food crops, microorganisms, and "essentially biological" processes and have called for the recognition of non-economic factors in environmental and biotechnology regulation (International Centre 1999). These ongoing disputes highlight the limitations of "free trade," economic efficiency, and private property as the paradigmatic principles of global governance. The growing perception that trade liberalization favors the economically strong helped to precipitate the WTO ministerial meltdown in Seattle and has contributed to continuing deadlocks in the WTO. The issues of biotechnology regulation and private property in organisms and their parts are especially inflammatory. They not only raise unprecedented questions about the powers and rights of individuals and companies to own and manipulate life but also are linked to controversies about international economic inequality and environmental justice.

THE CBD BATTLEGROUND

In contrast to the WTO, the Convention on Biological Diversity establishes an arguable basis in international law for taking non-economic criteria into account in biotechnology regulation. At the same time, contradictions built into the CBD make it a source of continuing conflict between market-oriented and equity-oriented approaches. Because the CBD is a framework treaty that requires further elaboration to be put into practice, its parties meet every two years to adopt guidelines for its implementation. CBD articles addressing access to genetic resources, distribution of the benefits these resources provide, the transfer of biotechnology, biosafety, and related intellectual-property issues have been hotly disputed throughout this process.[5] Some CBD articles commit signatory countries to goals that, at least implicitly, conflict with the privatization and market-based valuation of nature.

The CBD recognizes the sovereignty of states over genetic and other resources within their territories (Preamble; Art. 15.1). It calls for the in situ and ex situ conservation of biological diversity, including crop genetic resources (Arts. 8 and 9), for protection of the "traditional lifestyles relevant for the conservation and sustainable use of biological diversity" of "local and indigenous" communities (Art. 8, Sec. j) and of the "customary use of biological resources in accordance with traditional cultural practices" (Art. 10, Sec. c). The CBD also calls for prior informed consent as a precondition for access to local genetic resources (Art. 15, Sec. 5), for national policies to promote conservation and sustainability (Arts. 6 and 10), and for equity and "fairness" in genetic-resource trade and in the distribution of technology and its benefits (Arts. 16 and 19).

Given the disparities in economic power between transnational corporations and most developing countries and communities, and the ubiquitous economic incentives and opportunities for short-term exploitation of natural resources, none of the above objectives is likely to be achieved by means of the market mechanisms and private-property systems fostered by the WTO. In addition, resolutions by the CBD's Conference of the Parties have recognized alternatives to individual or corporate property rights, such as collective property and indigenous traditions of shared knowledge, concepts not recognized in the WTO (Drahos 1999; McAfee 1999a). However, there are other CBD provisions that foster a commodity-based framework for resource management. The influence of these market-oriented approaches has been amplified by the "green-developmentalist" bias of the Secretariat of the CBD.

Why—in a treaty initiated as a *conservation* compact, with a focus on wilderness, forests, and wildlife—have biotechnology and IPRs become so pivotal? The answer lies both in patterns from the past (the long history of removal of genetic and other resources from colonized regions) and in the political economy of the present (the importance of IPRs and other private-property rights to the global extension of commodity relations and the unequal impacts of economic globalization in different world regions). The controversies about life patents and genetic-resource access are linked to the economic agendas of countries with growing biotechnology industries. These agendas, in turn, arouse fears among food-import-dependent and genetic-resources-provider countries that the growth of giant biotechnology-agrochemical firms and the extension of IPRs will lead to their further impoverishment and dependency. To see these connections, we need to recall the context in which these CBD conflicts arose.

Contrasting Northern and Southern Goals for a Biodiversity Convention

The Convention on Biological Diversity is one of two international conservation treaties launched at the 1992 Earth Summit in Rio de Janeiro.[6] Its primary objectives are "the conservation of biological diversity, the sustainable use of its components and the fair and equitable sharing of the benefits arising out of the utilization of genetic resources, including by appropriate access to genetic resources and by appropriate transfer of relevant technologies, taking into account all rights over those resources and to technologies, and by appropriate funding" (UNEP/CBD 1994, Art. 1).

The original sponsors of the CBD definitely did not intend to investigate the degree to which existing international power relations, dominant development models, or present international distributions of resources contribute to environmental crises. These contentious issues, however, are proving to be inseparable from the more narrowly defined environmental goals of the treaty's original sponsors.

The Northern states (mainly Germany, France, and, later, the United States) that first called for a global conservation treaty in the mid-1980s wanted to limit the expansion of polluting industrialization in the global South, particularly increased emissions of greenhouse gases, and to preserve some critical mass of tropical forests as a carbon sink. They also hoped to slow the rate of species extinctions and the destruction of "wilderness" areas and to guarantee continued Northern access to the biological resources of Southern regions. In contrast, the immediate goal of most Southern-government signatories was to obtain additional foreign aid in the context of shrinking overall development assistance (Porter and Brown 1996). Some diversity-rich countries also hoped that the CBD would help them to establish their own biotechnology enterprises or at least to obtain revenues from the export of their genetic resources under the terms of bioprospecting contracts with Northern pharmaceutical firms and research institutions (Mugabe et al. 1997). Negotiation of the CBD from 1989 to 1992 involved intense disputes, mainly between the G77-plus-China bloc of Southern states and the more powerful industrialized nations of the OECD (Organization for Economic Cooperation and Development). When conflicts over the draft text could not be resolved, the disputed text was either excluded, as in the case of proposals for strong forest-conservation language, or diplomatically finessed (McConnell 1996). As a consequence, key provisions of the CBD are ambiguously worded and open to conflicting interpretations.

These contradictions might remain moot were it not for the activism of transnational alliances of social movements and NGOs (Dawkins 2000; Schurman and Munro, this volume). In contrast to other agencies of global governance (such as the WTO, the World Bank, and the International Monetary Fund) and in contrast to many other United Nations bodies, the CBD has permitted, and even depended on, the contributions of civil-society organizations. Mainstream conservationist NGOs have helped to draft CBD decisions. Advocacy-oriented networks of NGOs, in alliance with Southern states and some European states, have pushed for the CBD to take on issues of biotechnology and its environmental hazards and social consequences, much to the consternation of the U.S. government.

The paradoxical role of the United States in the CBD sheds light on the treaty's internal tensions and external pressures. The Reagan administration, lobbied by conservation biologists and mainstream environmental organizations, was an early supporter of plans for a single, global conservation accord (Takacs 1996). Less publicized was the desire of agricultural and biotechnology interests to guarantee continued access to Southern genetic resources (Shands 1995). During the CBD negotiations, the United States and the OECD negotiating bloc worked to ensure that the convention would make it easier for firms and research institutions to continue to survey and select crop varieties and pharmacologically active substances from the territories of other states. This goal took shape as CBD Article 15, "Access to Genetic Resources," which establishes that "Each Contracting party [to the CBD] shall endeavor to create conditions to facilitate access to genetic resources for environmentally sound uses by other contracting parties and not to impose restrictions that run counter to the objectives of this convention. . . . Access, where granted, shall be on mutually agreed terms . . . subject to prior informed consent" (Art. 15, Secs. 2, 4, and 5).

Crop Patents and Piracy

The concept of "genetic resources," which emerged in environmental discourse in the 1980s, refers to the information contained in the genomes of plants, animals, and microorganisms, many of them as yet "undiscovered"—that is, unknown to Western science—and in danger of extinction. Organisms containing pharmacologically active compounds, found in greatest abundance in tropical regions, are potential sources of medically and commercially important drugs or models for new synthetic drugs (see Scholz, this volume). As advances in biotechnology and information technology made possible the rapid screening, genetic mapping, and molecular manipulation of natural substances, genetic resources came to be seen as an important raw material for the U.S. economy. By the late 1980s, the perceived value of the medicinal genetic resources of the tropics, especially rainforests, had soared, albeit temporarily (Simpson and Sedjo 1994; Vogel 1994; Scholz, this volume).

Another form of genetic resources of great interest to U.S. negotiators was agricultural biodiversity: the myriad unique, locally specialized food-crop varieties bred and conserved by farmers worldwide (Fowler 1994). Genetic, varietal, and crop diversities are the cornerstones of the survival strategies of many small-scale cultivators, the sector that still produces most of the world's food (Rosset 1999; Pimbert 1999). Locally adapted crops and their wild relatives are also important to large-scale commercial agriculture as sources of traits for crop improvement because crop varieties, especially in industrial, monocrop farming systems, must be altered continually to defeat pests and diseases that have adapted to existing varieties and pesticides.

Most of the crops produced in the world's major agricultural exporting regions—Europe, the United States, Canada, Australia, Brazil, and South America's Southern cone—are derived from plants originally domesticated in Latin America, Southeast Asia, and western Asia (Kloppenburg and

Kleinman 1987). Samples of some of these varieties are conserved in public and private gene banks, and firms and research agencies from the relatively "gene-poor" global North have tapped these collections most frequently. But while the CBD was being framed, developing countries were already challenging the right to use crop genetic resources without compensation for their owners.

The decade preceding the CBD had seen unresolved North-South disputes over asymmetrical international flows of genetic resources and profits derived from them (Mooney 1983; Kloppenburg 1988; Busch 1995). Until the 1980s, genetic resources in fields, farms, and gene banks had been treated by seed companies, botanic gardens, and research institutions as a global commons, free for the taking (Sanchez and Juma 1994). In the early 1980s, however, governments of the South began to object to the treatment of genetic resources in their territories as a worldwide open-access resource (Juma 1989). They sought international recognition of their rights to produce and market useful plants and needed medicines, including those based on processes or substances patented in other countries.

Under pressure from Mexico and other diversity-rich states, the UN Food and Agricultural Organization's Commission on Plant Genetic Resources for Food and Agriculture adopted the International Undertaking on Plant Genetic Resources for Food and Agriculture (IU) in 1983. The original (1983) version of the IU declared *all* plant genetic resources, including varieties covered by intellectual-property claims in their countries of origin, to be part of the "common heritage" of humankind (Brush 1996). The Southern sponsors of this particular reinterpretation of "common heritage" intended it to mean that their farmers or enterprises would not be blocked by patents or other forms of IPRs from reproducing, breeding, and selling hybrid or genetically engineered plants or seeds. Industrial-country governments and transnational firms strenuously resisted this interpretation (Flitner 1998).[7]

In response to U.S. charges of patent "piracy," Southern spokespeople raised the issue of "biopiracy," pointing out that brand-name pharmaceuticals and crop varieties being exported to their countries were in many cases derived from medicines and crops discovered or bred in the global South. At least, they argued, the new biodiversity treaty ought to recognize their right to be compensated for the profitable development by others of their own biological patrimony (Fowler 1994). As a condition for promising access to their genetic resources, Southern governments and NGOs insisted that the CBD both recognize the principle of national sovereignty over genetic resources and also include provisions for the sharing of genetic-resource benefits with resource providers and for the transfer of new biotechnologies to developing countries. The United States and the OECD negotiating bloc agreed to accept this as a compromise, but declined to endorse any explicit formulas for defining "fair" compensation, "equitable" benefit sharing, or "appropriate" technology transfer (Porter and Brown 1996; McConnell 1996; Mooney 1998).

The U.S. delegation insisted that in addition to providing access to genetic resources, the new treaty should endorse "the adequate and effective protection [of] patents and other intellectual property rights" (CBD, Art. 16, Secs. 2 and 3). As a countermeasure, India won inclusion of a sentence to the effect that the IPR reference should not be applied in a way that undermined the CBD's objectives (Art. 16, Sec. 5).[8] Disputes over IPRs and biotechnology nearly derailed the CBD negotiations. Then, the Bush administration refused to sign the treaty when it was launched at the Earth Summit, on the grounds that its IPR references were not sufficiently strong. In short, the U.S. government's commitment to promote the international expansion of its agricultural, pharmaceutical, and technology industries prevailed over U.S. environmentalists' desire for a comprehensive conservation treaty.

U.S. Industry, the CBD, and Intellectual Property Rights

The White House alleged that the new convention "threatened to retard biotechnology and undermine the protection of ideas" (Boyle 1996; Blaustein 1996). This defensive, even paranoid, response has its roots in the importance of biotechnology and other high-technology sectors to the United States' international economic position and in the growing importance of intellectual property to U.S. industries.

By the 1980s, protection of U.S. proprietary technology and related intellectual property rights had become a cornerstone of U.S. trade policy (Busch 1995; Kevles 1998). Exports of new technologies—along with agrochemicals and the food surplus produced by state-subsidized agriculture— were seen as counterweighing negative U.S. trade balances in other sectors. Federal policymakers were swayed by industry arguments that genetic engineering was about to produce a bonanza of therapeutic compounds that would be commercialized only if they were covered by IPRs (Mossinghoff 1998). Biotechnology lobbyists were in close touch with White House officials during the early CBD talks, and the Japanese, British, and other OECD delegations shared many of their concerns (McConnell 1996; Val Giddings, Biotechnology Industry Organization, interview by author, Washington, D.C., October 1997). Industry representatives argued that the treaty could be invoked to pressure them to cede technological secrets to potential competitors and that it might undermine U.S. goals in the GATT IV trade talks.

The United States also tried to prevent the adoption of the CBD language calling for international regulation of genetically engineered organisms and their products. This CBD provision (Art. 19, Sec. 3) established the grounds for the biosafety protocol and was energetically advocated by a coalition of Southern states and transnational NGOs. It was included in the convention text over strong U.S. and Japanese objections, with the details to be negotiated at a later date (McConnell 1996, 66). Later, at the second conference of the CBD parties in 1994, a coalition spearheaded on the NGO side by the Third World Network, the German Green Party, and Greenpeace International, among others, convinced the CBD parties to begin protocol talks, a process that is still embroiled in controversy.

Six months after the CBD was introduced in 1992, the Clinton administration convened a review of the treaty by representatives of three biotechnology firms and three conservationist groups, who concurred that the CBD's IPR provisions were, after all, adequate. The president then signed the convention, but the Senate has not ratified it. In any case, conditions attached to the White House interpretation of the CBD would reduce U.S. obligations under the treaty to the same sort of market-based determination of genetic-resource and biotechnology distribution that would prevail even without the CBD. A proposed "statement of understanding" to be attached to the U.S. signature, should the Senate decide to ratify the CBD, declaims that "As such, the [WTO] TRIPs agreement will function as a 'floor' for substantive protection for intellectual property rights by GATT TRIPs parties under the biodiversity convention" (Wirth 1994).

This interpretation of the TRIPS Agreement is the opposite of the interpretation of the CBD by those NGOs and Southern states who see it as a basis for opposition to TRIPS and other WTO free-trade rules and to the uncompensated commoditization of biodiversity (e.g., GRAIN 1998). Indeed, the more that the United States has pressed in the WTO and other forums for genetic-resources IPRs and market-based resource valuation, the more that gene-rich countries have insisted on their right to limit access to their biological resources by taxonomists and plant breeders as well as by bioprospectors. Brazil and other "megadiversity" countries interpret the CBD provisions recognizing national sovereignty over biodiversity as a sort of national-level property right. They hope to sell their genetic resources or use biodiversity access as a bargaining chip to obtain aid, technology, or other benefits. Such a commodity-based approach is unlikely to work to their advantage, however, in a global genetic-resources market where providers have little power and supply exceeds demand.

SELLING NATURE TO SAVE IT?

Differing interpretations of the CBD and its purview continue to provoke controversy as its member governments, with the United States as a powerful, nonmember presence, battle over the treaty's implementation. I have argued that there is an internal tension in the CBD between an approach based on private property and globalized, market-based resource management, and a more pluralist approach that recognizes differences in the development needs, cultures, and property-rights systems of various countries and communities, as well as differences in how they use and value genetic resources. This tension grows out of global inequalities produced during the colonial era and compounded since then as would-be developing countries attempt to enter—or are pushed to join—an integrated world economy from a position of disadvantage.

The tension between market-based and equity-oriented frameworks also reflects disunity within the political-economic project of modern environmentalism. Over the past two decades, a green-developmentalist approach has come to dominate both the discursive practices of mainstream conservationist organizations and the greening policies of the World Bank (World Bank Environment Department 1997; McAfee 1999c). This approach has also influenced multilateral environmental institutions, including the CBD. Green developmentalism proposes that environmental problems can be corrected by market solutions. In this worldview, "natural capital" can be assigned property rights and can be traded transnationally (Perrings 1995; Serageldin 1996). Forest, mineral, and water resources and ecosystem services, as well as organisms and their parts, are assigned monetary prices based on actual or hypothetical markets. The result is a pan-planetary metric for valuing resources and managing their exchange. This universalizing discourse makes it possible to speak of the "global" management of environmental problems and to act on the assumption of compatibility between capitalist growth and ecological sustainability. The discursive practices of green developmentalism also further the shift from the direct appropriation, or "primitive accumulation," of genetic resources—the mode that prevailed for more than five hundred years—to the market exchange of genetic raw materials.

In theory, green developmentalism provides nature with the means to earn its own right to survive in a world-market economy. Conservation projects are to be financed by exports of environmental assets—access to ecotourism sites, rights to use ecological services (e.g., carbon emission credits), and intellectual property rights to medicinal plants, shamans' recipes, traditional crop varieties, and the genetic information they contain (Simpson and Sedjo 1994; Reid et al. 1993; Figueres 1997). Other green-developmentalist policies include "green conditionalities" attached to development aid; "capacity-building" projects to re-educate Southern inhabitants, train environmental managers, and construct environmental regulatory agencies within Southern states; and biodiversity surveys and assessments. These discursive practices revalue the South's natural resources from a "global" (read Northern) perspective (McNeeley 1988; World Bank Environment Department 1996; UNEP/CBD 1998b; McAfee

1999b). However, this revaluation of Southern resources according to methods of Western taxonomy and neoclassical economics constitutes a devaluation of those resources. The denomination of biodiversity values in dollars discounts the greater part of the values of Southern natural resources to the people who live in direct interdependence with those resources: their tangible use-values, their symbolic values, and their exchange values in local and domestic markets.

To obtain their "fair share" of the "benefits of biodiversity" as promised by the CBD, diversity-rich countries and indigenous communities are encouraged to assert their own intellectual property rights to genetic resources in their territories and then sell those rights. Prominent conservation biologists have argued that selling rights of access to living pharmacies will provide resources and incentives to preserve natural areas (Raven 1990; Janzen 1991; Eisner 1991). As the Smithsonian's leading conservation scientist told a World Bank workshop, prospects for saving biodiversity are now linked to biotechnology's new ability to "generate wealth at the level of the molecule."[9] Bioprospecting agreements have proliferated between Southern suppliers (governments, parastatals, and NGOs and Northern buyers (large and small pharmaceutical firms, universities, and agencies such as the U.S. National Institutes of Health) (Reid 1997; see also Scholz, this volume).

NGO critics of bioprospecting as a strategy for benefit sharing contend that it will facilitate the mining of Southern genetic raw material by bioprofiteers and reinforce the idea that, having paid a "fair market price" for this property, drug and seed firms are justified in selling products derived from collected materials back to their countries of origin at vastly higher prices (Nijar Singh 1996; Shiva 1997). Meanwhile, some of the early proponents of bioprospecting have since concluded that "regrettably, . . . genetic prospecting may not help much in the struggle to preserve habitats rich in biological diversity" and that the prospects of substantial bioprospecting resource transfers from North to South are negligible (Simpson, Sedjo, and Reid 1998). These analysts acknowledge that, given the economic and legal resources of transnational biotechnology firms and the fact that genetic-resource supplies already exceed industry's demand, most gene-source countries are in a weak position to bargain for "fair" compensation (Vogel 1997a; Scholz, this volume). Most local, direct providers of organic samples and knowledge are in a worse position, especially when national governments do not acknowledge their rights. Furthermore, the United States holds that if there is to be any sharing of the benefits of genetic resources, it should be at this initial, bioprospecting stage—when the commercial value of the resources sold is unproved and the sale price low—rather than after higher-priced products have been made by altering the natural materials or "discovering" new uses for them (International

Centre 2000). This early valuation would offer little to providers of medicinal and crop samples but is consistent with the U.S. position that genetic resources "enhanced" by biotechnology are ordinary commodities subject to free-market rules.

CBD Support for the Commodification of Genetic Resources

The administrative body of the CBD has been markedly influenced by the green-developmentalist perspective of Western governments and environmental organizations such as the World Conservation Union (IUCN) (McNeeley 1988). Interpretations of the CBD mandate prepared by the Secretariat of the CBD reflect this influence. One such document's proclamation that "modern biotechnology offers the potential to invent sustainable systems of the future, to be accompanied by a new paradigm for industry" reveals how central biotechnology has been to the interpretation of the treaty (UNEP/CBD 1998b, 5). Indeed, the word *biotechnology* appears six times in the CBD text and merits an entire section, Article 19, the only CBD article heading that addresses the distribution of the benefits of biodiversity. "The private sector is the key player in benefit-sharing arrangements," the aforementioned secretariat document states flatly (10). Another secretariat note identifies a "policy setting" conducive to benefit sharing as one that encourages "access legislation, incentives, partnerships and contracts" (UNEP/CBD 1998a, 5). This emphasis on market transactions and business partnerships illustrates how CBD administrators have promoted the market-based management of genetic resources.

Case studies compiled by the secretariat interpret biodiversity benefit sharing almost exclusively in terms of North-South bioprospecting deals (UNEP/CBD 1998c). In effect, access to "biodiversity benefits" under the CBD is being made contingent on the participation of diversity-rich countries in a global genetic-resource market. But when CBD documents define biodiversity benefits as benefits to be derived from the commercialization of genetic resources by biotechnology industries, they fail to recognize that biodiversity benefits already exist—that is, that the benefits of natural resources are known and valued by people who depend on them directly for sustenance, shelter, aesthetic pleasure, and spiritual significance. This equation of biodiversity benefits with genetic resources reduces biological variety to its purported essence as a commodity, separable from its complex interrelationships with the rest of nature and society. It is as if the values of biological variety come into existence only when its genetic information is "developed"—codified, counted, and commercialized—by biotechnology. A broader conceptualization would center on the incalculable present and future benefits of healthy ecosystems and diversity-based farming systems both to people locally and—insofar as such eco-social systems may conserve and generate biodiversity—to people in all countries.

Measuring the value of a country's biological resources on the basis of their commercial potential, or in terms of the market costs of replacing them, is compatible with the dominant discourse of environmental managerialism.[10] However, this green-developmentalist approach privileges those aspects of nature that can be removed from their local contexts, transformed by investment, and sold. The approach fosters a view of ecosystems as warehouses of potential commodities to meet the demands of foreign consumers rather than as the bases of local and national life, as the sources of material necessities and meanings, and as the biophysical contexts of cultures (McAfee 1999b). In this way, green developmentalism divorces the problems of biotechnology and genetic-resource management from the development needs of gene-rich but hard-currency-poor countries.

The globalized, market-based management of biodiversity requires clear property rights to natural resources, and the CBD secretariat has devoted what might seem, in a conservation treaty, inordinate attention to intellectual property. Conference decisions and secretariat documents display an almost schizophrenic ambivalence. The predominant assumptions in these documents support Northern intellectual-property models and their international extension, but references to IPRs are counterbalanced in nearly every statement by references to "alternative systems" or to the "concerns of indigenous and local peoples" about the impacts of IPRs.

This controversy has been kept alive by the active influence in the CBD and related international forums of social movements that oppose the privatization of genes and associated knowledge. On the basis of ethical, equity, and ecological concerns, the NGOs and indigenous peoples' and farmers' organizations that constitute this transnational movement have denounced the patenting and commoditization of life (e.g., "The Thammasat Resolution" 1998). With the support of Sweden and a number of Southern states, these organizations have energetically resisted Northern proposals that the CBD recognize the WTO as the appropriate body for settling international disputes over property rights to organisms and knowledge about nature. In light of fears among many Southern delegations of losing sovereignty to multilateral trade bodies; growing doubts about the benefits of industrial agriculture and the safety of genetic engineering; and questions about the fairness of intellectual-property regimes, these NGOs have found a growing audience among developing-country delegations.

CONTINUING BATTLES OVER BIOTECHNOLOGY AND "PROPERTY IN LIFE"

What became known as the Cartagena Protocol on Biosafety of the CBD was finally negotiated, after significant concessions from the United States, in January 2000. Because the protocol stipulates that countries may decline to accept exports of genetically engineered "living modified organisms" (LMOs), U.S.-based agribusiness interests have seen it as a threat to their export markets.[11] Nevertheless, a united front of European and developing-country delegations forced significant concessions from the United States delegation. The United States-led Miami Group of six grain-exporting states gave up its opposition to protocol rules for the labeling of exports of genetically altered organisms meant for release into the environment, and dropped its proposed language that would have asserted the primacy of the WTO over the CBD. Included over U.S. objections was a provision allowing governments to take account of the socioeconomic impacts of transgenics in deciding whether to permit imports of particular organisms. This principle may yet collide with WTO rules against "unfair" barriers to trade, rules in which criteria of economic efficiency are preeminent.

Although thirty-eight states had ratified the protocol as of November 2002, it will not become international law until 50 governments also ratify it. Substantial disagreements remain over whether states or enterprises will be held liable for environmental or health damages resulting from the use of their genetically engineered products; over specific requirements for labeling, transport, and "contained use" of genetically engineered organisms; and over the interpretation of the precautionary "principle" or precautionary "approach"—both terms appear in the protocol—which contrasts with the guidelines that frame U.S. biotechnology regulatory policy (see Buttel, this volume).[12]

In June 1999, a coalition of developing-country CBD members asked the CBD's scientific advisory body to call for a worldwide moratorium on the field testing and commercialization of "terminator technologies." These genetic engineering methods are being developed by the U.S. Department of Agriculture and commercial biotechnology firms to produce crops with seeds that will not germinate. By hardwiring property rights into plant genomes, these technologies would enable companies to control their privately-held crop genetic resources in cases and places where their IPR claims are not recognized. The advent of terminator technology, which confers no agronomic value to plants, has added to widespread skepticism about industry claims that transgenic crops are designed to benefit the hungry and increase the productivity of poor farmers in the developing world (see, for instance, Horst and Fraley 1998; Borlaug 2000).[13] Although the economic purpose of the technology—enlarging seed markets by preventing farmers from saving seed—is perfectly in keeping with the letter and spirit of the WTO, it is arguably at odds with the CBD's commitments to conserving crop biodiversity and the relevant practices of local communities.

In regional forums such as the European Union Parliament and the Organization of African Unity, governments, environmental ministries, and

NGOs have called for recognition of the CBD's precedence over the WTO in matters pertaining to biodiversity. The negotiation of the International Undertaking on Plant Genetic Resources for Food and Agriculture was deadlocked for seven years over debates about IPRs, genetic-resource benefit sharing, and biopiracy. The treaty that finally emerged from this process in November 2001 reflects an uneasy compromise that has not yet resolved issues of access to an valuation of crop genetic resources.[14] Disputes about private property in genetic information and in biotechnology tools have also embroiled the Consultative Group on International Agricultural Research (CGIAR), which is the world's largest multilateral network of seed banks and crop-research centers, the World Intellectual Property Organization, and even the World Bank.

In August 2001, the UN Sub-Commission for the Promotion and Protection of Human Rights passed a stinging resolution against the WTO TRIPS Agreement, noting conflicts between TRIPS and "economic, social and cultural rights" in relation to the need for technology transfer and

> the consequences for the enjoyment of the right to food of plant variety rights and the patenting of genetically modified organisms, "bio-piracy" and the reduction of communities' (especially indigenous communities') control over their own genetic and natural resources and cultural values, and restrictions on access to patented pharmaceuticals and the implications for the enjoyment of the right to health. (United Nations Sub-Commission 2001)

The report on which the resolution was based, which described the WTO as a "nightmare" for poor countries, prompted an official complaint by top WTO officials (Oloka-Onyango and Udagama 2000; "WTO Protests" 2000).

The repercussions of these disputes echo in the WTO. A United States-backed proposal to establish a WTO body on biotechnology, seen by critics as an attempt to outflank the Cartagena Protocol on Biosafety, was rejected by Europe and by developing countries at the failed 1999 WTO ministerial session in Seattle (World Trade Organization 1999c; Boadle 1999). Developing countries continue to call for reform of the TRIPS requirement that all countries enforce patents on microorganisms and property rights to animals and plants (Khor 1999a, 1999b). The African Group wants to remove references to plants and all life forms from TRIPS, whereas India wants language inserted that would require disclosure of the source of genetic material on patent applications (International Centre 2000; World Trade Organization 1999b). The Philippines Department of Agriculture has recommended that governments "get life forms (plants and animals) and biodiversity (and indigenous knowledge) out of the jurisdiction of WTO" (Republic of the Philippines 1999). India, Brazil, and the African negotiating bloc, among others, have asked that the WTO's Council for TRIPS take into account biodiversity, traditional knowledge, benefit sharing, farmers' rights to save and share seeds, socioeconomic welfare, and the ethics of patenting of life forms (Singh 1999; International Centre 1999). The majority of council delegations have asked the council to "harmonize" TRIPS with the CBD. The U.S. delegation adamantly opposes this and objects to granting the CBD secretariat observer status in the council, insisting that the only issue to be discussed is the progress of TRIPS implementation (International Centre 2000; South-Center 2000; Third World Network 2001).

Even if the majority is able to block or slow TRIPS implementation at the international level, the United States may achieve its goal of standardized IPRs by pressuring reluctant countries to include IPR promises in bilateral trade pacts or by threatening to reduce aid to countries that do not comply. Regional trade accords, including the North American Free Trade Agreement and the U.S.-proposed Free Trade Area of the Americas, include requirements that signatories maintain IPR regimes compatible with those of the United States. Bilateral trade deals, such as the recent agreement between the United States and the government of Vietnam, contain provisions requiring the new U.S. trade partner to join the UPOV (International Union for the Protection of New Varieties of Plants) convention, the international IPR agreement which the United States regards as the acceptable regime for plant-variety protection ("Agreement" 2000).

Nevertheless, enforcement of IPRs at the local level may be difficult in the face of growing defiance by social movements. Even where governments feel forced to comply with globalized IPR rules, many citizens are refusing to do so (see, e.g., Knight 1999). In India and Bangladesh, Thailand and the Philippines, and many Latin American countries, organizations of farmers have linked their demands for land tenure and support of domestic agriculture and rural livelihoods to their opposition to crop-variety IPRs, life patenting, and food-crop biopiracy. International farmers' organizations such as Via Campesina and NGOs such as Genetic Resources Action International, the Malaysia-based Third World Network, and the United States-based Institute for Agriculture and Trade Policy stress the connections between food security (of people), food sovereignty (of nations), and preservation of agro-biodiversity and diversity-based farming systems.

Thus, a high-stakes battle continues over whether food, farming, and biotechnology will be understood and governed as a problem of corporate technoscience, economic efficiency, and universal legal standards, or whether the broader issues of who really benefits and who loses from genetic engineering of crops, privatization of research, and world-scale consolidation of agro-economic power will be addressed by emerging institutions of global governance. In the CBD and in the WTO, these international battles have brought to the surface deep discontent with persistent and widening inequalities in the postcolonial world order.

NOTES

Research for this chapter was supported by the Social Science Research Council and the MacArthur Foundation Program on International Peace and Security and by a University of California President's Postdoctoral Fellowship. I am especially grateful to Margaret Fitzsimmons, David Goodman, Julie Guthman, Gillian Hart, Volker Heins, Elizabeth Oglesby, Scott Prudham, Rachel Schurman, and Michael Watts for their insightful comments on this work.

1. A natural substance or genetic construct may be patented in the United States once it has been isolated and characterized in formal scientific terms and a feasible useful application has been proposed for it.

2. The South is far from homogenous, of course. Splits between grain-exporting and food-import-dependent states of the South, and between those with biotechnology capacity and those without, are becoming more significant in the disputes I describe.

3. Philomenon Yang, statement to the Intersessional Meeting of the UN Convention on Biodiversity (CBD), Montreal, July 1999.

4. Under the 1991 version of the Union for the Protection of Plant Varieties (UPOV), which the United States sees as the model that countries should follow to comply with TRIPS, products of informal innovation are not protected by IPRs, because they are generally not genetically uniform enough to be reproduced consistently.

5. In theory, all member states have an equal voice at Conferences of the Parties (COPs). However, Northern nations—including the nonmember United States—generally have more representatives, credentialed experts, and communication resources, as well as power over CBD financing and foreign aid. Votes are rarely taken, and decisions often reflect behind-the-scenes pressure for "consensus."

6. The other is the Framework Convention on Climate Change, meant to address global warming.

7. Biotechnology industry backers later won revision of the IU in favor of recognition of private plant-breeders' rights (PBR) (Flitner 1998). Southern states countered by insisting on farmers' rights to save and replant seeds (Mooney 1998). The United States has pressed ever since for a more restrictive interpretation of the farmers' rights language and for recognition of private rights to patent crop varieties from any source, as long as they have been modified by the patent holder.

8. This provision provides a toehold for arguments against the extension of IPRs to food crop varieties and microorganisms, on the grounds that such IPRs can inhibit farmers' access to and sustainable use of biological diversity, that they may block the equitable sharing of diversity's benefits, and that property rights to living things are contrary to the "traditional practices . . . relevant to biodiversity" that CBD parties are pledged to protect.

9. Thomas Lovejoy, address to the Conference on Environmentally and Socially Sustainable Development, special session titled Biotechnology and Biosafety, orga-

nized by Ismail Serageldin, then World Bank Vice President for Environment, Washington, D.C., October 1997.

10. In the World Bank's version of this discourse, the world comprises four forms of capital—produced, natural, human, and social—which can be quantified and thus made commensurable and tradable so that the global distribution of goods and costs can be optimized (Serageldin 1996).

11. Should a country such as Brazil, the United States' biggest international competitor in soy, decide to continue restricting the planting of genetically altered soy, it could retain an advantage in markets in Europe and Japan, where there is great demand for LMO-free soy products. U.S. agribusiness firms have been reluctant to take on the costs of segregating genetically engineered from non-engineered crops and would prefer not to compete with producers of GMO-free foods. Their lack of preparedness for segregation was dramatized by the StarLink corn debacle.

12. The U.S. Food and Drug Administration presumes the "substantial equivalence" of genetically engineered and conventional products—that is, there is no difference between them that poses a health risk—whereas the U.S. Environmental Protection Agency permits planting of transgenic crops after short-term field trials if seed companies' reports of those trails do not contain evidence of hazards. A precautionary approach, in contrast, would address the possibility that the effects of transgenic crops on human health or on soil biota, crop-eating insects, and other elements of the agro-ecosystem might not be detectable by current, narrowly focused evaluation methods, or in the short time frame of one harvest cycle. The Cartagena Protocol's use of the precautionary principle is also in tension with the interpretation of "sound science" in the WTO, including its provisions on sanitary and phytosanitary (SPS) regulations and technical barriers to trade (TBT).

13. The USDA clearly indicated that the main purpose of technologies for seed sterility is to protect the investments of U.S. agribusiness firms and expand their markets (Glickman 1999).

14. The treaty provides for a multilateral system of crop-sample exchange and specifies that crop genetic resources may not be patented "in the form received" from provider countries or gene banks. Interpretations differ over how the treaty's IPR provisions will apply to genetically nonhomogenous crop strains and genetic constructs in engineered varieties derived from seed samples provided under the system. Meanwhile, China and some Latin American and African countries are withholding their indigenous food crop varieties from the multilateral system; they hope to sell access to those varieties separately from the treaty or to obtain better benefit-sharing terms.

8

From Molecules to Medicines

The Use of Genetic Resources in Pharmaceutical Research

Astrid J. Scholz

Before genetically altered food products reach the supermarket shelves, before genetically engineered crop varieties are planted in the fields, and before genetic material from one organism is transferred into another, there is a critical first step: a trait that is desirable for one organism must be discovered in another. Biochemical compounds elicit desirable traits, such as disease resistance, by affecting cellular activity. Gene-encoded proteins called enzymes produce these compounds. Discovering and characterizing these compounds is a long and costly procedure, which has historically taken place in the field and garden through slow, selective breeding. Today, the discovery of biochemically active compounds—those that produce desirable traits in living organisms like plants and animals, including humans—relies on technologies that are shared between agricultural and pharmaceutical research divisions in many companies.

In this chapter I focus on the drug discovery process in pharmaceutical research to illustrate how deeply the new biotechnologies constitute the politics and economics of genetic resources. My analysis concerns the interest of the pharmaceutical industry in biological diversity and draws on interviews with researchers, managers, and policymakers and on participant observation at sites of drug research—including industry, university, and government laboratories.[1]

The politics of access to, use of, and benefits from biodiversity in general, and genetic resources in particular, are interwoven with technological changes that have swept the pharmaceutical industry. Current policy discourses are founded on a "utilitarian rationale" for protecting biological diversity. Simply put, this rationale characterizes biologically diverse regions as repositories of raw materials for science and industry, especially for medical science and the pharmaceutical industry. The utilitarian rationale dominates international policy debates about protecting biological diversity and at one time appeared to give developing countries considerable negotiating power.

The search for new drugs from natural sources has made the pharmaceutical industry into a key player in the international environmental-policy arena. As a result, changes within the pharmaceutical industry—technological developments, industry dynamics, and institutional mechanisms for using genetic and other natural resources—have influenced global power distributions in biodiversity negotiations over the past ten years. As the importance of natural products in drug discovery has waxed and waned, so too has the strength of the utilitarian rationale. The weakening of this rationale for biodiversity conservation has also reduced the negotiating leverage of developing countries.

THE UTILITARIAN RATIONALE FOR PRESERVING BIODIVERSITY

Since their commercialization in the early 1980s, the new biotechnologies have been discursively linked to the use and conservation of biological diversity, especially through a utilitarian rationale for biodiversity preservation. The core theme of this rationale is that biologically diverse regions may yield desirable traits and compounds for agricultural and pharmaceutical innovations. As the biologist Tom Eisner argued to the U.S. Congress in 1981:

> In these days of genetic engineering, a species is to be viewed as a depository of genes that are potentially transferable. . . . The extinction of a species, in light of these [technological] advances, takes on a new meaning. It does not simply mean the loss of one volume from the library of nature, but the loss of a loose leaf book whose individual pages, were the species to survive, would remain available in perpetuity for selective transfer and improvement of other species (quoted in Takacs 1996, 209).

This line of reasoning is central to the discourse of biodiversity as a global resource and the problems surrounding its management (Escobar 1998).

Scientists and environmental nongovernmental organizations (NGOs) have played a significant role in propounding this utilitarian rationale. In a brief written to educate President George Bush on biodiversity, in preparation for the 1992 Rio Earth Summit, the biologist Thomas Lovejoy highlighted biodiversity's importance as a "significant new source of wealth drawn from the variety of nature" (Takacs 1996, 208). At around the same time, another biologist coined the term *bioprospecting* to describe the systematic search for novel compounds in nature (Eisner 1989, 1991), and Northern environmental organizations started promoting bioprospecting as a conservation strategy (see, e.g., the widely cited Reid et al. 1993).

Bioprospecting came to underlie the Convention on Biological Diversity

(CBD), which was signed at the Rio conference in 1992 and has now been ratified by some 177 countries. According to Article 1 of this international legal framework, the "objectives of this Convention . . . are the conservation of biological diversity, the sustainable use of its components and the fair and equitable sharing of the benefits arising out of the utilization of genetic resources" (Secretariat 2000). Although communities and social movements in the South at first resisted the suggestion that commercialization of biological diversity would contribute to its conservation (Shiva 1993), the utilitarian argument took hold, at least at the nation-state level (Escobar 1998). Subsequently, the policy debate shifted to how the South, as the holder of genetic resources, could capitalize on its bargaining power without revisiting the past injustices of colonialism and large-scale appropriation of both seed stock and traditional knowledge (Juma 1989; Kloppenburg and Rodriguez 1992; Vellvé 1992).

From its inception, the utilitarian rationale for conserving biodiversity has been tied to the pharmaceutical industry. Claims that genetic modification of crops will provide better foods for more people, with less environmental harm from the use of pesticides and other toxic inputs, have been strongly contested by industry critics (Fowler and Mooney 1990; Lappé and Bailey 1998; Rifkin 1998). However, the parallel claim that advances in biotechnology and genomics will help scientists find cures for cancer, AIDS, and other human diseases is generally less controversial; the discovery of new drugs is widely considered a good thing. This public-health rationale—that biodiversity may yield valuable new drug discoveries—is so well established in environmental politics (Burger 1990; A. C. Keller 2000) that from the earliest preparatory negotiations for the CBD, health experts from public and private sectors have been invited to participate on its technical committees.

The pharmaceutical industry, in addition to being validated by the public-health rationale as a political player in North-South biodiversity debates, has always commanded substantially higher revenues than its agricultural counterpart. At $300 billion, the market for prescription drugs is estimated to be six times that for seeds (ten Kate and Laird 1999, 9). It is therefore not surprising that biotechnology companies since the 1980s have tried to compete or affiliate with the multibillion-dollar pharmaceutical companies.

Early biotech start-up companies, such as Biogen, Genentech, and Chiron, embarked on drug research and became the vanguard for the use of biotechnology, especially recombinant DNA techniques, for drug design. The biotechnological trajectory then taken by the pharmaceutical industry neatly coincided with the rhetorical deployment of genetic resources as the source of new drugs. However, the quest for high mark-up pharmaceuticals has led the industry to adopt research strategies that undermine the reliance upon naturally occurring biological diversity as the source of drugs. This search has also changed the institutional mechanisms (for harnessing

genetic resources) in ways that benefit the industry but not the other entities that protect and use biodiversity. The result has been the erosion of biodiversity's utilitarian value in the drug discovery process—an ironic development from within the very industry that seemed best poised to manifest
this value.

The phrase that forms the title of this essay, "from molecules to medicines,"
is drawn from the promotional material of the National Cancer Institute,
where it serves as shorthand for the ten- to fifteen-year drug design process
during which researchers identify bioactive chemicals, repeatedly test and
modify the chemicals into prototype drugs, and then subject the drugs to
extensive clinical trials. The phrase also captures the current paradigm in
pharmaceutical research: the search for molecules that can be modified for
therapeutic purposes. This paradigm, and the tenuous place of genetic
resources in it, is the outcome of the institutional and intellectual history of
drug discovery.

A Brief History of Drug Discovery

The rise of the modern pharmaceutical industry since the beginning of the
twentieth century has been marked by the cyclical popularity of natural
products for drug discovery,[2] which mirrors the periodic preference given to
one or the other of two predominant approaches to drug research. The first
of these—random, or empirical, screening—originated in biology and the
plant-based traditions of medicine. The isolation, purification, and manufacture of plant-derived medicines was the extension of the study of drugs
such as opium, hemlock, and belladonna, which were well known and systematically studied in ancient Greece. In modern times, H. E. Merck, the
founder of the eponymous company, began manufacturing purified plant
extracts, notably alkaloids, on a large scale in 1827. Other large pharmaceutical companies such as GlaxoSmithKline, Bristol-Myers Squibb, and
Pfizer likewise trace their origins to the traditional apothecary, and natural
products have maintained a strong position in these companies as well.[3]

The other approach, "rational" drug design, grew out of the chemical-
manufacturing roots of the other major strand of the pharmaceutical industry. Initially motivated by wartime shortages of drugs, the Swiss dyestuff manufacturer Sandoz (which became part of Novartis in 1996 and is now
Syngenta) turned to pharmaceutical research. Sandoz also founded one of
the first dedicated industrial research departments in 1917, following a
trend set by the founders of Burroughs, Wellcome and Company (now
GlaxoSmithKline) in the 1880s. The rational approach involves designing
novel molecules that target key components of disease pathways. The evo-

lution of the industry along these two lines—medicinal-biological and chemical-manufacturing—partly explains why some companies have remained "friendlier" toward natural products than others.

During the first half of the century, basic scientific research in industry laboratories and national medical research institutes turned to increasingly sophisticated experiments to study diseases and their biochemical mechanisms. Alexander Fleming's observation of the bacteria-inhibiting activity of penicillin in 1929 led other scientists in the late 1930s to investigate the compounds produced by the soil microbe *Streptomyces* in the hope of finding other antibiotic activity.[4] In what was perhaps the first instance of a systematic screening effort, the antituberculosis agent streptomycin was discovered via a combination of laboratory tests and subsequent methodical screening of great numbers of microorganisms (Albers-Schönberg 1995).

Knowledge about the biochemical functioning of vitamins and steroid hormones also greatly increased during the early 1900s. Scientists isolated and synthesized these compounds to study the metabolic processes of which they were part. Scientists viewed these newly identified compounds as potential templates for drugs that could intervene in metabolic processes. The steroid hormone cortisone eventually became the first therapy for arthritis and inflammatory disease (Albers-Schönberg 1995). Such biochemistry-driven efforts were the beginning of rational drug discovery (Aylward 1995).

The division between the empirical-screening approach and rational drug design persists in pharmaceutical research, and it frames the debate about biological diversity's role in drug discovery. By the middle of the twentieth century, the two approaches coexisted and were increasingly integrated within companies. The growing prowess of chemists in synthesizing compounds *de novo* was thus coupled with the roots of medicinal research in plant therapeutics. With the increasing systematization of screening efforts and the demand for new sources of compounds such as alkaloids,[5] firms turned to natural products to feed their research pipelines. On the basis of the historical success of plant and microbial compounds, they began to undertake massive biological collection efforts.

Natural Products: Lore and Lure

Some of the best-known drugs derived from natural products were discovered in the 1950s and 1960s, and these drugs contributed to a body of anecdotes about the potential of natural products. In the 1950s, researchers at Ciba isolated the alkaloid reserpine, which is used in the treatment of high blood pressure. The plant from which this compound was isolated is a climbing shrub used in India as a sedative. Other often-cited examples are vinblastine and vincristine, developed by Eli Lilly in the 1960s from the Madagascar rosy periwinkle *(Catharanthus roseus),* and effective against

Hodgkin's disease and acute childhood leukemia, respectively. Such discoveries resulted from concerted screening efforts that drew on local ethnobotanical knowledge of medicinal plants (Aylward 1995; Chivian 1997).

Successful development of natural products depends on access to and collection of the biological source materials. Early discovery work was conducted without any contractual agreements with source countries and without any other provisions for sharing benefits arising from commercialization of the resulting drugs. Pharmaceutical firms either collaborated with botanical gardens to get plants for extraction, as they had done since the early twentieth century, or established programs to facilitate foreign collections by their own employees. The story of the immune-suppressant drug cyclosporin A illustrates this apparently widespread practice.[6] A Sandoz employee and his wife collected more than fifty soil samples while on vacation in Norway in 1969. One of those samples eventually yielded a compound (produced by a fungus) that was marketed as a drug in the 1980s (Svarstad and Dhillion 2000a). It is now one of the best-selling drugs in the portfolio of Syngenta (which acquired Sandoz), with annual sales of more than $1 billion. No royalty agreement was arranged, although at the going rate, 2 percent of net sales, Norway would have received an annual payment of $24 million from the use of its soil (Svarstad and Dhillion 2000a).

Such narratives contribute to the lore of natural products—and by extension biological diversity—as repositories of tremendous promise and hidden treasures. However, by the 1970s the industry was looking for novel approaches to drug design that would obviate the lengthy screening processes required to move from raw sample to pharmaceutical product.

Rationality in Sight

With the rise of molecular biology in the 1970s and biotechnology in the 1980s, a host of novel technologies started making their way from university labs into biotech start-ups, and rational drug design made a comeback. The business approach of these biotech companies depended on the notion that with molecular and genetic knowledge of diseases within reach, new drugs could finally be tailored to the biochemical pathways of diseases. Recall that rational drug design is premised on the notion that molecular pathways that lead to diseases can be known and manipulated, to prevent HIV from replicating or cancer cells from growing, for example. The first wave of rational drug design focused on inhibiting specific enzyme targets, as in the case of Roche's HIV protease inhibitor Saquinavir (Bains 1998).

Initially, biotechnology companies set out to compete with the large pharmaceutical companies that dominated the industry. Whereas the approach in the industry at the time was to screen large numbers of compounds, looking for molecules that interacted with specific disease-related molecular targets, the small biotech firms made use of new biochemical technologies to design therapeutic molecules, especially proteins, from scratch.

Companies such as Biogen, Genentech, and Chiron embarked on full-scale drug discovery and development endeavors by focusing on the production of proteins.[7] Each protein has unique functions in the body, for example, as hormones (e.g., insulin), enzymes, or antibodies encoded by specific gene sequences. Genentech makes human growth hormone (hGH)—one of the first biotech drugs marketed—whose sales exceeded $150 million in 1990 (Bains 1998, 204). Another class of therapeutic proteins, the interferons produced by Biogen and a number of other companies, have been approved for the treatment of a variety of cancers and hepatitis C. The protein-production approach ushered in the era of drug discovery based on genetic sequences, coincident with the rapid deciphering of the human genome beginning in the mid-1990s.

The vast majority of biotech companies, however, have not had the success of Genentech, Amgen, and a handful of other companies. The sector is extremely volatile, as reflected in the fact that the average company is less than ten years old (Dibner 1999, 6). Unable to raise the hundreds of millions of dollars needed for development and clinical trials, many biotechnology firms shifted to the provision of proprietary technological platforms for large pharmaceutical companies. Once seen as the key to revolutionizing drug discovery, these platforms have become the end products themselves, and they account for the major share of revenues. For example, automated techniques like polymerase chain reaction (PCR) allow fast and easy production of customized sequences of DNA (Bains 1998), and technologies for computer-based molecular design and analysis enable the modeling and manipulation of therapeutic compounds. Firms that specialized in automating and accelerating the analytical stages of drug discovery expanded the technological frontier of screening and investigation. Today, 72 percent of the roughly $320 million biotech market is comprised of diagnostics, supplies, and services (Biotechnology Industry Organization 2000).

Pharmaceutical companies that had moved away from rational drug design as a sole strategy for drug design (interviews by author, 1999 and 2000) quickly realized the advantage of having a highly competitive and innovative biotechnology sector to develop new technologies that could conveniently be bought or licensed without costly in-house research and development (R&D) efforts.[8] The doubling of pharmaceutical R&D expenditures in the United States from 1986 to 1990 reflects the concomitant capital investments in drug discovery and auxiliary technologies pioneered by biotech firms (PhRMA 2002).

The resulting "biomolecular bandwagon" consisted of redefining diseases in terms of their molecular processes and embracing rational drug design, utilizing technology packages produced in the biotechnology sector

(Fujimura 1997). Private industry was not alone in committing large resources to this approach. The National Institutes of Health (NIH) followed suit, and in the 1980s, the NCI temporarily discontinued its program of plant collection and screening.

Screening Redux

Despite large capital investments, rational drug design did not deliver on its promise to make trial-and-error screening obsolete, as its proponents had claimed (Waldrop 1990; "Plans" 1992). Despite rapidly advancing biomolecular knowledge, many disease mechanisms remain elusive. In the 1990s, the pharmaceutical industry returned to random screening, incorporating the current biotechnologies. Rational drug design principles were not discarded but were integrated into the drug design process at a later stage, following the high-throughput screening of large compound libraries. This screening step is designed to find compounds that will interact with a specific molecular target—for example, inhibit an enzyme implicated in a biochemical pathway of a disease. Instead of trying to create a single therapeutic molecule from scratch, companies now screen hundreds of thousands of synthetic and natural compounds against biochemical targets and, in a second step, chemically (rationally) modify any active compounds.

However, a great deal of uncertainty remains in the search for new drugs because the progression of many diseases, from inception to symptoms to pathology, is still poorly understood. The medical community hypothesizes a variety of mechanisms for each disease and for particular biochemical and cellular pathways. For most diseases, there is as yet no consensus as to which models and which mechanisms are the correct ones.

The many possible targets for each proposed disease mechanism exacerbate this uncertainty. For example, in cancer treatment, attention has recently shifted to inhibiting the growth of new blood vessels that supply the tumor mass. Scientists have focused their efforts on identifying biochemical targets that could be intercepted to prevent the formation of tumor blood vessels. Chemical experiments, or assays, detect changes in the target in response to active compounds. These assays must be developed and adapted for high-throughput screens, in which thousands of different compounds are tested simultaneously. New biochemical targets emerge almost daily in the scientific literature, and companies dedicate entire departments to developing assays based on these new targets. However, the rate at which new targets can be found and new assays developed far outpaces the speed with which companies can interpret the results (PhRMA 2002; Drews 2000).

The differences between natural and synthetic medicinal compounds can be illustrated with reference to an idealized "molecular space" (figure 2), a metaphor widely used in industry descriptions of the search for thera-

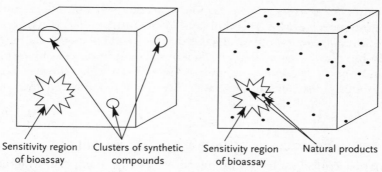

Figure 2. Drug discovery in molecular space. Adapted from Artuso 1997.

peutics. The dimensions of molecular space represent characteristics, such as size, atomic composition, and valence, that give any compound its therapeutic properties.[9] For any target, active compounds that match the target's molecular characteristics occupy only a small region of this molecular space. For example, many molecules within the molecular space may have the appropriate size or shape yet may not be able to interact with the disease-related target.

It therefore makes sense to screen a diverse collection of compounds, which, if they fall within the sensitivity region defined by a particular assay, will show up as active "hits" in a screen. Natural products are one source of such compounds, but they compete with massive "libraries," or collections, of synthetic compounds. Combinatorial chemistry ("combichem") libraries contain hundreds of thousands of compounds that may be screened. These compounds generally incorporate some of the desirable molecular properties needed for activity. The logic of combinatorial chemistry is aptly summarized in the words of one senior scientist I interviewed: "we can create all the diversity we need in the lab" (interview by author, 1999). The many hundreds of thousands of compounds in a typical combinatorial library are synthesized in batch processes and tend to be variations on a theme. Because they share various desired molecular properties, the combichem library molecules are tightly clustered in molecular space.

If the clusters of synthetic compounds in the combinatorial library are too far away from the assay's sensitivity region, even the largest compound library will not yield a hit. Because of this limitation, many researchers and managers in the industry suggest that combinatorial chemistry has failed to deliver on its promise to streamline the discovery process. Many firms therefore screen natural-product libraries, alongside combichem libraries, in their assays. Because natural molecules are more complex, they are more widely distributed in molecular space and thus have a higher chance of falling within an assay's sensitivity region. The complexity of natural molecules cannot be generated by combinatorial chemistry methods. The comparative advantage of natural products is that "you can't do better chemistry than Mother Nature," as a number of scientists put it (interviews by author, 1999 and 2000). Screening natural products from widely diverse taxonomic groups yields a higher molecular diversity of potentially active compounds.

TAXOL AND THE NICHE FOR NATURAL PRODUCTS

The pharmaceutical industry's predilections for "screening" and rational approaches resulted in cycles that have alternately favored and dismissed natural products. Taxol, approved in 1992 for the treatment of ovarian cancer, was the first new drug from a natural product to be released since the 1960s. Gordon Cragg, the head of NCI's natural-products branch, credits biotechnology with the belated discovery of Taxol.[10] The current paradigm of drug discovery—high-throughput screening followed by rational modifications of active compounds—has had a defining effect on the political economy of genetic resources. However, this paradigm clashes with the expectations generated by the discovery of Taxol.

After its isolation in 1969 from the bark of the Pacific yew tree (*Taxus brevifolia*), the active compound, paclitaxel, had been shelved because it showed insignificant activity in the assays then current. After instituting new screening processes in the early 1980s, researchers systematically went through the NCI's entire collection of compounds, including those that had previously failed. Paclitaxel now showed considerable activity in the modern, molecular screens and was promoted to development. The first phase of clinical trials proceeded slowly, owing to difficulties with the considerable toxicity of paclitaxel caused by its poor solubility in water. The compound eventually proceeded to the next stage in 1987, generating intense interest throughout the drug industry when it demonstrated significant efficacy in patients with terminal ovarian cancer.

As the demand for the trial drug intensified, supply difficulties arose—a problem characteristic of natural products. The initial hit may come from a single, small sample; chemical follow-up work and clinical trials require substantially larger amounts. Because it takes thirty pounds of bark to generate one gram of paclitaxel, and two grams of paclitaxel to treat one patient, Taxol's use for ovarian cancer stood to destroy thirty-six thousand trees a year (Cragg et al. 1999), a number projected to increase because paclitaxel also showed activity against late-stage breast cancer and other forms of advanced malignancies. Bristol-Myers Squibb (BMS), the company developing the drug under license from the NCI, spent a number of years negotiating and carrying out collections on public lands, in collaboration with the U.S. Forest Service (USFS) and Bureau of Land Management (BLM). BMS financed research that eventually yielded more sustainable sources of paclitaxel (derived from the needles, as opposed to the bark, of yew trees), resolving the supply issue and preventing further public and media scrutiny.

When Taxol was approved for treatment of ovarian cancer in 1992 and breast cancer in 1994, it brought natural products back into the limelight of drug design, concurrent with the signing of the CBD in 1992. Taxol quickly became part of the natural-products lore that invoked the "healing" capacity of forests (Balick and Mendelsohn 1992; Mendelsohn and Balick 1995). This capacity underscored the utilitarian rationale for preserving biological diversity and was seized as a bargaining chip by developing countries, which tried to leverage their biological wealth in the new round of global negotiations ushered in by the Rio Earth Summit (Escobar 1998; see also McAfee, this volume).

Taxol illustrates two characteristics of natural products that have become significant in the discourse about genetic resources. The first is that the reliable resupply of biological source material for natural products can be challenging because it threatens the very organisms that yielded the drug in the first place. Even within the friendly regulatory climate of the United States and in the context of broad public support for the "war on cancer," the development of Taxol was slowed by congressional inquiries into resupply solutions proposed by BMS, the USFS, and the BLM. This supply issue serves as a disincentive to pharmaceutical companies, and these manufacturers experience dealings with suppliers outside the United States as even more difficult (interviews by author, 2000).

A second important characteristic of natural products is that they tend to be very potent, containing tannins and sugars that may wreak havoc with sensitive high-throughput assays. Their potency is often accompanied by considerable toxicity: Taxol, for example, is too dangerous for all but terminally ill cancer patients. Drug development efforts therefore focus on modifying the molecular structure and chemical properties of such products so that they pose less risk not only to the screening process but also to patients.

THE ECONOMIC SPACE FOR NATURAL PRODUCTS SINCE 1992

By the 1990s, technological, political, and economic forces coincided to shape the biodiversity discourse. Bolstered by the success of Taxol, cyclosporin, and other drugs derived from natural products, the use of biological entities and their genetic codes for drug design was proposed as a win-win strategy that would result in environmental conservation, new medicines, and economic opportunities for source countries and the pharmaceutical industry (Reid et al. 1993; ten Kate 1995). The players in the biodiversity discourse endorsed bioprospecting for a number of reasons: environmental groups such as the World Resources Institute saw it as an avenue to the large-scale protection of biodiversity; developing countries saw it as a mechanism for capitalizing on "sustainable development" and for mitigating the effects of past economic exploitation; and the pharmaceutical industry saw it as a supply mechanism to sustain the rediscovered technological and economic potential of natural products.

The Pharmaceutical Industry as a Political Player

Given the renewed interest in natural products as a source of diverse compounds for drug discovery, it is not surprising that the chemical and resupply challenges associated with natural products featured prominently in the way the industry framed the value of genetic resources and the conditions for their acquisition and use. Realizing that the free-collection days of the past were over, two early models of collaboration helped define the political economy of natural products use in the 1990s (see, e.g., Mugabe et al. 1997; ten Kate and Laird 1999). The first was the agreement between Merck & Co. and the Instituto Nacional de Biodiversidad (INBio) in Costa Rica, and the second was a collaboration between Eli Lilly and Co. and the biotechnology company Shaman Pharmaceuticals.

The 1991 agreement between Merck and INBio is a prime example of an arrangement between a transnational pharmaceutical company and a developing country. The Merck-INBio agreement is significant for the particular institutional form it takes: an agreement between a large, transnational, for-profit corporation and a private, national, nonprofit agency. INBio is a private, nonprofit organization founded in 1989 to serve as the national coordinating center for all bioprospecting agreements with Costa Rica. In addition, INBio conducts national biodiversity inventories, trains local people as research aides ("parataxonomists"), and runs educational programs for schoolchildren (Gamez 1993; Imfeld 1994; Sittenfeld, Lovejoy, and Cohen 1997). The agreement with INBio gave Merck two years of exclusive access to plant, insect, and environmental samples collected by INBio, in exchange for a $1 million up-front payment and royalties on any commercial products resulting from samples.

The direction taken by Eli Lilly reflects a second approach to natural products that emerged in the 1990s. Despite its blockbuster success with vinblastine and vincristine, Lilly had terminated its entire plant-screening program in the 1980s and retooled its drug pipeline using rational drug design. In 1992, Lilly signed a $4 million collaborative agreement with Shaman Pharmaceuticals, a California biotechnology company specializing in natural products (Aylward 1995). Shaman Pharmaceuticals had initiated its ethnomedically guided drug discovery effort in 1990, embarking on a series of community projects in exchange for extensive consultations with traditional healers on medicinal plants commonly used to treat diseases (King, Carlson, and Moran 1996). Although Shaman Pharmaceuticals commanded considerable media attention, it ultimately failed to bring a drug to market and eventually folded. However, Lilly developed potential antifungal agents from the compounds discovered by Shaman.

Both of these approaches allow large pharmaceutical companies to avoid some of the problems associated with natural products by contracting, as needed, chemical and technological expertise that they would formerly have kept in-house. Such collaborations, aided by source country "one-stop" arrangements such as the Merck-INBio relationship, have become the preferred modus operandi for the pharmaceutical industry. The difficulties with natural-products chemistry and with raw-material resupply, which underlie this restructuring of the pharmaceutical industry, are also themes around which the industry articulates its position in the biodiversity discourse. The industry invokes the former to argue that the raw materials for natural products—plants and soil samples, for example—are a cumbersome and crude component of the drug pipeline, thus warranting only small benefit payments to suppliers. Pharmaceutical companies invoke the latter to call for national one-stop regulatory agencies that make access to genetic resources easy and convenient for them.

"Just One More Taxol!"

Martin Kenney argues that biotechnology has led to the creation of a new "economic space," in which public science generates possibilities for private appropriation (Kenney 1998). Not only are natural products located as commodities in this new economic space, but their use also frames particular institutional outcomes and broader political debates. Emerging economic and political institutions in the biodiversity arena are driven by the value to the pharmaceutical industry of natural products and their associated genetic resources, value that is constrained by technological commitments geared toward reducing the time required for discovery and development.

Research expenses in the pharmaceutical industry have mushroomed since the turn of the twentieth century, when basic research first became part of the core business activity of drug manufacturers. The largest companies invest between 10 and 20 percent of their revenues in research and development each year—more than $30 billion dollars in the United States alone in 2001 (PhRMA 2002, 12).[11] Companies aim to bring five to seven novel chemical entities to the market every year; even mid-sized firms (five thousand employees or fewer) aim to have at least one "blockbuster" drug each year. For each drug passing through the long and expensive development phase, a set of "leads" is generated in a one- to three-year discovery-phase of screening and analysis that costs $20-50 million.[12] During this time, compound libraries from both combinatorial chemistry and natural

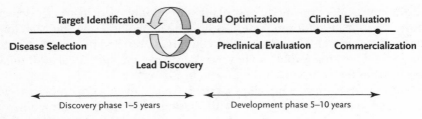

Figure 3: The drug pipeline.

sources are screened; and the resulting active compounds are isolated, dereplicated,[13] and modified for safety, efficacy, and bioavailability (the ease with which they are absorbed and metabolized by the body).

Figure 3 situates this iterative process in the overall drug pipeline, which typically takes over a decade and costs on the order of $500 million per drug (Agnew 2000). Drug discovery and development are organizationally and operationally distinct, since the latter has to be geared to Food and Drug Administration (FDA) specifications and requirements. All data generated in toxicological, metabolic, and animal studies and eventually in human clinical trials are subject to FDA review.

Because the development phase is an order of magnitude more expensive than the discovery phase, firms have a strong incentive to eliminate potential failures as early as possible. As a result, internal standards for a "good" lead are so strict, many senior scientists complain, that hardly any compounds make it through the process (interviews by author, 2000). Companies are constantly revising their criteria, strategies, and management to optimize the discovery process. A number of large pharmaceutical companies are undergoing such dramatic internal reorganizations that their scientists and managers joke about not understanding the new acronyms denoting stages in the drug pipeline.

There are, however, certain commonalities in the structure and organization of research conducted at different companies. At a fairly high level of management, disease areas are chosen for investigation. Cancer and AIDS are priorities in most pharmaceutical companies; interest in other diseases, such as cardiovascular, infectious, or central nervous system conditions, is largely determined by each company's historical strengths and emphases. For each disease area, a "target team" is convened to identify particular molecular or genetic targets, representing a commitment to one or a few of the many possible disease mechanism models. Depending on the disease area, targets are relatively few and well defined.

Once targets are identified, assays are developed either in-house or through contracts with biotech companies specializing in this rapidly expanding market niche. The total number of targets under investigation, and the biochemical assays based on these targets, are projected to increase six- to twenty-fold in the next few years, from the current total of less than 500 (for all diseases) to 3,000-10,000 (Drews 2000, 1962). This increase is due to innovations afforded by the sequencing of the human genome. As more human genes are identified, the biochemical products for which they code may be targeted.

Large pharmaceutical companies increasingly have difficulty keeping up with this biotechnological treadmill, which is fueled by the smaller, less risk-averse biotech companies. Therefore, the pharmaceutical firms either dedicate specialized departments to the development of new targets and assays, or they rely on outside contractors. Companies have substantial screening capacity—they often run a half dozen high-throughput screening suites in parallel—but there is a danger of screening the wrong kind of compound for the assay in question. With targets and assays in place, the target team hands over the process to a specialized project team that decides what kinds of compounds to screen.[14]

Trial runs help narrow the choice from the millions of compounds that are often available in commercial or in-house libraries to the hundreds of thousands that can be screened in a matter of days or weeks. By contrast, in the 1970s companies screened hundreds of compounds per year at the benchtop. According to the executive director for lead discovery at Bristol-Myers Squib, scientists at BMS a decade ago screened 10,000 to 30,000 compounds yearly. Now BMS uses ultra-high-throughput screening to handle 100,000 compounds per week and will soon be able to do 250,000 samples in a single day (interview by author, 2000). These increases in screening speed and throughput capacity work against natural products because their complex chemistry interferes with sensitive assays and requires more follow-up work, which in turn conflicts with the tight schedule.

Although the pharmaceutical industry realizes the logical case for natural products and needs ever more compounds to feed the screens, the practical configuration of the drug discovery process is biased against natural products. To compete with combinatorial chemistry libraries internally, natural-products proponents have to "constantly justify [their] existence," as one group leader in a large pharmaceutical company put it (interviews by author, 1999). The drug discovery process is the battleground where proponents of natural products lock horns with proponents of chemical libraries. Usually both classes of compounds are screened; but natural-products chemists and ecologists tend to identify strongly with "nature's chemistry," whereas their synthetic chemist and molecular biologist colleagues prefer combinatorial compounds.

Scientists make the case for natural products in the early meetings of a project team, when it is choosing the compound libraries that will enter the screening process. Natural-products advocates draw on extensive ethnobotanical and ethnomedical databases to establish why a particular drug project would benefit from the screening of natural products. For example, the fact that certain classes of plants are known for their steroidlike compounds makes them candidates for a steroidal project. Although the value of these compounds may be obvious to chemical ecologists, synthetic chemists may not be aware that these plants have the desired therapeutic potential.

In other stages of the process, scientists seek to get around the molecular complexity of natural products by teasing out active compounds from complex biochemical mixtures. Once there is a natural-product lead, however, it tends to generate whole classes of new active compounds. Taxol and another anticancer drug, bryostatin, are cases in point. Not surprisingly, the feeling among proponents of natural products—both within and outside pharmaceutical companies—is that "all we need is one more Taxol!" to turn the tide and put natural products back on the R&D map for large pharmaceutical companies.[15] The dominant sentiment of the industry, however, is that if natural products are going to stay in pharmaceutical R&D, they must fit readily and inexpensively into the screening process, just as the combichem libraries do.

THE NEW OLD POLITICS OF BIOPROSPECTING

Over the past ten years, as the pharmaceutical industry's investments, technological commitments, and modes of drug discovery have changed, so has the power of the various players in the 1992 Convention on Biological Diversity (CBD). The CBD provides the international legal framework for achieving the conjoined objectives of conservation, sustainable development, and commercial gains. The details of its implementation were left to ongoing negotiations among the contracting parties. Over the course of the 1990s, what had opened as a window of opportunity, allowing the South to leverage its power as the source of much of the world's biological diversity, quickly closed as the economic space for natural products was defined by the pharmaceutical industry.

The CBD Process

At the beginning of the CBD negotiating process, countries of the South embraced their advantage as sources of biological diversity and sought to leverage that advantage for the transfer of financial and technical resources and to establish national sovereignty over resources (Escobar 1998). Because biochemical products from natural sources—for example, those with pharmaceutical potential—are encoded by specific gene sequences, an early negotiating point in the CBD was how to extend the principle of sovereignty to genetic resources. This sovereignty is now enshrined in Article 15 of the CBD (Mugabe et al. 1997). The same article requires contracting parties to establish national regulatory and legal systems for access to genetic resources. From the inception of the CBD, there was considerable urgency to create institutions, particularly in source countries, to handle applications, carry out negotiations, and issue necessary permits (Bugge and Tvedt 2000).

On the basis of the natural-products lore, bolstered by successes such as Taxol, the pharmaceutical potential of biodiversity conferred substantially more bargaining power on Southern countries than did the agricultural potential of biodiversity (Dutfield 2000). Some countries, such as the Philippines, tried to leverage this power by temporarily suspending trade in genetic resources or by exacting steep fees for samples. For the most part, however, countries began a rapid process of instituting national biodiversity policies based on the model of the INBio-Merck arrangement (World Resources Institute 1995).

This model has been widely disseminated, for example, in official "information papers" filed with the CBD secretariat and distributed to all delegates, or in expert testimonies at intersession meetings of technical working groups. These materials propagate the pharmaceutical companies' stance that access to genetic resources must be easy and predictable to make bioprospecting worth their investment. Northern NGOs help enact this discourse in national institution-building, as they pursue their particular conservation agendas and draw on their relationships with countries in the South to implement these agendas (Brand 2000).

The CBD process also forces contracting parties to resolve domestic institutional issues, notably between the government and the local communities where biological resources have grown and been maintained for a long time. This mandate is encapsulated in Article 8(j), which requires countries to respect, preserve, and compensate local and indigenous communities for their contributions to the conservation and sustainable use of biological diversity (Bugge and Tvedt 2000). It is largely around this article that Southern NGOs and social movements articulate an alternative to the utilitarian biodiversity discourse, an alternative that centers on themes of territory, cultural autonomy, and alternative epistemologies of nature (Escobar 1998).[16]

This institutional flux within countries has two significant effects. First, local communities themselves are actively engaged in building institutions to deal with biodiversity issues—creating national, regional, and international governing bodies and political alliances. An example from Peru illustrates the new governance structures. In the early 1990s, during access negotiations for an NIH project that involved U.S. academic scientists and the pharmaceutical branch of Monsanto (Monsanto-Searle, now Pharmacía), Aguaruna communities in Peru retained a lawyer to represent their interests vis-à-vis both the national government and outside interests in the contract negotiations and also took action to resolve a host of local governance issues (Tobin 1997b; Argumedo, personal communication, 2000). Subsequently, the Aguaruna began to collaborate with other indigenous groups regionally and internationally, and to represent their interests at CBD negotiations, both as national delegates and as part of the NGOs participating in these meetings.

The biodiversity discourse and its associated political negotiations have thus brought greater prominence and visibility to local communities, which—in the second effect of these institutional developments—translates into the potential for greater power, at least nationally. In Peru, to continue the example, indigenous communities are being consulted extensively in the drafting of national biodiversity legislation, in a new system of participatory decision-making processes that did not previously exist (interviews by author, 2000).

As the CBD process continues, institutional issues are accompanied by struggles over who sits at the inter- and intranational negotiating tables. Although the Merck-INBio agreement, for example, created a new national organization as well as a blueprint for others to follow, the agreement may have displaced alternative mechanisms for trading biological resources. At least one study suggests that INBio effectively has a monopoly on biodiversity negotiations in Costa Rica, and its funding of the system of national conservation areas undermines the areas' historical autonomy to manage resources as they see fit (Simoncelli 2000). According to one observer, the Merck-INBio deal supplanted a decentralized, informal network of botanical field assistants, taxonomists, and merchants dealing in biological specimens (Charles Weiss, personal communication, 1997).

These processes are shaped by the political-economic landscape of genetic resources and by the CBD framework that set them in motion. Even more influential, however, is the pharmaceutical industry's success in mobilizing the discourse of biodiversity as having only marginal value to utilitarian objectives.

Wolves in (Cloned) Sheep's Clothing

The pharmaceutical industry has become a major player in the biodiversity arena for what are now obvious reasons. The industry relies on biological diversity for drug discovery, both directly and as part of biotechnological methods. However, these biotechnological approaches entail commitments that limit the success and value of natural products. Large firms increasingly rely on small biotech companies to provide technology platforms and processes for modifying natural products so that they fit into the existing capital infrastructure. Small firms such as Shaman use natural products as part of the R&D services around which they have reinvented their biotech business models. Furthermore, the pharmaceutical industry relies on private and academic collaborators to negotiate and guarantee the supply and resupply of biological samples.

The technological and scientific developments of the past ten years are manifested in a discourse propagated by the pharmaceutical industry and its advocates at the CBD negotiations—typically delegations from Northern countries with strong life sciences industries. In this discourse, biological diversity is of only marginal value to drug discovery. It is just one source of inputs for a complex and expensive production process. Natural products must be inexpensive and readily available, or they will not be chosen over alternatives such as combinatorial chemical libraries. Furthermore, drug discovery will continue to be profitable only if the industry can recoup its substantial R&D costs through patent-protected revenues. The industry is willing to share these revenues via "best practice" policies that have emerged over the past ten years, including up-front payments to local communities, conservation projects and technology, milestone payments, and royalties ranging from 1 to 3 percent of the net sales from resulting commercial products (ten Kate and Laird 1999). Not coincidentally, these best practices for handling genetic resources mirror the technology-licensing agreements used in the pharmaceutical industry.

I do not mean to suggest that there is some sort of sinister conspiracy. Rather, the discourse about the marginal value of biodiversity for drug discovery is enacted by a variety of players in mutually reinforcing ways. The Merck-INBio deal set a precedent for bilateral agreements between private parties. Because all the existing agreements are confidential, countries have no opportunity to compare notes and bargain for favorable royalty rates or other terms. Even the International Collaborative Biodiversity Group projects funded by the NIH cannot share information on royalty agreements, promising drug leads, or other data with one another (interviews by author, 2000). This confidentiality protects commercial objectives at the expense of the conservation and sustainable-development objectives that are explicit in the biodiversity discourse.

Furthermore, the industry uses the ambivalent status of natural products as a threat. A number of large companies assert that "we have so much material, we will never have to make another collection" (interviews by author, 2000). That is, rather than bear the substantial costs of collection, they will instead screen their existing naturally derived and synthetic libraries. This assertion is somewhat disingenuous because these same large companies now rely on biotech and academic collaborators to do the collecting and provide specific natural-products derivatives.

The argument about the marginal value of biodiversity has been adopted by influential advocates of bioprospecting as a form of sustainable development. Program directors at the NCI's and the NIH's International Collaborative Biodiversity Group premise their presentations to potential academic collaborators with the warning that industry may jettison the natural-products approach (Artuso 1997; Cragg, Newman, and Snader 1997;

Grifo and Rosenthal 1997; Cragg et al. 1999). Because academic scientists frequently become policy advisers who broker new agreements, the dominant discourse continues to be reenacted in countries like Panama and Palau (observations and interviews by author, 1999 and 2000). At the international level, experts who are working out the details of the CBD similarly echo the exhortation for countries and communities to get the best deal they can in light of the economic realities (ten Kate 1995; ten Kate and Laird 1999).

Prevalent institutional mechanisms combine with the marginal-value discourse to create a momentum that precludes biodiversity-rich countries from forming a resource cartel, as Joseph Henry Vogel has suggested they should (1994, 1997b). Other strategies include regional agreements, such as the Andean Pact's Decision 391 (Bugge and Tvedt 2000), and shifting responsibility to the commercial users of biodiversity, for example, through certificates of origin as a requirement for patent applications (Tobin 1997a). These particular ideas for institutional change have become part of a counterdiscourse to the utilitarian framing of biodiversity conservation.[17]

The overall effect of these institutional dynamics is to shift key risks of drug discovery away from the pharmaceutical industry and onto countries of the South. Although the biotech sector embraces the need for streamlined use of natural products to secure a niche in which it can command some comparative advantage, the burden on source countries is considerable. They bear the responsibility for creating the legal institutions that enable smooth and efficient access to genetic resources. Because available tools are now limited to private agreements between countries and companies, Southern countries have lost the opportunity to advocate alternative access and trading regimes, including those arrangements that existed before the CBD (as in the case of Costa Rica) and the more favorable relationships that can be imagined today.

DEFINING THE DEBATE AND CLOSING THE POLITICAL SPACE

The utilitarian rationale for protecting biodiversity, which has been advanced by scientists, Northern NGOs and policymakers, fall short of meeting the conservation, sustainable development, and commercial objectives attached to this rationale. In particular, the bioprospecting discourse, arising from the search for new drugs from natural sources, introduced the pharmaceutical industry as a key player in the international environmental-policy arena. The changes in that industry, driven by technological commitments to more rational, genetics-based approaches to drug discovery, have influenced global power distributions in biodiversity negotiations over the past ten years.

The pharmaceutical industry was quick to colonize the new economic space for natural products opened up by biotechnology. The use of natural products is now defined in terms of the capital costs that have already been sunk into high-throughput screening and analytical biochemistry. For the most part, the exchange of access to genetic resources and the benefits to suppliers of such access are now structured analogously to other research collaborations; the agreements even follow the same royalty rates and other contractual forms used in the industry. The international debate has been framed in terms of pharmaceutical companies' need for inexpensive, relatively nonrisky, and readily available inputs. This debate has shifted toward property rights over and access to biodiversity and the benefits of its use, and away from sovereignty, equity, and cultural autonomy. By defining the terms of the debate, the pharmaceutical industry has been instrumental in closing the political space for countries of the South to negotiate a good bargain for their genetic resources.

The onus of creating institutions for preserving genetic resources under the premises of their usefulness for pharmaceutical and other uses has been laid upon countries and communities in the South. Countries in the biologically rich South have for the most part embraced the call for national biodiversity policies and central biodiversity-management institutions. The legal framework of the CBD necessitates that countries find a way to involve local communities in the governance of genetic resources, which in many cases involves political struggles over representation, territory, and roles of traditional knowledge.

The well-intentioned strategy to package conservation issues in terms of economics has been politically problematic. Given the changes in the pharmaceutical industry and the political prominence it was afforded by the biodiversity discourse, the utilitarian argument for preserving biodiversity is a Trojan horse. Over the past ten years, the objectives of the CBD have been subordinated to commercial motives, and the debate—including the counterdiscourse—has been framed in terms of Northern industry's concerns.

NOTES

The research for this chapter was conducted as part of my doctoral studies at the University of California, Berkeley, and was funded by a number of grants from the university and a grant from the National Science Foundation (No. 9975929). I thank my academic advisers for their support and guidance during the thesis-writing process, as well as members of the biotech working group and members of my dissertation-writing group, for their invaluable comments and repeated readings of drafts. The largest debt of gratitude, however, I owe to the informants who graciously submitted themselves and their work to my questions and scrutiny, and the gatekeepers to the various fieldsites who made my presence there possible—often in spite of the express skepticism of their organizations. Among the more than eighty individuals I met during my research, I especially remember R.C., whose death in a car crash weeks after we met is a reminder that in qualitative research one forms relationships, however fleeting, with real people.

1. In this chapter, *genetic resources* denotes the object of pharmaceutical research and of the biodiversity discourse. Until recently, the biochemicals for which genes code, rather than the genetic code itself, were of interest in drug design. In what Francis Crick, the co-discoverer of the helical shape of DNA, termed the "central dogma" of molecular biology, genes code for proteins and secondary metabolites (Kay 2000, 174) and are thus at the front end of the biochemical pathways that underlie life itself. Although I recognize that the genetic determinism inherent in the central dogma is problematic (see Rolston 1999; Fox Keller 2000; and Kay 2000), I do not pursue that issue in this chapter.

I use *biological diversity* and *biodiversity* with the following connotative difference, depending on the context. *Biological diversity* is "stuff out there," the sum total of plants, animal*s*, and microorganisms. *Biodiversity* is a neologism coined by conservation biologists in the early 1980s to denote this organismic world, plus the complex linkages within and between species, ecosystems, and humans (Takacs 1996).

I observed the drug discovery process up to the point where drug candidates reach the development phase. This phase typically entails chemical modifications of the newly discovered leads, followed by toxicity and metabolism studies in animals. Human clinical trials begin next and lead to the filing of a New Drug Application with the Food and Drug Administration and eventually to marketing.

2. This section draws on the comprehensive history of European medicine by Mark Weatherall (1990). *Natural products* is the collective term for extracts and other samples derived from plants, fungi, microbes, or, more recently, marine organisms. It refers to secondary metabolites produced by organisms over and beyond what they need for the primary processes of metabolism, respiration, and basic biological functioning (Albers-Schönberg 1995). Secondary metabolites, which include chemicals for skin or hair color and defensive toxins and secretions, generally are common only to a particular family, genus, or even species (Aylward 1995).

3. The 2000 merger of GlaxoWellcome and SmithKline Beecham created GlaxoSmithKline, the largest drug company in the world, with a market share of just under 8 percent (Sorkin and Petersen 2000).

4. A chemical is considered to be (bio)active when it demonstrates a desired effect in an experiment, such as inhibiting cell growth, killing organisms (the basis of the penicillin discovery), or otherwise intervening in a chemical reaction.

5. Alkaloids, a group of potent nitrogen-containing organic compounds chiefly found in vascular plants, have been used for therapeutic purposes for centuries; examples include nicotine, quinine, cocaine, and morphine.

6. A number of my informants confirmed this practice. One retired scientist said he received soil collection kits complete with plastic bags, tags, and data recording sheets before going on vacation.

7. Proteins are comparatively large molecules, composed of at least one chain of amino acids arranged in a specific order. The order of the amino acids is determined by the base sequence of nucleotides in the gene coding for the protein. Proteins are required for the structure, function, and regulation of the body's cells, tissues, and organs.

8. To date, few drugs created entirely by rational design are on the market. A notable exception is the class of drugs known as protease inhibitors, such as Roche's Saquinavir (Bains 1998).

9. *Valence* refers to the number of sites on a molecule where chemical reactions take place.

10. The discussion of the Taxol discovery draws on interviews with Gordon Cragg in March 1999 and May 2000 at the National Cancer Institute, as well as on the account in Cragg et al. 1999. See also Goodman and Walsh 2001.

11. These transnational corporations, with markets in all regions of the world, cover the spectrum of human medicine. Revenues are typically in the tens of billions of U.S. dollars, and each corporation employs more than twenty thousand people. Companies in this category include GlaxoSmithKline, Novartis, and Lilly.

12. The goal of the lead-discovery phase is to generate novel chemical entities, that is, compounds that are patented and approved by the Food and Drug Administration (FDA). Patentability is a major factor in the lead discovery process because only those compounds that can be sold exclusively for a time will allow the firm to recoup its investment.

13. To *dereplicate* means to avoid replication by checking experimental data on a compound—including its signature structure, molecular weight, and other identifying characteristics—against commercial databases of known compounds.

14. The various phases a compound undergoes in the drug discovery and development process are reflected in the organizational structure. The main organizational unit is the project team. This team is a flexible unit, and its membership changes with the stage of a project. Initially a physician specializing in the disease might lead the team, but senior applied scientists take over during the discovery phase. In the transitional stages before lead development, medicinal chemists typically lead the project team; as the drug candidate moves into clinical trials and toward FDA filing status, the regulatory group (which includes physicians) takes over.

15. Some firms are now taking natural-products research out of the increasingly fast-paced drug pipeline by dedicating separate pots of money for benchtop tinkering that is based on ecological and other rationales (Sal Forenza, Lead Discovery, Bristol-Myers Squibb, personal communication, 2000; interviews by author 2000).

16. Bioprospecting is the central trope of the dominant discourse, whereas the counternarrative invokes the notion of biopiracy (Shiva 1997) to highlight the fact that local communities and holders of traditional knowledge are not sufficiently consulted or compensated (Svarstad 2000).

17. There is a growing literature on alternative discourses of biodiversity, roles of traditional knowledge, and notions of ownership and sovereignty (see Escobar 1998 or Svarstad and Dhillion 2000b).

9

The Brave New Worlds
of Agricultural Technoscience

*Changing Perspectives, Recurrent Themes,
and New Research Directions in Agro-Food Studies*

David Goodman

At the turn of the millennium, even casual acquaintance with the media in advanced capitalist economies reveals the palpable unease and mistrust enfolding the nature-society coproductions more conventionally known as agro-food systems. This unease is more acute in Western Europe, where cases of "extreme food events" and the systemic breakdown of food provision, particularly in livestock production, have occurred with disturbing frequency in recent years. A litany of these "extreme food events" would include mad cow disease in Britain and its pandemic translation throughout Western Europe in 2000-2001, episodic yet recurrent food-contamination scares, the Belgian dioxin crisis, and 1999 reports of untreated sewage, septic tank residues, and slaughterhouse effluent being used in several animal-feed-processing plants in France. Nor is food safety the only register of public disquiet, which would give the entirely misleading impression that this mistrust can be rectified by appropriate regulatory measures and better risk-management techniques.

Mistrust of industrial food-provisioning, at least in Western Europe, also reflects ethical opposition to the environmental harms wrought by industrial agriculture and intensive-confinement livestock practices, and fears that the centralizing and homogenizing forces of agro-food globalization are threatening the material and symbolic content of foodways, which are potent bearers of cultural identity. To adapt Jean Brillat-Savarin's aphorism, there is unease about what we eat, how we produce it, and what it means for what we are and might become. More than ever, food is a signifier for political, social, and cultural struggles over the metabolic reciprocities between nature and society, which are the material and discursive metrics of everyday life. As Daniel Miller (1995) and others have realized, personal choices about food can give voice to socioecological commitments whose cumulative expression in biopolitical activism potentially can change the way we live in the world.

Agricultural biotechnologies (ABTs) and genetically engineered organisms contribute to the general disquiet over food provisioning in distinctive ways, exacerbating the instinctive anxieties of the omnivore's paradox, already fully aroused by the events recounted above. ABTs sound the alarm on virtually all registers: food safety, environmental harms, and the further concentration of economic power over the food supply—that is, power over our habitual metabolic interactions with agricultural nature and, hence, over the material and cultural expressions of our corporeal identity. At this fundamental level, extreme food events and novel, genetically engineered foods create unease because of what they reveal about society's relations with nature and their possible transformation.

Starting in Western Europe and some developing countries, but now gathering momentum in the United States and Canada, social mobilization against ABTs and genetically engineered foods is manifest at different scales, from the street protests against the World Trade Organization in Seattle and nongovernmental organizations' efforts to influence the regulation of the Convention on Biological Diversity to the destruction of test sites of GE crops and consumer movements to deny shelf space to genetically engineered food products in supermarkets. ABTs and the new realities they portend are now being interrogated on a radically more comprehensive scale than at any time over the past two decades. This interrogation already has successfully exposed points of weakness and vulnerability in this technoscientific enterprise: its life-sciences business model has been summarily abandoned, the material and discursive claims of the technology have been called into question, and it is losing ground in national and international regulatory struggles. In short, the commercial deployment of ABTs and the threatened ubiquity of genetically engineered foods have opened a new front of biopolitical mobilization. Here, if only incipiently, spaces for an ecological politics and forms of social organization are emerging that reject modernist instrumentalist relations with nature.

With this background, I offer some reflections on the main theoretical approaches to ABTs in agro-food studies, as well as discussion of critical engagement with the "new" biopolitics of agriculture and food. For present purposes, the field of agro-food studies is identified with the "critical" rural sociology and the "new" political economy of agriculture, which emerged from the later 1970s (Buttel and Newby 1980; Newby 1983, 1985; Falk and Gilbert 1985; Friedland 1991, 1992; Marsden et al. 1986.) The imprint of classical Marxism and "agrarian question" problematics is still discernible in the agro-food studies literature on ABTs. This legacy is particularly evident in the conceptual primacy of the labor process and the consequent privileging of production-centered analytics. Within this conceptual armature, I examine several subthemes that elaborate the "vectors of incorporation" of ABTs by private capitals. A schematic survey of this literature is undertaken in the chapter's first section.

Although the labor process-commodification perspective remains pre-eminent in the agro-food studies literature on ABTs, several contributors recently have begun to explore the advantages of the nondualist, relational ontology of actor-network theory in understanding the new socioecological constellations of human and nonhuman entities associated with agricultural technoscience.[1] These recent developments are reviewed in the second section. A concluding section notes several lacunae in the literature and considers future directions of research on ABTs.

AGRI-BIOTECHNOLOGIES AND AGRO-FOOD STUDIES

Until quite recently, analyses of ABTs in agro-food studies were firmly rooted in the agrarian question problematics and deductivist epistemology of classical Marxism.[2] This importation typically was mediated by neo-Marxist debates in development theory and peasant studies, with their focus on agrarian transition and the fate of Third World peasantries as com-moditization processes intensified (Newby 1985; Long et al. 1986). In these classical agrarian question problematics, inflected by Third World debates, family-labor forms of production and the immediate labor process consti-tuted the key units of analysis.

Theoretical trajectories in the new agro-food studies thus were strongly informed by the recovery of the classical Marxist tradition and embraced its production-centered analysis of agrarian change. These epistemological foundations and problematics were not seriously interrogated until the later 1980s (Long et al. 1986; Marsden 1988; Buttel and Goodman 1989; Buttel and McMichael 1990). Even so, the labor process, a cornerstone of Marxist political economy, with its embedded ontological and epistemolog-ical priorities, has retained an unexplained place in putatively revised, post-structuralist and actor-oriented approaches in agro-food studies (van der Ploeg 1986, 1993; Goodman 2001).

These comments are a rather circuitous way of recognizing the continu-ing preeminence of the labor process as a meso-level organizing concept in agro-food studies. The corollary is that social and technical relations of pro-duction are privileged analytically. These legacies are easily detected in those "first generation" approaches to ABTs, which attempt to furnish a gen-eral framework of analysis (Goodman, Sorj, and Wilkinson 1987; Kloppen-burg 1988). Although ABTs are represented as a new technoscientific par-adigm, the analysis is anchored in the agricultural labor process and its transformation via commodification of seed production and plant breed-ing. In an italicized passage, Jack Kloppenburg (1988, 201) stresses that "the seed, as embodied information, becomes the nexus of control over the determination and shape of the entire crop production process." The wider structural implications of ABTs in terms of industrial appropriationism and substitutionism, or institutional change and new property forms, for example, are similarly ushered through the privileged gateway of production. This obligatory passage-point into the circuits of capital also is seen in the preoccupation with industrial concentration, reflecting the redistribution of power toward upstream farm-input sectors as agrochemical and pharmaceutical companies take up dominant positions in ABTs and the seed industry. Broadly speaking, this labor process-commodification perspective has provided the general, overarching analytical framework of choice for addressing ABTs in agro-food studies.

The "first generation" analyses approached ABTs by problematizing the boundaries between agriculture and industry. This analytic move provided the basis for more systemic and historically informed studies of agro-industrial development by drawing attention to the contingent nature of this division of labor. Nevertheless, the farm labor-process is taken as the privileged locus of the transformative contradictions generated by agro-technoscientific innovation.

The work of Kloppenburg (1988), for example, is first situated generally on the classical Marxist terrain of agriculture as a "recalcitrant sector" and then takes up the specific theme of the vectors of capitalist penetration of public plant-science and its gradual institutional reconfiguration as "capitalist property" (Braverman 1974, 156). The commodification of the seed is conceptualized as a process of primitive accumulation, a process whose highlights are the innovation of hybridization—which "functions to uncouple agricultural producers from the autonomous reconstitution of their own means of production" (Kloppenburg 1988, 281)—politically driven shifts in the institutional division of labor between public and private plant-breeding, and changes in intellectual-property regimes to facilitate the private appropriation of plant genetic resources. Kloppenburg's purpose is to explain how the seed, "which is perhaps the element of agricultural means of production most central to the entire farm production process" (39), is commodified and becomes a capitalist force of production. Agricultural biotechnologies are emblematic of this historical trajectory because "what is now occurring in the seed sector is one instance of a much broader technological transformation that is galvanizing changes in the social organization of all production processes in which organic substances or life forms play a significant role" (193).

My colleagues and I (Goodman, Sorj, and Wilkinson 1987) apply the commodification approach to on-farm means of production more widely (implements, motive power, nutrient cycles, pest control, seeds, energy) and argue that the biophysical processes of agricultural production and food consumption have constituted natural, though historically contingent, constraints to the industrialization of agricultural use-values. Unable to reproduce natural production processes fully by direct transformation, industrial capitals have adapted in singular ways to the sectorally differentiated properties of agricultural nature (biological time, photosynthesis, land, climate) and the physiology of human nutrition. These differences, we argue, are analytically significant as a major source of variation in the historical dynamics, specificities, and contemporary configurations of social production in agro-food commodity networks. The concept of appropriationism is used to designate the historically discontinuous, piecemeal "but persistent undermining of discrete elements of the agricultural production process, their transformation into industrial activities, and their re-incorporation into agriculture as inputs" (Goodman, Sorj, and Wilkinson 1987, 2). Elements of natural production processes are progressively internalized by industrial capitals via proprietary science and technology as individual sectors of capitalist accumulation and reproduction. In brief, in agriculture, where industrial capitals confront a natural production process, agricultural biotechnologies constitute "a generalized advance in the capacity of industrial capitals to manipulate nature" (98).

Whether in explicit or implicit terms, the framework adopted by my colleagues and I (Goodman, Sorj, and Wilkinson 1987) and by Kloppenburg (1988) posits a contingent, ongoing *tension* between agriculture as a recalcitrant sector and its full assimilation by industrial capital. Though with differing emphases, these studies broadly explore the cumulative effects and convergence of several interdependent processes of incorporation—cognitive, technoscientific, economic, and regulatory—that progressively extend the commodity form to new spheres of the farm labor-process.[3] In this context, the technoscientific paradigm constituted by biotechnology is identified as the catalyst of assimilation. Nature is transmuted into a force of production. This reconfiguration represents the vector of "domestication" of recalcitrant biological processes, hitherto inaccessible to technoscientific manipulation and the reductionist endeavors of industrial capitals.[4]

In this framework, biotechnology, actually or potentially, has swept away the *technological* foundations of the recalcitrance or exceptionalism of agriculture.[5] For example, we formulated the basic question of the agricultural labor process-commodification approach in the following terms: "If biotechnology represents a qualitative breakthrough in that nature can now be reconstituted industrially, does that mean that the food system is open to assimilation within the broader transformations of the industrial system?" (Goodman, Sorj, and Wilkinson 1987, 188). The answer we gave at that time could not be clearer; the dichotomous tension is sundered definitively. "In this perspective, biotechnology . . . mark[s] the end of the pre-history of the food industry and its incorporation within the broader dynamics of the industrial system and post-industrial society" (189). However, with what now seems fortunate prescience in the light of contemporary biopolitical activism, we suggested that "The frontiers of substitutionism are likely to be defined as much by consumer tastes and loyalty to organic whole foods as technical and engineering constraints" (139).

Vectors of Incorporation

The labor process-commodification approach clearly has furnished the preferred analytical framework for research on ABTs in agro-food studies. A recent critique and extension of "first generation" analyses attests to the continuing influence of this approach (Boyd, Prudham, and Schurman 2001). This same theoretical perspective also frames a number of subsidiary research themes, which emerged in the 1980s and early 1990s as social scientists came to grips with the wider implications of ABTs. A full account of these complementary studies, whose scope ranges from the institutional intricacies of regulatory change to the ethics of genetic engineering, exceeds the more limited purview of this essay. However, with some qualifications, these subsidiary studies follow the same analytical threads Kloppenburg (1988) traces in his history of plant improvement: that is, "the commodification of the seed, the changing division of labor between public and private research institutions, and the appropriation of plant genetic resources" (192).

A particularly rich vein of scholarship on ABTs is devoted to the constellation of political-economic forces that determine the shifting demarcation line between basic and applied research, and the corresponding realignment of the institutional division of labor between public- and private-sector research. The changing division of labor in the U.S. agricultural research establishment, and notably the institutional "capture" of the land-grant university system, dominated work on ABTs in the 1980s. These studies grappled with the political-economic and ideological issues raised by the mounting evidence of corporate penetration of American research universities, where "biotechnology was born" (Kenney 1986, 5). As Edward Yoxen puts it, the capitalist incorporation of molecular biology has reached the point where "the industrial exploitation of recombinant DNA research by corporate capital can be serviced directly from the academic research laboratory" (1981, 67).

With remarkably few exceptions (e.g., Busch et al. 1991), the agro-food studies literature has been reluctant to follow Yoxen's lead and venture seriously into the history of science. However, the emergence of the "university-industrial complex" and the vital contribution of academic scientists to the nascent biotechnology industry are explored fully in Martin Kenney's outstanding and prescient book *Biotechnology: The University-Industrial Complex*

(Kenney 1986). This study crowned a wave of related papers investigating the emerging social division of labor in agricultural biotechnology and plant-breeding research. Much of this work on institutional change is associated with Fred Buttel and his colleagues, then in the Department of Rural Sociology at Cornell University (Buttel 1986b; Buttel et al. 1986; Kenney and Kloppenburg 1983). The rapidly changing matrix of agricultural research policy, scientific practices, and public research institutions and the international reach of agricultural biotechnologies also distinguish the scholarship of Lawrence Busch, Bill Lacy, and their collaborators in this same period (Busch and Lacy 1983, 1986; Busch et al. 1991).

A second strong theme of agro-food studies research on ABTs in the 1980s focused on patterns of innovation and industrial concentration, and their impacts on agricultural production and rural social structures. In a pioneering paper, Jack Kloppenburg (1984) assesses the prospective structural consequences of ABTs by extending the historical tendencies already observed in the development and diffusion of hybrid corn. As in this earlier case, "Biotechnology, too, promises to create a vast new space for the accumulation, concentration, and centralization of capital" (30). This Schumpeterian notion is reinforced by other analytical foci, including the capitalist subordination of public agricultural research and plant breeding, the development of herbicide-resistant crops, the loss of farmer autonomy, acceleration of the technological treadmill, and continued genetic erosion (Kloppenburg 1984). If the concentration of intellectual-property ownership in corporate hands is added to these foci, a remarkable continuity emerges between the scholarship of the early 1980s and the contemporary political-economic analysis of ABTs. A further parallel can also be drawn with current activist opposition to the rising corporate control of global agro-food systems, opposition that has captured public attention since the street battles at the 1999 WTO meetings in Seattle.

Other contributors approached the socioeconomic impacts of ABTs by examining innovation patterns, typically through the prism of new opportunities for accumulation, the implosion of sectoral barriers to entry, and the industrial reorganization and concentration in the agro-food system as a whole. These studies focus on the upstream and downstream industrial sectors, notably the chemical-pharmaceutical complex, to draw out the implications of ABT innovation for farming and for social-production relations in farming. For example, John Wilkinson and I suggest that the generic capacity to engineer living organisms "prefigures a new bio-industrial paradigm" (1990, 132). "Biotechnologies now threaten to *implode* the long-standing organization of the food system around specialized commodity chains. . . . There is the capacity simultaneously to relocate agricultural production in factories and industrial production in fields" (134). Although countervailing tendencies are likely to set up tensions between alternative models and trajectories, we argue that ABTs will accentuate the shift toward a more demand-oriented agro-food system (see also Wilkinson 1993).

Biotechnology as the generic catalyst of wider impulses toward bioindustrialization also underpins projected scenarios of change in the social organization of agriculture (Goodman, Sorj, and Wilkinson 1987; Goodman and Wilkinson 1990). These processes include the amplification of the observed trend toward large-scale, intensive, continuous production systems and the introduction of all-purpose agricultural "biomass refineries." Such developments are predicted to lead to greater concentration of land ownership and more widespread contract production and part-time farming.

From the early 1980s, innovation studies with a more action-oriented policy research perspective began to appear in the agro-food studies literature. These studies were galvanized by the field testing and approaching commercial adoption of genetically engineered organisms, which gave concrete expression to concerns about environmental safety, rural structural change, and demands for regulatory processes with greater democratic participation. Struggles over the licensing of recombinant bovine growth hormone (rBGH) crystallized these issues acutely in the United States (Buttel 1986a; Comstock 1988; Buttel and Geisler 1989; Geisler and DuPuis 1989). The rBGH controversy also exposed the conflicted politics of ABT research in the U.S. land-grant university system and other public institutions involved in the innovation process.

A third and continuing strand of agro-food studies scholarship on ABTs examines the political-economic repercussions and contested politics of changing intellectual-property regimes in plant breeding and genetic resources. As in the case of rBGH, the academic literature in the 1980s was strongly informed, if not led, by parallel activist contributions, notably from members of RAFI, or the Rural Advancement Foundation International (Mooney 1979, 1983; Fowler et al. 1987). These interactions have intensified since the 1992 Earth Summit in Rio as part of the ongoing struggles to shape the emerging supranational institutions of global environmental governance, and notably in this context, the Convention on Biological Diversity (CBD) and the Cartagena Protocol on Biosafety, which regulates international commerce in living modified organisms.

Contributors in the 1980s quickly grasped the import of the landmark rulings that extended and consolidated property rights to microorganisms, plant germplasm, and rDNA techniques and other processes involved in plant genetic research. The dramatic institutional shift to allow the commodification of life forms—"ownable artifacts, whilst also being a part of nature" (Yoxen 1981, 111)—has been analyzed from various angles in agro-food studies.

Several accounts trace the institutional origins and evolving structures of intellectual property rights in plant breeding before 1980, when the U.S.

Supreme Court's decision in *Diamond v. Chakrabarty* overturned the "product of nature" principle, which had earlier dominated this field of patent law (Kloppenburg 1988). Other scholars surveyed this same terrain but from specific institutional standpoints to evaluate the implications of these new legal and social conventions for particular groups of actors. This scholarship, for example, investigated university-industry relations (Kenney 1986) and the public and private communities of agricultural scientists and research administrators (Busch et al. 1991).

However, in agro-food studies, the issues arising from the patenting of life forms were explored most vigorously at the international level. Academics and activists exposed the institutional dimensions of North-South power asymmetries and the inequalities embedded in the governance structures of international agricultural research, such as the Consultative Group on International Agricultural Research (CGIAR) system, and the associated collection and transfer of germplasm as "common heritage" resources. Jack Kloppenburg deserves much credit for bringing the "North-South seed wars" and questions of political-economic control over international plant genetic resources into agro-food studies, and other scholars soon followed his lead (Goodman and Redclift 1991; Busch 1995).

More recently, issues of access to and ownership and conservation of international genetic resources have faded from prominence in this literature. This decline, paradoxically, has coincided with the rising salience of these questions on national and international policy agendas as Greenpeace, Friends of the Earth, and other leading environmental groups have reinforced the longstanding campaigns of more specialized, agrienvironmental organizations, such as RAFI and Genetic Resources Action International (GRAIN).

Although incomplete, this survey of the earlier literature on ABTs reveals some strong continuities with contemporary scholarship, in terms of both theoretical perspective and more specific concerns, such as genetic erosion, decline of farmer autonomy, and centralized control of agro-food networks on a global scale. Discursive continuities also persist, despite Fred Buttel's suggestion that the days of extravagant rhetoric characteristic of biotechnology in "its formative years, roughly the mid-1970s to late 1980s," are now past (Buttel 1993, 6). In this period, Buttel argues, virtually all the protagonists—leading molecular biologists, venture capitalists, small start-up firms, government officials, and environmental and public-interest groups—embraced it as epoch-making and revolutionary. "As late as the end of the 1980s, most academic, policy and activist treatments of biotechnology were essentially agreed on its magic bullet character and transformative potential" (10-11). At the turn of the millennium, the implication that this viewpoint is no longer shared seems premature, even if more pragmatic assessments can increasingly be found. The tropes of these formative

years are still actively deployed in the rancorous exchanges between supporters and opponents of ABTs. For each group, the discursive starting
point remains the promise of the technology: golden rice versus Frankenfoods, precision breeding versus superweeds, and so on.

A brave new socionatural world is on offer, which, if realized, would
empower the networks of human and nonhuman entities involved in its
construction. Some recent work on technoscience and relational ethics in
agro-food studies, particularly extensions of actor-network theory, seek to
elucidate such biopolitical choices by adopting an explicitly nondualist
framework of analysis. These new approaches represent a reflexive theoretical project to overcome the abstraction of nature in mainstream agro-food
studies by interrogating its modernist ontological foundations.

NEW PERSPECTIVES ON AGRO-TECHNOSCIENCE

Although the labor process-commodification perspective retains analytical
appeal, it is clearly a product of its times. As Kloppenburg observes, "The
model of change that emerges from this analysis is fundamentally dialectical—the forces and relations of production are mutually conditioning"
(1988, 281). Human praxis is ontologically central, and nature is firmly
located on the opposite side of the modernist divide. At best, nature is
endowed with certain qualities of "resistance," which are identified, for
example, with "biological barriers" to capital and "secrets of life" that are
inaccessible to science. However, in this characterization, nature is figured
as a passive entity whose latent properties will be revealed only if it is *acted
upon* by industrial technoscience. Following the Enlightenment antinomy
between nature and society, nature is other, which industrial society is driven to subjugate and appropriate.

As depicted in *From Farming to Biotechnology* (Goodman, Sorj, and
Wilkinson 1987), the agricultural labor process has indeed presented historically contingent biophysical limits to industrial appropriation and substitution. Yet, although nature and industry are drawn as oppositional categories, in analytical terms, industry is the only actor. This unexamined
ontological choice precludes the conceptualization of nature as a lively,
active, and formative presence and so *underplays* what arguably are the truly
revolutionary material dimensions of biotechnology. Unwittingly and
implicitly, with this choice the analysis is captured by the *engineering*
metaphor of life propagated by industrial capital, with its omnipotent tech-
nocratic discourse of precision, efficiency, and benign evolutionary improvement (Levidow and Tait 1995).

This observation is not intended to deny the incisiveness of the labor
process framework as an analytical vantage point to address social *cui bono*
issues and rural structural change as nature is reconfigured as a productive

force. Clearly, such a denial would fly in the face of historical and contemporary evidence of the salience of production as a terrain of theory and praxis. Nevertheless, the ontological critique of late post-industrial capitalist political economy can fruitfully be extended by bridging the modernist divide between nature and society in order to imagine and construct alternative socioecological worlds. As already noted, agency in "first generation" approaches to ABTs is uniquely identified with human intentionality and human action on an objectified, but now less recalcitrant, nature. This instrumentalist ontology, with its purified categories of nature and society, is closed to notions of the relational materiality of nature, offers no theorization of the lively entities emerging as social partners in these technoscientific practices, and fails to entertain nonhuman perspectives and shared consequences.

An alternative conceptualization of nature, one that attributes active properties to nonhuman entities, would focus analytical attention on the interrelational negotiation of new socionatural realities, which are now being constituted with the commercial diffusion of genetically engineered crops in the United States. Such an approach also would make explicit the ethical, environmental, and political choices associated with different human-nonhuman assemblages and "socio-ecological projects" (Harvey 1996). However, as argued elsewhere, mainstream agro-food studies remains transfixed by the modernist ontology (FitzSimmons and Goodman 1998; Goodman 1999, 2001). Encouragingly, there are recent signs of a reflexive "turn" to give analytical salience to "the status of nature" (Marsden, Murdoch, and Banks 2000) and to interrogate the modernist divide (Murdoch and Miele 1999; Lockie and Kitto 2000).

Actor-Network Theory: Natural-Technical
Intermediaries and Agro-Social Networks

The analytical richness and potential of actor-network theory (ANT) in agro-food studies have been expressively revealed in these reflexive explorations (Murdoch 1994; Murdoch 1997a, 1997b; Whatmore 1997). However, apart from an illustrative vignette (Goodman 1999), these analytical resources so far have not been deployed in work on ABTs. This is a major omission in agro-food studies, and efforts to rectify this position deserve high priority on the ABT research agenda.

Lawrence Busch and his colleagues in a recent series of papers on the rapeseed (canola) commodity sector have undertaken the most systematic work on agricultural technoscience from an actor-network perspective. This impressive research elucidates the endogeneity of technical change and the processes by which knowledge-commodity transformations become eco-socially embedded. ANT is used to analyze the rise and institutionalization of rapeseed technoscience by conceptualizing technological innovation as a process of network building. Thus, instead of considering technology as an exogenous factor to the system of commodity production, the network approach does not differentiate between human and nonhuman elements. In such analyses, society does not transform technology, nor does technology cause the transformation of society. Rather, "the very actor-networks . . . simultaneously give rise to society and to technology." (Callon 1987, 99, cited in Juska and Busch 1994, 582)

Moreover, Arunas Juska and Lawrence Busch find ANT to be particularly helpful in uncovering points both of analytical entry and of political action in cases where, as with ABTs, processes of network formation, extension, and reconfiguration are dynamic and in flux. In this perspective, "it becomes evident that the relationships mediated through the network are contingent in nature: they can be disrupted; they can collapse; they can be organized according to different principles; they can be constantly changed and renegotiated" (Juska and Busch 1996, 583-84).

In a second paper, Busch and Keiko Tanaka (1996) deploy the concept of symmetry, which ANT extends to nonhumans, to give "an explicit portrayal of non-human actors over time and space" in "the complex networks known . . . as commodity chains" (4), such as rapeseed (canola). The product grades and standards constitutive of commodities represent "rites of passage" for both nature and people. "Thus, by transforming nonhumans and subjecting them to multiple rites of passage, we coproduce nature, society, [and] the capitalist market" (5). The symmetry of these qualification processes also extends to their ethical dimensions, which infuse these modes or "rites" of mutual socialization of humans and nonhumans.

In a later analysis of the globalization of rapeseed networks, Busch and Juska (1997) contend that the political economy of agriculture perspective and its "categorical apparatus" are "inadequate" to the task at hand (701). The political economy approach is underspecified because "in true Baconian style, nature is recast as resources to be transformed" (691), as passive. In contrast, the political economy of actor networks reveals how the strategic positions of human and nonhuman actors and the geometry of power in networks are negotiated, modified, and transformed temporally and spatially. A more recent paper investigates these questions in finer historical detail by examining the reciprocal and contingent relationships between agricultural research and agricultural production, and the changing strategic positions of nation-states as the rapeseed sector has become more globalized since the mid-1970s (Tanaka, Juska, and Busch 1999).

This brief review of rapeseed technoscience provides some indication of the purview and analytical purchase of ANT. With its symmetrical ontology and method, ANT offers a penetrating conceptual repertoire for the analysis of ABTs. Lively eco-social coproductions and category fusions of the natural and artifactual are particularly in evidence in the everyday practices of agro-food networks in an era of genetically engineered organisms. Thus Bruno Latour (1994) extends an invitation to reject the purified categories of "society" and "nature" and focus instead on "the blind spot where society and matter exchange properties" (41). These transactions are brought center stage in order to expose the inescapable sociomateriality of the entities mobilized into the heterogeneous associations that hold society together. The constant interchange of human and nonhuman properties in network formation has created "mixtures between two entirely new types of being, hybrids of nature and culture" (Latour 1993, 10). These processes of mediation, in turn, constitute the foundation of modern technosciences, which "multiply the non-humans enrolled in the manufacturing of collectives and . . . make the community that we form with these beings a more intimate one" (Latour 1993, 108).

Rather than engage in a lengthy exposition of ANT, its merits and limitations, the point to emphasize is that we have a nondualist, relational, and processual framework in which nonhumans are actively present, performative, and consequential. In this significant respect, although otherwise confessedly modest in its claims (Law 1994), ANT challenges the silences and abstractions of production-centered analyses. That is, it furnishes an ontology and conceptual language with which to address the implosions, nature-culture hybrids, and newly socialized intermediaries emerging from the heterogeneous engineering practices of agro-food technoscience.

ANT's terms of engagement and insistence on "the permeable boundary running between humans and non-humans" (Pels 1996, 297) resonate strongly with the ethical and relational concerns of biopolitical activism. An ethical standpoint, a relational moral philosophy, is discernible in ANT's framing of the construction of our world, its insistent reference to crossovers and the exchange of properties between human and nonhuman entities (Koch 1995; Whatmore 1997; Shapiro 1997). As Jonathan Murdoch notes, actor-network theorists "force us to look afresh at the categories, divisions and boundaries that frequently divert our attention away from the nonhuman multitudes which make up our world" (1997a, 753).

This imperative recalls Latour's analysis of Louis Pasteur's research on the anthrax bacillus (Latour 1983, 1988). That is, the bacilli, once "translated" from the natural competition found in the farmyard to Pasteur's laboratory in Paris, encounter a new environment, an altered state, where they can thrive. Following Latour (1983), Elizabeth Bird (1987) observes that "In the laboratory, nature—in the form of Pasteur's "natural-technical object"—becomes an actor negotiating a *new reality*. In the terms of that context, the microbes become actors in shaping a new environment" (258, original emphasis). Latour continues, "Training microbes and domesticating them is a craft. . . . Once these skills have accumulated inside laboratories, many cross-overs occur that had no reason to occur anywhere else before" (1983, 148). Similarly, when analyzing Pasteur's discovery of the microorganism responsible for lactic fermentation, Latour draws attention to the change in ontological status that this step involved and observes that "in his laboratory in Lille Pasteur is *designing* an *actor*" (1990, 122, original emphasis). The analytical parallels and possibilities of extending this approach to the transgenic "natural-technical objects" of ABTs—such as Roundup Ready soybeans and Bt corn, not to mention the unintended progeny of horizontal gene transfer—are clear.

In a brief vignette on ANT, I suggest that agri-biotechnological innovation can be analyzed in terms of the practices deployed to reconfigure or "translate" existing agro-food networks by enrolling genetically engineered organisms (GEOs) and foods (Goodman 1999). In effect, corporate networks, such as Aventis, DuPont, and Syngenta, are seeking to displace previous socionatural orderings and to realign agro-food networks in ways that support and "naturalize" the diffusion of GEOs into rural environments, crops, and animals. Thus, " agri-biotechnologies introduce new mediators into the intimate corporeal relations of agro-food networks, promising new corporealities and, quite literally, new bodies" (30).

Biopolitical mobilization, notably in Western Europe, has raised material and ethical concerns against this reordering of agro-food networks in marshaling opposition to the environmental release of GEOs and the incorporation of genetically engineered foods into human bodies. This mobilization directly challenges the industrial, technoscientific problematization of ABTs, variously framed as the answer to world hunger, as an improvement on nature, or in terms of the inevitability of technical change. In this modernist instrumental perspective, nature is objectified as a field of resources awaiting domination and exploitation by the relentless advance of technoscience. Against this dualist rationality, green biopolitical activism is informed by a relational ethics and by precepts of shared community. These biopolitics of ABTs reveal the "clash of divergent ontologies" (Goodman 1999, 31) provoked by struggles to realign agro-food networks into new socionatural orderings.

By undermining the modernist ideology of nature as externalized and objectified, ANT provides theoretical resources to address nature and its lively materiality directly. This attention to how "socionatures" are constructed broadens critical engagement with capitalist technoscience and political economy and informs our understanding of the heterogeneous associations fostered by this ordering of the socioecological. The dimensions of this political space are amplified if we interpret ANT as an ethical discourse of how to live in the world. This perception of ethical, as well as material, embeddedness speaks directly to the problematics of biopolitical activism, as noted above.

Even a cursory understanding of ABTs brings recognition of the new socionatural assemblages emerging, under the aegis of capitalist techno-science, to construct new worlds. In turn, this recognition suggests the need for conceptual frameworks that explicitly bring normative judgment and political critique to bear on these new collectives and respond to Donna Haraway's interrogation of technoscience: how, for whom, and at what cost? (Haraway 1997). Acknowledgment of our partnership in these human-nonhuman assemblages would be an initial step toward the devel-opment of forms of social organization that encourage democratic choice between alternative orderings and the worlds they bring forth. For these purposes, we need ontologies that reveal, not abstract, our interactive, relational production of worlds we inhabit with others. The novel socio-natural assemblages of capitalist agro-food technoscience, which herald new actors and new realities, underline the significance of theoretical and political choice.

CONCLUSION AND RESEARCH AGENDA

In this re-encounter with agro-food studies research on ABTs, the theoreti-cal and thematic continuities of this literature emerge insistently. Indeed, in theoretical terms, there is a powerful sense of déjà vu, of involution even, and alternative perspectives remain firmly on the margins. In the preceding sections of this chapter, I emphasized both the primacy of the labor process-commodification approach and its ontological limitations for compre-hending the new socionatures constituted by ABTs. This framework con-strains efforts to find common ground with the relational ontology and moral economy that inform the biopolitics of environmental movements and Green activists. Such serious limitations, in short, lend urgency to the-oretical renewal in agro-food studies and, more generally, to the "greening" projects and explorations of Red-Green rapprochement now under way in various fields of critical social theory.

These projects unmask the political agendas and instrumentalist ethics imbricated in modernist ontological antinomies and their reification. At the risk of repetition, the agro-food studies literature on ABTs has as its analyt-ical focus the ensemble of institutional processes and social relations that have led to the commodification of nature or, as Yoxen (1981) has it, to "capitalizing life" (cf. Boyd, this volume). This labor process conceptualiza-tion, with its emphasis on the subsumption of nature and its manipulation as a productive force, sees this transition exclusively from the standpoint of the social. Nature is subsumed by purposive social agency, whose dynamic is to be found in the laws of accumulation and social relations of the capital-ist mode of production (FitzSimmons and Goodman 1998). There is no place here for the relational materiality of nature, its liveliness, or its "boomerang" qualities (Beck 1992, 23). This framework does not entertain either notions of natural-social coproductions or the consequences of these assemblages for entities with whom we share this world.

The labor process perspective, in short, does not lend itself to an assured engagement with the new constituencies of agro-food biopolitics. However, "this is not to dismiss the strengths of this perspective. Rather, it is . . . to observe that this theoretical lens or 'framing' device does not focus directly, for example, on the new socionatural relations, interspecies metabolisms and exotic corporealities unleashed by agricultural biotechnologies. . . . these new constellations or assemblages of nature-society relations are key catalytic elements of bio-political activism in agro-food networks" (Goodman 2001, 196).

This review also has drawn attention to thematic continuities, although clearly the scale and intensity of social mobilization have grown sharply with the accelerating deployment of ABTs. These thematic links are amply reflected in this volume. Issues of governance, although not known as such in the 1980s, form a recurrent body of concern. Two themes, already identified previously, have retained particular salience. The first theme concerns the ways in which ABTs heighten the concentration of industrial control in agro-food systems—"a global oligopoly" in William Boyd's estimation (this volume). Exploring the "deep structures of monopoly" within a commodification of nature framework, Boyd extends the analysis of ABTs into the era of life sciences multinationals, genomics, and the competitive imperative to capture value by integrating vertically from proprietary intellectual-property platforms to seed marketing and contract farming.

A social constructivist-commodification perspective also frames the contributions of Scott Prudham and Dennis Kelso to this collection. Following Richard White (1995), Prudham adopts the metaphor of nature as an organic machine to describe the transformation of living organisms into technologies and commodities. Within this framework, he is particularly concerned to track the harnessing of public science to private innovation in the development of forestry biotechnology, the concomitant restructuring of university-industry-state relations, and how this trajectory is shaped by the specificity of recalcitrant nature. In warning against technological fetishism, Prudham insists that biotechnologies be seen not as things but as bundles of social relations with historical lineages in order to emphasize that technological change is socially produced.

Although Kelso's analysis of the deployment of biotechnology in commercial salmon aquaculture broadly fits with the labor process-agrarian transition problematic of agro-food studies, his main concern is to reject its technological determinist inflections. This endeavor brings Kelso into closer engagement with issues that have been strangely muted in this literature until recently and especially with the sources, forms, and resources of social resistance to biotechnological innovation. Kelso's account of transgenic salmon embraces not only mobilization around questions of food safety and environmental risk but also the defensive stance of salmon farmers against the perceived technological threat to the aquaculture industry as presently constituted. In elaborating these questions, Kelso draws attention to the politics of scientific uncertainty and state regulation, highlighting the strategic importance of discursive struggles to form public perceptions of nature and the natural. This discussion, together with the chapters by Julie Guthman, Frederick Buttel, and Rachel Schurman and William Munro, begins to address important lacunae in the agro-food studies literature.

The second thematic grouping is around governance issues and focuses on continued First World-Third World tensions over access to genetic resources and the perceived asymmetries of power articulated by intellectual property rights regimes and, notably, the 1994 WTO TRIPS accord. These ongoing tensions find expression in the contested politics, shifting alliances, and arcane regulatory processes of new multilateral institutions of global governance—the WTO and CBD—and their disputed mandates in the conjoined policy arenas of international economics, trade, and environment (McAfee, this volume). Environmental governance emerges in another contemporary guise in the chapter by Astrid Scholz (this volume). Her analysis traces the vagaries of the utilitarian rationale for biodiversity conservation as the importance of natural product screening in the R&D strategies of transnational pharmaceutical corporations waxes and wanes, exacerbating the inequities of power embedded in private bioprospecting agreements.

The contribution by Frederick Buttel similarly can be situated within the global governance thematic; however, like Kelso's chapter, it also provides a bridge to some neglected issues. Buttel's wide-ranging account encompasses the institutional architecture of the globalization regime, the power brokering of the GATT-WTO transition and the "spoiling" role of agro-food issues—festering EU-U.S. "food wars" (bananas, beef, GEOs), unilateral trade sanctions, the "environmentalization" of ABTs, the global farm crisis—in revealing potential fault lines and pressure points in this accumulation regime. Taken in the aggregate, these individually contentious issues have cumulatively resonated with growing force in political, cultural, and institutional domains. Whether or not GEOs prove to be the Achilles' heel of the globalization regime, Buttel is surely right to stress that EU-U.S. disputes, and their potential to galvanize social protest, are less about trade liberalization than about the perceived threat of institutional convergence, and especially the forced harmonization of national regulatory structures and the further erosion of cultural identity.

The bridge in Buttel's account rests on recognition of the crucial nexus formed by the politics of scientific research and policy, environmental risk, food safety, regulation, and consumption. These politics are complexly intertwined and varied in their manifestation, ranging from agro-food movements, environmental coalitions, and many forms of direct action, including street theater and green sabotage, to NGO involvement in regulatory processes and consumer pressure on food retailers and manufacturers. This terrain remains largely unexplored in agro-food studies, apart from limited incursions into one or other of its arenas, such as the politics of rBGH consumption (Buttel 2000; DuPuis 2000) or the role of ABTs in facilitating transition to demand-driven food systems (Wilkinson 1993, 2000). This neglect is surprising in view of the considerable prominence of these research themes in other fields of critical social theory. In this context, work on the institutional matrix of science, science policy, and regulation, as undertaken more generally by Yoxen (1981), Kay (1993), Bud (1993), and Wright (1994), could fruitfully be extended to developments in agriculture and food since the 1980s.

In the present volume, the chapters by Guthman and by Schurman and Munro set some markers to follow in addressing the research nexus identified above. Guthman examines the contradictions that GEO labeling and right-to-know legislation in the United States present for movements seeking to build an effective politics of consumption, especially the privatization of risk management for genetically engineered foods and the political disarticulation that labeling implies. In calling for research on "an emerging political economy of risk," Guthman follows Haraway (1997) in emphasizing the centrality of struggles for "the power to define what counts as technical or political" (89). In this respect, it would be interesting to explore how European consumer groups and environmental organizations have avoided the pitfalls of labeling and convinced national governments and the EU to redraw the boundary between the technical and the political by agreeing to reopen previous regulatory decisions to public scrutiny (Levidow, Carr, and Wield 2000).

Demarcation struggles and boundary changes are the central theme of Schurman and Munro's chapter. The chronology of events in the rising social opposition to ABTs is becoming well-known, but there is a dearth of careful analyses of antibiotech activism, its strategies and modus operandi. Schurman and Munro begin to address this hiatus by examining antibiotech movements in the North, primarily in the United States. In their view, the marked shift in public sentiment against genetically engineered foods is not attributable to inchoate consumer resistance or to spontaneous protest. Rather, this dramatic change, and its economic and regulatory repercussions, have been orchestrated by the social-movement organization and mobilization of established civil-society actors. In pressing this argument, the authors provide valuable insights into the wide array of social organizations articulated by this movement, its tactical sophistication, and its networking skills, which facilitate operation across a variety of institutional and spatial scales and in different regulatory spheres and discursive arenas. Schurman and Munro leave unanswered the thorny questions of representation and the transformative potential of the antibiotechnology movement. However, it is to be hoped that this initial exploration will encourage others to join them in investigating this serious gap in the politics of agricultural technoscience.

In December 2000, completion of the plant genome sequence of thale cress *(Arabidopsis thaliana)* was announced, the first of some 250,000 plant species. Agro-food technoscience, here represented by the public-private consortium, including Monsanto, which comprises the Multinational Coordinated *Arabidopsis thaliana* Genome Research Project, goes marching on. Now, as in the 1980s, it is vital that critical social scientists join with the antibiotech movement and other progressive forces in the struggle to submit this enterprise and the worlds it would create to democratic debate and public assent.

NOTES

1. The *commodification-labor process perspective* referred to throughout this chapter has its conceptual and political roots in the agrarian question debates of classical Marxism in the later nineteenth century. These debates concerned the fate of the peasantry in industrializing societies, where market relations and capitalist commodity production were becoming increasingly pervasive in all spheres of economic activity. *Agrarian question problematics* refers to the framing of political economic analyses whose overriding purpose is to determine the path, or trajectory, of rural social relations and structural change in capitalist societies. That is, more specifically, would agriculture replicate the capitalist-proletarian class structure of manufacturing industry or, alternatively, provide opportunities for the reproduction of peasant family labor-based farms? Since these debates turned on the dynamics of the social differentiation of production relations as the commodity form became ubiquitous, the farm labor process was the privileged unit of analysis in making these determinations. For further discussion, see Hussain and Tribe 1981; Goodman and Redclift 1981; and Long et al. 1986.

2. Parts of this discussion draw on my recent paper titled "Ontology Matters" (Goodman 2001).

3. As Martin Kenney observes on the rise of the biotechnological industry more generally, it is necessary to "create the social, legal and economic institutions within which the product is embedded. . . . Each strand has its own logic, which is not entirely derived from the other strands, and yet the strands also interact" (1998, 132).

4. This line of thought also is represented in the seminal work of Susan Mann and James Dickenson (1978) and Mann (1990).

5. This view also finds some resonance in the work of William Boyd, Scott Prud-

ham, and Rachel Schurman (2001), who borrow from Marx's value theory to conceptualize the formal and real subsumption of nature, with the latter arising when "capital circulates through nature (albeit unevenly) as opposed to *around* it" (22, original emphasis). This focus on the social agency of capital in making or reducing nature into a productive force recalls the earlier formulation by Edward Yoxen (1981), whose work is better known in science studies (Fox Keller 1995; Kay 1998).

CONCLUSION

Recreating Democracy

Dennis Doyle Takahashi Kelso

"No one wants to eat his science fair experiment," chuckled the head of a major seafood marketing organization, asserting that well-informed consumers will be reluctant to embrace genetically engineered foods (interview by author, 1998). Another seafood industry leader, the president of a wild-salmon-processing company, went a step farther to argue that genetically engineered organisms are a bad idea because of their possible ecological effects, and he could hardly contain his enthusiasm about the opportunities to differentiate his natural product from the genetically engineered version: "As for marketing, bring 'em on!" (interview by author, 2000).

This confidence in retail-level resistance suggests that consumers will be key actors in constraining the adoption of genetically engineered foods. In that role, consumers, as well as nongovernmental organizations (NGOs), serve as imperfect surrogates for democratic institutions that have been slow to address the range of social issues associated with these new technologies. As Rachel Schurman and William Munro describe in this volume, a globally networked coalition of skeptics and opponents has argued tenaciously in favor of a cautious approach to these technologies. The current success of this resistance is all the more remarkable in light of the active regulatory and political support that some national governments have provided for commercial deployment of genetically engineered organisms.

As companies with interests in these products have sought "to capitalize on the wave of innovations and proprietary technologies associated with recombinant DNA techniques," changes in the intellectual-property regime and other elements of the legal framework have enabled rapid technology acquisition and concentration in a few multinational firms (Boyd, this volume). Critics charge that as companies have capitalized, government regulatory authorities have capitulated and thereby reduced opportunities for citizens to consider the potential effects of these rapidly evolving technologies before they have been adopted. In effect, consumers and their activist allies—some of whom reject genetic engineering under any circumstances, whereas others merely seek to place some conditions on the technologies' deployment—have begun to take up the regulatory slack.

As Rachel Schurman notes in the introduction to this volume, many people have started to question the assumption that any single segment of society should have the prerogative to intervene in virtually every form of life. They argue that a broader set of interests reflecting a wider set of societal values must have the opportunity to participate in decisions about what precautions and institutional structures will be deemed adequate to mediate our engagement with these technologies. Much of the controversy has focused on whether genetic engineering is safe for humans and other animals and whether it is capable of producing the results that its proponents promise. However, the politics of these technologies—Who has the power to make decisions about the distribution of risks and benefits from genetic engineering?—have implications that may be as profound as any technology-induced changes in human interactions with nonhuman nature. The effects of these technologies on access to, and exclusion from, decision-making power fundamentally challenge a democratic society.

The contributors to this volume have explored some of the diverse mechanisms by which genetic engineering is changing our relationships with the rest of nature, the character of commodity production, and conflicts over the content (both material and symbolic) of food. Even at this early stage of application, biotechnology has stimulated major shifts in knowledge-acquisition and -transfer systems, intellectual property rights, environmental and social risks, concentrations of industrial power, production processes and control, and agro-food systems. The preceding chapters have also traced the countercurrents of resistance that are, in turn, shaping the technologies. Through the interactions of change and resistance runs a fundamental question that requires a sustained, public conversation: How should a democracy ensure that the uses of these powerful new technologies serve the public interest rather than just the interests of private firms?

AN IMPERFECT SURROGATE FOR DEMOCRACY

Activists have successfully broadened the discussion about genetically engineered goods by leveraging the role of consumers. By posing food-safety questions and other objections that matter to consumers, they have raised the threat of consumer rejection of these food products and, as a result, have constrained deployment of some technologies. These consumer-resistance-based constraints constitute a kind of nongovernmental regulatory effect.

Consumer strength in the agro-food sector derives from activists' ability to impinge upon the profit strategies of biotechnology firms, strategies that depend upon successful linkages between scientific research, technical innovation, intellectual property, agricultural production, food processing, and consumer acceptance (Boyd, this volume). In the execution of this strategy, however, consumers have proven difficult to control, especially outside the United States. Indeed, Frederick Buttel (2001, 172) suggests that "in most countries of the industrial world other than [the United States,] biotechnology and genetic engineering have shaky public support and active political opposition." More recently, Buttel (2002, 7) has observed that the adoption of genetically engineered crops is "becoming deeper but narrower": most GE production is concentrated in herbicide-resistant soybeans, and most of that acreage is in the United States. As of 2001, perhaps only 2 million hectares in genetically engineered crops were planted outside the United States, Canada, and Argentina, and adoption of genetically engineered varieties in the world's staple crop sectors is limited.

Industry's difficulty in controlling consumers is due, in part, to its inability to keep the terms of debate narrow for its ultimate client base; this inability contrasts with industry's success in controlling the scope of policy discussions. Consumer advocates and other activists have mobilized around issues that extend well beyond the technical questions defined by industry and government experts. By contrast, government regulatory agencies have sharply delimited their discussions about potential unintended effects of genetic-engineering applications. In the rush to facilitate the commercialization of biotechnologies and to promote global trading advantages, government policy has excluded nontechnical concerns from the debate. Deregulation policies also have changed the regulatory ground rules to make it more difficult to achieve strong governmental oversight. The narrowed policy debate and an onerous burden of proof have had the effect of passing the functions of participatory democracy to consumers and NGOs.

NARROWING THE FIELD OF POLICY DISCUSSION

Even before recombinant DNA applications were ready for deployment, their proponents had successfully limited the discussion of public policy by narrowing the scope of the questions deemed relevant for consideration. Susan Wright argues that by the mid-1970s "the social problems of controlling the use of a powerful and possibly hazardous technology" had been transformed "into the technical problem of containing the organisms used in research." Issues associated with controlling applications of these new technologies were "virtually excluded from formal consideration," and this exclusion constrained subsequent policy deliberations (1998, 86).

During the 1975 Symposium on Science, Ethics, and Society at Asilomar,

California, the scientific community debated the precautions that scientists should undertake to contain genetically engineered organisms in research. A number of participants in the symposium, which was convened by scientists who were concerned about responsible control of risks from use of these technologies, believed that no regulation of research practices would occur unless scientists initiated self-regulation. Wright (1998) argues, however, that the Asilomar discussions ultimately emphasized technical issues rather than any larger social and value implications of the applications of these technologies (Wright 1998). Subsequent legislative efforts to establish regulatory control failed under pressure from research and commercial interests that promoted genetic-engineering technologies as essential to U.S. competitiveness in international markets (Kevles 1998). Wright notes that by the early 1980s, "the political climate was changing from support for control . . . to support for deregulation" (1998, 94).

In the United States, the regimes of intellectual-property law and antitrust law provided the foundation for this trend, as William Boyd shows in chapter 1 of this volume. He points out that the commercial development of genetic engineering in the United States has been linked to an increase in the "specificity and frequency with which proprietary claims can be made over novel life forms." The result has been a more formal, increasingly privatized intellectual-property protection system that reaches into the early stages of biotechnology development and covers property interests ranging from particular genes to basic transformation technologies used in genetic engineering of new varieties. In 1992, the Office of the President announced policies that reduced regulatory barriers even further. The record of federal regulatory-policy development strongly supports Boyd's argument that government regulation or, in some cases deregulation, has promoted the commercial viability of these technologies in several ways.

STREAMLINING REGULATORY OVERSIGHT, INCREASING BURDENS OF PROOF

In addition to having eliminated most social issues from the agenda, federal policy has also facilitated biotechnology development by leaving resolution of many technical issues either to the industry or to government agencies with sharply curtailed regulatory discretion. In some instances, the government has allowed the industry to provide data or to implement safety measures on a voluntary basis and, perhaps more important, has failed to conduct its own studies or to sponsor independent research on genetically engineered food products.

In the United States, federal agency oversight of biotechnology products is subject to the Coordinated Framework for Regulation of Biotechnology, adopted by the president's Office of Science and Technology Policy (OSTP) in 1986 (51 *Fed. Reg.* 23302, June 26, 1986).[1] In its proposal for the framework, the OSTP predicted enormous benefits from biotechnology: superior services and products that would "alleviate many problems of disease and pollution and increase the supply of food, energy, and raw materials." Accordingly, support for these technologies was essential: "The tremendous potential of biotechnology to contribute to the nation's economy in the near term, and to fulfill society's needs and alleviate its problems in the longer term, makes it imperative that progress in biotechnology be encouraged" (49 *Fed. Reg.* 50856, December 31, 1984).

The Reagan administration sought a regulatory balance that would ensure, on the one hand, health and environmental safety and, on the other, "regulatory flexibility to avoid impeding the growth of an infant industry." The Coordinated Framework presumed that existing laws "as currently implemented" for the regulation of products developed by "traditional genetic manipulation techniques" (i.e., not by genetic engineering), would be adequate for genetically engineered organisms (51 *Fed. Reg.* 23302-3, June 26, 1986). Therefore, additional legislation was unnecessary.

To support that approach, the Coordinated Framework continued the narrow, technical terms of debate by focusing only on specific safety and efficacy characteristics of each product. In other words, the framework and subsequent related policies expressly dismissed issues associated with the genetic-engineering process itself; instead, the regulatory framework dealt only with the use of the resulting product. Consequently, GE foods and other products would be reviewed by the Food and Drug Administration, the Department of Agriculture, and the Environmental Protection Agency "in essentially the same manner for safety and efficacy as products obtained by other techniques" (51 *Fed. Reg.* 23304, June 26, 1986).

Six years later, in the first Bush administration's policy limiting the exercise of federal agency discretion to regulate the planned introduction of biotechnology products into the environment, the OSTP reiterated, in somewhat stronger language, that "the process of modification is . . . independent of the safety of the organism" (57 *Fed. Reg.* 6753, February 27, 1992). That foundation was essential to the presumption that GE organisms phenotypically similar to traditionally bred (i.e., artificially selected rather than genetically engineered) organisms are substantially equivalent and should not be regulated more rigorously. However, the administration took the additional step of increasing the burden of proof for proponents of precautionary regulatory oversight.

The 1992 policy provided that where an applicable statute allows for the exercise of agency discretion, "oversight will be exercised *only where the risk* posed by the introduction *is unreasonable,* that is, when the value of the reduction in risk obtained by additional oversight is greater than the cost thereby imposed" (57 *Fed. Reg.* 6753, February 27, 1992; emphasis added).

In the absence of demonstrable harm, anyone seeking regulatory oversight to address risks on a precautionary basis faces the substantial problem of establishing a degree of risk and a value of risk reduction sufficient to justify protective regulation.

In its 1992 policy announcement, the OSTP made this burden clear by relying upon other policy documents, including the Competitiveness Council Fact Sheet on Critical Technologies (April 1991), which the OSTP paraphrased as follows: "Regulations should be issued *only on evidence* that their potential benefits exceed their potential costs. . . . Regulations that seek to reduce health or safety risks should be based upon scientific risk-assessment procedures, and should address *risks that are real and significant rather than hypothetical or remote*" (57 *Fed. Reg.* 6761-62, February 27, 1992; emphasis added).

Even within the "health and safety" risk limitation of the 1992 policy (which excluded other potential social impacts entirely), the task of demonstrating sufficiently concrete risk—in the absence of evidence proving harm that has already occurred—is a significant burden. Yet control of theoretical risks—"hypothetical or remote" risks, in the eyes of some proponents of genetic engineering—may be the only tool for preventing potential harms that could be irreversible in the long run. There are few meaningful opportunities for citizens to consider either the nature of the risks or their acceptability in the larger social context of the potential harms.

In some situations, the burden of proof is further increased. For example, the FDA's consideration of potential environmental impacts of new animal drugs may follow a path that has neither specific, substantive standards nor public scrutiny of the process. The genetically engineered growth-hormone-delivery systems of transgenic salmon are examples. No statute sets substantive environmental safety standards for these organisms.[2] Only the standards of the Federal Food, Drug and Cosmetic Act (FFDCA, 21 U.S.C. §§301-60bbb-2) and the procedural requirements of the National Environmental Policy Act apply (NEPA, 42 U.S.C. §§4321-47). NEPA's usefulness derives primarily from disclosure requirements that provide the opportunity for public discussion of potential environmental impacts. However, to comply with the Trade Secrets Act, FDA regulations drastically limit the disclosure of information to the public in the NEPA environmental review process (see 21 C.F.R. 25.50[b]).[3]

Indeed, this proprietary information may never be available to the public, even if it is essential to the FDA's decision (21 C.F.R. 25.51[a]). For example, if the FDA determines that an Environmental Assessment or Environmental Impact Statement (EIS) is necessary for investigations or approvals of animal drugs, the EIS "will become available only at the time of the approval of the product" (21 C.F.R. 25.52[a]). The public then has the extremely heavy burden of submitting comments *after* the agency's approval, but without access to the excluded information, in an attempt to convince the FDA to reverse its decision (21 C.F.R. 25.52[b]). In effect, this system protects not the public but rather the intellectual property and commercial opportunities of the applicant seeking approval of the technology.

This approach is consistent with the OSTP's 1992 policy announcement, which made clear that competitiveness considerations are primary concerns for federal regulatory agencies. Whenever statutes do not preclude agency discretion, the policy constrains the agency's actions in its oversight of biotechnologies (57 *Fed. Reg.* 6757). Referring to the report of the President's Council on Competitiveness (February 1991), the OSTP stated:

> The Administration has sought to eliminate unneeded regulatory burdens for all phases of the development of new biotechnology products—laboratory and field experiments, products development, and eventual sale and use. Existing regulatory structures . . . provide an adequate framework for regulation of biotechnology in those limited instances where private markets fail to provide adequate incentives to avoid unreasonable risks to health and the environment. In these instances, regulation also can help shield industry from avoidable incidents that could tarnish its image and impair its development. (6761)

Reinforced by this industry-centered view of regulatory oversight, the structure of the regulatory framework, the burden of proof, and the proprietary control of information all impede or nullify opportunities for the practice of democracy.

WHO GETS THE BENEFIT, WHO BEARS THE RISK?

Social conflict over the deployment of genetically engineered products is exacerbated by the fact that, at least to date, the entities receiving the purported benefits from the products are often completely different from those bearing most of the risks. For example, the farmers whose corn crops were no longer marketable because of genetic material introgression from StarLink pollen obviously suffered economic harm that was not paired with benefit. In another example, organic farmers are unlikely to derive benefits from genetic engineering, but they must bear the risk that their crops will be affected by genetically engineered varieties grown nearby or by insect resistance to non-genetically engineered Bt-insecticide products.[4] Similarly, non-GE canola producers in Canada or corn farmers in Mexico bear the burden of risk from inadvertent transfer of genetic material through open pollination by GEOs.

In a different context, transgenic salmon, which have not yet been deployed, may impose ecological and social risks for the wild-salmon industry and the human communities that depend upon the wild-salmon catch. The degree of ecological risk depends on a number of factors, including the extent to which fertile transgenic fish escape into the ecosystems of wild fish. The economic effects of the StarLink corn incident were the result of unintentional contamination, but the economic risks of transgenic fish may arise not only from the unintended results of consumers' difficulty in differentiating natural from genetically engineered products but also from intentional competitive effects. Regardless of the type and degree of risk, however, the benefits of transgenic growth-hormone-enhanced fish would go primarily to the patent holders and their licensees. Consumers might also benefit if prices were driven down by substantially higher yields, but whether this will actually happen is difficult to predict.[5]

If current agriculture serves as a guide, consumer benefits from GE salmon—as well as other foods—may prove elusive. The agricultural economist Neil Harl suggests that consumers have been "largely unimpressed" with genetically engineered agricultural crops thus far because they have not seen foods with lower prices or superior qualities (2003, 2). Without those benefits, "any concern about food safety leads to consumer discounting" of genetically engineered foods and a preference for non-GE foods. Whether or not consumers perceive benefits from GE salmon and accept them in the market, questions about the mixture of benefits and risks are important subjects for public discussion and decision making. The issues take on added importance because consumer benefits from GE salmon would accrue mainly to relatively wealthy consumers in the industrial North, whereas most of the risks would be borne by those living near and dependent on the ecosystems of which wild salmon are a part.

More generally, the economic benefits of output-increasing genetically engineered organisms, whether fish or crops, will likely go primarily to the firms that own the patents on the organisms and to the producers who are early adopters of the technologies (Harl 2003). Despite the controversy that has surrounded genetically engineered foods, farmers in the United States and a few other countries do see significant benefits in the production of these crops. However, if genetically engineered crops ultimately increase output, they (like other output-increasing agricultural technologies) may exacerbate the problem of low prices faced by the farm sector as a whole.[6]

Some farmers who grow GE crops perceive additional risks to their farming operations—risks that are beyond the scope of current policy consideration. In the words of a potato farmer who adopted Monsanto's NewLeaf potato, which is genetically engineered for resistance to the Colorado potato beetle (NatureMark 2002), "There is a cost. It gives corporate America one more noose around my neck" (quoted in Pollan 1998, 92).[7]

These examples demonstrate that a meaningful discussion of the nature and distribution of the risks, including not only health and safety issues but also potential social and economic impacts, is essential to a policy outcome that maximizes the gain to society as a whole. William Lacy (2000) argues that in some European countries, various formulations of the "precaution-ary principle" provide an indirect way of considering unintended social con-sequences and of choosing among the possible configurations of risks and benefits. Once deployment has occurred and harms have been realized, of course, it may be too late to revisit and revise the choice. Consequently, the precautionary approach may provide a one-time-only opportunity for con-sidering the distribution of risks and benefits and making reasoned choices. The precautionary principle essentially buys time to allow for consideration of the potential severity of risks and for selection among the possible risks.

The real issue is the necessity for serious consideration of potential risks and other social effects, even if that means delaying or placing conditions on some uses of the technologies. Such considerations may or may not result in the rejection of these technologies. Some applications of genetic engineering—in pharmaceutical or other medical uses, for example—already enjoy substantial social acceptance, perhaps because the potential benefits are more apparent, or may be widely shared. Genetic engineering in the food sector does not enjoy a similar base of support. Under these cir-cumstances, a sustained, thoughtful public conversation about the nature of the risks and their relation to the benefits seems essential. Indeed, the rush to approve and use these technologies without discussion is warranted only if all other interests are considered subordinate to those of the corporations that own the intellectual property being promoted.

Several commentators argue that the overall benefits to society may also be reduced by unintended disincentives to scientific research and innova-tion. In his chapter, William Boyd highlights the complex of effects that are driven by the biotechnology industry's imperatives to acquire and control intellectual property in order to secure competitive position, effects that are enabled by U.S. intellectual-property and antitrust law. Interlocking patents, reinforced by private litigation that strengthens the patents' blocking effect, have not only concentrated intellectual-property assets but also constrained the practice of applied and basic science by other firms and university researchers, thus deterring innovation. Two leading legal scholars charac-terize the current configuration of intellectual property and antitrust law as an "anti-commons" (see Heller and Eisenberg 1998). The negative effects of this legal thicket are compounded by the trend toward increasingly pri-vate control of information and the processes for generating knowledge.

Other analysts also document a decades-long shift toward an increasing private-sector role in public agricultural research (see, e.g., Busch 1994; Buttel 2001; Kenney 1986; Kloppenburg 1988). When this shift is com-bined with the growing commitment to intellectual property rights inhering in genetic information and the technologies for deriving that information, the meaningful evaluation of risks, benefits, and unintended social impacts becomes even more problematical.

IN SEARCH OF THE PUBLIC INTEREST

Missing from our current approach to genetic engineering is a serious commitment to the exercise of democracy in pursuit of the public interest. It is neither necessary nor desirable to conclude that all applications of genetic engineering pose unacceptable risks or that society should forgo the potential benefits of molecular genetics in the production of food and raw materials. However, a vigorous democracy requires a meaningful public conversation about where the power to make decisions and to allocate the risks and benefits of these technologies should reside. The public has a fundamental interest in deciding what risks are acceptable, in knowing who will bear those risks, and who is in a position to receive the benefits. Without the effective practice of democracy, members of the public whose concerns have been excluded from the policy discussion have few alternatives but to reject and attack the uses of these technologies across the board.

Proponents of the status quo may object that democratic institutions—the Congress and executive branch administrative agencies—have set the current standards, that these institutions are politically accountable, and that by definition the public interest is reflected in their decisions. However, that argument mistakenly equates the existence of public institutions with the meaningful practice of democracy. When existing public entities systematically exclude from consideration substantial areas of social concern and place the burden of proof in such a way as to give private actors freedom to impose risks—not only on their own populace and environment but also on those of the rest of the world—the practice of democracy needs attention so that the state's "fundamental social duty" can be reconciled with opportunities for private gain. To address this larger public interest, the authors in this volume have suggested several issues that require the participation of a broader set of interests than are currently included in the policy discussion. In U.S. law, the concept of pursuing the public interest, even where important private property rights are involved, is hardly new; and it may therefore be useful to consider settings in which public policies have explicitly required government regulatory agencies to protect the public interest.

For example, modern water law (primarily state law) in the American West has integrated specific public-interest content into a conditional property rights system that depends on the extraction and beneficial use of water from natural watercourses. Under appropriative water rights law in the western states, private users of water are able to obtain a limited property interest in the use of water as long as the appropriator makes beneficial use of the water—a requirement that conditions the water right and makes the property interest less than absolute. Today, the overwhelming majority of states have permit systems that impress water rights with an explicit public-interest requirement. That is, state government water agencies may condition or deny water rights permits in order to ensure that the grant of the water right is compatible with the public interest (Sax et al. 2000).

Reflecting this principle, California's water code requires the State Water Resources Control Board to allow water appropriation under terms and conditions that will best develop, conserve, and utilize the water "in the public interest" (California Water Code, Section 1253) and to reject applications for water rights when the proposed appropriation "would not best conserve the public interest" (Section 1255). As early as the mid-1960s, the California courts held that the "public interest" is the primary standard that the State Water Resources Control Board must implement in acting upon applications to appropriate water. The board's public-interest determination process includes consideration of not only technical issues but also social impacts. In an area where extremely valuable resources, socioeconomic effects, and property interests are enmeshed, California requires engagement with the public interest.[8]

The point is that although property interests in appropriated water could have been absolute, they are not. Instead, water policy in most of the western United States has recognized an essential public interest that travels with the water through its various uses. Private markets may be useful in moving water from uses of lower economic value to uses of higher value, but society has allowed water markets to operate only in a modified form. This approach reflects the state's policy of ensuring that the public's interest in the use of water is not consigned entirely to private decisions.

A second example of a mandatory, active search for the public interest is the public trust doctrine. Based upon principles of Roman law transported to England and then to the British colonies in North America, the public trust doctrine is a body of law articulated primarily by state courts to protect the public's interest in certain services provided by nature (Sax 1970). The doctrine arose out of the need to protect public access to and use of navigable waters, fisheries resources, seabeds, streambeds, lake bottoms, and adjacent lands. Protected uses originally included navigation, commerce, and fisheries; but many states have now added recreation to these uses and extended public trust principles to include broader protected interests such as environmental quality and ecosystem functions (see Johnson 1989; Johnson and Galloway 1994).[9]

Despite variations among states in the scope of the doctrine, Joseph Sax—the leading commentator on the theory underpinning the doctrine—has identified a "central substantive thought" underlying public trust litigation: "When the state holds a resource which is available for the free use of the general public, a court will look with considerable skepticism upon *any* governmental conduct which is calculated *either* to reallocate that resource to more restricted uses *or* to subject public uses to the self-interest of private parties" (Sax, 1970, 490, emphasis in original).

The doctrine does not prevent a state from granting to a private party (or to any group narrower than the general public) a portion of the resources associated with the trust and thereby reducing the traditional public uses. However, courts have demanded that decisions about such grants be made in a clearly articulated, publicly visible way by a governmental entity that is sufficiently broad-based to be accountable for the contemplated changes.[10] That is, courts have required that democracy function to ensure that the broader public, not just the narrower interests that benefit from the change, has the opportunity to shape the outcome and to protect its shared interests.

Neither water appropriation nor public trust doctrine provides a template for the public-policy questions at issue in the conflicts over food and raw materials produced by genetic engineering. The point is that we already have models that directly engage in the search for a public interest that is not merely the aggregated private interests associated with use of public resources or with subjecting those resources to risks. In moving away from this basic democratic principle, as we seem to be doing in the case of biotechnology, society is poised to suffer a serious loss.

The exploration of public interest outcomes for the new biotechnologies may involve, as Boyd suggests, rethinking basic patent law issues and considering stronger antitrust oversight to address the concentration of strategic assets in the hands of only a few firms. Adjustments to the burden of proof may be necessary in situations where the risk is borne by the public but the benefit goes to private actors. The public interest may require, in some instances, protective standards that apply during the process of generating information adequate for an evaluation of potential risks and reliable safeguards. It may also be desirable to revisit some of the technical issues, including the assumptions that have limited the inquiry, as well as the processes for evaluating those issues. In the words of one scientist, that means not only "getting the science right" but also "doing the right science" (Kapuscinski 2002, 387). Finally, meaningful engagement with the public interest will certainly entail addressing concerns about broad social effects, not merely technical details.

Lacy (2000) has argued that biotechnology policy discussions in the United States have been limited to three areas: human safety, animal and environmental safety, and the efficacy of the technology for its intended uses. Evaluation of a fourth criterion—social and economic effects—should be a prerequisite for approval and regulation of a product or technology application. To avoid unintended adverse effects, those who make decisions about the uses of technologies need to consider "the balance between the different worldviews and values" by engaging in "social, economic and moral as well as scientific analysis" (77-78). Lacy's suggestion highlights a serious gap in our public policy formulation. Much of U.S. regulatory policy on genetic engineering has assumed that the public interest is substantially equivalent to the interests of private firms. The constraints on federal agency oversight and the narrow, technical terms of the policy debate reflect that assumption.

Our opportunities, whether in policy development or in further research, lie in helping society to benefit from the promise of these powerful new technologies while ensuring that affected human and nonhuman communities are represented as partners in the decisions about how to share those benefits and their associated risks. Toward that end, as we consider the use of genetic engineering, we would be wise to improve the workings of our national democracy.

However, the issue of democratic decision making about biotechnology extends beyond the domestic policies of the United States, as do the potential effects of these technologies and the economic activities of the multinational firms that own most of the technologies. As Frederick Buttel and Kathleen McAfee indicate in this volume, the United States and other industrialized countries that are committed to genetic engineering have come into sharp conflict with many developing countries over control of the new biotechnologies, particularly in relation to agro-food systems. Led by the United States, the North has challenged the authority of these countries to regulate technology deployment, even though the ecological and social effects could be significant. The strains in North-South power relations arise from the sense that a handful of countries are deciding for the rest. At an international level, this tension mirrors domestic concerns about how democracy is being overridden in the rush to commercialize applications of genetic engineering. These international political struggles, exacerbated by preexisting power inequalities between countries, raise additional questions about equity and justice, which are fundamentally questions about who has the power to decide for whom.

Unlike selective breeding and culture techniques, which are informed by centuries of human experience with incremental modifications of plants and animals, genetic engineering can make abrupt changes that would otherwise be extremely unlikely to occur. Human society has had little chance to adjust to these leaps, which extend beyond our social institutions and shared experience. However, challenges and conflicts arise not only from the changes in food, fiber, and pharmaceuticals generated by genetic engineering but also from the potential for radical changes in the structure of production systems and regulatory institutions. Some countries that produce agricultural commodities—Australia, Brazil, India, and Thailand, to name a few—have perceived an opportunity to differentiate their non-genetically engineered products from GE commodities to exploit a market advantage (Harl 2003; see also Buttel 2002). But the gap is more fundamental than merely market specialization, for it highlights differences in ideas about human welfare, self-determination, and food security. For example, from the perspective of the biotechnology industry, concentration among seed-producing companies may be seen as a by-product of international competition, an artifact of the quest for greater efficiency in production, and an opportunity created by intellectual property rights. But in a world bound tightly by ties of global trade and multinational economic agreements, the loss of control over such a basic element of human welfare—seeds—may undercut the foundation of food security and cultural identity for some nations.

This volume has explored some of the ways in which we have become more globally interconnected by the new biotechnologies. Genetic engineering has increased at such a rapid pace, and has introduced such significant transformations, that the horizon is rushing toward us with a complex array of potential benefits and risks for humankind. If genetic engineering lives up to the claims of its proponents, it may provide the tools to remake our world. But at this moment of exhilarating new developments, our most important challenge may be as old as the struggle for democracy, equity, and justice. For it is human values, not technical innovation, that will determine how choices about these new technologies are made.

NOTES

1. Subject to the Coordinated Framework are the regulatory policies of the Food and Drug Administration (FDA), Environmental Protection Agency (EPA), Occupational Safety and Health Administration (OSHA), and Department of Agriculture (USDA) The framework also pertains to the research policies of the National Institutes of Health, National Science Foundation, EPA, and USDA. Where more than one agency has authority to provide regulatory oversight, the Coordinated Framework streamlines the regulatory process by establishing a lead agency and requiring that all reviews be consolidated or coordinated by that agency.

2. In specific, limited circumstances, provisions of the Endangered Species Act of 1974 (ESA), as amended, may provide substantive standards. For example, the Gulf of Maine distinct population segment of Atlantic salmon has been listed under the ESA. See 65 Fed. Reg. 69459 (November 17, 2000). As a consequence, the provisions of ESA Sections 7 and 9 would apply. See 16 U.S.C. §§1531-44; see also Mary Colligan, National Marine Fisheries Service, and Michael J. Bartlett, U.S. Fish and Wildlife Service, to Charles Eirkson, FDA, October 30, 2001, regarding interagency consultation under ESA Section 7(a)(2) with respect to the ESA-listed Gulf of Maine distinct population segment of Atlantic salmon and the FDA's consideration of Aqua Bounty Farms' application seeking FDA approval for "production and marketing of genetically modified Atlantic salmon" (1). A scanned photocopy of the letter appears at www.centerforfoodsafety.org/gefish/legal/fws&nmfscomment.pdf (as of December 8, 2002).

3. The regulations cite the Trade Secret Act, 18 U.S.C. §§1905 and 301(j).

4. Commercial *Bacillus thuringiensis* (Bt) products, sold under a variety of trade

names, are available as microbial insecticides and are used by organic farmers. Insect-resistant lines of Bt-transformed tobacco, cotton, corn, tomatoes, potatoes, and other plants are now available. Monsanto Company, the dominant producer of these genetically engineered plants, has argued that Bt resistance is "very unlikely to occur" from Bt-transformed crops (Monsanto Company 2002).

5. The effect that transgenic salmon could have on the salmon market is hard to predict for several reasons. First, the yield effects of the new GE technologies are not known, and they may vary between the short and the long run, particularly if nature "fights back" in unexpected ways. Second, if salmon prices do fall, this decline could force some producers—not only salmon fishers but also salmon farmers—out of business, likely resulting in further industry concentration and increased market power for those firms that remain. Third, salmon market differentiation (segmentation) over time, could offset potential consumer benefits and might even result in price premiums for certain types of salmon (e.g., wild salmon and "GEO-free" farmed salmon).

6. In the case of a yield-increasing technology like Bt corn, an increase in aggregate output will result in lower prices (Harl 2003). In the face of inelastic demand for corn, higher output will reduce profitability for all producers. In the case of a cost-reducing technology like Roundup Ready soybeans, the technology may increase output by extending production to areas where it would otherwise be uneconomical. The result again will be a "disproportionate drop in price and in profitability for the producer" (8).

7. Monsanto's rebuttal to Pollan's (1998) article focuses on safety issues and is available at www.monsanto.co.uk/news/98/november98/110198_MonsantoPR.html (as of December 6, 2002). In 2001, Monsanto removed the NewLeaf potato from the market (see Schurman and Munro, this volume).

8. The California Water Code contains several provisions that require consideration of the public interest in water rights determinations (see, for example, Sections 1256, 1257, 1257.5, and 1258). California appellate courts have emphasized that the "public interest" requirements of the California Water Code are the primary statutory standard that guides appropriation of water. See, for example, *United States v. State Water Resources Control Bd.*, 182 Cal. App. 3d 82; 227 Cal. Rptr. 161 (Cal. App. 1 Dist. 1986) and *Johnson Rancho County Water Dist. v. State Water Rights Bd.* 45 Cal. Rptr. 589; 235 Cal. App. 863 (Cal. App. 3 Dist. 1965). The importance of social effects in the California approach to water rights is underscored by the state's area-of-origin laws, which are intended to take account of potential effects on local communities or areas from which water may be transferred. See, for example, Sections 11460 and 11463.

9. See *National Audubon Society v. Superior Court of Alpine County*, 33 Cal. 3d 419; 189 Cal. Rptr. 346; 658 P. 2d 709 (California Supreme Court 1983); *Marks v. Whitney*, 6 Cal. 3d 251; 98 Cal. Rptr. 790; 491 P. 2d 374 (California Supreme Court 1971); *Orion Corp. v. State*, 747 P. 2d 1062, 1073 (Washington Supreme Court 1987).

10. Sax (1980) has argued that some courts' articulations of the public trust doctrine go beyond procedure assurances of democracy to require satisfaction of substantive standards.

GLOSSARY

We use most terms in their common, dictionary senses. However, some issues require a more specialized vocabulary. This glossary provides basic definitions of terms that are used in this book's chapters or that may be useful in understanding the concepts presented. Except as otherwise indicated, the definitions are taken or adapted from the Scientists' Working Group on Biosafety's *Manual for Assessing Ecological and Human Health Effects of Genetically Engineered Organisms (Part 1)* (1998) and from *The Language of Biotechnology: A Dictionary of Terms,* by John M. Walker and Michael Cox (1995).

Antibody	A protein that is synthesized by plasma cells in response to invasion by an antigen and that confers immunity against subsequent invasions by the same antigen.
Antigen	A molecule that stimulates production of neutralizing antibody proteins when introduced into a vertebrate animal.
Bacillus thuringiensis (Bt)	A bacterium that occurs naturally on plants and in soil ("Bacteria" 2002). Different Bt varieties produce proteins that are toxic to specific insect groups.
Diploid (*see* Ploidy).	
DNA sequencing	Determination of the order of nucleotides in a sample of DNA.
Gene flow	The exchange and movement of genes within and between populations and species.
Gene introgression	Incorporation of a gene into the gene pool of a population.

Genetic swamping	Inundation of a population by new or alternate genotypes of the same species or by hybrid derivatives descended from that species, with consequent change in genetic structure.
Genome	The genetic constitution of an organism; the complete set of chromosomes and all associated genes.
Haploid (see Ploidy).	
Immunoglobulin	An antibody secreted by mature plasma cells (King and Stansfield 1997, 175).
Monoclonal antibody	An immunoglobulin that is produced by a single clone of plasma cells (lymphocytes), is chemically and structurally identical to all immunoglobulins produced by the cell or the clone of the cell, and has specific antigen-binding properties (King and Stansfield 1997, 220; Walker and Cox 1995, 184).
Nonreproductive interference	Interference by one organism or species with the nonreproductive functions of another organism or species (e.g., through changes in competition, predation, parasitism, etc.).
Novel trait	Expression of a phenotypic trait not normally found in the species.
Nuclear transplantation	The process by which the haploid nucleus of an egg is removed and a genetically different diploid nucleus is implanted. This process causes the organism to develop the genetically determined characteristics of its new nucleus.
Phenotype	The observable physical or biochemical characteristics of an organism as determined both by its genetic makeup and by environmental influences.
Ploidy	A multiple of the basic number of full sets of homologous chromosomes in a cell. (Homology refers to the degree of identity between two nucleotide sequences.) Haploidy indicates a single set of chromosomes. Diploidy indicates two full sets of homologous chromosomes. Higher ploidy levels (e.g., triploidy, tetraploidy, hexaploidy, etc.) are also known. In general, polyploidy refers to a number of chromosome sets that is multiplied by an integer greater than two.
Polymerase chain reaction (PCR)	An enzymatic method for selectively amplifying a specific nucleotide sequence several millionfold in a few hours. This method allows amplification of as little as a single molecule of DNA to provide sufficient amounts of material for analysis, cloning, or other oper-

ations. The three steps in the PCR cycle are summarized in Walker and Cox 1995, 216-18.

Protein-encoding DNA sequences	Either a stretch of DNA coding for a single protein or a part of a complete, spliced protein-coding sequence. Splicing is accomplished by transcribing the gene's DNA sequence into RNA and then removing the non-coding portions (called intervening sequences or introns) located between the stretches of DNA that contain the coding sequences (called exons). These coding parts are then joined to produce a molecule of RNA that provides instructions for the exact amino acid sequence of the final protein product.
Protoplast fusion	Genetic modification (unique to plants) that involves fusing protoplasts (plant cells from which the cell wall has been removed). The fused protoplasts regenerate a cell wall.
Recombinant DNA	A DNA molecule formed in vitro by ligating DNA molecules that are not normally joined.
Regulatory DNA sequences	Gene sequences that do not code for proteins that go into the structure or metabolism of an organism but instead control or regulate the expression of other genes. These sequences may turn other genes on or off and may increase or decrease the activity of protein-encoding genes (yielding more or less production from these genes).
Stochastic variability	Changes or differences resulting from chance or random events.
Tissue culture	The process by which small pieces of living tissue (explants) are isolated from an organism and grown aseptically in a defined or semidefined nutrient medium. The term covers both organ culture and cell culture (in which explant tissue is dispersed enzymatically or mechanically and propagated as a cell suspension or attached monolayer).
Transgenic organism	An organism whose genetic composition has been altered to include selected genes from other organisms of the same or different species by methods other than those used in traditional breeding (artificial selection). Methods for creating transgenic organisms include microinjection of DNA into the zygote, introduction of DNA by retroviral infection, and DNA transfection into cultured embryonic stem cells that are injected into a blastocyst.

Zygote   A diploid cell that results from the union of a haploid
                                female gamete and a haploid male gamete (King and
                                Stansfield 1997, 370).

ADDITIONAL RESOURCES

Standard references (e.g.,Walker and Cox 1995) provide more extensive
discussions of these terms and concepts. The *Manual for Assessing Ecological
and Human Health Effects of Genetically Engineered Organisms* prepared by the
Scientists' Working Group on Biosafety (1998) contains a concise glossary
and is available online at www.edmonds-institute.org/manual.html (as of
December 8, 2002). In addition to these references, several Internet
resources provide background information about biotechnologies and
their processes. Useful materials, produced by organizations with sharply
different perspectives, are available at the web sites of the Biotechnology
Industry Organization (2002a, 2002b) and the Union of Concerned
Scientists (2002).

CONTRIBUTORS

William Boyd is a 2003–4 AAAS Science and Technology Policy Congressional Fellow. He received his J.D. from Stanford Law School and his Ph.D. from the Energy and Resources Group at the University of California, Berkeley.

Frederick H. Buttel is Professor in the Department of Rural Sociology; Professor of Environmental Studies; and Co-Director of the Program on Agricultural Technology Studies at the University of Wisconsin, Madison. Buttel has published widely in the areas of environmental sociology; the sociology of agriculture, agricultural research, and technological change; and the sociology of economic change and development. Most recently, Buttel has coedited *Environment and Global Modernity* (2000), *Hungry for Profit* (2000), and *Sociological Theory and the Environment* (2002). A new edition of his *Environment, Energy, and Society* was published in 2002.

David Goodman is Professor and Chair in the Department of Environmental Studies at the University of California, Santa Cruz. His work explores the interrelationships between agro-food sectors, technological innovation, and environmental change. He is coauthor of *From Farming to Biotechnology* (1987) and *Refashioning Nature: Food, Ecology, Culture* (1991) and coeditor of *Globalising Food: Agrarian Questions and Global Restructuring* (1997), and he has written numerous articles on food and agrarian issues.

Julie Guthman is Assistant Professor of Community Studies at the University of California, Santa Cruz. Her research interests are in agro-food sector change and environmental politics, with a focus on California and the American West. She has published several articles on the production, consumption, and regulation of organic food. Her forthcoming book with

University of California Press examines the political economy of organic agriculture in California.

Dennis Doyle Takahashi Kelso is Assistant Professor of Environmental Studies at the University of California, Santa Cruz, where he teaches and conducts research on environmental issues at the intersection of law, policy, and science. Between 1986 and 1990, he was Alaska Commissioner of Environmental Conservation and, before that, Deputy Commissioner of Fish and Game in Alaska. He received a J.D. from Harvard University and a Ph.D. from the Energy and Resources Group at the University of California, Berkeley.

Kathleen McAfee is Assistant Professor of Geography at the Yale School of Forestry and Environmental Studies. Her recent research concerns new biotechnologies, intellectual property rights to genetic information and living organisms, and related challenges for food security and sovereignty, the conservation of food-crop biodiversity, and rural livelihoods. She is the author of *Storm Signals: Structural Adjustment and Development Alternatives in the Caribbean* (1991) and many articles on community development, gender, race, and social and environmental justice.

William A. Munro is Assistant Professor in the Department of Political Science at Illinois Wesleyan University. He works on agrarian change and state formation in Southern Africa and is the author of *The Moral Economy of the State: Conservation, Community Development, and State-Making in Zimbabwe* (Ohio University Press, 1998). Currently, he is working with Rachel Schurman on a book about social resistance to biotechnology.

W. Scott Prudham is Assistant Professor in the Department of Geography, the Program in Planning, and the Institute for Environmental Studies at the University of Toronto. His research interests are in the politics, economics, and regulation of natural-resource appropriation and environmental change. Most of his current work concerns forests and forestry in western North America. He is author of a forthcoming book titled *The Nature of Capital: Political Ecology on the Pacific Slope* (Routledge Press, forthcoming in 2004).

Astrid J. Scholz received her Ph.D. from the Energy and Resources Group at the University of California, Berkeley. Her chapter is based on her dissertation, titled "Green Gold: The Science, Politics, and Business of Harnessing the World's Biological Riches for Novel Pharmaceuticals," which she is preparing for publication. She is also collaborating on a book about the linkages between local knowledge and global environmental governance (MIT Press, forthcoming in 2004). She works as an ecological economist with Ecotrust, a nonprofit organization that promotes a conservation economy in the Pacific Northwest.

Rachel A. Schurman is Assistant Professor of Sociology at the University of Illinois in Urbana-Champaign. She teaches and publishes in the areas of environmental sociology, development studies, and the political economy of agriculture and rural change. She has worked in Latin America and the western Pacific region and is now collaborating with William Munro on a book on social resistance to biotechnology and its effects on firms, states, and the trajectory of biotechnology.

BIBLIOGRAPHY

Abley, M. 2000. "The Bio-Battle of Words." *The Gazette* (Montreal), January 29.

Adams, W. T., V. D. Hipkins, J. Burczyk, and W. K. Randall. 1997. "Pollen Contamination Trends in a Maturing Douglas-Fir Seed Orchard." *Canadian Journal of Forest Research* 27:131-34.

A/F Protein Inc. 1997. "Aqua Bounty Farms' Response." *Aqua Bounty Farms Update: News from Aqua Bounty Farms and the World of Ag-Biotech* (promotional brochure) 1 (3): 2-3.

————. [1998]. *Aqua Bounty Farms Update: News from Aqua Bounty Farms and the World of Ag-Biotech.* (promotional brochure).

————. 1999. "Aqua Bounty Farms: Broodstock Development." Retrieved March 15, 2000, from www.afprotein.com/bounty.htm.

Agnew, B. 2000. "When Pharma Merges, R&D Is the Dowry." *Science* 287 (March 17): 1952.

"Agracetus Soybean Patent Challenged by Monsanto, Public Interest Groups." 1994. *Biotechnology Newswatch,* December 19, 5.

"Agreement between the United States of America and the Socialist Republic of Vietnam on Trade Relations." 2000. July 13. Retrieved December 11, 2002, from www.vietsandiego.com/vietnews/archives/us-vntrade.html.

Agricultural Statistics Board, National Agricultural Statistics Service, U.S. Department of Agriculture. 2001. June Agricultural Survey, Biotechnology Varieties. Retrieved November 24, 2002, from www.ers.usda.gov/Briefing/biotechnology/Data/nasscrop2001.pdf.

Albers-Schönberg, G. 1995. "The Pharmaceutical Discovery Process." In *Intellectual Property Rights and Biodiversity Conservation,* ed. T. Swanson. Cambridge: Cambridge University Press.

Alexander, T. D. 1999. "The Patentability of Algorithms." *Nature Biotechnology* 17 (4): 395.

Allen, G. 1978. *Life Sciences in the Twentieth Century.* Cambridge: Cambridge University Press.

Allen, P., and M. Kovach. 2000. "The Capitalist Composition of Organic: The Potential of Markets in Fulfilling the Promise of Organic Agriculture." *Agriculture and Human Values* 17 (3): 221-32.

Alliance for Better Foods. 2001. "Accurate and Informative Product Labeling." Retrieved June 1 from www.betterfoods.org/Regulations/Labeling/Labeling.htm.

Altieri, M., and P. Rosset. 1999. "Ten Reasons Why Biotechnology Will Not Ensure Food Security, Protect the Environment, and Reduce Poverty in the Developing World." *AgBioForum* 2 (3-4): 155-62.

American Forest Council. 1987. *Forest Industry-Sponsored Research Cooperatives at U.S. Forestry Schools.* Washington, D.C.: American Forest Council.

Artuso, A. 1997. *Drugs of Natural Origin: Economic and Policy Aspects of Discovery, Development, and Marketing.* New York: The Pharmaceutical Products Press.

Atlantic Salmon Watch Program. 2002. "Reported BC Atlantic Salmon Escapes." Fisheries and Oceans Canada—Pacific Region. Retrieved December 8, 2002, from www.pac.dfo-mpo.gc.ca/sci/aqua/pages/atlsalm.htm.

Aylward, B. 1995. "The Role of Plant Screening and Plant Supply in Biodiversity Conservation, Drug Development, and Health Care." In *Intellectual Property Rights and Biodiversity Conservation,* ed. T. Swanson. Cambridge: Cambridge University Press.

Aylward, B., and E. Barbier. 1996. "Capturing the Pharmaceutical Value of Biodiversity in a Developing Country." *Environmental and Resource Economics* 8:157-81.

"Aventis Wins Appeal against Monsanto." 2000. *Chemical Week,* March 1, 10.

"Bacteria." 2002. *Biological Control: A Guide to Natural Enemies in North America,* ed. C. R. Weeden, A. M. Shelton, Y. Li, and M. P. Hoffmann. Retrieved May 5 from www.nysaes.cornell.edu/ent/biocontrol/pathogens/bacteria.html.

Bains, W. 1998. *Biotechnology from A to Z.* 2d ed. Oxford: Oxford University Press.

Balick, M. J., and R. Mendelsohn. 1992. "Assessing the Economic Value of Traditional Medicines from Tropical Rainforests." *Conservation Biology* 6 (1): 128-30.

Barboza, D. 1999a. "DuPont Buying Top Supplier of Farm Seed." *New York Times,* March 16.

———. 1999b. "Biotech Companies Take On Critics of Gene-Altered Food." *New York Times,* November 11.

———. 1999c. "Monsanto Sued over Use of Biotechnology in Developing Seeds." *New York Times,* December 15.

———. 2000a. "Industry Moves to Defend Biotechnology." *New York Times,* April 4.

———. 2000b. "AstraZeneca to Sell a Genetically Engineered Strain of Rice." *New York Times,* May 16.

———. 2001a. "As Biotech Crops Multiply, Consumers Get Little Choice." *New York Times,* June 10.

———. 2001b. "Consumers Get Little Choice: Altered Types Found Even in Organic Food." *New York Times,* June 17.

Barrett, A. 2000. "Rocky Ground for Monsanto?" *Business Week,* June 12, 72-76.

Barton, J. H. 1998. "The Impact of Contemporary Patent Law on Plant Biotechnology Research." In *Intellectual Property Rights III, Global Genetic Resources: Access and Property Rights,* ed. S. A. Eberhardt, H. L. Shands, W. Collins, and R. L. Lower. Madison, Wisc.: Crop Science Society of America.

———. 1999. "Intellectual Property, Biotechnology, and International Trade: Two

Examples." Discussion Paper for World Trade Forum, Berne, Switzerland, August 1999.

———. 2000. "Rational Limits on Genomic Patents." *Nature Biotechnology* 18 (8): 805.

———. 2002. "Antitrust Treatment of Oligopolies with Mutually Blocking Patent Portfolios," *Antitrust Law Journal* 69:851.

B.C. Salmon Farmers Association. 2002a. "Salmon Farming in BC Today." Retrieved January 3, 2003, from www.salmonfarmers.org/industry/today.html.

———. 2002b. "The Global Industry." Retrieved April 4, 2003, from www .salmonfarmers. org/industry/global.html.

———. Undated-a. "Environmental and Other Issues: Pollution, Water Quality, and Benthic Impacts." *Net Work: Information from the BC Salmon Farmers.* Vancouver, B.C.: B.C. Salmon Farmers Association.

———. Undated-b. "Environmental and Other Issues: Use of Antibiotics in Salmon Farming." *Net Work: Information from the BC Salmon Farmers.* Vancouver, B.C.: B.C. Salmon Farmers Association.

Beck, U. 1992. *Risk Society: Towards a New Modernity.* Translated by M. Ritter. Theory, Culture, and Society, ed. M. Featherstone. Thousand Oaks, Calif.: Sage.

Belsie, L. 2000. "Superior Crops or 'Frankenfood'? Americans Begin to Reconsider Blasé Attitude toward Genetically Modified Food." *Christian Science Monitor,* March 1.

Bender, K., and R. Westgren. 2001. "Social Construction of the Market(s) for Genetically Modified and Non-Modified Crops." *American Behavioral Scientist* 44 (8): 1350-70.

Bernton, H. 2000. "Hostile Market Spells Blight for Biotech Potatoes." *Seattle Times,* April 30.

Bijker, W. E., T. P. Hughes, and T. J. Pinch. 1987. *The Social Construction of Technological Systems: New Directions in the Sociology and History of Technology.* Cambridge: MIT Press.

Bijker, W. E., and J. Law. 1992. *Shaping Technology/Building Society: Studies in Sociotechnical Change.* Inside Technology. Cambridge: MIT Press.

Biotechnology Industry Organization. 2000. "Biotechnology Industry Statistics." Retrieved October 28, 2000, from www.bio.org/aboutbio/guide1.html#stats.

———. 2002a. "A Collection of Technologies." Retrieved May 5 from www.bio.org/er/technology_collection.asp.

———. 2002b. "The Technologies and Their Applications." Retrieved May 5 from www.bio.org/er/applications.asp.

Bird, E. 1987. "The Social Construction of Nature: Theoretical Approaches to the History of Environmental Problems." *Environmental Review* 11, no. 4 (winter): 255-64.

Blaustein, R. 1996. "Convention on Biological Diversity Draws Attacks." *National Law Journal* 19 (9): C39-40.

Boadle, A. 1999. "EU Ministers Rap EC on WTO Biotechnology Concession." Reuters, December 1. Retrieved from www.reuters.com.

Boal, I. A. 2001. "Damaging Crops: Sabotage, Social Memory, and the New Genetic Enclosures." In *Violent Environments,* ed. N. L. Peluso and M. Watts. Ithaca, N.Y.: Cornell University Press.

Bonanno, A., L. Busch, W. H. Friedland, L. Gouveia, and E. Mingione, eds. 1994.

From Columbus to ConAgra: The Globalization of Agriculture and Food. Rural America. Lawrence: University Press of Kansas.

Bordelon, M. A. 1988. "Genetic Improvement Opportunities." In *Assessment of Oregon's Forests: A Collection of Papers,* ed. G. J. Lettman. Salem: Oregon State Department of Forestry.

Borlaug, N. 2000. "Ending World Hunger. The Promise of Biotechnology and the Threat of Antiscience Zealotry." *Plant Physiology* 1 (24): 487-90.

Boyd, W., S. Prudham, and R. Schurman. 2001. "Industrial Dynamics and the Problem of Nature." *Society and Natural Resources* 14 (7): 555-70.

Boyle, A. E. 1996. "The Rio Convention on Biological Diversity." In *International Law and the Conservation of Biological Diversity,* ed. M. Bowman and C. Redgwell. London: Kluwer Law International.

Brand, U. 2000. *Nichtregierungsorganisationen, Staat und Ökologische Krise: Konturen Kritischer NRO-Forschung.* Münster: Westfälisches Dampfboot.

Brasher, P. 2001. "More Genetic Soybeans Planned." *San Francisco Chronicle,* April 2.

Braverman, H. 1974. *Labor and Monopoly Capital.* New York: Monthly Review Press.

Broydo, L. 1998. "Engineering an Organic Standard." *Mother Jones,* May/June.

Brunner, Amy M., Rozi Mohamed, Richard Meilan, Lorraine A. Sheppard, William H. Rottman, and Steven H. Straus. 1998. "Genetic Engineering of Sexual Sterility in Shade Trees." *Journal of Arboriculture* 24 (5): 263-73.

Brush, S. 1996. "Is Common Heritage Outmoded?" In *Valuing Local Knowledge: Indigenous People and Intellectual Property Rights,* ed. S. B. Brush and D. Stabinsky. Washington, D.C.: Island Press.

Brush, S. B., and D. Stabinsky, eds. 1996. *Valuing Local Knowledge: Indigenous People and Intellectual Property Rights.* Washington, D.C.: Island Press.

Bryan, J. 1997. "Agricultural Biodiversity in Indigenous Communities." In *Protecting What's Ours: Indigenous Peoples and Biodiversity,* ed. D. Rothschild. Oakland, Calif.: South and Meso-American Indian Rights Center.

Bud, R. 1993. *The Uses of Life: A History of Biotechnology.* Cambridge: Cambridge University Press.

————. 1998. "Molecular Biology and the Long-Term History of Biotechnology." In *Private Science: Biotechnology and the Rise of the Molecular Sciences,* ed. A. Thackray. Philadelphia: University of Pennsylvania Press.

Bugge, H. C., and M. W. Tvedt. 2000. "A Legal Look at Article 15 in the Convention on Biological Diversity: Access to Genetic Resources." In *Responding to Bioprospecting: From Biodiversity in the South to Medicines in the North,* ed. H. Svarstad and S. S. Dhillion. Oslo: Spartacus Forlag.

Bugos, G. E., and D. J. Kevles. 1992. "Plants as Intellectual Property: American Practice, Law, and Policy in World Context." *Osiris,* 2d ser., 7:75-104.

Burger, E. J., Jr. 1990. "Health as a Surrogate for the Environment." *Daedalus* 119 (4): 133-53.

Burns, G., and P. X. Chiem. 1999. "Food Fight for the FDA: Dozens Protest Use of Altered Ingredients." *Chicago Tribune,* November 19.

Busch, L. 1994. "The State of Agricultural Science and the Agricultural Science of the State." In *From Columbus to ConAgra: The Globalization of Agriculture and Food,* ed. A. Bonanno, L. Busch, W. H. Friedland, L. Gouveia, and E. Mingione. Rural America. Lawrence: University Press of Kansas.

————. 1995. *Making Nature, Shaping Culture: Plant Biodiversity in Global Context.* Lincoln: University of Nebraska Press.

Busch, L., and A. Juska. 1997. "Beyond Political Economy: Actor Networks and the Globalization of Agriculture." *Review of International Political Economy* 4 (4): 688-708.

Busch, L., and W. B. Lacy. 1983. *Science, Agriculture, and the Politics of Research.* Boulder, Colo.: Westview.

Busch, L., and W. B. Lacy, eds. 1986. *The Agricultural Scientific Enterprise.* Boulder, Colo.: Westview.

Busch, L., and W. B. Lacy, J. Burkhardt, and L. R. Lacy. 1991. *Plants, Power, and Profits: Social, Economic, and Ethical Consequences of the New Biotechnologies.* Oxford: Basil Blackwell.

Busch, L., and K. Tanaka. 1996. "Rites of Passage: Constructing Quality in a Commodity Subsector." *Science, Technology, and Human Values* 21:3-27.

Buttel, F. H. 1986a. "Agricultural Research and Farm Structure Change: Bovine Growth Hormone and Beyond." *Agriculture and Human Values* 3:88-98.

————. 1986b. "Biotechnology and Public Agriculture Research Policy." In *Agricultural Science Policy in Transition,* ed. V. J. Rhodes. Bethesda, Md.: Agricultural Research Institute.

————. 1993. "Ideology and Agricultural Technology in the Late Twentieth Century: Biotechnology as Symbol and Substance." *Agriculture and Human Values* 10 (2): 5-15.

————. 1999. "Agricultural Biotechnology: Its Recent Evolution and Implications for Agrofood Political Economy." *Sociological Research Online* 4 (3).

————. 2000. "The Recombinant BGH Controversy in the United States: Toward a New Consumption Politics of Food?" *Agriculture and Human Values* 17 (3): 5-20.

————. 2001. "Land-Grant/Industry Relationships and the Institutional Relations of Technological Innovation in Agriculture." In *Knowledge Generation and Technical Change: Institutional Innovation in Agriculture,* ed. S. A. Wolf and D. Zilberman. Boston, Mass.: Kluwer Academic Publishers.

————. 2002. "The Adoption and Diffusion of GM Crop Varieties: The 'Gene Revolution' in Global Perspective, 1996-2001." Program on Agricultural Technology Studies, no. 6, University of Wisconsin.

Buttel, F. H., and C. C. Geisler. 1989. "The Social Impacts of Bovine Somatotropin: Emerging Issues." In *Biotechnology and the New Agricultural Revolution,* ed. J. J. Molnar and H. Kinnucan. Boulder, Colo.: Westview.

Buttel, F. H., and D. Goodman. 1989. "Class, State, Technology, and International Food Regimes." *Sociologia Ruralis* 29 (2): 86-92.

Buttel, F., M. Kenney, and J. Kloppenburg Jr. 1985. "From Green Revolution to Biorevolution: Some Observations on the Changing Technological Bases of Economic Transformation in the Third World." *Economic Development and Cultural Change* 34 (1): 31-55.

Buttel, F. H., M. Kenney, J. Kloppenburg Jr., J. T. Cowan, and D. Smith 1986. "Industry/Land Grant University Relationships in Transition." In *The Agricultural Scientific Enterprise,* ed. L. Busch and W. B. Lacy. Boulder, Colo.: Westview.

Buttel, F. H., and P. McMichael. 1990. "New Directions in the Political Economy of Agriculture." *Sociological Perspectives* 33 (1): 89-109.

Buttel, F. H., and H. Newby, eds. 1980. *The Rural Sociology of the Advanced Societies: Critical Perspectives.* Montclair, N.J.: Allanheld, Osmun.

Caldwell, D. J. 1998. *Ecolabeling and the Regulatory Framework—A Survey of Domestic and International Fora.* Retrieved October 30 from Consumer's Choice Council Web site at www.consumerscouncil.org.

Callon, M. 1987. "Society in the Making: The Study of Technology as a Tool of Sociological Analysis." In *The Social Construction of Technological Systems: New Directions in the Sociology and History of Technology,* ed. W. Bijker, T. Hughes, and T. Pinch, 83-103. Cambridge: MIT Press.

Carlberg, J. M. 1999. Presentation at a technical session titled "Genetically Engineered Advances in Aquaculture: Reshaping America's Seafood Supply," San Francisco Seafood Show, San Francisco, November 4.

Carr, S., and L. Levidow. 1999. "Coping with Environmental Uncertainty by Social Learning: The Case of Agricultural Biotechnology Regulation in Europe." In *Systems for Sustainability,* ed. F. A. Stowell, R. L. Ison, R. Armson, and J. Holloway. New York: Plenum.

Castells, M. 1996. *The Rise of the Network Society.* Vol. 1, *The Information Age: Economy, Society, and Culture.* Cambridge, Mass.: Blackwell.

Castree, N. 1995. "The Nature of Produced Nature: Materiality and Knowledge Construction in Marxism." *Antipode* 27 (1): 12-48.

Center for Media and Democracy. 1997. "Shut Up and Eat: The Beef Industry's Lawsuit against Oprah Winfrey." *PR Watch* 4 (2).

CEQ/OSTP. 2001. CEQ and OSTP Assessment: Case Studies of Environmental Regulations for Biotechnology. Case Study no. 1: Growth-Enhanced Salmon. Washington, D.C.: Council on Environmental Quality and Office of Science and Technology Policy. Retrieved December 8, 2002, from www.ostp.gov/html/ceq_ostp_study2.pdf.

Charles, D. 2001. *Lords of the Harvest: Biotech, Big Money, and the Future of Food.* Cambridge, Mass.: Perseus Publishing.

Cheliak, W. M., and D. L. Rogers. 1990. "Integrating Biotechnology into Tree Improvement Programs." *Canadian Journal of Forest Research* 20 (4): 452-63.

Chen, L., and F. H. Buttel. 2000. "Adoption and De-Adoption of GMO Crop Varieties in Wisconsin." Paper presented at the Annual Meeting of the Rural Sociological Society, Washington, D.C., August.

Chivian, E. 1997. "Global Environmental Degradation and Biodiversity Loss: Implications for Human Health." In *Biodiversity and Human Health,* ed. F. Grifo and J. Rosenthal. Washington, D.C.: Island Press.

Churchill, L. U. 1996. *Maine Finfish Aquaculture: An Overview.* West Boothbay Harbor: Maine Department of Marine Resources.

Clapp, S., and S. Romero Melchor. 2001. "EU Member States Balk at Endorsing Biotech Regime." *Food Traceability Report* 1 (6): 24.

Clunies-Ross, T. 1990. "Agricultural Change and the Politics of Organic Farming." Ph.d. diss., University of Bath.

Cohen, R. 1999. "Fearful over the Future, Europe Seizes on Food." *New York Times,* August 29.

Comstock, G. 1988. "The Case against BGH." *Agriculture and Human Values* 5 (3): 36-52.

"Concurrent USDA-DOJ Merger Review Debated at Senate Agriculture Hearing." 2000. *FTC Watch*, no. 544, May 8.

Cosbey, A. 2000. *Institutional Challenges and Opportunities in Environmentally Sound Trade Expansion: A Review of the Global State of Affairs*. The North-South Agenda, paper no. 41. Miami: Dante B. Fascell North-South Center, University of Miami.

Cosbey, A., and S. Burgiel. 2000. *The Cartagena Protocol on Biosafety: An Analysis of Results*. Winnipeg, Canada: International Institute for Sustainable Development.

Cragg, G. M., M. Boyd, R. Khanna, D. Newman, and E. Sausville. 1999. "Natural Product Drug Discovery and Development: The United States National Cancer Institute Role." In *Phytochemicals in Human Health Protection, Nutrition, and Plant Defense*, ed. J. T. Romeo. New York: Kluwer Academic/Plenum Publishers.

Cragg, G., D. Newman, and K. Snader. 1997. "Natural Products in Drug Discovery and Development." *Journal of Natural Products* 60 (1): 52-60.

Crane, S. E., S. B. Kelber, and M. R. Labgold. 2000. "Degeneracy in the Legal Code: Can the Patent and Trademark Office (PTO) and the Federal Circuit Reach a Consensus regarding Patenting Biotech Inventions?" *Journal of Biolaw and Business* 4 (1): 39-42.

Crook, S. 1998. "Biotechnology, Risk, and Sociocultural (Dis)Order." In *Altered Genes*, ed. R. Hindmarsh, G. Lawrence, and J. Norton. St. Leonards, Australia: Allen & Unwin.

"Crop Biotech Leaders DuPont, Monsanto Taking Different Roads." 1999. Dow Jones Newswires, March 17.

Cummins, R. 2000. "News & Analysis on Genetic Engineering, Factory Farming, & Organics." *BioDemocracy News*, no. 29.

Dana, S. T., and S. K. Fairfax. 1980. *Forest and Range Policy, Its Development in the United States*. 2d ed. McGraw-Hill Series in Forest Resources. New York: McGraw-Hill.

Danaher, K., and R. Burbach, eds. 2000. *Globalize This: The Battle against the World Trade Organization and Corporate Rule*. Monroe, Maine: Common Courage Press.

Daniels, J. D. 1984. "Role of Tree Improvement in Intensive Forest Management." *Forest Ecology and Management* 8:161-95.

Dawkins, K. 2000. "Battle Royale of the 21st Century." *Seedling: The Quarterly Newsletter of Genetic Resources Action International* 17 (1): 2-8.

"Dekalb Genetics Alleges Infringement of Patent on Insect-Resistant Corn." 1996. *Mealey's Litigation Reports: Intellectual Property* 4 (23).

DeLind, L. B. 1993. "Market Niches, 'Cul De Sacs,' and Social Context: Alternative Systems of Food Production." *Culture and Agriculture*, no. 47: 7-12.

Demeritt, D. 2001. "Scientific Forest Conservation and the Statistical Picturing of Nature's Limits in the Progressive-Era United States." *Environment and Planning D: Society and Space* 19:431-59.

Deogun, N., R. A. Langreth, and T. M. Burton. 1999. "Pharmacia & Upjohn, Monsanto Boards Approve $27 Billion Merger of Equals." *Wall Street Journal*, interactive edition, December 20.

Devlin, R. H. 1997. "Transgenic Salmonids." In *Transgenic Animals: Generation and Use*, ed. L. M. Houdebine. Amsterdam, Netherlands: Harwood Academic Publishers.

Devlin, R. H., C. A. Biagi, T. Y. Yesaki, D. E. Smailus, and J. C. Byatt. 2001. "Growth of Domesticated Transgenic Fish—A Growth-Hormone Transgene Boosts the Size of Wild but Not Domesticated Trout." *Nature* 409 (6822): 781-82.

Devlin, R. H., and E. M. Donaldson. 1992. "Containment of Genetically Altered Fish with Emphasis on Salmonids." In *Transgenic Fish*, ed. C. L. Hew and G. L. Fletcher. Singapore: World Scientific.

Devlin, R. H., T. Y. Yesaki, C. A. Biagi, E. M. Donaldson, P. Swanson, and W. K. Chan. 1994. "Extraordinary Salmon Growth." *Nature* 371 (6494): 209-10.

Diamond v Chakrabarty, 447 U.S. 303 (1980).

Dibner, M., ed. 1999. *Biotechnology Guide USA*. Research Triangle Park, N.C.: Institute for Biotechnology Information.

Directorate-General for Agriculture. Commission of the European Communities. 2000. "Economic Impacts of Genetically Modified Crops on the Agri-Food Sector: A Synthesis." Working paper B1049, European Commission, Brussels.

"DOJ Approves $2.3 Billion Merger of Genetic Technology Corporations." 1998. *Andrews Mergers & Acquisitions Litigation Reporter*. December.

Doll, J. J. 1998. "The Patenting of DNA." *Science* 280 (May 1): 689-90.

Donaldson, E. M., R. H. Devlin, F. Piferrer, and I. I. Solar. 1996. "Hormones and Sex Control in Fish with Particular Emphasis on Salmon." *Asian Fisheries Science* 9:1-8.

Donaldson, E. M., R. H. Devlin, I. I. Solar, and F. Piferrer. 1993. "The Reproductive Containment of Genetically Altered Salmonids." In *Genetic Conservation of Salmonid Fishes*, ed. J. G. Cloud and G. H. Thorgaard. New York: Plenum Press.

Dove, M. 1996. "Center, Periphery, and Biodiversity: A Paradox of Governance and a Developmental Challenge." In *Valuing Local Knowledge: Indigenous People and Intellectual Property Rights*, ed. S. B. Brush and D. Stabinsky. Washington, D.C.: Island Press.

"Dow, Monsanto Sign DNA Research Deals." 1980. *Chemical Week*, October 29, 17.

Doyle, J. 1985. *Altered Harvest: Agriculture, Genetics, and the Fate of the World's Food Supply*. New York: Viking.

Drahos, P. 1999. "The TRIPs Review." Paper presented at the Conference on Strengthening Africa's Participation in the Review and Revision of the TRIPs Agreement of the World Trade Organization, Nairobi, Kenya, February 6-7.

Drews, J. 2000. "Drug Discovery: A Historical Perspective." *Science* 287 (March 17): 1960-64.

Du, S. J., Z. Gong, G. L. Fletcher, M. A. Shears, and C. L. Hew. 1992. "Growth Hormone Gene Transfer in Atlantic Salmon: Use of Fish Antifreeze/Growth Hormone Chimeric Gene Construct." In *Transgenic Fish*, ed. C. L. Hew and G. L. Fletcher. Singapore: World Scientific.

Dunkley, G. 2000. *The Free Trade Adventure: The WTO, the Uruguay Round, and Globalism*. London: Zed.

"DuPont Claims Monsanto Stole Technology for Herbicide-Resistant Soybeans." 2000. *Delaware Law Weekly*, April 4.

"DuPont Files Two Antitrust Lawsuits against Monsanto." 2000. *Chemical Week*, April 5.

"DuPont Licenses 'Gene Gun' Technology to Dekalb Genetics." 1996. *Biotech Patent News* 10 (1).

"DuPont Says Court Ruling Doesn't Prevent Roundup Marketing." 2001. Dow Jones Newswires, March 21.

DuPuis, M. 2000. "Not in My Body: rBGH and the Rise of Organic Milk." *Agriculture and Human Values* 17 (3): 285-95.

Dutfield, G. 2000. *Intellectual Property Rights, Trade, and Biodiversity.* London: Earthscan Publications.

Economic Research Service. U.S. Department of Agriculture. 1999. "Competition Facing U.S. Aquaculture in 2000 and Beyond." *Aquaculture Outlook,* October 4.

Egziabher, T. B. G. 2000. "Biosafety Negotiations—Flashbacks." *Third World Resurgence,* no. 114/115.

Eichenwald, K., G. Kolata, and M. Petersen. 2001. "Biotechnology Food: From the Lab to a Debacle." *New York Times,* January 25.

Eisenberg, R. S. 1996. "Public Research and Private Development: Patents and Technology Transfer in Government-Sponsored Research." *Virginia Law Review* 82:1663.

———. 2000. "Re-Examining the Role of Patents in Appropriating the Value of DNA Sequences." *Emory Law Journal* 49:783.

Eisner, M. A. 1993. *Regulatory Politics in Transition.* Baltimore: Johns Hopkins University Press.

Eisner, T. 1989. "Prospecting for Nature's Chemical Riches." *Issues in Science and Technology* 6 (2): 31-34.

———. 1991. "Chemical Prospecting: A Proposal for Action." In *Ecology, Economics, and Ethics: The Broken Circle,* ed. F. Bormann and R. Kellert. New Haven, Conn.: Yale University Press.

Ellefson, P. V. 1995. "Forestry Research Undertaken by Private Organizations in Canada and the United States: A Review and Assessment." In *The Role of the Private Sector in Forestry Research: Recent Developments in Industrialized Countries,* ed. R. Romeo. Rome: Food and Agriculture Organization of the United Nations.

Ellis and Associates. 1996. *Net Loss: The Salmon Netcage Industry in British Columbia.* Report prepared for the David Suzuki Foundation, Vancouver, B.C., October 1996.

Endres, M. G., and A. B. Endres. 2000. "Regulation of Genetically Modified Organisms in the European Union." *American Behavioral Scientist* 44 (3): 378-434.

Enriquez, J. 1998. "Genomics and the World Economy." *Science* 281 (August 14): 925-26.

———. 2000. "The Life Science Revolution: A Rough Map." *Journal of Biolaw and Business* 4 (1).

Entis, E. 1997. "Aquabiotech: A Blue Revolution?" *World Aquaculture* 28 (1): 12-15.

———. 1999. Presentation at a technical session titled Genetically Engineered Advances in Aquaculture: Reshaping America's Seafood Supply, San Francisco Seafood Show, San Francisco, November 4.

Environmental Assessment Office. 1997. *The Salmon Aquaculture Review Final Report.* Vol. 1, *Report of the Environmental Assessment Office.* Victoria, B.C.: Environmental Assessment Office. August 20.

Ernst & Young. 2000. *The Economic Contributions of the Biotechnology Industry to the U.S. Economy.* Report prepared for the Biotechnology Industry Organization, Washington, D.C., May.

Escobar, A. 1998. "Whose Knowledge, Whose Nature? Biodiversity, Conservation, and the Political Ecology of Social Movements." *Journal of Political Ecology* 5:53-82.

Evans, P. B. 1995. *Embedded Autonomy: States and Industrial Transformation.* Princeton Paperbacks. Princeton, N.J.: Princeton University Press.

"Extreme Tides, Strong Currents Cause Break-Up at Washington Farm." 1999. *Northern Aquaculture* 5 (7): 14.

Fairley, P. 1998a. "Dow Ups Mycogen Stake on Eve of Bt Patent Suit." *Chemical Week,* January 28, 10.

———. 1998b. "Monsanto Prevails in Mycogen Suit." *Chemical Week,* February 18, 13.

———. 1998c. "Monsanto Outspends Rivals for Dekalb, Snaps Up Cotton Giant." *Chemical Week,* May 20, 10.

———. 1998d. "Genomics Race Is On." *Chemical Week,* July 29, 9.

———. 1998e. "Zeneca Claims Monsanto Is 'Monopolizing' the Herbicides Market." *Chemical Week,* August 12, 8.

———. 1998f. "Justice Approves Monsanto's Dekalb Purchase." *Chemical Week,* December 9, 12.

———. 1998g. "The Genomics Race." *Chemical Week,* December 23/30, 18.

Falk, W. W., and J. Gilbert. 1985. "Bringing Rural Sociology Back In." *Rural Sociology* 50 (4): 561-77.

Feder, B. J. 1998. "Getting Biotechnology Set to Hatch." *New York Times,* May 2.

Federal Bureau of Investigation. 2002. "Statement for the Record of Dale L. Watson, Executive Assistant Director, Counterterrorism and Counterintelligence, Federal Bureau of Investigation, on the Terrorist Threat Confronting the United States, before the Senate Select Committee on Intelligence." Congressional Statement, Federal Bureau of Investigation, Washington, D.C. Retrieved April 25 from www.fbi.gov/congress/congress02/watson020602.htm.

Ferrara, J. 1998. "Revolving Doors: Monsanto and the Regulators." *The Ecologist* 28 (5): 280-86.

Figueres, C. 1997. "Partnerships with the Private Sector in Biodiversity Development and Ecosystem Services." Presentation at the Latin America Associated Event, World Bank Conference on Environmentally and Socially Sustainable Development, Washington, D.C., October 8.

FitzSimmons, M., and D. Goodman. 1998. "Incorporating Nature: Environmental Narratives and the Reproduction of Food." In *Remaking Reality: Nature at the Millennium,* ed. B. Braun and N. Castree. London: Routledge.

Flitner, M. 1998. "Biodiversity: Of Local Commons and Global Commodities." In *Privatizing Nature,* ed. M. Goldman. New Brunswick, N.J.: Rutgers University Press.

Forster, J. 1999a. "Aquaculture Chickens, Salmon—A Case Study." *World Aquaculture* 30 (3): 33-40, 69-70.

———. 1999b. Presentation at a session titled "Aquaculture Debate," Fish Expo WorkBoat Northwest, Seattle, Washington, November 19.

Fortun, M. 1998. "The Human Genome Project and the Acceleration of Biotechnology." In *Private Science: Biotechnology and the Rise of the Molecular Sciences,* ed. A. Thackray. Philadelphia: University of Pennsylvania Press.

Foucault, M. 1994. *The Order of Things.* 2d English ed. New York: Vintage Books.

Fowler, C. 1994. *Unnatural Selection: Technology, Politics, and Plant Evolution.* Yverdon, Switzerland: Gordon and Breach Scientific Publishers.

Fowler, C., E. Lachkovics, P. Mooney, and H. Shand. 1987. *The Laws of Life: Another Development and the New Biotechnologies.* Special issue of *Development Dialogue* (Dag Hammarskjöld Centre, Upsalla, Sweden), nos. 1-2.

Fowler, C., and P. R. Mooney. 1990. *Shattering: Food, Politics, and the Loss of Genetic Diversity.* Tucson: University of Arizona Press.

Fox, N. 1997. *Spoiled: Why Our Food Is Making Us Sick and What We Can Do about It.* New York: Penguin.

Fox Keller, E. 1995. *Refiguring Life: Metaphors of Twentieth-Century Biology.* New York: Columbia University Press.

———. 2000. *The Century of the Gene.* Cambridge: Harvard University Press.

Frewer, L. J., C. Howard, and R. Shepherd. 1997. "Public Concerns in the United Kingdom about General and Specific Applications of Genetic Engineering: Risk, Benefit, and Ethics." *Science, Technology, and Human Values* 22:98-124.

Friedland, W. H. 1991. "Introduction: Shaping the New Political Economy of Advanced Capitalist Agriculture." In *Towards a New Political Economy of Agriculture,* ed. W. H. Friedland, L. Busch, F. H. Buttel, and A. P. Rudy. Boulder, Colo.: Westview.

———. 1992. "The End of Rural Society and the Future of Rural Sociology." *Rural Sociology* 47 (4): 589-608.

Friedlin, J. 2000. "New Theme for Shareholder Activism: Policing Genetically Modified Food." *New York Times,* May 4.

Friedmann, H., and P. McMichael. 1989. "Agriculture and the State System: The Rise and Fall of National Agricultures, 1870 to the Present." *Sociologia Ruralis* 29 (3/4): 93-117.

Fujimura, J. 1997. "The Molecular Biological Bandwagon in Cancer Research: Where Social Worlds Meet." In *Grounded Theory in Practice,* ed. A. Strauss and J. Corbin. Thousand Oaks, Calif.: Sage.

Funk Brothers Seed Co. v. Kalo Inoculant Co., 333 U.S. 127 (1948).

Gamez, L. 1993. "Costa Rica's Conservation Program and National Biodiversity Institute (INBio)." In *Biodiversity Prospecting: Using Genetic Resources for Sustainable Development,* ed. W. V. Reid. Washington, D.C.: World Resources Institute.

Geisler, C. C., and E. M. DuPuis. 1989. "From Green Revolution to Gene Revolution: Common Concerns about Agricultural Biotechnology in the First and Third Worlds." In *Biotechnology and the New Agricultural Revolution,* ed. J. J. Molnar and H. Kinnucan. Boulder, Colo.: Westview.

Gertler, M. S., and T. J. Barnes. 1999. *The New Industrial Geography: Regions, Regulations and Institutions.* Routledge Studies in the Modern World Economy, no. 22. London: Routledge.

Glickman, D. 1999. U.S. Department of Agriculture press release no. 0229.99, May 24. Retrieved April 30, 2002, from www.usda.gov/news/releases/1999/05/0229.

Gold, E. R. 2000. "Moving the Gene Patent Debate Forward." *Nature Biotechnology* 18 (12): 1319-20.

Goldberg, G. 2000. Comments of Gary Goldberg, Chief Executive Officer, American Corn Growers Association, before the U.S. Department of Agriculture Advisory Committee on Agricultural Biotechnology. Retrieved April 28.

Goldburg, R., J. Rissler, H. Shand, and C. Hassebrook. 1990. *Biotechnology's Bitter Harvest: Herbicide Tolerant Crops and the Threat to Sustainable Agriculture.* Report of the Biotechnology Working Group, Environmental Defense Fund, New York, March 1990.

Goldburg, R., and T. Triplett. 1997. *Murky Waters: Environmental Effects of Aquaculture in the United States.* Washington, D.C.: Environmental Defense Fund. October.

Golden, F. 2000. "Make Way for Frankenfish! What Happens to These Ordinary Salmon If the Genetically Modified Lunkers Ever Get Loose?" *Time* 155 (9): 62.

Goldsmith, P. D. 2001. "Innovation, Supply Chain Control, and the Welfare of Farmers." *American Behavioral Scientist* 44 (8): 1302-27.

Gonzales, S. 2000. "Biofood Opponents Protest at Safeway Meeting." *San Jose Mercury News,* May 10.

Gonzáles, T., and J. Kloppenburg Jr. 1993. "¡Prohibido Cazar! Expoliacíon Científica, Los Derechos Indígenas Y La Biodiversidad Universal." In *Biotechnología, Recursos Fitogeneticos Y Agricultura en los Andes,* ed. T. Gianella and J. Aragon. Lima, Peru: Comisíon de Coordinacíon de Tecnología Andina.

Goodman, D. 1999. "Agro-Food Studies in the 'Age of Ecology': Nature, Corporeality, Biopolitics." *Sociologia Ruralis* 39 (1): 17-38.

———. 2001. "Ontology Matters: The Relational Materiality of Nature and Agro-Food Studies." *Sociologia Ruralis* 41 (2): 182-200.

Goodman, D., and M. Redclift. 1991. *Refashioning Nature: Food, Ecology, and Culture.* London: Routledge.

Goodman, D., B. Sorj, and J. Wilkinson. 1987. *From Farming to Biotechnology: A Theory of Agro-Industrial Development.* New York: Basil Blackwell.

Goodman, D., and M. Watts. 1997. *Globalising Food: Agrarian Questions and Global Restructuring.* London: Routledge.

Goodman, D., and J. Wilkinson. 1990. "Patterns of Research and Innovation in the Modern Agro-Food System." In *Technological Change and the Rural Environment,* ed. P. Lowe, T. Marsden, and S. Whatmore. London: David Fulton.

Goodman, J. and D. Walsh. 2001. *The Story of Taxol. Nature and Politics in the Pursuit of an Anti-Cancer Drug.* New York: Cambridge University Press.

Gottweis, H. 1998. "The Political Economy of British Biotechnology." In *Private Science: Biotechnology and the Rise of the Molecular Sciences,* ed. A. Thackray. Philadelphia: University of Pennsylvania.

GRAIN (Genetic Resources Action International). 1998. "CBD over TRIPs: Yes, Please!" *Seedling: The Quarterly Newsletter of Genetic Resources Action International* 15 (4).

———. 2000. "Last Chance for an Open Access Regime?" *Seedling: The Quarterly Newsletter of Genetic Resources Action International* 17 (2).

Granovetter, M. 1985. "Economic Action and Social Structure: The Problem of Embeddedness." *American Journal of Sociology* 91:481-510.

Greider, W. 2000. "The Last Farm Crisis." *The Nation* 271 (16): 11-18.

Grifo, F., and J. Rosenthal, eds. 1997. *Biodiversity and Human Health.* Covelo, Calif.: Island Press.

Grisham, J. 2000. "New Rules for Gene Patents." *Nature Biotechnology* 18 (9): 921.

Guidera, J. 1999. "Justice Dept Widens Monsanto Probe as Acquisition Stalls." *Wall Street Journal,* interactive edition, December 17.

Gura, T. 2000. "Reaping the Plant Gene Harvest." *Science* 287 (January 21): 412-14.

Guthman, J. 2000. "Agrarian Dreams? The Paradox of Organic Farming in California." Ph.D. diss., University of California, Berkeley.

Hagenstein, W. D. 1973. *Growing 40,000 Homes a Year.* S.J. Hall Lectureship in Industrial Forestry. Berkeley, Calif.: School of Forestry and Conservation, University of California, Berkeley.

Hallerman, E. M., and A. R. Kapuscinski. 1992. "Ecological and Regulatory Uncertainties Associated with Transgenic Fish." In *Transgenic Fish*, ed. E. L. Hew and G. L. Fletcher. Singapore: World Scientific.

Hamilton, N. D. 1994. "Why Own the Farm If You Can Own the Farmer (and the Crop)? Contract Production and Intellectual Property Protection of Grain Crops." *Nebraska Law Review* 73:48.

Haraway, D. J. 1991. *Simians, Cyborgs, and Women: The Reinvention of Nature.* New York: Routledge.

———. 1997. *Modest_Witness@SecondMillennium.FemaleMan(c)_Meets_OncoMouse^a.* New York: Routledge.

———. 2002. "Cloning Mutts, Saving Tigers: Ethical Emergents in Technocultural Dog Worlds." Paper presented at the Yale Program in Agrarian Studies, New Haven, Conn., April 12.

Harl. N. E. 2003. "Biotechnology: Global Environmental Issues." Paper presented at the Annual Meeting of the Minnesota Chapter of the American Society of Farm Managers and Rural Appraisers, Mystic Lakes Casino Hotel, Prior Lake, Minnesota, February 6.

———. 1999. "Possible Consequences in Input Supply in Agriculture." Testimony to the U.S. Senate Committee on Agriculture, Nutrition, and Forestry, October 6.

Harris, M., and D. T. Massey. 1968. *Vertical Coordination via Contract Farming.* U.S. Department of Agriculture Miscellaneous Publication, MP1073. Washington, D.C.: U.S. Department of Agriculture.

Harvey, D. 1982. *The Limits to Capital.* Chicago, Ill.: University of Chicago Press.

———. 1989. *The Condition of Postmodernity: An Enquiry into the Origins of Cultural Change.* Cambridge, Mass.: Blackwell.

———. 1996. *Justice, Nature, and the Geography of Difference.* Oxford: Basil Blackwell.

Harvie, D. 2000. "Alienation, Class, and Enclosure in UK Universities." *Capital and Class* 71 (summer): 103-33.

Hays, W. M. 1905. "Address to the First Meeting of the American Breeders' Association." *American Breeders' Association I.* Washington, D.C.

Hee, S. 1992. "Intensive Silviculture Stewardship: The Weyerhaeuser Experience." In *The Silviculture Conference: Stewardship in the New Forest,* 72-78. Vancouver, B.C.: Forestry Canada.

Heffernan, W. D., and D. H. Constance. 1994. "Transnational Corporations and the Globalization of the Food System." In *From Columbus to ConAgra: The Globalization of Agriculture and Food,* ed. A. Bonanno, L. Busch, W. H. Friedland, L. Gouveia, and E. Mingione. Rural America. Lawrence: University of Kansas Press.

Held, D., and A. McGrew, eds. 2000. *The Global Transformations Reader.* Cambridge: Polity.

Heller, M. A., and R. S. Eisenberg. 1998. "Can Patents Deter Innovation? The Anticommons in Biomedical Research." *Science* 280 (May 1): 698-701.

Henderson, G. 1998. "Nature and Fictitious Capital: The Historical Geography of an Agrarian Question." *Antipode* 30 (2): 73-118.

Hew, C. L., and G. L. Fletcher. 1996. *Transgenic Salmonid Fish Expressing Exogenous Salmonid Growth Hormone.* U.S. Patent No. 5,545,808. August 13.

Hindmarsh, R. A., G. Lawrence, and J. Norton. 1998. *Altered Genes: Reconstructing Nature: The Debate.* St. Leonards, Australia: Allen & Unwin.

Hirst, P., and G. Thompson. 1999. *Globalization in Question.* Cambridge: Polity.

Hobbelink, H. 1991. *Biotechnology and the Future of World Agriculture.* London: Zed.

Hollingsworth, J. R., and R. Boyer. 1997. *Contemporary Capitalism: The Embeddedness of Institutions.* Cambridge Studies in Comparative Politics. Cambridge: Cambridge University Press.

Holmberg, M. 1999. "Bundling of Seeds and Services Paves the Way for More Vertical Integration of Crop Production." *Successful Farming* 97 (1): 31.

———. 2000. "High Hopes for Genomics." *Successful Farming* 98 (4).

Hornstein, D. T. 1992. "Reclaiming Environmental Law: A Normative Critique of Comparative Risk Analysis." In *Law and the Environment,* ed. R. V. Percival and D. C. Alevizatos. Philadelphia: Temple University Press.

Horst, R. B., and R. T. Fraley. 1998. "Biotechnology Can Help Reduce the Loss of Biodiversity." In *Protection of Global Biodiversity: Converging Strategies,* ed. J. A. McNeeley and L. D. Guruswamy. Durham, N.C.: Duke University Press.

Howard, R. 1996. "Salmon Farming Spokesman Blasts Critical Report." *Toronto Globe and Mail,* October 25.

Howie, M. 1999. "DuPont Makes Move in Purchase of Pioneer." *Feedstuffs* 71 (12).

Hughes, T. P. 1989. *American Genesis: A Century of Invention and Technological Enthusiasm.* New York: Viking.

Hussain, A., and K. Tribe. 1981. *Marxism and the Agrarian Question.* 2 vols. London: Macmillan.

Imfeld, T. 1994. "Implementing Sustainable Development in Costa Rica: Lessons from the Instituto Nacional De Biodiversidad." Master's thesis, Florida International University.

Institute of Forest Genetics. 2002. "Conifer Molecular Genetics and Genomics." Retrieved December 17, 2002, from www.psw.fs.fed.us/ifg/genomic.htm.

International Centre for Trade and Sustainable Development. 1999. "North-South Divide Splits TRIPS Council." *BRIDGES Weekly Trade News Digest* 3 (2). Retrieved April 30, 2002, from www.ictsd.org.

———. 2000. "WTO Members Continue to Wrangle over TRIPs." *Bridges Weekly Trade News Digest* 4 (36). Retrieved September 26, 2000, from www.ictsd.org.

———. 2002. "U.S. Pressures WTO Members on GMOs." *BRIDGES Trade Bio Res* 2 (1): 1-2. Retrieved April 30, 2002, from www.ictsd.org/biores.

ISAAA (International Service for the Acquisition of Agri-Biotech Applications). 2002. ISAAA in Brief. Retrieved April 22, 2002, from www.isaaa.org.

Isaksson, A. 1991. "Culture of Atlantic Salmon." In *Culture of Salmonid Fishes,* ed. R. R. Stickney. Boca Raton, Fla.: CRC Press.

ISFA. 1998. *World Farmed Salmon Supply/Demand Review.* Hobart, Tasmania, Australia: International Salmon Farmers Association. May.

Jacob, F. 1973. *The Logic of Life: A History of Heredity.* Translated by B. E. Spillman. Princeton, N.J.: Princeton University Press.

Jacobs, P. 2000. "Monsanto Offers Up Draft of Genetic Code of Rice Plant." *Los Angeles Times,* April 5.

Jaffe, A. B. 1999. "The U.S. Patent System in Transition: Policy Innovation and the Innovation Process." Working paper no. 7280, National Bureau of Economic Research, Cambridge, Mass.

Jaffee, D. 1999. "Constructing Free Trade as an Environmental Issue: U.S. Environmental Groups, the WTO, and the Challenge to Capital." Master's thesis, University of Wisconsin.

James, C. 1998. *Global Review of Commercialized Transgenic Crops: 1998.* Ithaca, N.Y.: International Service for the Acquisition of Agri-Biotech Applications.

————. 1999. *Global Review of Commercialized Transgenic Crops: 1999.* Ithaca, N.Y.: International Service for the Acquisition of Agri-Biotech Applications.

————. 2000. *Global Status of Commercialized Transgenic Crops: 2000.* Ithaca, N.Y.: International Service for the Acquisition of Agri-Biotech Applications. Available on the Web at www.isaaa.org/publications/briefs/Brief_24.htm (as of November 24, 2002).

————. 2001. *Global Review of Commercialized Transgenic Crops: 2001.* Ithaca, New York: International Service for the Acquisition of Agri-Biotech Applications.

James, R. R. 1997. "Utilizing a Social Ethic toward the Environment in Assessing Genetically Engineered Insect-Resistance in Trees." *Agriculture and Human Values* 14:237-49.

James, R. R., S. P. DiFazio, A. M. Brunner, and S. H. Strauss. 1998. "Environmental Effects of Genetically Engineered Woody Biomass Crops." *Biomass and Bioenergy* 14 (4): 403-14.

Janzen, D. 1991. "The National Biodiversity Institute of Costa Rica: How to Save Biodiversity." *American Entomologist* 37 (3): 159-71.

"Japan's Stand on GM Food Draws Attention." 2001. *Kyodo News,* April 13.

Jepperson, R. 1991. "Institutions, Institutional Effects, and Institutionalism." In *The New Institutionalism in Organizational Analysis,* ed. W. W. Powell and P. DiMaggio. Chicago: University of Chicago Press.

Johnson, R. W. 1989. "Water Pollution and the Public Trust Doctrine." *Environmental Law* 19:485.

Johnson, R. W., and W. C. Galloway. 1994. "Protection of Biodiversity under the Public Trust Doctrine." *Tulane Environmental Law Journal* 8:21.

Josling, T. 1999. "Who's Afraid of the GMOs? EU-US Trade Disputes over Food Safety and Biotechnology." Seminar paper presented at the Center for Advanced Studies and the European Center of California, University of Southern California, March 11.

"Judge Upholds $65 Mil. Verdict." 2000. *Delaware Law Weekly,* February 15.

Juma, C. 1989. *The Gene Hunters: Biotechnology and the Scramble for Seeds.* London: Zed.

Juska, A., and L. Busch. 1994. "The Production of Knowledge and the Production of Commodities: The Case of Rapeseed Technoscience." *Rural Sociology* 59 (4): 581-97.

Kahn, L. 2001. Paper presented at the Future of Food Biotechnology Conference, Washington, D.C., October 29-30.

Kalaitzandakes, N. 1998. "Biotechnology and the Restructuring of the Agricultural Supply Chain." *AgBioForum* 1 (2): 40-42.

Kapuscinski, A. R. 1995. "Implications of Introduction of Transgenic Fish into Natural Ecosystems." In *Environmental Impacts of Aquatic Biotechnology.* Paris: Organisation for Economic Co-Operation and Development.

————. 2002. "Controversies in Designing Useful Ecological Assessments of Genetically Engineered Organisms." In *Genetically Engineered Organisms: Assessing Envi-*

ronmental and Human Health Effects, ed. D. K. LeTourneau and B. E. Burrows. Boca Raton, Fla.: CRC Press.

Kapuscinski, A. R., and E. M. Hallerman. 1991. "Implications of Introduction of Transgenic Fish into Natural Ecosystems." *Canadian Journal of Fisheries and Aquatic Sciences* 48 (supp. 1): 99-107.

———. 1994. *Benefits, Environmental Risks, Social Concerns, and Policy Implications of Biotechnology in Aquaculture.* Springfield, Va.: U.S. Congress, Office of Technology Assessment. October. Available on microfiche through the National Technical Information Service (NTIS order no. PB96-107586).

Kapuscinski, A. R., T. Nega, and E. M. Hallerman. 1999. "Adaptive Biosafety Assessment and Management Regimes for Aquatic Genetically Modified Organisms in the Environment." In *Towards Policies for Conservation and Sustainable Use of Aquatic Genetic Resources,* ed. R. S. V. Pullin, D. M. Bartley, and J. Kooiman. Makati, Philippines: International Center for Living Aquatic Resources Management (ICLARM).

Kaufman, M. 2001a. "Going Backwards: U.S. Will Buy Back Corn Seed, Firms to Be Compensated for Batches Mixed with Biotech Variety." *Washington Post,* March 8.

———. 2001b. "Farmer Liable for Growing Biotech Crops." *Washington Post,* March 30.

Kay, L. E. 1993. *The Molecular Vision of Life: Caltech, the Rockefeller Foundation, and the Rise of the New Biology.* New York: Oxford University Press.

———. 1998. "Problematizing Basic Research in Molecular Biology." In *Private Science: Biotechnology and the Rise of the Molecular Sciences,* ed. A. Thackray. Philadelphia, Penn.: University of Pennsylvania Press.

———. 2000. *Who Wrote the Book of Life? A History of the Genetic Code.* Writing Science. Stanford, Calif.: Stanford University Press.

Keck, M. E., and K. Sikkink. 1998. *Activists beyond Borders: Advocacy Networks in International Politics.* Ithaca, N.Y.: Cornell University Press.

Kelch, D. R., M. Simone, and M. L. Madell. 1998. *Biotechnology in Agriculture Confronts Agreements in the WTO.* Washington, D.C.: Economic Research Service, U.S. Department of Agriculture. December.

Keller, A. C. 2000. "Discourse and Deposition: Decentralizing Scientists in the U.S. Acid Rain Program." Paper presented at Society for Social Studies of Science and the European Association for the Study of Science and Technology Conference 2000, Vienna, September 27-30.

Keller, E. F. 1993. *Refiguring Life: Metaphors of Life in Twentieth-Century Biology.* New York: Columbia University Press.

Kenney, E. A. 1997. *Net Gain: The Salmon Farming Industry in B.C.* Vancouver: B.C. Salmon Farmers Association. January.

Kenney, M. 1986. *Biotechnology: The University-Industrial Complex.* New Haven, Conn.: Yale University Press.

———. 1998. "Biotechnology and the Creation of a New Economic Space." In *Private Science: Biotechnology and the Rise of the Molecular Sciences,* ed. A. Thackray. Philadelphia: University of Pennsylvania Press.

Kenney, M., and J. Kloppenburg Jr. 1983. "The American Agricultural Research System: An Obsolete Structure?" *Agricultural Administration* 14:1-10.

Kevles, D. J. 1998. "*Diamond v. Chakrabarty* and Beyond: The Political Economy of the Patenting of Life." In *Private Science: Biotechnology and the Rise of the Molecular Sciences,* ed. A. Thackray. Philadelphia: University of Pennsylvania Press.

Khor, M. 1999a. "WTO Biotech Working Party Opposed by Majority." *SUNS—South-North Development Monitor,* November 9. Retrieved December 12, 2002, from www.sunsonline.org.

———. 1999b. "Trade: The Revolt of Developing Nations." *SUNS—South-North Development Monitor.* Retrieved December 11, 2002, from www.twnside.org.sg/title/revolt-cn.htm.

Kilman, S. 1998. "Monsanto Is Ordered to Pay Damages Totaling $174.9 Million to Mycogen." *Wall Street Journal,* interactive edition, March 23.

———. 1999. "Antitrust Regulators Are Investigating Monsanto's Control of Cotton Genes." *Wall Street Journal,* interactive edition, December 17.

———. 2001. "Bioengineered Bugs Stir Dreams of Scientists, but Will They Fly?" *Wall Street Journal,* January 26.

———. 2002. "Monsanto Delays Debut of Wheat Bioengineered to Resist Herbicide." *Wall Street Journal,* February 27.

Kimmelman, B. A. 1983. "The American Breeders' Association: Genetics and Eugenics in an Agricultural Context, 1903-1913." *Social Studies of Science* 13:163-204.

King, S., T. Carlson, and K. Moran. 1996. "Biological Diversity, Indigenous Knowledge, Drug Discovery, and Intellectual Property Rights: Creating Reciprocity and Maintaining Relationships." *Journal of Ethnopharmacology* 51:45-57.

King, R. C., and W. D. Stansfield. 1997. *Dictionary of Genetics.* New York: Oxford University Press.

Kingsnorth, P. 1998. "Bovine Growth Hormones." *The Ecologist* 28 (5): 266-69.

Klee, K. 1999. "Frankenstein Foods?" *Newsweek,* September 13, 33.

Kloppenburg, J. R., Jr. 1984. "The Social Impacts of Biogenetic Technology in Agriculture: Past and Future." In *The Social Consequences and Challenges of New Agricultural Technologies,* ed. G. M. Berardi and C. C. Geisler. Boulder, Colo.: Westview.

———. 1988. *First the Seed: The Political Economy of Plant Biotechnology, 1492-2000.* 1st ed. Cambridge: Cambridge University Press.

Kloppenburg, J. R., Jr., and M. Kenney. 1984. "Biotechnology, Seeds, and the Restructuring of Agriculture." *The Insurgent Sociologist* 12 (3): 3-17.

Kloppenburg, J. R., Jr., and D. L. Kleinman. 1987. "The Plant Germplasm Controversy." *Bioscience* 37 (3): 190-98.

Kloppenburg, J. R., Jr., and S. Rodríguez. 1992. "Conservationists or Corsairs?" *Seedling: The Quarterly Newsletter of Genetic Resources Action International* 9 (2-3): 12-17.

Knickerbocker, B. 2000. "Concerns Rise as Ecoterrorists Expand Aim." *Christian Science Monitor,* April 3.

Knight, D. 1999. "Amazon Groups Challenge US Plant Patent." *Inter Press Service News Bulletin,* March 31. Retrieved December 11, 2002, from www.forests.org/archive/brazil/amgroupc.htm.

Knutson, P. 1999. Presentation at a session titled "Aquaculture Debate," Fish Expo WorkBoat Northwest, Seattle, Washington, November 19.

Koch, R. 1995. "The Case of Latour." *Configurations* 3:319-347.

Krimsky, S. 1991. *Biotechnics and Society: The Rise of Industrial Genetics.* New York: Praeger.

―――. 1998. "The Cultural and Symbolic Dimensions of Agricultural Biotechnology." In *Private Science: Biotechnology and the Rise of the Molecular Sciences,* ed. A. Thackray. Philadelphia: University of Pennsylvania Press.

Krimsky, S., and R. P. Wrubel. 1996. *Agricultural Biotechnology and the Environment: Science, Policy, and Social Issues.* The Environment and the Human Condition. Urbana, Ill.: University of Illinois Press.

Kuhn, T. S. 1969. *The Structure of Scientific Revolutions.* 2d ed. Chicago: University of Chicago Press.

Lacy, W. B. 2000. "Agricultural Biotechnology, Socioeconomic Issues, and the Fourth Criterion." In *Encyclopedia of Ethical, Legal, and Policy Issues in Biotechnology,* ed. T. H. Murray and M. J. Mehlman. New York: John Wiley & Sons.

Lambrecht, B. 2001. *Dinner at the New Gene Café: How Genetic Engineering Is Changing What We Eat, How We Live, and the Global Politics of Food.* 1st ed. New York: Thomas Dunne Books.

Lander, E. S., and R. A. Weinberg. 2000. "Genomics: Journey to the Center of Biology." *Science* 287 (March 10): 1777-82.

Lang, M. 2002. "Price of Growing GM Wheat Too High: Farmers Would Lose Millions." *The Star Phoenix,* February 26.

Lappé, M., and B. Bailey. 1998. *Against the Grain: Biotechnology and the Corporate Takeover of Your Food.* Monroe, Maine: Common Courage Press.

Latour, B. 1983. "Give Me a Laboratory and I Will Raise the World." In *Science Observed,* ed. K. D. Knorr-Cetina and M. J. Mulkay. Beverly Hills, Calif.: Sage.

―――. 1988. *The Pasteurization of France.* Cambridge: Harvard University Press.

―――. 1993. *We Have Never Been Modern.* Translated by C Porter. Brighton, U.K.: Harvester Wheatsheaf.

―――. 1994. "On Technical Meditation—Philosophy, Sociology, Geneology." *Common Knowledge* 3 (2): 29-64.

―――. 1999. *Pandora's Hope: Essays on the Reality of Science Studies.* Cambridge: Harvard University Press.

Law, J. 1992. "Notes on the Theory of Actor-Network: Ordering, Strategy, and Heterogeneity." *Systems Practice* 5 (4): 379-93.

―――. 1994. *Organizing Modernity.* Oxford: Blackwell.

Lehrman, S. 1996. "Mycogen Renews Patent Battle with Monsanto over Bt Resistance Genes." *Biotechnology Newswatch,* November 18, 12.

"Let Them Eat Fishmeal." 1997. *Seafood Leader* 17 (3): 14-15.

Levidow, L. 1998. "Democratizing Technology—or Technologizing Democracy? Regulating Agricultural Biotechnology in Europe." *Technology in Society* 20:211-26.

―――. 2000. "Pollution Metaphors in the UK Biotechnology Controversy." *Science as Culture* 9 (3): 325-51.

―――. 2001. "The GM Crops Debate: Utilitarian Bioethics?" *Capitalism, Nature, Socialism* 12 (1): 44-55.

Levidow, L., S. Carr, and D. Wield. 2000. "Genetically Modified Crops in the European Union: Regulatory Conflicts as Precautionary Opportunities." *Journal of Risk Research* 3 (3): 189-208.

Levidow, L., and C. Marris. 2001. "Science and Governance in Europe: Lessons from the Case of Agricultural Biotechnology." *Science and Public Policy* 28 (October): 345-60.

Levidow, L., and J. Tait. 1995. "The Greening of Biotechnology: GMOs as Environment-Friendly Products." In *Biopolitics*, ed. V. Shiva and I. Moser. London: Zed.

Lewontin, R. C. 2000. *The Triple Helix: Gene, Organism, and Environment.* Cambridge: Harvard University Press.

———. 2001. "Genes in the Food!" *New York Review of Books* 48 (10): 81-84.

Lim, L. L. 2000. "Biosafety Talks End on Mixed Note." *Third World Resurgence,* no. 114/115.

Lin, W., G. Price, and E. Allen. 2001. "StarLink: Impacts on the US Corn Market and World Trade." *Feed Situation and Outlook Yearbook,* USDA-ERS, FDS-2001, April, 46-54.

Ling, C. Y. 2000a. "Delayed, but Better, Biosafety Protocol." *Third World Resurgence,* no. 114/115.

———. 2000b. "The Way Forward." *Third World Resurgence,* no. 114/115.

Lockie, S., and S. Kitto. 2000. "Beyond the Farm Gate: Production-Consumption Networks." *Sociologia Ruralis* 40 (1): 3-19.

Loewenberg, S. 1999. "Cultivating Allies in Genetic Food Fight." *Legal Times* 22 (30).

Long, N., J. D. van der Ploeg, C. Curtin, and L. Box. 1986. *The Commodization Debate: Labour Process, Strategy, and Social Network.* Wageningen, Netherlands: Agriculture University.

Losey, J. E., L. S. Rayor, and M. E. Carter. 1999. "Transgenic Pollen Harms Monarch Larvae." *Nature* 399 (May 20): 214.

Lourie, L. S. 1998. "The U.S. Position on Developing Trade Agreements concerning Intellectual Property." In *Intellectual Property Rights III. Global Genetic Resources: Access and Property Rights,* ed. S. Eberhart. Madison, Wisc.: Crop Science Society of America, American Society of Agronomy.

Loy, W. 2000. "'Organic' Label Sought for Salmon." *Anchorage Daily News,* Internet edition, April 13. Available at www.adn.com/stories/T00041330.html.

Lutz, E., and S. E. Serafy. 1988. *Environmental and Resource Accounting: An Overview.* Washington, D.C.: World Bank Environment Department.

Mann, S. 1990. *Agrarian Capitalism in Theory and Practice.* Chapel Hill, N.C.: University of North Carolina Press.

Mann, S., and J. Dickinson. 1978. "Obstacles to the Development of a Capitalist Agriculture." *Journal of Peasant Studies* 5 (4): 466-81.

Marris, C. 2000. *Swings and Roundabouts: French Public Policy on Agricultural GMOs, 1996-1999.* Saint-Quentin-en-Yvelines, France: Centre d'Economie et d'Ethique pour l'Environnement et le Développement, Université de Versailles Saint-Quentin-en-Yvelines.

Marsden, T. 1988. "Exploring Political Economy Approaches in Agriculture." *Area* 20:315-322.

Marsden, T., R. Munton, S. Whatmore, and J. Little. 1986. "Towards a Political Economy of Capitalist Agriculture: A British Perspective." *International Journal of Urban and Regional Research* 10:498-521.

Marsden, T., J. Murdoch, and J. Banks. 2000. "Quality, Nature, and Embeddedness:

Some Theoretical Considerations in the Context of the Food Sector." *Economic Geography* 76 (2): 107-25.

Marshall, Andrew. 1997. "Millennium Signs Away Plant Kingdom to Monsanto." *Nature Biotechnology* 15 (12): 1334.

Martin, R. 2000. "Institutional Approaches in Economic Geography." In *A Companion to Economic Geography*, ed. T. J. Barnes. Oxford: Blackwell Publishers.

Martineau, B. 2001. *First Fruit: The Creation of the Flavr Savr Tomato and the Birth of Genetically Engineered Food*. New York: McGraw-Hill.

Martinez-Alier, J. 2000. "Environmental Justice, Sustainability, and Valuation." Unpublished manuscript. New Haven, Conn.: Program in Agrarian Studies, Yale University.

Marx, K. 1967a. *Capital: A Critique of Political Economy*. Edited by F. Engels. Vol. 2, *The Process of Circulation of Capital*. New York: International Publishers.

———. 1967b. *Capital: A Critique of Political Economy*. Edited by F. Engels. 3 vols. New York: International Publishers.

Matheson, J. C. I. 1999. "Transgenic Fish Developments: Are Transgenic Fish and Shellfish in Our Future?" Paper presented at technical session titled Genetically Engineered Advances in Aquaculture: Reshaping America's Seafood Supply, San Francisco Seafood Show, San Francisco, November 4. Available on the Web at www.fda.gov/cvm/biotechnology/shellfish/index.htm (as of December 8, 2002).

May, C. 1998. "Thinking, Buying, Selling: Intellectual Property Rights in Political Economy." *New Political Economy* 3 (1): 59-78.

Mayr, E. 1982. *The Growth of Biological Thought: Diversity, Evolution, and Inheritance*. Cambridge, Mass.: Belknap Press.

McAfee, K. 1999a. "Biodiversity and the Contradictions of Green Developmentalism." Ph.D. diss., University of California, Berkeley.

———. 1999b. "Biodiversity and the Global Economic Paradigm." In *Cultural and Spiritual Values of Biodiversity*, ed. D. Posey. London: United Nations Environmental Program/Intermediate Technology Publications.

———. 1999c. "Selling Nature to Save It? Biodiversity and Green Developmentalism." *Environment and Planning D: Society and Space* 17:133-54.

———. 2003. "Economic and Genetic Reductionism in Biotechnology Battles." *Geoforum*. Forthcoming.

McCluskey, J. J. 2000. "Read the Warning: This Product May Contain GMOs." *Choices (American Agricultural Economics Association)*, 2d quarter, 39-42.

McConnell, F. 1996. *The Biodiversity Convention: A Negotiating History*. London: Kluwer Law International.

McGloughlin, M. 1999. "Ten Reasons Why Biotechnology Will Be Important to the Developing World." *AgBio Forum* 2 (3-4): 163-74.

McGonigle, J. 1998. Presentation at a session titled "Environmental Sustainability," Northeast Aquaculture Conference and Exposition, Rockport, Maine, November 19.

McKinnell, S., and A. J. Thomson. 1997. "Recent Events concerning Atlantic Salmon Escapees in the Pacific." *ICES Journal of Marine Science* 54:1221-25.

McMichael, P. 1994. *The Global Restructuring of Agro-Food Systems, Food Systems, and Agrarian Change*. Ithaca, N.Y.: Cornell University Press.

————. 1995. *Food and Agrarian Orders in the World-Economy.* Contributions in Economics and Economic History, no. 160. Westport, Conn.: Greenwood Press.

————. 1996. "Globalization: Myths and Realities." *Rural Sociology* 61:25-55.

————. 1999. "Global Food Politics." *Monthly Review* 50 (3): 97.

————. 2000. *Development and Social Change.* 2d ed. Thousand Oaks, Calif.: Pine Forge Press.

McMichael, P., and D. Myhre. 1991. "Global Regulation vs. The Nation-State: Agro-Food Systems and the New Politics of Capital." *Capital & Class* 43 (spring): 83-105.

McNeeley, Jeffrey. 1988. *Economics and Biological Diversity: Developing and Using Economic Incentives to Conserve Biological Resources.* Gland, Switzerland: International Union for the Conservation of Nature (IUCN).

Mendelsohn, R., and M. J. Balick. 1995. "The Value of Undiscovered Pharmaceuticals in Tropical Forests." *Economic Botany* 49 (2): 223-28.

Miller, D. 1995. "Consumption as the Vanguard of History." In *Acknowledging Consumption,* ed. D. Miller. London: Routledge.

Miller, H. I. 1997. *Policy Controversy in Biotechnology: An Insider's View.* Austin, Tex.: R. G. Landes Company.

Mistiaen, V., and I. Boucq. 1999. "A War against Techno-Food: Europeans Fighting to Block Engineered Crops Are Having a Global Impact." *San Francisco Chronicle,* August 16.

Mittal, A., and P. Rosset. 2001. "Genetic Engineering and the Privatization of Seeds." *Dollars and Sense,* March/April, 24-27.

"Monsanto Alleges Farmer Infringed Seed Patent." 2000. *Mealey's Litigation Reports: Patents,* September 1.

"Monsanto, Calgene in Biotech Pact." 1983. *Chemical Week,* May 5.

Monsanto Company. 2000. Prospectus, SEC Form S-1, filed October 17

————. 2002. *Bt Crops Not a Threat to Bt Sprays.* Retrieved May 5 from www.monsanto. com/monsanto/biotechnology/background_information/00mar22nothreat. html.

"Monsanto, DuPont Dismiss Suits on Seeds." 2002. *Chicago Tribune,* April 3, Business section, p. 2.

"Monsanto Lab in Crystal Closes Amid Food Protests." 2000. *Bangor Daily News,* May 3.

"Monsanto Puts Human Gene into Plant, Unveils $150-Million Biocenter." 1984. *Biotechnology Newswatch* 4 (21): 1.

"Monsanto Takes Control of Calgene." 1996. *Chemical Week,* August 7, 5.

"Monsanto to Acquire All of Calgene." 1997. *Biotechnology Newswatch,* April 7, 2.

"Monsanto Unveils Three Herbicide-Resistant Plants." 1985. *Biotechnology Newswatch* 5 (22): 3.

Mooney, P. R. 1979. *Seeds of the Earth: A Private or Public Resource?* Ottawa: Inter Pares.

————. 1983. *The Law of the Seed: Another Development and Plant Genetic Resources.* Special issue of *Development Dialogue* (Dag Hammarskjöld Centre, Upsalla, Sweden) 1 (2): 1-172.

————. 1998. *The Parts of Life.* Special issue of *Development Dialogue* (Dag Hammarskjöld Centre, Upsalla, Sweden), nos. 1-2.

Moore, J. A. 2001. "More Than a Food Fight." *Issues in Science and Technology Online,* summer 2001. Retrieved February 25, 2002, from www.nap.edu/issues/17.4/p_moore.htm.

Morange, M. 1998. *A History of Molecular Biology*. Cambridge: Harvard University Press.

Morgan, H. E. 1969. *The Environment of High-Yield Forestry* S. J. Hall Lecture Series in Industrial Forestry. Berkeley, Calif.: School of Forestry and Conservation, University of California, Berkeley.

Morgenstern, E. K. 1996. *Geographic Variation in Forest Trees: Genetic Basis and Application of Knowledge in Silviculture*. Vancouver. B.C.: UBC Press.

Mossinghoff, G. 1998. "The Biodiversity Convention and Intellectual Property Rights: Conflict or Harmony?" *Patent World,* no. 106: 27-30.

Mugabe, J., C. V. Barber, G. Henne, L. Glowka, and A. La Viña, eds. 1997. *Access to Genetic Resources: Strategies for Sharing Benefits*. Nairobi, Kenya: African Centre for Technology Studies.

Muir, W. M., and R. D. Howard. 1999. "Possible Ecological Risks of Transgenic Organism Release When Transgenes Affect Mating Success: Sexual Selection and the Trojan Gene Hypothesis." *Proceedings of the National Academy of Science* 96 (24): 13853-56.

Mullin, T. J., and S. Bertrand. 1998. "Environmental Release of Transgenic Trees in Canada: Potential Benefits and Assessment of Biosafety." *The Forestry Chronicle* 74 (2): 203-19.

Munasinghe, M. 1993. *Environmental Economics and Sustainable Development*. Washington, D.C.: World Bank.

Murdoch, J. 1994. "Weaving the Seamless Web: A Consideration of Network Analysis and Its Potential Application to the Study of Rural Economy." Working Paper 3, Centre for Rural Economy, University of Newcastle-upon-Tyne.

———. 1997a. "Inhuman/Nonhuman/Human: Actor-Network Theory and the Prospects for a Nondualist and Symmetrical Perspective on Nature and Society." *Environment and Planning D: Society and Space* 15:731-56.

———. 1997b. "Towards a Geography of Heterogeneous Associations." *Progress in Human Geography* 21 (3): 321-37.

Murdoch, J., and M. Miele. 1999. "'Back to Nature': Changing 'Worlds of Production' in the Food Sector." *Sociologia Ruralis* 39 (4): 465-83.

Murphy, S. 1998. *Market Power in Agricultural Markets: Some Issues for Developing Countries*. Geneva, Switzerland: The South Centre.

"Mycogen Proceeds with Suit." 1996. *Chemical Week,* May 22, 33.

"Mycogen Stock Tumbles after Monsanto Files Suit over Bt Patent." 1996. *Biotechnology Newswatch,* April 1, 4.

Nash, C. F., ed. 2001. *The Net-Pen Salmon Farming Industry in the Pacific Northwest*. Springfield, Va.: U.S. Department of Commerce, National Oceanic and Atmospheric Administration. NOAA Technical Memorandum, NMFS-NWFSC-49.

National Research Council. 1990. *Forestry Research: A Mandate for Change*. Washington, D.C.: National Academy Press.

———. 2002a. *Animal Biotechnology: Science-Based Concerns*. Washington, D.C.: National Academy Press. Available at www.nap.edu/books/0309084393/html/ (as of December 8, 2002).

———. 2002b. *Environmental Effects of Transgenic Plants: The Scope and Adequacy of Reg-*

ulation. Washington, D.C.: National Academy Press. Available at www.nap.edu (as of October 2002).

National Science Foundation. 1996. *National Patterns of R&D Expenditures: 1996.* Washington, D.C.: National Science Foundation.

NatureMark [subsidiary of Monsanto Company]. 2002. "Biotechnology: What's So Special about This Potato?" Retrieved May 5 from www.naturemark.com/pages/ TOP_BIO_Special.html.

Nelson, G. C., T. Josling, D. Bullock, L. Unnevehr, M. Rosegrant, and L. Hill. 1999. *The Economics and Politics of Genetically Modified Organisms in Agriculture: Implications for WTO 2000.* Bulletin no. 809. Urbana, Ill.: Office of Research, College of Agricultural, Consumer and Environmental Sciences, University of Illinois at Urbana-Champaign.

———, ed. 2001. *Genetically Modified Organisms in Agriculture: Economics and Politics.* San Diego, Calif.: Academic Press.

Neubar, M. 1999. "Lawsuits Follow Introduction of Genetically Altered Seeds." Associated Press Newswires, May 8.

Newby, H. 1983. "The Sociology of Agriculture: Toward a New Rural Sociology." *Annual Review of Rural Sociology* 9:67-81.

———. 1985. "Twenty-Five Years of Rural Sociology: Some Reflections on the Conclusion of the 25th Volume of *Sociologia Ruralis.*" *Sociologia Ruralis* 25 (3-4): 207-13.

Niiler, E. 2000. "Demise of the Life Science Company Begins." *Nature Biotechnology* 18 (1): 14.

Nijar Singh, G. 1996. *TRIPs and Biodiversity: The Threat and Responses. A Third World View.* Penang, Malaysia: Third World Network.

Noble, D. F. 1977. *America by Design: Science, Technology, and the Rise of Corporate Capitalism.* New York: Knopf.

———. 1984. *Forces of Production: A Social History of Industrial Automation.* 1st ed. New York: Knopf.

"Novartis Sues Monsanto, Dekalb for Infringement of Corn Larvae Patent." 1997. *Mealey's Litigation Reports: Intellectual Property* 5 (10).

OECD (Organization for Economic Cooperation and Development). 2000. *Multifunctionality: Toward an Analytical Framework.* Paris: OECD.

Office of Technology Assessment. U.S. Congress. 1991. *Biotechnology in a Global Economy.* Washington, D.C.: Office of Technology Assessment.

"Of Greens and American Beans." 1997. *The Economist,* January 4, 62.

Oh, C. n.d. "Third World Network Briefing: Ten Questions on TRIPS, Technology Transfer, and Biodiversity." Retrieved December 9, 2002, from www.twnside .org.sg/title/trips10-cn.htm.

Oloka-Onyango, J., and D. Udagama. 2000. *The Realization of Economic, Social, and Cultural Rights: Globalization and Its Impact on the Full Enjoyment of Human Rights.* UN Sub-Commission on the Promotion and Protection of Human Rights. June 15.

Olson, J. 1998. "Accessing Seed Technologies: Will Your Local Seed Supplier Have the Seeds You Want?" *Farm Industry News,* December 30.

Oregon State University, College of Forestry. 1995. *Forest Research Laboratory, Biennial Report 1992-1994.* Corvallis: Oregon State University, College of Forestry.

————. 1997. *Forest Research Laboratory, Biennial Report 1994-1996.* Corvallis: Oregon State University, College of Forestry.

Organic Consumers Association. 2000. "Shareholders Challenge Kellogg over Genetically Engineered Foods." Retrieved December 10, 2002, from www .organicconsumers.org/ge/kelloggshareholders.cfm.

"Organic Will Calm GE Controversy, US Says." 1999. *Organic View* 1 (8). E-mail publication of the Organic Consumers Association. Retrieved June 30 from www .organicconsumers.org/Organic/oca18.cfm#Organic.

Pacific Northwest Tree Improvement Research Co-operative. 1996. *Annual Report 1995-1996.* Corvallis: Forest Research Laboratory, Oregon State University.

"Patent Covers All Transgenic Cotton." 1992. *Biotechnology Newswatch* 12 (22): 5.

Paul, D. B., and B. A. Kimmelman. 1988. "Mendel in America: Theory and Practice, 1900-1919." In *The American Development of Biology,* ed. R. Rainger, K. R. Benson, and J. Maieschein. Philadelphia: University of Pennsylvania Press.

Pels, D. 1996. "The Politics of Symmetry." *Social Studies of Science* 26:277-304.

Penman, D. J., M. Woodwark, and B. J. McAndrew. 1995. "Genetically Modified Fish Populations." In *Environmental Impacts of Aquatic Biotechnology.* Paris: Organisation for Economic Co-operation and Development.

Perkins, J. 2001. "If StarLink Fouls Crop, Farmers Will Get Aid." *Des Moines Register,* October 18.

Perrings, C. 1995. "Economic Values of Biodiversity." In *Global Biodiversity Assessment,* ed. V. H. Heywood and R. T. Watson. New York: United Nations Environmental Program.

Petersen, M. 1999. "New Trade Threat for U.S. Farmers: Dislike of Gene-Altered Food Is Now Proving Contagious." *New York Times,* August 29.

Pezzella, M. 1996. "Monsanto to Sell Chem Biz in Bid to Dominate Ag Bio." *Biotechnology Newswatch,* October 21, 1.

PhRMA (Pharmaceutical Researchers and Manufacturers of America). 2002. *Pharmaceutical Industry Profile 2002.* Available at www.phrma.org/publications/ publications/profile02/index.cfm (as of January 10, 2003).

Pickering, A. 1995. *The Mangle of Practice: Time, Agency, and Science.* Chicago: University of Chicago Press.

Pimbert, M. 1999. *Agricultural Biodiversity.* Rome: FAO/Netherlands Conference on the Multifunctional Character of Agriculture and Land.

Pimm, S. L. 1991. *The Balance of Nature? Ecological Issues in the Conservation of Species and Communities.* Chicago: University of Chicago Press.

"Plans Gone Awry." 1992. *The Economist,* December 5.

"Plant Biotech; Transgenic Crops Head to Market." 1995. *Chemical Week,* September 27, 25.

"Plant Biotechnologists Tell AAAS Meeting of Transforming Corn, Cotton." 1989. *Biotechnology Newswatch* 9 (3): 5.

Pollack, A. 2000. "Kraft Recalls Taco Shells with Bioengineered Corn." *New York Times,* September 23.

————. 2001. "The Green Revolution Yields to the Bottom Line." *New York Times,* May 15.

Pollack, M., and G. Shaffer. 2000. *The Challenge of Reconciling Regulatory Differences:*

Food Safety and Genetically Modified Organisms in the Transatlantic Relationship. Madison: Department of Political Science, University of Wisconsin.

Pollan, M. 1998. "Playing God in the Garden." *New York Times Magazine,* October 25, 44-51, 62-63, 82, 92.

Pollution Control Hearings Board. 1997. *Marine Environmental Consortium et al. v. State of Washington, Department of Ecology et al.,* Pchb. nos. 96-257, 96-258, 96-259, 96-260, 96-261, 96-262, 96-263, 96-264, 96-265, 96-266, and 97-110. First Order on Summary Judgment. Lacey, Washington: Washington Pollution Control Hearings Board. May 27.

Porter, G., and J. W. Brown. 1996. *Global Environmental Politics.* 2d ed. Boulder, Colo.: Westview.

Powell, D., and W. Leiss. 1997. *Mad Cows and Mother's Milk: The Perils of Poor Risk Communication:* Montreal: McGill-Queen's University Press.

Powell, W. W., and P. DiMaggio. 1991. *The New Institutionalism in Organizational Analysis.* Chicago: University of Chicago Press.

Power, T. M. 1997. "Ideology, Wishful Thinking, and Pragmatic Reform." In *The Next West: Public Lands, Community, and Economy in the American West,* ed. J. A. Baden and D. Snow. Washington, D.C.: Island Press.

Press, E., and J. Washburn. 2000. "The Kept University." *Atlantic Monthly* 285 (3): 39-54.

Pritchard, B., and R. Fagan. 1999. "Circuits of Capital and Transnational Corporate Spatial Behaviour: Nestle in Southeast Asia." *International Journal of Sociology of Agriculture and Food* 8:3-20.

Pueppke, S. 2001. "Agricultural Biotechnology and Plant Improvement." *American Behavioral Scientist* 44 (8): 1225-32.

Purdue, D. 1995. "Hegemonic Trips: World Trade, Intellectual Property, and Biodiversity." *Environmental Politics* 4 (1): 88-107.

————. 2000. *Anti-GenetiX: The Emergence of the Anti-GM Movement.* Ashgate Studies in Environmental Policy and Practice. Aldershot: Ashgate.

Rajala, R. 1998. *Clearcutting the Pacific Rain Forest: Production, Science, and Regulation.* Vancouver, B.C.: UBC Press.

Ratner, M. 1998. "Competition Drives Agriculture's Genomics Deals." *Nature Biotechnology* 16 (9): 810-11.

Rauber, C. 1997. "$200m Patent Runs Out." *San Francisco Business Times* 12 (14).

Raven, P. 1990. "The Politics of Preserving Biodiversity." *Bioscience* 40:769-74.

Regal, P. J. 1993. "The True Meaning of 'Exotic Species' as a Model for Genetically Engineered Organisms." *Experientia* 49:225-34.

————. 1994. "Scientific Principles for Ecologically Based Risk Assessment of Transgenic Organisms." *Molecular Ecology* 3:5-13.

Reichmann, J. L., J. Zhang, and P. Broun. 1999. "Plant Genomics: The Next Green Revolution." *Chemistry and Industry,* June 21, 12.

Reid, W. V. 1997. "Technology and Access to Genetic Resources." In *Access to Genetic Resources: Strategies for Sharing Benefits,* ed. J. O. Mugabe, C. V. Barber, G. Henne, L. Glowka, and A. La Viña. London: Sweet & Maxwell.

Reid, W. V., S. A. Laird, C. A. Meyer, R. Gámez, A. Sittenfield, D. H. Janzen, M. A. Gollin, and C. Juma. 1993. *Biodiversity Prospecting: Using Genetic Resources for Sustainable Development.* Washington, D.C.: World Resources Institute.

Reisner, A. 2001. "Social Movement Organizations' Reactions to Genetic Engineering in Agriculture." *American Behavioral Scientist* 44 (8): 1389-404.

"Rep. Kucinich Introduces Labeling Bill for GE Foods." 1999. *Organic View* [e-mail publication of the Organic Consumers Association] 1 (17). Retrieved November 12 from www.organicconsumers.org/newsletter/ov117.cfm#Kucinich.

Republic of the Philippines. 1999. *Review of TRIPS Article 27.3(B)*. Diliman, Quezon City, Philippines: Department of Agriculture, Office of the Secretary. April 14.

Rifkin, J. 1998. *The Biotech Century: Harnessing the Gene and Remaking the World*. New York: Jeremy P. Tarcher/Putnam.

Rissler, J., and M. Mellon. 1996. *The Ecological Risks of Engineered Crops*. Cambridge : MIT Press.

Robbins, W. G. 1982. *Lumberjacks and Legislators: Political Economy of the U.S. Lumber Industry, 1890-1941*. 1st ed. Environmental History Series, no. 5. College Station: Texas A&M University Press.

Robinson, M. 2002. "Judge Approves $9 Million Settlement in Bioengineered-Corn Suit." March 8. Retrieved April 23, 2002, from www.enn.com.

Rolston, H., III. 1999. *Genes, Genesis, and God: Values and Their Origins in Natural and Human History*. Cambridge: Cambridge University Press.

Rosenberg, C. E. 1997. *No Other Gods: On Science and American Social Thought*. Rev. ed. Baltimore: Johns Hopkins University Press.

Rosset, P. 1999. "The Multiple Functions and Benefits of Small Farm Agriculture in the Context of Global Trade Negotiations." Policy brief prepared for Cultivating Our Futures, the FAO/Netherlands Conference on the Multifunctional Character of Agriculture and Land, Maastricht, The Netherlands, September 12-17.

Rothschild, D., ed. 1997. *Protecting What's Ours: Indigenous Peoples and Biodiversity*. Oakland, Calif.: South and Meso-American Indian Rights Center.

Rotman, D. 1993. "Agchem Producers Sow Plans for a Rich Harvest." *Chemical Week*, August 18, 33.

———. 1995. "Mycogen Sues Monsanto in Patent Fight." *Chemical Week*, May 31, 9.

———. 1996a. "DowElanco Takes Mycogen Stake." *Chemical Week*, January 24.

———. 1996b. "Monsanto Gains Patent, Launches Infringement Suit." *Chemical Week*, March 27, 9.

———. 1996c. "Monsanto Snaps up Agracetus." *Chemical Week*, April 17, 8.

———. 1996d. "Monsanto Pays $17 Million for Calgene's Oils Know-How." *Chemical Week*, June 5, 10.

———. 1996e. "Monsanto Buys Asgrow Seed Business." *Chemical Week*, October 2, 14.

———. 1997a. "Monsanto Spends $1.02 Billion for Corn Seed Business." *Chemical Week*, January 15, 7.

———. 1997b. "Monsanto Buys More Gene Know-How." *Chemical Week*, November 5, 14.

The Royal Society. 2001. *The Use of Genetically Modified Animals*. London: The Royal Society. May.

Rubenstein, B. 1999. "Growing Agro-Biotech Business Fuels Patent Battles, Dominance of a New Industry at Stake." *Corporate Legal Times*, February, 29.

Runge, C. F., and L. A. Jackson. 2000. "Labeling, Trade, and Genetically Modified Organisms: A Proposed Solution." *Journal of World Trade* 34:111-22.

Sagoff, M. 1991. "On Making Nature Safe for Biotechnology." In *Assessing Ecological Risks of Biotechnology,* ed. L. Ginsburg. Stoneham, Mass.: Butterworth-Heinemann.

Sanchez, V., and C. Juma. 1994. *Biodiplomacy: Genetic Resources and International Relations.* Nairobi, Kenya: African Centre for Technology Studies.

Sax, J. L. 1970. "The Public Trust Doctrine in Natural Resources Law: Effective Judicial Intervention." *Michigan Law Review* 68:471.

————. 1980. "Liberating the Public Trust Doctrine from Its Historical Shackles." *U.C. Davis Law Review* 14:185.

Sax, J. L., J. D. Leshy, B. H. Thompson Jr., and R. H. Abrams. 2000. *Legal Control of Water Resources: Cases and Materials.* St. Paul, Minn.: West Group.

Saxenian, A. 1994. *Regional Advantage: Culture and Competition in Silicon Valley and Route 128.* Cambridge: Harvard University Press.

Schmidt, S. 1999. "Frankenfish or Salmon Saviour?" *National Post,* September 4.

Schumpeter, J. A. 1950. *Capitalism, Socialism, and Democracy.* 3d ed. New York: Harper.

Schweiger, T. G. 2001. "Europe: Hostile Lands for GMOs." In *Redesigning Life? The Worldwide Challenge to Genetic Engineering,* ed. B. Tokar. London: Zed.

Scientists' Working Group on Biosafety. 1998. *Manual for Assessing Ecological and Human Health Effects of Genetically Engineered Organisms.* Edmonds, Wash.: Edmonds Institute.

Scott, J. C. 1998. *Seeing Like a State: How Certain Schemes to Improve the Human Condition Have Failed.* Yale Agrarian Studies. New Haven, Conn.: Yale University Press.

Seay, N. J. 1993. "Intellectual Property Rights in Plants." In *Intellectual Property Rights: Protection of Plant Materials,* ed. P. S. Baenziger, R. A. Kleese, and R. F. Barnes. Madison, Wisc.: Crop Science Society of America.

Secretariat of the Convention on Biological Diversity. 2000. *Handbook of the Convention on Biological Diversity.* London: Earthscan.

Serageldin, I. 1996. *Sustainability and the Wealth of Nations.* Washington, D.C.: World Bank Department of Environmentally and Socially Sustainable Development.

Service, R. F. 2001. "Gene and Protein Patents Get Ready to Go Head to Head." *Science* 294 (December 7): 2082-83.

"72 Firms in 9 Countries Buy Licensing Rights to Cohen-Boyer Basic Patent." 1981. *Biotechnology Newswatch* 1 (18): 4.

Shands, H. L. 1995. "Forming a Global Plant Genetics Insurance Policy." *Agricultural Research* 43 (10): 2.

Shapiro, C. 2000. "Navigating the Patent Thicket: Cross Licenses, Patent Pools, and Standard-Setting." Paper presented at the National Bureau of Economic Research Conference on Innovation Policy and the Economy, Washington, D.C., April 11.

Shapiro, S. 1997. "Caught in the Web: The Implications of Ecology for Radical Symmetry in STS." *Social Epistemology* 11 (1): 97-110.

Shimoda, S. M. 1998. "Agricultural Biotechnology—Master of the Universe?" *AgBio Forum* 1 (2): 62-68.

Shiva, V. 1993. *Monocultures of the Mind: Perspectives on Biodiversity and Biotechnology.* London: Zed.

————. 1997. *Biopiracy: The Plunder of Nature and Knowledge.* Boston: Southend Press.

Shoemaker, R., ed. 2001. *Economic Issues in Agricultural Biotechnology.* Agriculture

Information Bulletin 762. Washington, D.C.: U.S. Department of Agriculture, Economic Research Service.

Shulman, S. 1994. "A New King Cotton? Genetically Engineered Cotton." *Technology Review* 97 (5).

Silen, R. R. 1966. *A Simple, Progressive Tree Improvement Program for Douglas-Fir.* Portland, Ore.: United States Department of Agriculture, Forest Service, Pacific Northwest Range and Experiment Station.

————. 1978. "Genetics of Douglas-Fir." Edited by S. Forest. USDA Forest Service Research Paper WO-35, U.S. Department of Agriculture, Forest Service, Washington, D.C.

Simoncelli, T. 2000. "ACG and INBio: Diverging Approaches to Saving, Knowing, and Using Costa Rica's Biodiversity." Master's thesis, University of California, Berkeley.

Simpson, R. D., and R. A. Sedjo. 1994. "Commercialization of Indigenous Genetic Resources." *Contemporary Economic Policy* 12 (4): 34-44.

Simpson, R. D., R. A. Sedjo, and J. Reid. 1998. "The Commercialization of Indigenous Genetic Resources as Conservation and Development Policy." In *Protection of Global Biodiversity: Converging Strategies,* ed. L. D. Guruswamy and J. A. McNeely. Durham, N.C.: Duke University Press.

Singh, S. 1999. "Trade: Patents on Life Forms Should Be Re-Examined, Says India." *SUNS—South-North Development Monitor.* Retrieved October 28, 1999, from www.sunsonline.org.

Sissell, K. 2000a. "Court Overturns $175 Million Damage Award to Mycogen." *Chemical Week,* July 5/12, 23.

————. 2000b. "California High Court Takes up Bt Dispute." *Chemical Week,* November 8.

Sittenfeld, A., A. Lovejoy, and J. Cohen. 1997. *Managing Biodiversity for Agriculture Research: Building Awareness from the INBio Experience—The Case of Costa Rica.* San Jose: INBio.

Skaala, Ø. 1995. "Possible Genetic and Ecological Effects of Escaped Salmonids in Aquaculture." In *Environmental Impacts of Aquatic Biotechnology.* Paris: Organisation for Economic Co-operation and Development.

Slaughter, S., and L. L. Leslie. 1997. *Academic Capitalism: Politics, Policies, and the Entrepreneurial University.* Baltimore: Johns Hopkins University Press.

Smith, M. 2001. "The Rice Stuff—Big Payoff Predicted from Genome Completion." *Biotechnology Newswatch,* February 5.

Smith, M. P., and L. Guarnizo, eds. 1998. *Transnationalism from Below.* New Brunswick, N.J.: Transaction Publishers.

Smith, R. 1998. "Monsanto to Secure Biotech Leadership." *Feedstuffs* 70 (20).

Sorkin, A. R., and M. Petersen. 2000. "Glaxo and SmithKline Agree to Form Largest Drugmaker." *New York Times,* January 17.

South-Center. 2000. "Trade: The Push and Pull for a New Round." *South Bulletin,* no. 14. Retrieved December 11, 2002, from www.southcentre.orfginfo/southbulletin/bulletin14/southbulletin14.htm.

Spalding, B. J. 1988. "The Big Plant Biotechnology Shootout." *Chemical Week,* August 31, 16.

Steinberg, R. H., ed. 2002. *The Greening of International Trade Law.* Boulder, Colo.: Rowman and Littlefield.

Steingraber, S. 1997. *Living Downstream: An Ecologist Looks at Cancer and the Environment.* New York: Addison-Wesley.

Steyer, R. 1998. "Seed Industry Goes through Wave of Mergers and Acquisitions." *St. Louis Post-Dispatch,* May 6.

Stickney, R. R. 1994. *Principles of Aquaculture.* New York: John Wiley & Sons.

"Still Bananas." 2000. *The Economist,* July 22.

Stillwell, M. 1999. *Implications for Developing Countries of Proposals to Consider Trade in Genetically Modified Organisms (GMOs) at the WTO.* Geneva: Center for International Environmental Law.

Stoll, M. 1999. "Designer Fish Flounder over Legal Hurdles." *Christian Science Monitor,* March 4. Retrieved December 2, 2002, from www.csmonitor.com/durable/1999/03/04/p19s1.htm.

Storper, M. 1997. *The Regional World: Territorial Development in a Global Economy,* Perspectives on Economic Change. New York: Guilford.

Storper, M., and R. Walker. 1989. *The Capitalist Imperative: Territory, Technology, and Industrial Growth.* New York: Basil Blackwell.

Strauss, S. H., S. P. DiFazio, and R. Meilan. 2001. "Genetically Modified Poplars in Context." *The Forestry Chronicle* 77 (2): 271-79.

Strauss, S. H., G. T. Howe, and B. Goldfarb. 1991. "Prospects for Genetic Engineering of Insect Resistance in Forest Trees." *Forest Ecology and Management* 43:181-209.

Strauss, S. H., S. A. Knowe, and J. Jenkins. 1997. "Benefits and Risks of Transgenic Roundup Ready Cottonwoods." *Journal of Forestry* 95 (5): 12-19.

Strauss, S. H., A. M. Rottmann, and L. A. Sheppard. 1995. "Genetic Engineering of Reproductive Sterility in Forest Trees." *Molecular Breeding* 1:5-26.

Stringer, J. 1997. "DowElanco Moves into the Biotech Big Leagues." *Chemical Week,* February 5, 55.

Svarstad, H. 2000. "Reciprocity, Biopiracy, Heroes, Villains, and Victims." In *Responding to Bioprospecting: From Biodiversity in the South to Medicines in the North,* ed. H. Svarstad and S. S. Dhillion. Oslo: Spartacus Forlag.

Svarstad, H., and S. S. Dhillion. 2000a. "Responding to Bioprospecting: Rejection or Regulation." In *Bioprospecting: From Biodiversity in the South to Medicines in the North,* ed. H. Svarstad and S. S. Dhillion. Oslo: Spartacus Forlag.

Svarstad, H., and S. S. Dhillion, eds. 2000b. *Responding to Bioprospecting: From Biodiversity in the South to Medicines in the North.* Oslo: Spartacus Forlag.

Takacs, D. 1996. *The Idea of Biodiversity: Philosophies of Paradise.* Baltimore: Johns Hopkins University Press.

Tanaka, K., A. Juska, and L. Busch. 1999. "Globalization of Agricultural Production and Research: The Case of the Rapeseed Subsector." *Sociologia Ruralis* 39 (1): 54-77.

ten Kate, K. 1995. *Biopiracy or Green Petroleum? Expectations and Best Practice in Bioprospecting.* London: Overseas Development Agency.

ten Kate, K., and S. A. Laird. 1999. *The Commercial Use of Biodiversity: Access to Genetic Resources and Benefit Sharing.* London: Earthscan.

Thackray, A., ed. 1998. *Private Science: Biotechnology and the Rise of the Molecular Sciences.* Philadelphia: University of Pennsylvania Press.

"The Thammasat Resolution." 1998. *Synthesis/Regeneration* 16 (summer 1998). Retrieved December 11, 2002, from www.greens.org/s-r/16/16-13.html.

Third World Network. 2001. *Seattle WTO Ministerial Conference: The Process, Events, and Positions.* Penang, Malaysia: Third World Network. Retrieved April 30, 2002, from www.twnside.org.sg/title/seattlemain.htm.

Thomas, J. 2001. "Princes, Aliens, Superheroes, and Snowballs: The Playful World of the UK Genetic Resistance." In *Redesigning Life? The Worldwide Challenge to Genetic Engineering,* ed. B. Tokar. London: Zed.

Tobin, B. 1997a. "Certificates of Origin: A Role for IPR Regimes in Securing Prior Informed Consent." In *Access to Genetic Resources: Strategies for Sharing Benefits,* ed. J. Mugabe, C. V. Barber, G. Henne, L. Glowka, and A. La Viña. Nairobi, Kenya: African Centre for Technology Studies.

———. 1997b. "Know-How Licenses: Recognising Indigenous Rights over Collective Knowledge." *Bulletin of the Working Group on Traditional Resource Rights,* no. 4, 17-18.

Tokar, B. 2001. *Redesigning Life? The Worldwide Challenge to Genetic Engineering.* London: Zed.

Tree Genetic Engineering Research Cooperative. 1997. *TGERC Annual Report, 1996-97.* Corvallis: Forest Research Laboratory, Oregon State University.

———. 1999. "TGERC Profile: History, and Structure." Retrieved December 13, 1999, from www.fsl.orst.edu/tgerc/hist.htm.

Trewhitt, J., and M. Bluestone. 1985. "Agrichemical Firms Turn to Genetic Engineering." *Chemical Week,* April 3, 34.

"UM Researcher Suggests Growth Hormone to Create Super Trout." 1994. *Aquaculture News* 2 (9): 6.

UNEP/CBD. 1994. "Convention on Biological Diversity: Text and Annexes." Châtelaine, Switzerland: United Nations Environment Programme.

———. 1998a. *Addressing the Fair and Equitable Sharing of the Benefits Arising out of Genetic Resources.* UNEP/CBD/COP4/22e. Montreal: UNEP/CBD Secretariat. Available at www.biodiv.org/convention/cops.asp (as of January 10, 2003).

———. 1998b. *Measures to Promote and Advance the Distribution of Benefits from Biotechnology in Accordance with Article 19.* Montreal: UNEP/CBD Secretariat, UNEP/CBD/COP4/21e. Available at www.biodiv.org/convention/cops.asp (as of January 10, 2003).

———. 1998c. *Synthesis of Case-Studies on Benefit Sharing.* Montreal: UNEP/CBD Secretariat, UNEP/CBD/COP4/Inf.7. May. Available at www.biodiv.org/convention/cops.asp (as of January 10, 2003).

Union of Concerned Scientists. 2002. "Food and Environment. Fact Sheet: Genetic Engineering Techniques." Retrieved January 17, 2003, from the Union of Concerned Scientists Web site www.ucsusa.org/food_and_environment/biotechnology/page.cfm?pageID=35.

United Nations Sub-Commission on the Promotion and Protection of Human Rights. 2001. *The Realization of Economic, Social and Cultural Rights.* Document E/CN.4/Sub.2/res/2001/21. Geneva: United Nations Sub-Commission on the Promotion and Protection of Human Rights.

"University of Washington Researchers Map Rice Genome." 2000. Associated Press Newswires. April 4.

U.S. Patent and Trademark Office. 2001. "Utility Examination Guidelines." *Federal Register* 66 (4): 1092.

"U.S. Wants TRIPs off Seattle Agenda." *Washington Trade Daily,* August 5. Retrieved April 30, 2002, from www.washingtontradedaily.com/.

Utter, F., K. Hindar, and N. Ryman. 1993. "Genetic Effects of Aquaculture on Natural Salmon Populations." In *Salmon Aquaculture,* ed. K. Heen, R. L. Monahan, and F. Utter. New York: Halsted Press.

Vanderburg, W. H. 2000. *The Labyrinth of Technology.* Toronto: University of Toronto Press.

van der Ploeg, J. D. 1986. "The Agricultural Labour Process and Commodization." In *The Commodization Debate: Labour Process, Strategy, and Social Network,* ed. N. Long. Wageningen, Netherlands: Agricultural University.

———. 1993. "Rural Sociology and the New Agrarian Question: A Perspective from the Netherlands." *Sociologia Ruralis* 32 (2): 240-60.

Veblen, T. 1964. *Essays in Our Changing Order,* ed. L. Ardzrooni. New York: A. M. Kelley.

Vellvé, R. 1992. *Saving the Seed: Genetic Diversity and European Agriculture.* London: Earthscan.

Vogel, J. H. 1994. *Genes for Sale: Privatization as a Conservation Policy.* New York: Oxford University Press.

———. 1997a. "The Recognition of Non-rational Behavior in the Design of Environmental Policy: Non-rational Behavior Analysis and the Convention on Biological Diversity." Paper presented at the Minds and Matter: An Interdisciplinary Exploration, Washington and Lee University, Lexington, Va.

———. 1997b. "An Economic Analysis of the Convention on Biological Diversity: The Rationale for a Cartel." Paper presented at the IV Foro del Ajusco, UNEP, Mexico, November 19-21.

Volpe, J. P., E. B. Taylor, D. W. Rimmer, and B. W. Glickman. 2000. "Evidence of Natural Reproduction of Aquaculture-Escaped Atlantic Salmon in a Coastal British Columbia River." *Conservation Biology* 14 (3): 899-903.

von Schomberg, R. 2000. "Agricultural Biotechnology in the Trade-Environment Interface: Counterbalancing Adverse Effects of Globalisation." In *Biotechnologie,* ed. D. Barben and Gabriele Abels. Berlin: Edition Sigma.

Waknitz, F. W., T. J. Tynan, C. E. Nash, R. N. Iwamoto, L. G. Rutter. 2002. *Review of Potential Impacts of Atlantic Salmon Culture on Puget Sound Chinook Salmon and Hood Canal Summer-Run Chum Salmon Evolutionarily Significant Units.* Springfield, Va.: U.S. Department of Commerce, National Oceanic and Atmospheric Administration. NOAA Technical Memorandum NMFS-NWFSC-53.

Waldrop, M. 1990. "The Reign of Trial and Error Draws to a Close." *Science* 247 (January 5): 28-29.

Walker, J. M., and M. Cox. 1995. *The Language of Biotechnology: A Dictionary of Terms.* 2d ed. Washington, D.C.: American Chemical Society.

Washington Department of Fish and Wildlife. 1999. "Commercial Production of Atlantic Salmon, Escapes and Recoveries in Washington State." Retrieved December 8, 2002, from www.wa.gov/wdfw/fish/atlantic/comcatch.htm.

Watts, M. J. 1994. "Life under Contract: Contract Farming, Agrarian Restructuring, and Flexible Accumulation." In *Living under Contract,* ed. P. D. Little and M. J. Watts. Madison: University of Wisconsin Press.

Weatherall, M. 1990. *In Search of a Cure: A History of Pharmaceutical Discovery.* Oxford: Oxford University Press.

Weiss, R. 1999. "Seeds of Discord: Monsanto's Gene Police Raise Alarm on Farmers' Rights, Rural Tradition." *Washington Post,* February 3.

Welch, M. 1998. "Novartis Earmarks $600m for Agricultural Genomics." *Bioworld Today* 9 (140).

Whatmore, S. 1997. "Dissecting the Autonomous Self: Hybrid Cartographies for a Relational Ethics." *Environment and Planning D: Society and Space* 15:37-53.

White, R. 1995. *The Organic Machine: The Remaking of the Columbia River.* New York: Hill and Wang.

"White House Clears Major Cloud over Food Biotechnology." 1992. *Biotechnology Newswatch* 12 (11): 1.

Wilkinson, J. 1993. "Adjusting to a Demand-Oriented Food System: New Directions for Biotechnology Innovation." *Agriculture and Human Values* 10 (2): 31-39.

———. 2000. "'From the Dictatorship of Supply to the Democracy of Demand?' Transgenics, Organics and the Dynamics of Demand in the Agrofood System." Paper presented at the 10th International World Congress of the Rural Sociology Association, Rio de Janeiro, July-August.

Williams, M. 1989. *Americans and Their Forests: A Historical Geography.* Studies in Environment and History. Cambridge: Cambridge University Press.

Wills, P. R. 1998. "Disrupting Evolution: Biotechnology's Real Result." In *Altered Genes,* ed. R. Hindmarsh, G. Lawrence, and J. Norton. St. Leonards, Australia: Allen and Unwin.

Wirth, Timothy E. 1994. "Ratification Sought for the Convention on Biological Diversity." *Dispatch* (U.S. Department of State) 5, no. 16 (April 18). Published by the Bureau of Public Affairs. Retrieved November 24, 2002, from dosfan .lib.uic.edu/ERC/briefing/dispatch/1994/html/Dispatchv5no16.html.Wood, A., and P. Fairley. 1998. "Biotech Crops Flourish." *Chemical Week,* February 4/11, 27.

World Bank Environment Department. 1996. *Mainstreaming Biodiversity in Agricultural Development: Toward Good Practice (Draft).* Washington, D.C.: The World Bank.

———. 1997. *Expanding the Measure of Wealth: Indicators of Environmentally Sustainable Development.* Environmentally Sustainable Development Studies and Monograph Series, no. 17. Washington, D.C.: The World Bank.

World Resources Institute. 1995. *National Biodiversity Planning.* Washington, D.C.: World Resources Institute.

World Trade Organization. 1996. *Final Act Embodying the Results of the Uruguay Round of Multilateral Trade Negotiations, Annex I C Agreement on Trade-Related Aspects of Intellectual Property Rights, Marrakesh.* April 15.

———. 1998. "Preparations for the 1999 Ministerial Conference: General Council Discussion on Mandated Negotiations and the Built-in Agenda." Communication received November 19 from the Permanent Mission of the United States, World Trade Organization document WT/GC/W/115.

———. 1999a. "Measures Affecting Trade in Agricultural Biotechnological Products." Communication received July 27 from the United States, World Trade Organization document WT/GC/W/288.

———. 1999b. "The WTO TRIPs Agreement: Communication from Kenya on Behalf of the African Group." Communication received July 29 from the Permanent Mission of Kenya, World Trade Organization document WT/GC/W/302.

———. 1999c. "Preparations for the 1999 Ministerial Conference: Proposal for Establishment of a Working Party on Biotechnology in WTO." Communication received October 4 from the Permanent Mission of Canada, World Trade Organization document WT/GC/W/359.

———. 2001. *Views of the United States of America on the Relationship between the Convention on Biological Diversity and the TRIPs Agreement.* Geneva: World Trade Organization Document Dissemination Facility. April 3. World Trade Organization document IP/C/W/257.

Wright, A. 1990. *The Death of Ramón González: The Modern Agricultural Dilemma.* Austin: University of Texas Press.

Wright, S. 1994. *Molecular Politics: Developing American and British Regulatory Policy for Genetic Engineering, 1972-1982.* Chicago: University of Chicago Press.

———. 1998. "Molecular Politics in a Global Economy." In *Private Science: Biotechnology and the Rise of the Molecular Sciences,* ed. A. Thackray. Philadelphia: University of Pennsylvania Press.

"WTO Protests to UN over 'Nightmare' Report on TRIPS." 2000. *Financial Times,* August 25.

Yoon, C. K. 2000a. "Altered Salmon Lead the Way to the Dinner Plate, but Rules Lag." *New York Times,* May 1.

———. 2000b. "If It Walks Like a Cow and Moos Like a Cow, It's a Pharmaceutical Factory." *New York Times,* May 1.

Yoxen, E. 1981. "Life as a Productive Force: Capitalising the Science and Technology of Molecular Biology." In *Science, Technology, and the Labour Process: Marxist Studies,* ed. L. Levidow and R. M. Young. London: CSE Books.

"Zeneca Files Antitrust Suit against Monsanto." 1998. *Chemical Week,* August 5, 6.

Zobel, B. 1974. *Increasing Productivity of Forest Lands through Better Trees.* The S. J. Hall Lectureship in Industrial Forestry. Berkeley, Calif.: School of Forestry and Conservation, University of California, Berkeley.

———. 1981. "Forest Tree Improvement—Past and Present." In *Advances in Forest Genetics,* ed. P. K. Khosla. New Delhi, India: Ambika.

INDEX

academic capitalism: corporate funding, 22, 76; forestry models, 17–18, 73, 75–76; graduate student role, 66, 81; impact of, 37; intellectual enclosure, 64, 175, 247; IPRs and, 34, 37, 41, 61, 64–66, 247; Monsanto and, 29, 56; pharmaceutical industry, 212–14; studies of, 223, 226. *See also* Bayh-Dole Act; TGERC

actor-network theory (ANT), of agro-food systems, 228–32

Advanta, seed sales statistics, 27

A/F Protein Inc., 84–91, 96–99, 101–3, 105–8

Africa: antibiotech movement, 121–22; IPR policies, 176, 177, 194

African Group, 121, 171, 191

ag-biotech industry: agronomic promise of, 11, 125–26, 134, 170–71, 174, 243, 252; government support for, 111, 128, 135, 181–93, 239, 242–45; industry focuses, 25; institutional changes, 14–19; revenues, 6; start-up companies, 32, 42, 48; WTO agreements favorable to, 152–64, 167–69, 171. *See also* academic capitalism; antibiotech movement; food supply, control of; GE foods, labeling; governmental regulation; IPRs; pharmaceutical industry; salmon, transgenic; *specific companies*; technology-licensing agreements

ag-biotech industry, financial setbacks: Monsanto, 25, 51, 52, 54, 123, 126, 129, 169;

public distrust and, 122–26, 169, 219, 241; regulatory costs, 13, 112; shareholder actions, 123, 129

ag-biotech industry, legal issues: antidisparagement complaints by, 138–39; antitrust actions against, 51, 54, 61, 76, 123, 247; contract farming arrangements, 30, 50–51, 53, 54

ag-biotech industry, marketing: CBI, 125, 129; public relations campaigns, 120, 121, 125–27, 129, 169–70

ag-biotech industry, vertical and horizontal integration, 7, 30, 51–54, 175; alliances with food processors, 51; alliances with genomics firms, 4, 16, 22, 34–35, 41, 46–47, 55–57, 61; alliances with pharmaceutical industry, 16, 22, 52, 175, 197, 200–203, 206–7, 209, 212; alliances with seed companies, 16, 26–28, 30, 48–50, 52–53, 61, 175, 221; chemical company origins, 16, 26–28, 34–35

Agracetus: gene gun technology, 43, 55–56, 61; licensing strategies, 43, 55–56; Monsanto and, 29, 61; patents, 43, 45, 59, 61; as pioneer, 32

Agreement on the Application of Sanitary and Phytosanitary Measures. *See* SPS

Agreement on Trade Related Intellectual Property Rights. *See* TRIPS

agricultural biotechnology: defined, 2, 20. *See also* ag-biotech industry; transgenic crops

Roundup Ready crops *(continued)*
78; economic impact, 253; Monsanto and, 28, 29, 33, 50, 62; soybeans, 28, 50–51, 55, 62
Rural Advancement Fund International (RAFI), 128, 225, 226

Sakata, seed sales statistics, 27
salmon, commercially farmed: competition, 95, 96; environmental concerns, 92, 102, 105, 109; growth hormones, artificial, 95–96; hatchery procedures, 84–85, 88, 108; pharmaceutical use, 92; production statistics, 90–91; public distrust of, 81; selective breeding, 85, 88, 98, 102, 108, 109; species grown, 91; vertical integration, 92–93, 108; vs. wild salmon fishermen, 91–92
salmon, transgenic: adoption pressures, 92–94, 96, 104, 109, 234; attributes, 84, 85, 87; ecological fitness of, 102–5, 109, 110; environmental concerns, 85–87, 100–106, 109–10, 234, 244–46, 252; exports of, 106–7, 129; growth hormones, 84–85, 87–88, 97–99, 105–6, 109–10, 244, 246, 252; licensing agreements, 91; moratoriums on, 17; as natural vs. unnatural, 97–98; in net pens, 89, 100–102; production costs, 89; regulation of, 88, 97, 101, 105–7, 110; sterile, 89–90, 102–3; tank-raised, 88–89; triploid, 90, 102–4, 108, 110; vertical integration, 96, 108. *See also* antibiotech movement, aquaculture
salmon, wild: vs. farmed and GE salmon, 90–92, 98, 239, 245–46, 253; harmed by escaped GE salmon, 100–104
salmon industry resistance to GE salmon: economic concerns, 93, 246; environmental concerns, 92, 101, 104–6, 253; social resistance concerns, 13–14, 86, 91–92, 94–95, 98–99; technological threat concerns, 92–94, 104, 234
Sandoz (Novartis), 198, 200
Seagram's, 124
Seattle Ministerial Conference (1999): Cartagena Protocol discussion, 191; protests, 153, 156, 160–62, 172–73, 179, 219, 224
seed companies: ag-biotech acquisition of, 48–50, 53, 61, 221; alliances with geno-

mics firms, 34–35, 41; alliances with universities, 34; chemical company acquisitions of, 16, 26–28, 175; contract farming arrangements, 30; corn seed market shares, 27; top ten, 27
seeds: commodification of, 22–23, 220–21, 223; cost of transgenic, 62; distribution channels, 48–49, 52–53, 252; fraudulent guarantees, 123; as patentable material, 39; technology-licensing agreements for, 29, 40
seed saving: lawsuits against farmers, 40, 50, 62, 175; Plant Variety Protection Act and, 59; private plant-breeders' rights, 193; terminator technology, 22–23, 61, 190, 194
sexual sterility: GE cottonwoods, 67; GE salmon, 89–90, 102–3; self-pollination problems, 74
Shaman Pharmaceuticals, 206–7
Shapiro, Robert, 52, 111
Sierra Club, 115, 161
silvaculture cooperatives, 73–75, 78, 82. *See also* forests and forestry; TGERC
Smith-Lever Act, 71
smolts/smoltification, 84, 87–88, 108
socially embedded or socially produced technological innovations, 64, 81
social resistance. *See* antibiotech movement
South (global): antibiotech movement, 10–12, 120–22; defined, 22; foreign aid to, 181, 192; G77 group, 163, 181; homogeneity of, 193; opposition to TRIPS, 177–79, 193; vs. WTO, 155–56, 160–61, 168–70, 171–73, 176
South (global), genetic resources of: biopiracy from, 10–11, 182–84, 191, 192, 217; green development, 180, 186–89; vs. IPRs, 10–11, 120, 162, 175, 177–79, 181–85, 193–94; pharmacologically active substances, 8, 179, 195–98, 205–6, 213–15; threatened by GEOs, 120, 162, 181–82; withholding from market, 194
soybeans: GE-free, suppliers, 157–58, 166, 194; monopolistic control of, 51
soybeans, transgenic: acreage statistics, 4, 5, 26, 55, 152–53, 171, 241; Agracetus' patent on, 59, 61; contraband, 172; economics of growing, 49–50, 166, 253; labeling requirements, 143; Monsanto's

Indexer:	Ellen Davenport
Compositor:	BookMatters, Berkeley
Text:	10/12 Baskerville
Display:	Baskerville
Printer and Binder:	Edwards Brothers, Inc.